Microsoft® SQL Server® 2008

ADMINISTRATION
for ORACLE® DBAs

About the Authors

Mark Anderson is a data platform technical specialist working in the Enterprise and Partner Group at Microsoft UK. Specializing in the SQL Server relational engine, Mark works with Microsoft's top enterprise customers and partners, helping them to design and architect Tier-1 solutions on the Microsoft platform. Migrating and integrating with non-Microsoft platforms such as Oracle and IBM also form part of his role. Mark holds certification in both the Microsoft and Oracle database platforms. He can be contacted at markand@microsoft.com.

James Fox is an independent consultant and director of Datagility, a company dedicated to helping businesses make their information work harder using the Microsoft Business Intelligence platform, including SQL Server and SharePoint. Prior to this, James has worked for Microsoft and Oracle partners, building and supporting data-driven solutions and providing SQL Server training to experienced Oracle DBAs. He can be contacted at dba@datagility.co.uk.

Christian Bolton is the technical director for Coeo Ltd., a leading provider of SQL Server consulting and managed support services in the UK and Europe. Prior to this, Christian worked for five years at Microsoft, leading the SQL Server Premier Field Engineering team in the UK. He is a Microsoft Certified Architect, Master, and MVP for SQL Server, and lead author of *Professional SQL Server 2008 Internals and Troubleshooting*. Christian works out of London and lives in the south of England with his wife and children. He can be contacted at christian@coeo.com.

About the Technical Editor

David Browne is a technology architect at the Microsoft Technology Center in Dallas, focusing on SQL Server solutions. He is a developer and has been writing solutions in SQL Server, .NET, Java, and Oracle for over ten years.

Microsoft® SQL Server® 2008

ADMINISTRATION for ORACLE® DBAs

Mark Anderson
James Fox
Christian Bolton

New York Chicago San Francisco Lisbon
London Madrid Mexico City Milan
New Delhi San Juan Seoul Singapore
Sydney Toronto

The McGraw·Hill Companies

Library of Congress Cataloging-in-Publication Data

Anderson, Mark, 1977-
    Microsoft SQL server 2008 administration for Oracle DBAs / Mark
Anderson, James Fox, Christian Bolton. — 1
        p.   cm.
    ISBN 978-0-07-170064-1 (pbk.)
    1. SQL server.   2. Client/server computing.   3. Database management.
    4. Oracle (Computer file)   I. Fox, James, 1976-   II. Bolton, Christian.   III. Title.
    QA76.9.D3A6434   2010
    005.75'85—dc22   2010035643

McGraw-Hill books are available at special quantity discounts to use as premiums and sales promotions, or for use in corporate training programs. To contact a representative, please e-mail us at bulksales@mcgraw-hill.com.

Microsoft® SQL Server® 2008 Administration for Oracle® DBAs

1234567890   DOC DOC   109876543210

ISBN   978-0-07-170064-1
MHID   0-07-170064-1

Sponsoring Editor
    Wendy Rinaldi

Editorial Supervisor
    Patty Mon

Project Manager
    Vastavikta Sharma, Glyph International

Acquisitions Coordinator
    Joya Anthony

Technical Editor
    David Browne

Copy Editor
    Bill McManus

Proofreader
    Julie Searls

Indexer
    Jack Lewis

Production Supervisor
    Jean Bodeaux

Composition
    Glyph International

Illustration
    Glyph International

Art Director, Cover
    Jeff Weeks

Cover Designer
    Jeff Weeks

I wish to dedicate this book to two people; firstly, to my wife and best friend, Wendy, and secondly, to a constant in my life who was there when I started this book but sadly not when I finished it: "Nana" Lillian O'Conner, 1925–2010.

—Mark Anderson

This is for Caroline and Charlie, who helped me in their own ways from the start, and for Chloe and Alice, who only arrived when we were nearly finished.

—James Fox

For my parents, the often unsung heroes of my career, who I always strive to make proud.

—Christian Bolton

Contents at a Glance

Contents

Acknowledgments

The list of people to thank is huge, but without a shadow of a doubt, my first thanks must go to my wife Wendy. For over a year, Wendy has had to put up with my spending all of our weekends glued to my laptop writing this book. As a result, I need to also say thank you to all my family and friends for being so patient with us when they heard the regular excuse of "Sorry, we can't come over. Mark needs to work on the book this weekend."

Thanks also go to my co-authors, James Fox and Christian Bolton, with a special thank you to James, who, following the joint delivery of one of our SQL Server for Oracle DBA training courses, thought I was initially joking when I said, "We should write a book about this!" Christian, thank you for joining us on this journey and for writing two great chapters.

In addition to the official technical editor, David Browne, who has done an amazing job and provided great wisdom and insight, we would also like to thank Benjamin Wright-Jones and Jens K. Süßmeyer, two of Microsoft's top SQL Server consultants from the UK and Germany, respectively, for reviewing the book and providing feedback and ideas as well as ensuring technical accuracy.

A huge thanks must go to David Stewart, the Microsoft UK Librarian. Those of you who have seen Steven Seagal films know that he often masquerades as a normal guy but then turns out to be some form of Navy SEAL or other special forces operative; David is a real-life version of this, masquerading as a librarian hidden away in Building 1 of the Microsoft UK Campus, but ultimately a "Navy SEAL" of book knowledge. David, your insight, guidance, and ability to help me translate some of my technobabble into something that someone other than myself can read have been invaluable. Writing a book has been an amazing experience, which would have been much harder if it was not for your assistance, and I truly thank you.

The list of other people who have all played their part is huge. From colleagues in Microsoft to friends in the industry and customers with whom I have worked, I apologize for not being able to name you all, but you know who you are! There are a few people for whom I want to make a special mention. In no particular order, I would like to say thank you to Graeme Scott, John Plummer, Shaun Beasley, Ken England, Paul West, Gareth Ford, Simon Eckford, and all of the Microsoft Application Platform Team in the UK.

A mention must go to the core team at McGraw-Hill, Wendy Rinaldi and Joya Anthony. Wendy and Joya, thank you both for your guidance and patience in guiding me through writing my first book.

The final thank you must go to you for reading this book! This book has taken many hours of work from all involved, and we hope you enjoy reading it and that it inspires you to want to learn more about SQL Server.

—Mark Anderson

Thanks are due to everyone who has had to listen to me talk about this book, everyone who put up with something I didn't do because I was writing it, and all the clients and training course attendees who acted as unknowing guinea pigs for the content.

—James Fox

First and foremost, I would like to thank my wife, Gemma, for her support and patience for yet another authoring project; I wouldn't be anywhere without her never-ending support for my "crazy" ideas. I'd also like to thank my children, Ava and Leighton, for helping me to balance work with home life by pulling me away from my desk to oversee a princess wedding or to be a volunteer patient for two trainee doctors.

I'd like to thank Mark Anderson for allowing me to be involved in this book and for his limitless patience.

Finally, I'd like to thank my parents, to whom I have dedicated my contribution to this book. As a parent of two young children, I am now fully aware of the sacrifices they made for my sister and me when we were young, and I want them to know how much I appreciate it.

—Christian Bolton

Introduction

It is said that during a polite dinner conversation, the topics of politics and religion should be left alone because they can be emotionally charged subjects that can lead to heated conversation and the ruination of a good evening meal. Discussing the choice of database platform among DBAs and architects of different backgrounds also falls into this category! For that reason alone, this book is not about who has more widgets and features or who can hold the most data.

These days, many organizations run multivendor database environments. DBAs who traditionally administered systems from only one vendor, such as Oracle, are now being asked to administer other environments as well, such as Microsoft SQL Server. A DBA who has skills in more than one database platform is very attractive to potential new employers. It is probably due to one or both of these reasons that you decided to read this book.

The authors of this book have worked with many Oracle DBAs over the years who have made the transition to becoming cross-skilled as SQL Server DBAs. When an Oracle DBA is introduced to SQL Server, they naturally make constant references to their base knowledge of terms and concepts in the Oracle platform. For example, as you would expect, both platforms have the concept of an entity known as a "database," and although the comparison of a "database" in both platforms may initially seem to be logical, you will soon realize that the comparison is not so straightforward and the feature or function is not comparable. In the book, we will make clear where any comparisons start and end, thus capitalizing on your existing knowledge while making sure it is not a hindrance.

This book has been written to give you an understanding of the principles of how SQL Server works in comparison to Oracle. We will guide you through the architecture of SQL Server, through basic administration tasks, and through advanced scenarios such as high availability and performance tuning. The first two chapters give you an overview of the components and toolset of the SQL Server platform and an understanding of the relational engine architecture. With this foundational knowledge, Chapter 3 walks you through installing and configuring an instance of SQL Server. Chapter 4 explores the database objects, such as schemas, tables, views, and programmable objects. You then need to make sure your SQL Server database is secure, and in Chapter 5 we show you how to do this by creating users and roles and encrypting data. In Chapter 6 we address how you access data, control transactions, and perform DML operations through the T-SQL language. As a DBA, backing up is fundamental to everything you do, so to ensure you don't lose your data (and your job!), Chapter 7 covers SQL Server backup and explains recovery techniques from full database recovery to fine-grained repair in the event that you suffer a database failure.

Chapter 8 looks at how you maintain and monitor the health and performance of your database server to give your users the best possible service. We move on to evaluate various business continuity solutions in Chapter 9 to show you how SQL Server can be implemented in high availability and disaster recovery scenarios. In Chapter 10, we introduce the automation and scheduling capabilities alongside the alerting mechanisms built into the core SQL Server product.

As a DBA, you'll likely need to import and export data between line-of-business applications as well as move and copy data to test and develop environments. Chapter 11 covers the tools and techniques available within SQL Server. We finish in Chapter 12 by looking at how you upgrade between different releases of SQL Server as well as how you migrate to SQL Server from Oracle.

We recommend that you begin by reading the first two chapters to give you an overview of the components and toolset of the SQL Server platform and an understanding of the relational engine architecture. The rest of the chapters can be read in any order, such that you can concentrate on areas of specific interest. Thus, to fully grasp what is being said in later chapters, you need the foundation given in the first two chapters. For example, if you were tasked with backing up a SQL Server database, you would want to read Chapter 7 for the relevant information. However, you will need to have read Chapters 1 and 2 for an introduction to the tools and concepts discussed in Chapter 7.

After reading this book, when you are tasked with a SQL Server job, you will have enough understanding of the tools and skills required to complete the task and how they relate to your existing Oracle skills and experience.

Mark Anderson and James Fox have both been delivering cross-platform database training courses for several years. The "Oracle DBA Q&A" sections in this book have been drawn directly from real questions raised by students in their classes or by Oracle DBAs who were involved in the review process for this book.

The "On the Job" sections offer tips, tricks, and advice arising from the authors' experiences of architecting, administering, and troubleshooting database platforms in a wide variety of customer environments.

Chapter 1

Introduction to the SQL Server Platform

In This Chapter

- ▶ SQL Server Editions
- ▶ SQL Server—What's in the Box?
- ▶ Operating System Platforms
- ▶ SQL Server Documentation and Sample Databases
- ▶ SQL Server Resources, Support, and Software Patches

Before delving into the technical side of Microsoft SQL Server, it is worth taking time to look at what exactly SQL Server is. Most people know SQL Server as a relational database engine, but the SQL Server brand is now an overarching banner for the Microsoft Data Platform vision. Today, the Microsoft SQL Server brand encompasses more than just a relational database engine that you install on your own servers; it now includes business intelligence features, a complex event-processing engine, highly scalable data warehousing solutions, and a version of SQL Server running in the cloud.

This chapter takes a look at the various editions of SQL Server that are available today, what is included out of the box, and where to go for help and assistance.

SQL Server Editions

As with Oracle, SQL Server is available in multiple editions. Each SQL Server edition is targeted at different scenarios that span from mobile and embedded devices through to data center environments and into the cloud.

For SQL Server 2008 R2, Microsoft breaks down the editions into five categories with the following editions:

- ▶ Premium editions
  - ▶ Datacenter
  - ▶ Parallel Data Warehouse
- ▶ Core editions
  - ▶ Enterprise
  - ▶ Standard
- ▶ Specialized editions
  - ▶ Workgroup
  - ▶ Web
  - ▶ Developer
- ▶ Free editions
  - ▶ Express
  - ▶ Compact
- ▶ Cloud services
  - ▶ SQL Azure

This book concentrates on the core editions, and in particular Enterprise Edition, but the skills gained from this book are transferable up and down the editions stack.

Premium Editions

Datacenter is the top SQL Server offering from Microsoft and currently allows for scale of up to 256 processing cores. (Note: The 256-core restriction is imposed by the operating system; SQL Server Datacenter edition will support more cores as the OS is able to support more cores.) Datacenter Edition is targeted at Tier-1 applications, which typically have high data volume, user concurrency, and availability requirements.

Parallel Data Warehouse is a scale-out data warehousing solution aimed at large-scale data warehouses. It is covered in detail in the "Data Warehousing with SQL Server" section of this chapter.

Core Editions

The core editions of SQL Server are likely to be the editions that you encounter most frequently in your data center environments. Enterprise Edition is targeted at business-critical applications that require enterprise-class availability and scalability. Enterprise Edition supports up to 8 CPUs with a total of up to 64 cores of processing power and contains features such as table and index partitioning, data compression, transparent database encryption, and online re-indexing, all of which are included in the license.

Standard Edition is targeted at small- to medium-scale OLTP (online transaction processing) applications and is limited to 4 CPUs. It does not contain features such as online re-indexing and table partitioning, which would typically be required in the larger databases with 24×7 database availability requirements.

It should be noted that in the previous paragraphs we have spoken about CPUs and cores. When licensing SQL Server using the per processor licensing model, Microsoft only charges per physical socket not per core or a percentage of core as per other vendors. Therefore, a server with 8 sockets each with 8 cores would only be 8 CPU licenses.

Specialized Editions

Workgroup Edition with its limit of 2 CPUs and 4GB RAM is targeted at small organizations and remote branch scenarios. For example, a retail organization that has many stores may use Workgroup Edition because it allows the organization not only to store and report sales and stock data locally at the retail branch level, but also to synchronize data back to the corporate headquarters for sending sales figures back, downloading the latest product price lists, and so forth.

Web Edition is targeted at web-hosting scenarios and is primarily aimed at Internet service providers (ISPs). It can only be used to support public, Internet-accessible web pages, sites, applications, and services. It cannot be used for line-of-business applications.

Developer Edition is effectively SQL Server 2008 R2 Datacenter Edition but is licensed for development, demonstration, and testing purposes only, meaning it cannot be used for production systems.

Free Editions

The two free editions of SQL Server are Compact and Express. Compact Edition is an embedded database used for developing mobile phone or desktop applications. Compact Edition is a different codebase from the server editions of SQL Server, and is an embedded database engine rather than a client/server database (like Oracle). Compact has a very small client footprint—just a couple of DLL libraries—and supports only a subset of T-SQL (the SQL Server version of PL/SQL). It does not have stored procedures or views, and is used mainly for applications that need to take relatively simple datasets offline and synchronize them back with the central server.

SQL Server Express Edition is the free edition of the full SQL Server relational database engine. It shares the same codebase with the Core and Premium editions, and to an application developer or a DBA it behaves like those editions. Express Edition has a database size limit of 10GB and will only use one CPU and up to 1GB RAM per instance. Express is used both as a desktop database for applications that need the full power of SQL Server locally, and as a client/server database engine to support small workgroup or branch office scenarios. It is quite commonly redistributed by independent software vendors (ISVs) that want to embed a small amount of database capability within their applications.

SQL Azure (SQL Server in the Cloud)

In recent years, the trend of cloud-based computing has gained traction. Microsoft's brand of cloud-based computing components is called the Windows Azure platform. As part of that platform, Microsoft provides a SQL Server offering called Microsoft SQL Azure. SQL Azure provides a relational database service in the cloud. When running in the SQL Azure cloud, you no longer need to worry about server management and elements such as scalability, high availability, fault tolerance, and patch management because these are provided by the platform. From a development perspective, the database still uses T-SQL for development as per a normal on-premise database solution.

To manage databases both on premise and off premise, the database management tools provided with Microsoft SQL Server 2008 R2 allow a DBA to connect to a database hosted in the cloud in the same way they would to one hosted on their local machine.

Data Warehousing with SQL Server

For building data warehousing solutions using SQL Server, there are two approaches that can be taken. The first is a scale-up, single-server approach, and the second is a scale-out approach that utilizes the power of multiple servers.

Scale-up data warehousing is achieved using the off-the-shelf Enterprise and Datacenter editions of SQL Server (it is possible to use Standard Edition, but most of the data warehousing features such as partitioning, star join optimization, and data compression are only available in Enterprise Edition and above). To help accelerate scale-up data warehousing projects, Microsoft provides a series of reference architectures that have been developed by the Microsoft Data Warehouse Product Unit in conjunction with various hardware vendors. These reference architectures, known as Fast Track reference architectures, specify a complete system kit list, including the disks, storage array, storage area network (SAN) components, CPU, and memory for a given workload and data volume requirement. In addition, Fast Track describes how to set up and lay out SQL Server on top of this hardware. The Fast Track specification is designed around a concept known as a "balanced architecture." This means that each component in the solution, from disk to CPU, is able to supply the next component with the right amount of throughput, therefore ensuring that you have not over- or underspecified a component. The idea behind Fast Track is to provide a system that can be installed very quickly to deliver consistent data warehouse performance at a known price point. A balanced architecture helps to make sure you get the right price/performance—there is no point in having fast multicore CPUs and a huge array of disks if the networking infrastructure is so slow that the disks and CPUs spend their time idle, and yet this type of setup is all too common. Fast Track focuses on getting the balance right so you don't overspend on any particular component.

The Fast Track whitepapers, implementation guides, and best practices are available for free download at the Microsoft website. The hardware specified in the Fast Track architectures is standard hardware available from (at the time of writing) HP, Dell/EMC, IBM, and Bull.

ON THE JOB

To give you a real-world example, I worked with a customer that spent many weeks of their data warehousing project time in test labs building different combinations of server and storage configurations to try to find the optimal configuration for their workload. After settling on a design and deploying it into production, they found that the hardware choices were incorrect; many months of adding and swapping various hardware components eventually led to a solution that was massively oversized for the workload. The additional cost and downtime that was introduced into the project could have been avoided with a Fast Track solution. The Fast Track architectures have been designed and tested by both Microsoft and the hardware vendor engineers to ensure that the system performs from disk through to the CPU and that SQL Server is configured to make best use of the hardware. Even if you don't buy the specified hardware solution, the Fast Track methodology available in the free-to-download whitepapers will help you to build your own design or maybe tweak an existing solution.

For scale-out data warehousing, there is a specific edition of SQL Server called SQL Server Parallel Data Warehouse Edition that is aimed at high-volume, high-performance data warehousing workloads. It provides a linear scale-out solution that stretches from the tens to hundreds of terabytes of data using a massively parallel processing (MPP) architecture. Parallel Data Warehouse has been specifically tuned to manage complex, mixed-query workloads, and also has a particular focus on hub/spoke architectures where it can interoperate very effectively with either standard SQL Server or SQL Server Fast Track spokes. In this architecture, the hub acts as a powerful aggregation, calculation, and query engine, rapidly publishing data to the spokes for user analysis. Parallel Data Warehouse is an appliance-type solution similar to Oracle Exadata from the point of view that you buy it as a complete solution that has been preconfigured with both hardware and software. At the time of writing, Parallel Data Warehouse solutions are available from hardware vendors including HP, Dell/EMC, IBM, and Bull.

SQL Server—What's in the Box?

SQL Server comes with all the components that you need to set up and manage the SQL Server Data Platform. As you read in the previous section, Microsoft breaks down its editions in almost the same way as Oracle, with Express, Standard, and Enterprise editions being the main products. Unlike Oracle, Microsoft does not have additional Enterprise options that can be purchased separately, such as Partitioning, Spatial, OLAP, and Data Mining. Instead, Microsoft bundles all its features into the base product, and which edition you buy determines which features are available to you in the product. For example, if you wanted table partitioning, then you would need to buy at least the Enterprise Edition of the product.

In the interest of balance, there is an argument that says that, in some instances, what Oracle provides in its chargeable options is greater than what Microsoft provides out of the box. For example, Microsoft does not charge extra for the table partitioning feature that comes with its Enterprise (and above) Edition of the product, whereas in Oracle you need to purchase the partitioning pack. However, SQL Server only has range partitioning, whereas the Oracle partitioning pack contains range, list, and interval partitioning, among others. In other areas, such as online analytical processing (OLAP), it can be argued that Microsoft has the upper hand in the functionality and capability it provides.

You can break down what is provided out of the box in SQL Server into several categories:

- ▶ RDBMS features
- ▶ Tooling
- ▶ Business intelligence
- ▶ Complex event processing

RDBMS Features

Listing every RDBMS feature would be a very long and tiresome task. Every edition contains the basic capabilities for data management, security, backup, and so forth that you would expect an RDBMS solution to provide, but as you move up the edition stack, more features are included, as previously noted. For building enterprise-class, Tier-1 applications, the Enterprise and Datacenter editions of SQL Server contain all the data management, security, high-availability, and scalability features required to build these types of solutions; there are no additional options to purchase.

SQL Server Tools

Out of the box, SQL Server comes with a set of tools for management, tuning, monitoring, development, configuration, and data movement, all of which will be discussed and used throughout this book.

The tools that are used by a DBA include

- ▶ sqlcmd command-line interface
- ▶ SQL Server Management Studio (SSMS)
- ▶ SQL Server Configuration Manager
- ▶ SQL Server Profiler
- ▶ SQL Server Database Tuning Advisor
- ▶ Third-party tools

sqlcmd

sqlcmd is similar to SQL*Plus in Oracle. It is a command-line tool for issuing statements and queries against a SQL Server. However, unlike the relationship that Oracle DBAs have with SQL*Plus, which tends to be their preferred tool when issuing commands and queries against Oracle, SQL Server DBAs tend to use sqlcmd only for executing scripts in batch processes and for connecting to a SQL Server when the Management Studio tool is not available. Figure 1-1 shows sqlcmd connecting to a local SQL Server and issuing a query.

SQL Server Management Studio

When managing SQL Server, the main tool is SQL Server Management Studio (SSMS). SSMS can be thought of as the functionality of Oracle Enterprise Manager, SQL Developer, and SQL*Plus all rolled into one application. SSMS allows you to

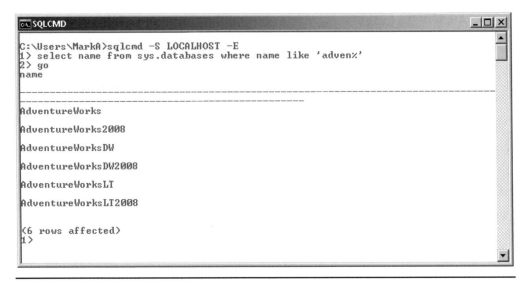

Figure 1-1 *sqlcmd connected to a local SQL Server and issuing a basic query*

graphically manage your SQL Server servers and instances across your estate and issue T-SQL statements and queries. The relationship that SQL Server DBAs have with SSMS is comparable to the relationship that Oracle DBAs tend to have with SQL*Plus.

SSMS is fully customizable, so you can lay out the look and feel as well as shortcut keys to suit your way of working. If you prefer to see only the query window and results, then you can close or collapse your other windows to the side of the tool.

Figure 1-2 shows SSMS in action with a typical window layout. The registered servers and server objects are located on the left side, and a connection to the server with the window to issue SQL statements and retrieve results is located on the right.

ON THE JOB

As you become more familiar with working with SSMS and SQL Server, you will come up with your own preferred window layout. This can also depend on the screen resolution at which you run your workstation. If you run at a high resolution, then you can probably keep more windows open, whereas working with a low resolution will probably mean you want to keep the number of visible windows to a minimum to allow for more workspace when typing queries and so forth.

Because SSMS is a graphical tool, it allows you to retrieve properties and details of objects by right-clicking the object as you would when working in most Microsoft Windows–based applications. For example, to retrieve the properties that are currently

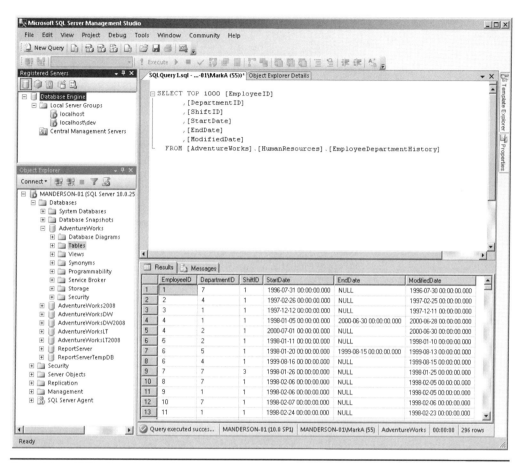

Figure 1-2   *SSMS—Typical window layout*

set for a database, you can either issue a T-SQL query or right-click the database and select Properties. Figure 1-3 shows the Database Properties window of the AdventureWorks database with the Options page selected, showing the current values for the database options.

In addition to the RDBMS side of SQL Server, SSMS is used to manage the Business Intelligence components of the stack. It can also be used to manage SQL Server Compact Edition databases and SQL Azure databases.

SSMS is extensible such that you can also write your own add-ins using Microsoft .NET (VB, C#, C++) to perform additional tasks.

Database Properties - AdventureWorks		

Select a page
- General
- Files
- Filegroups
- **Options**
- Change Tracking
- Permissions
- Extended Properties
- Mirroring
- Transaction Log Shipping

Script ▾ Help

Collation:	Latin1_General_CI_AS
Recovery model:	Full
Compatibility level:	SQL Server 2008 (100)

Other options:

☐ **Automatic**	
Auto Close	True
Auto Create Statistics	True
Auto Shrink	False
Auto Update Statistics	True
Auto Update Statistics Asynchronously	False
☐ **Cursor**	
Close Cursor on Commit Enabled	False
Default Cursor	GLOBAL
☐ **Miscellaneous**	
ANSI NULL Default	False
ANSI NULLS Enabled	True
ANSI Padding Enabled	True
ANSI Warnings Enabled	True
Arithmetic Abort Enabled	True
Concatenate Null Yields Null	True
Cross-database Ownership Chaining Enabled	False
Date Correlation Optimization Enabled	False
Numeric Round-Abort	False
Parameterization	Simple

ANSI NULL Default

Connection

Server:
MANDERSON-01

Connection:
MANDERSON-01\MarkA

View connection properties

Progress

Ready

OK   Cancel

Figure 1-3   *Database Properties window in SSMS*

ON THE JOB

In my experience, many Oracle DBAs prefer to use the SQL*Plus command-line tool instead of the graphical tools provided with Oracle (that is, SQL Developer and Oracle Enterprise Manager). Common reasons DBAs give for not wanting to use the graphical tools are that they think the tools provided by Oracle are not up to the job and not very user friendly, or they simply think that graphical tools "de-skill" a DBA because the DBA no longer needs to memorize the syntax.

Whatever the reason for avoiding graphical tools when working in Oracle, as an Oracle DBA learning SQL Server, it is worth trying out the very good set of SQL Server graphical tools. Even if you don't want to use the property pages and check boxes approach to management, you can still issue your T-SQL statements and queries in the SSMS tool to get nicely formatted output.

I do not fully agree with the argument that using graphical tools "de-skills" an individual, because as a DBA, the most important thing is to get the task done as quickly and efficiently as possible. I agree that you do need to understand the syntax and the detail behind what you are doing. In the graphical tools, if you just check boxes, adjust values, and click OK without understanding the ramifications of your actions, this will eventually lead to mistakes and potential outages of service. Equally, when working with a command-line tool, it is just as dangerous to copy syntax from a book, copy scripts from the Internet, or even just guess at the syntax for a command. Ultimately, you need to understand what it is that you are doing when running a command.

SSMS has a great feature that is a mix of the two approaches of GUI and command line when working with dialog boxes. Instead of clicking OK to perform an action, you can ask SSMS to script the action to a new query window, file, or the Windows Clipboard, or even to take the command and schedule it as a job to run later. That way, you get to see what SSMS was going to do had you clicked OK.

As an example, Figure 1-4 shows the Server Properties dialog box, which allows you to adjust instance parameters. In this example, we changed the Minimum Server Memory value to 1000MB. Instead of clicking OK,

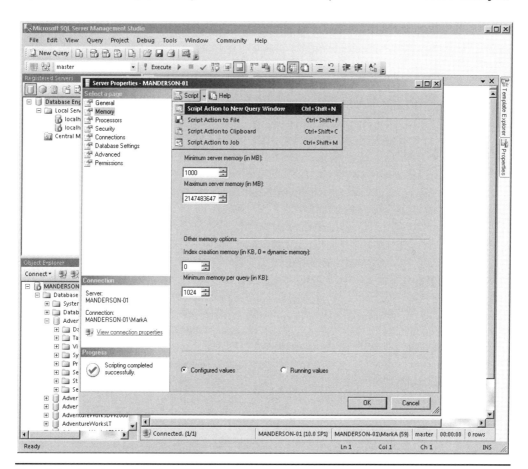

Figure 1-4   *Choosing a script action in SSMS*

we are selecting Script | Script Action to New Query Window, which causes SSMS to launch a new query window and place the commands that it was going to execute within it, as shown in Figure 1-5. In this case, it is a call to the sp_configure stored procedure.

The scripting option, which is available in almost every dialog box in SSMS, provides a great way of getting up to speed quickly on syntax and understanding how the tool works. Other examples of dialog boxes from which you can script out the results include those for creating new databases, running a backup, creating or rebuilding an index, and adjusting server parameters.

I strongly recommend that you spend more time working with SSMS than sqlcmd unless you have a real aversion to graphical utilities. Graphical tools are provided to make you more productive! If you are really a die-hard command-line junkie, try PowerShell. It is the next-generation command-line environment for administering Windows and Microsoft Server products. Everything that you can do in SSMS can be done in PowerShell, because both SSMS and PowerShell use the same underlying libraries, called the SQL Server Management Objects (SMO). SSMS builds a GUI on top of them, and PowerShell gives you an interactive scripting environment to work with them.

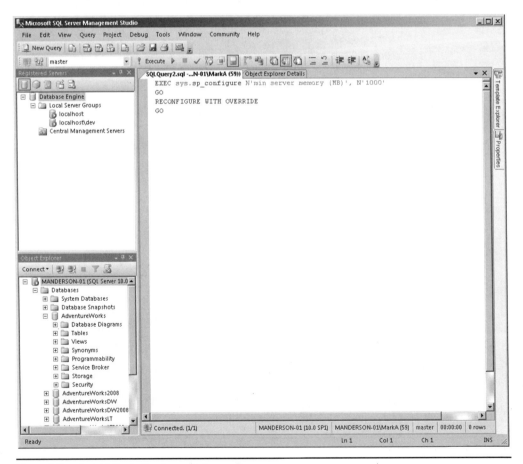

Figure 1-5 *Script Action to New Query window result*

SQL Server Configuration Manager

SQL Server Configuration Manager is used to configure and manage the networking protocols that SQL Server responds to and the service accounts under which the SQL Server services (processes) run. The SQL Server Configuration Manager is covered in more detail in Chapter 3.

Figure 1-6 shows SQL Server Configuration Manager with the SQL Server Services selected.

SQL Server Profiler

There are times when you want to monitor and log events that are taking place inside the engine, to troubleshoot performance issues, audit database activity, or capture a workload to replay into performance-tuning tools. For this, SQL Server contains a feature known as SQL Trace. SQL Trace allows you to specify which events you are interested in and any filters—for example, all stored procedure calls by user Fred. A SQL Trace can be defined in code using a set of system stored procedures, but a more intuitive and interactive way to do this is through SQL Server Profiler to create a trace definition that can then be set to run on the server side.

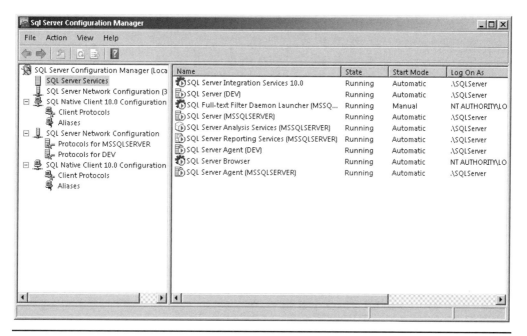

Figure 1-6   *SQL Server Configuration Manager*

SQL Profiler can also be used on the client side and run interactively with SQL Server to watch real-time activity on a SQL Server server. More information on using SQL Trace and SQL Server Profiler for performance tuning is available in Chapter 8. Figure 1-7 shows SQL Server Profiler in action capturing events.

SQL Server Database Engine Tuning Advisor

The SQL Server Database Engine Tuning Advisor (DTA) is used to analyze a workload against the physical implementation of one or more databases in order to make recommendations upon how best to tune the database based on the workload provided. Workloads can be provided as SQL Trace outputs (to capture real-world usage of the system) or as a script containing T-SQL statements.

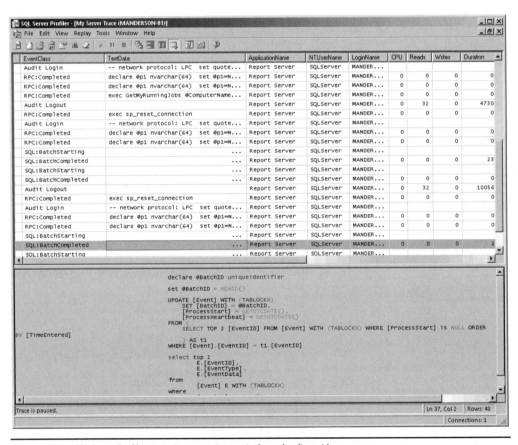

Figure 1-7   *SQL Server Profiler capturing events interactively on the client side*

DTA can recommend physical changes to your database design, such as the addition or removal of indexes, the implementation of a partitioning strategy, or simply the addition of statistics. DTA is covered in Chapter 8.

Figure 1-8 shows DTA's Tuning Options tab, where you can select what design decisions you allow DTA to consider.

Third-Party Tools

The ecosystem for third-party management and monitoring tools for SQL Server is very rich. Vendors such as Idera, Red Gate, and Quest, to name a few, all create tools that either fill gaps or extend existing functionality within the SQL Server product.

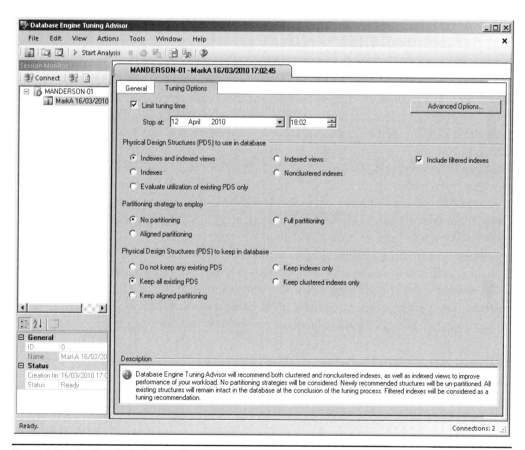

Figure 1-8   *Database Engine Tuning Advisor, Tuning Options tab*

Some tools that are popular on the Oracle platform such as Toad from Quest Software also have SQL Server equivalents. Therefore, if you use Toad on Oracle you can still keep the same familiar interface by using Toad for SQL Server.

Business Intelligence with SSIS, SSRS, and SSAS

SQL Server Integration Services (SSIS), SQL Server Reporting Services (SSRS), and SQL Server Analysis Services (SSAS) are the three components that make up the Business Intelligence (BI) part of the SQL Server stack. The structure of your organization will dictate how many of these components you will have exposure to, as you may have BI developers and analysts who are more likely to use these products than you are as a DBA—although it is highly likely you will be involved in administering some of the infrastructure to support these components.

SQL Server Integration Services

SSIS was introduced in SQL Server 2005 to replace a feature called Data Transformation Services (DTS). SSIS is an enterprise-class extract, transform, and load (ETL) product. To draw a comparison, think of SSIS as being in the same category as SAP BusinessObjects Data Integrator, Ab Initio, Informatica PowerCenter, and Oracle Data Integrator Enterprise Edition (formerly known as Oracle Warehouse Builder and Oracle Data Integrator).

SSIS can be used to build complex data movement operations. Its package format in which SSIS packages are saved and the execution engine for executing the packages is also used by some of the core SQL Server RDBMS features such as the Import and Export data wizards and SQL Server Maintenance Plans. We will take a brief look at SSIS in Chapter 11 when we discuss data movement. As a DBA, you may or may not get involved in creating SSIS packages, as this may fall to a data integration team. Even if you do not get involved in the development, it is highly likely you will be involved in the execution and monitoring of package execution. The SQL Server Maintenance Plans feature, which is aimed at DBAs for creating automated database maintenance tasks, also uses SSIS as its package format and uses the SSIS engine to execute them.

SQL Server Reporting Services

SSRS is Microsoft's enterprise reporting tool. It allows for the design, publishing, subscription, and delivery of reports. SSRS also contains features that allow end users to design, build, and publish their own reports using an application known as Report Builder. Again, to draw a comparison to competitive products, think of SSRS as being similar to SAP BusinessObjects Web Intelligence, Crystal Reports, and MicroStrategy Report Services. As with the SSIS packages, you may or may not be involved in the creation and development of the SSRS reports, but you will be involved in the backup and recovery of the databases that are part of the SSRS solution. SSRS has two databases, which by default are named ReportServer and ReportServerTempdb. These databases contain information such as report definitions, execution statistics, subscriptions, security settings, and other data associated with the SSRS solution. Although you may not create line-of-business reports, it should be noted that SSMS also hosts SSRS reports for reporting system status information such as disk space, top queries by CPU, etc. Therefore, if you want to extend SSMS with your own custom reports it is worth understanding how to write SSRS reports.

SQL Server Analysis Services

SSAS is the Microsoft OLAP engine. SSAS is used to create multidimensional data cubes that can support fast ad hoc querying. SSAS also incorporates data mining functionality to perform data analysis, looking for patterns in data for use in applications such as targeted marketing, retail basket analysis, and fraud detection. Comparison products include Oracle OLAP and IBM Cognos PowerPlay.

ON THE JOB

Microsoft has proven to be very strong in the Business Intelligence arena, and companies who are predominantly Oracle commonly use for their RDBMS platform SQL Server just for its BI tools. I have worked with customers who run their data warehouse on Oracle 11g but use SSIS to extract data from source systems and load it into Oracle, and then use SSAS to provide OLAP data analysis and SSRS for reporting over the top of the Oracle warehouse. All the components are interchangeable; a customer who uses SQL Server as the data warehouse can use other products to load, report, and analyze data. You can pick and choose which components to use.

Complex Event Processing with StreamInsight

In SQL Server 2008 R2, Microsoft introduced StreamInsight into the SQL Server technology stack. StreamInsight is a platform for developing and deploying complex event processing (CEP) applications. CEP applications are typically built for real-time data scenarios where there are very large data volumes with very low latency response time requirements. An example of a CEP application would be an algorithmic trading system used in financial services environments to make decisions to buy or sell assets rapidly based on data feeds from many different systems. A StreamInsight CEP application would be able to handle in near real time the high-speed event streams, filtering, and decision making based on this data. This type of processing speed and decision making would not be possible within any standard RDBMS platform. StreamInsight is a stand-alone solution in a similar way to SSAS and SSIS in that it can be used either independently or together with the RDBMS part of the platform. As a DBA, it is highly unlikely that you would be responsible for developing StreamInsight applications, as this would fall to a .NET developer, but you may be required to perform some of the management tasks. StreamInsight is not covered in this book.

Operating System Platforms

SQL Server is only available on the Microsoft Windows platform. The Enterprise and Datacenter editions of SQL Server are only able to run on the Windows Server platform (the Developer, Standard, Workgroup, and Express editions are able to run on a client operating system such as Windows 7). The choice of Windows Server version and edition is generally dependent on a few parameters.

Ideally, when choosing the version of Windows Server to use, you would automatically choose the latest supported edition because it contains the most recent advances in the operating system. However, in many enterprise environments, the choice of operating system can sometimes be restricted to the available (internally) supported operating systems. If your Windows deployment team does not currently have a build of the latest version of Windows Server, then you may have to raise an exception request or settle for an older version.

ON THE JOB

Sometimes it can be a real battle to obtain the latest operating system for a new project if the team managing the deployments does not yet have a build for that version, but in some areas it really is worth the fight. For example, in Windows Server 2008, the failover clustering capability and the TCP/IP stack were completely rewritten and simplified. In Windows Server 2008 R2, significant changes were made to the kernel that resulted in faster performance for SQL Server workloads. If your Windows team only supports Windows Server 2003, you will be sacrificing all these new features and performance enhancements.

The choice of which Windows Server edition—Standard, Enterprise, or Datacenter—to use usually boils down to two main criteria. First, choose the edition that matches your CPU and memory requirements. Second, decide whether you want to set up SQL Server in a high-availability failover cluster. Table 1-1 lists the various editions and the associated CPU and RAM limits.

Windows Server 2008 R2 Edition	CPU Sockets	RAM
Standard	4	32GB
Enterprise	8	2TB
Datacenter	64 (max. 256 cores)	2TB

Table 1-1 *Windows Server 2008 R2 CPU and RAM Limits*

If you want to build SQL Server into a Windows Server failover cluster, you need the Windows Server Enterprise Edition or above in order to have the Failover Clustering feature. It is worth noting that Windows Server 2008 R2 is only available on the x64 processor architecture or the Intel Itanium architecture (using Windows Server 2008 R2 for Itanium-Based Systems edition). If you require an x86 32-bit operating system, you need to select Windows Server 2008.

ON THE JOB

As a consultant working with some of the world's largest organizations who currently do not use Microsoft solutions in their Tier-1 environments, I often come across statements from Unix and mainframe professionals such as "The Windows Server platform is not a Tier-1 operating system" and "Windows Server is buggy, is not secure, and has to be constantly rebooted." As a consultant in the early days of Windows Server NT 3.51 and NT 4, I probably would have agreed that this was a fairly strong argument when comparing Windows Server to Unix-based solutions. However, Windows Server has evolved since then. Windows Server has made significant strides in the areas of performance, scalability, and security, with Windows Server 2008 R2 now supporting up to 256 cores of processing power. The old argument against the use of Windows Server in an enterprise environment is, in my opinion, now very much dated. A quick tour of the Microsoft Case Studies website (www. microsoft.com/casestudies/) will show that there are major well-known financial, retail, manufacturing, and government organizations running their mission-critical Tier-1 business applications on the Windows Server platform.

SQL Server Documentation and Sample Databases

The documentation that is provided with SQL Server is a stand-alone application known as SQL Server Books Online. The sample databases are called AdventureWorks.

SQL Server Books Online

Throughout this book, SQL Server Books Online is cited several times as a point of reference for further information on SQL Server features; this is done not because the authors are being lazy, but simply because this book focuses on the features and their most commonly used scenarios. To include in-depth information about every feature mentioned would probably have quadrupled the size of the book! At last count, Books Online contains in excess of 70,000 electronic pages of information for the SQL Server 2008 R2 platform. Becoming familiar with navigating and using SQL Server Books Online will save you time and help you become more productive. Figure 1-9 shows the SQL Server Books Online application.

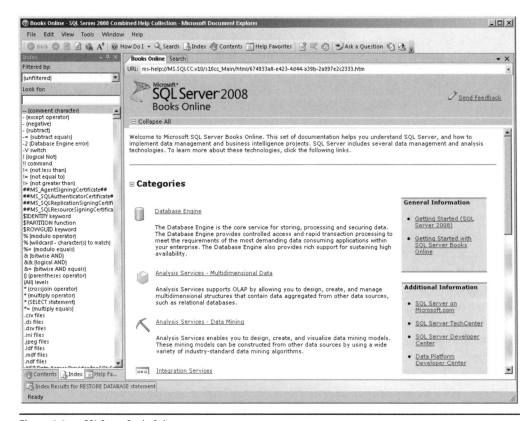

Figure 1-9   *SQL Server Books Online*

An example of using Books Online is shown in Figure 1-10. For this example, we want to know more about the dynamic management view (DMV) sys.dm_os_ schedulers (DMVs are the SQL Server equivalent of V$ views). Because we know what the feature is called, we can simply use the index lookup facility. Therefore, if we start typing **sys.dm_os_sche** in the Look For box, the index results jump to the closest match. Clicking the index entry takes us to the DMV's details—in this case, a description of the object and the details behind the return values, the permissions required to use it, and examples of usage.

NOTE

Books Online is also the help system for SSMS; therefore, typing the full DMV name in a query window and pressing F1 will take you to the same entry.

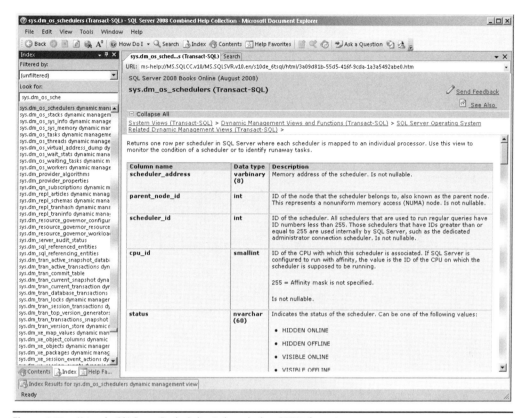

Figure 1-10   *Using the SQL Server Books Online index to look up DMV information*

The Books Online application also has a search facility. It will (if you permit it) search the Microsoft MSDN website, the MSDN forums, and a selection of non-Microsoft SQL Server community sites such as www.sqlservercentral.com and www.sqlserverfaq.com.

Figure 1-11 shows the available search options, which you access by selecting Tools | Options from the toolbar menu.

ON THE JOB

Books Online is updated and released independently of the main SQL Server release schedule. Therefore, it is quite probable that the version you install from the SQL Server media is already out of date. The latest, up-to-date version is available for free download from the Microsoft website. Visit www.microsoft.com/downloads and search for **SQL Server Books Online.** *Books Online is also available as online documentation at the Microsoft MSDN website, http://msdn.microsoft.com.*

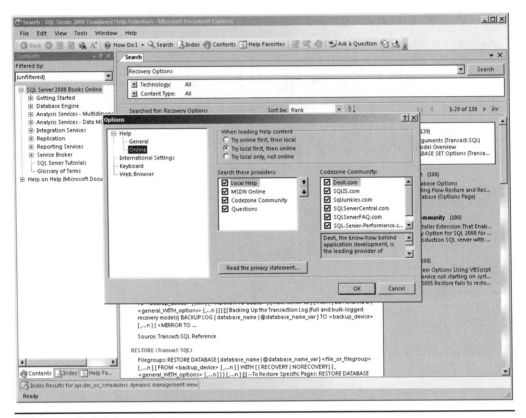

Figure 1-11   *Books Online search options*

AdventureWorks Sample Databases

In Oracle, the sample schemas include HR, SH, and PM, each designed to showcase different features and to provide a learning platform. SQL Server provides sample databases (note that schemas in Oracle are fairly analogous to databases in SQL Server; you'll read much more about this in Chapter 2). In older versions of SQL Server, you may notice sample databases called Northwind and Pubs; these have been superseded as of SQL Server 2005 with a set of sample databases known as AdventureWorks. The AdventureWorks databases, of which there are several types, including OLTP and data warehouse, are based on a fictitious company called AdventureWorks Cycles that sells bicycles and accessories. Microsoft uses this fictitious company to provide samples not only for databases but also for SSRS and SSAS. There are also SSIS packages that show how to ETL data from the AdventureWorks OLTP database to the data warehouse.

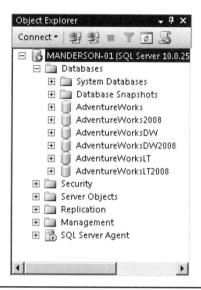

Figure 1-12   *AdventureWorks sample databases installed*

Figure 1-12 shows the AdventureWorks databases installed on a SQL Server instance.

The majority of the code samples in this book use the AdventureWorks databases. The samples can be found at http://sqlserversamples.codeplex.com/ (CodePlex is a Microsoft open source website; more on this shortly).

SQL Server Resources, Support, and Software Patches

The amount of SQL Server help and resources that are available is vast, from online community websites and blogs through to official, fee-based Microsoft support and independent consultancy and training.

Online Resources

If you are looking for less-formal support (that is, free!), there are many online resources available, including official Microsoft websites, forums, and community websites and blogs.

The main official Microsoft resources include

- **TechNet SQL Server TechCenter** http://technet.microsoft.com/sqlserver/
- **MSDN SQL Server Online Resources** http://msdn.microsoft.com/sqlserver/
- **Microsoft Support** http://support.microsoft.com/
- **Data Platform Insider** http://blogs.technet.com/dataplatforminsider/
- **SQL Server Customer Advisory Team** http://sqlcat.com/
- **CodePlex** www.codeplex.com/
- **MSDN Forums** http://social.msdn.microsoft.com/Forums/en/category/sqlserver/

TechNet and MSDN are the Microsoft equivalent of the Oracle Technology Network, providing online versions of the product documentation and best practice whitepapers and guidance. The Microsoft Support site is a searchable knowledge base of known issues, with details of how to fix or work around the problems.

To keep up to date with the latest SQL Server product announcements, the Data Platform Insider blog is regularly updated with news related to the Microsoft Data Platform.

The CodePlex website is a Microsoft-hosted open source site where developers can upload their projects for community involvement. It is worth looking there for SQL Server–related projects because there are many add-ins for tools such as SSMS and Business Intelligence Development Studio. Also, as mentioned in the previous section, CodePlex is used by Microsoft as the release mechanism for product samples such as the sample databases for SQL Server.

Some of the most interesting SQL Server articles come from the SQL Server community MVPs (Microsoft Most Valuable Professionals). MVPs are members of the SQL Server community who have been recognized by Microsoft as experts in the field and are regular contributors to educating the SQL Server community. The following list contains some of the authors' favorite MVP and Microsoft blogs (in alphabetical order by first name):

- **Aaron Bertrand** http://sqlblog.com/blogs/aaron_bertrand/
- **Brent Ozar** www.brentozar.com/
- **Buck Woody** http://blogs.msdn.com/buckwoody/
- **Cindy Gross** http://blogs.msdn.com/cindygross/
- **Erland Sommarskog** www.sommarskog.se/
- **Jens K. Suessmeyer** http://blogs.msdn.com/Jenss/

▶ **Kalen Delaney**   http://sqlblog.com/blogs/kalen_delaney/

▶ **Kimberley Tripp**   www.sqlskills.com/blogs/kimberly/

▶ **Paul Randal**   www.sqlskills.com/blogs/paul/

▶ **SQL Server Storage Engine Team**   http://blogs.msdn.com/
  sqlserverstorageengine/

▶ **Tony Rogerson**   http://sqlblogcasts.com/blogs/tonyrogerson

ON THE JOB

If you encounter a problem or a question you cannot solve or answer, even after reading through Books Online and searching the Internet, try the MSDN SQL Server Forums at http://social.msdn.microsoft.com/Forums/ en-US/category/sqlserver. Many of the MVPs just listed, as well as a huge number of other knowledgeable and helpful SQL Server professionals, monitor these forums. In addition to the MSDN Forums, there are also several Usenet forums named microsoft.public.sqlserver.*, accessible with a Usenet news reader or via Google Groups. As you search the Web, you will find the content from the MSDN and Usenet forums copied over and over again by content-aggregation websites, which is fine for searching. But if you want a question answered, post it on the MSDN or Usenet forums directly (after searching to make sure it hasn't been answered already).

Official Microsoft Support and Software Patches

For official Microsoft support, there is a range of options available depending on your requirements. The range is from e-mail and phone support for which you pay for each incident by credit card at the time of raising the support request, through to support contracts that have strict service-level agreements and dedicated support coordinators and personnel.

If you experience a problem with SQL Server that you cannot fix yourself, then it is time to contact Microsoft Support. If the problem turns out to be a software bug, you will be provided with a fix for that issue if one is available. Microsoft publishes several types of software fixes, ranging from the immediate fix of a critical problem through to the incremental service releases generally available to everyone.

The most granular type of patch is known as a hotfix. Hotfixes are fixes to a problem or set of problems that causes a specific issue (hotfixes are cumulative, so they may well contain other fixes for other issues.) Microsoft has two types of hotfix: Critical On-Demand and On-Demand. The hotfixes are categorized based on certain criteria such as whether a workaround is available and the effect the issue is having on the customer. Hotfixes by their nature are turned around in a short period of time and therefore do not go through long testing cycles before delivery to the customer. It is strongly recommended that you do not apply hotfixes unless instructed to do so by a Microsoft product support engineer.

A more predictable approach to hotfix availability is the Cumulative Update (CU) package. A CU is a rollup of all Critical On-Demand hotfixes to date as well as other hotfixes that meet the hotfix acceptance criteria (a workaround does not exist, the code that must be changed is complex and affects large parts of the system, and so forth). CUs have also been through better integration testing and engineering procedures than the stand-alone fixes. A CU is released every two months but you should not be compelled to install every CU released unless there is a fix contained in the CU that will repair a problem you are experiencing. It should be noted that CUs are based on Service Pack level, i.e., the CU3 for the RTM (Release To Manufacturing) version is not the same as the CU3 for SP1. You should always name the CU version along with Service Pack level.

A Service Pack is a rollup of CUs. Service Packs are fully regression tested by Microsoft and have been through extensive community testing through the Beta programs that allow customers to test and provide feedback on Service Packs before they are fully released. It is recommended that you apply Services Packs as they become available; the Service Pack level you are running at can affect the support you receive from Microsoft.

Finally, the last type of fix that Microsoft supplies is a General Distribution Release (GDR). A GDR is released when an issue or set of issues is found that has a broad customer impact or security implications. GDRs have no release cycle, as they are only released when Microsoft determines that the impact is great enough to produce a fix outside of the normal release cycle. GDRs are made available through the Microsoft Download Center website and also through the Windows Update capability available in the Microsoft Windows platform.

Hotfixes and CUs are only available through contacting Microsoft Support, but there is no charge for the supply of the fixes. Service Packs and GDRs are made publicly available for download on the Microsoft website, removing the need to contact Microsoft Support.

This approach to patch delivery is known as the Incremental Servicing Model (ISM). More information on the ISM can be found in the following Microsoft Support article: http://support.microsoft.com/kb/935897.

ON THE JOB

Unless the hotfix or CU addresses an issue you are experiencing, then it is a good idea to stay away from them. There is no point in trying to fix a problem you don't have, as you may break something else as a result. Service Packs, on the other hand, are always worth applying, especially because they can affect the support you receive from Microsoft. As of SQL Server 2008, it is possible to uninstall a Service Pack if you find that it introduces a problem; this was not possible in earlier versions of SQL Server. If you contact Microsoft for support, as part of the problem-resolution process, you might be asked to apply the latest CU by the Microsoft support engineer investigating your issue. CUs can also be uninstalled via the Add\Remove Programs facility in Windows.

Chapter 2

SQL Server Architecture

In This Chapter

- ► **High-Level Architecture Overview**
- ► **Database Architecture**
- ► **System Databases**
- ► **Database Snapshots**
- ► **Instances**
- ► **Client/Server Communication**

A s an Oracle DBA, you appreciate that understanding the concepts of instances, the SGA, databases, tablespaces, data files, and so on is vital to effectively managing an Oracle database solution. In this chapter we introduce you to the SQL Server architecture. SQL Server and Oracle have many concepts in common, some identical, others similar. There are also some concepts unique to each platform. There are areas where entities have the same name but mean something very different.

ON THE JOB

Naming this chapter "SQL Server Architecture" has given it the potential to turn itself into a book of its own. The aim of the chapter is to address the architecture at a level that enables you to get started with SQL Server. Therefore, some concepts have been loosely coupled for a "good enough" comparison, but if you dig deep enough, they would eventually differ.

For a deeper understanding of the SQL Server architecture, read Microsoft SQL Server 2008 Internals *by Kalen Delaney.*

High-Level Architecture Overview

In Oracle, if we consider high-level architecture, we think about a client, where a client is the consumer of the data, be that an end user, web server, or application tier. When the client wants to interact with the data stored in the database, it does so by connecting to an instance. The instance is a set of processes and memory structures that is responsible for handling the client request and returning results through interacting with the database. The database itself is a set of data files that reside on disk containing the actual data (see Figure 2-1).

At a very high level, Oracle and SQL Server would appear identical in that they both have the concept of instances and databases, and clients interact with an instance to get data from a database.

If we delve deeper, instances in Oracle and SQL Server are still identical in concept—they are the components responsible for servicing client requests and for interacting with the database data files. This conceptual equivalency does not hold completely true for the term "database," however, and this can be the first point of confusion when moving from Oracle to SQL Server. Both Oracle and SQL Server have the concept of an entity known as a "database" for storing data, which we described earlier as a set of files on disk containing the data that the instance connects to, but the role of the database in each technology differs.

In Oracle, the relationship between an instance and database is that an instance connects to only one database (or multiple instances connect to one database in a RAC configuration). The Oracle database then consists of multiple schemas. It has system-related schemas (for example, SYS), which contain information such as the data dictionary, and user schemas, which contain the user or application data.

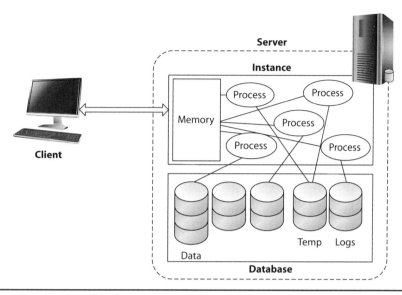

Figure 2-1   *Client, instance, and database*

In SQL Server, an instance always connects to multiple databases, of which there are system databases and user databases. Therefore, it is a good idea to conceptually think of schemas in Oracle as databases in SQL Server. For example, if you were to move the HR sample schema from Oracle to SQL Server, it would end up as the HR database in SQL Server. Conversely, if you were to migrate the AdventureWorks sample database from SQL Server to Oracle, it would be converted to the AdventureWorks schema.

Figure 2-2 shows the SQL Server Management Studio (SSMS) tool connected to an instance with the Databases node expanded. Under the databases node the user

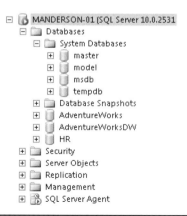

Figure 2-2   *SQL Server databases in SSMS*

databases such as AdventureWorks and HR are listed; also note the System Databases node, which separately groups the system databases together.

Each database is a physically separate entity in that it has its own set of data and transaction (redo and undo) log files. Figure 2-3 shows the default DATA directory containing all the data and log files. Note that the AdventureWorks database has an AdventureWorks_Data data file and an AdventureWorks_Log log file. More detail on the physical database architecture will be covered later in this chapter.

Now that you have grasped the concept that instances to databases is a one-to-many relationship in SQL Server, we need to consider the concept of schemas. In Oracle, a schema is a collection of objects owned by a user, and the schema has the same name as the user. In SQL Server, a schema is a namespace for a collection of objects within a database and is not tied to a user (although schemas do have owners). Think of a SQL Server schema as a container for objects inside a SQL Server database. For example, Figure 2-4 shows the AdventureWorks database expanded to show a filtered list of tables. In this example, SSMS is set to filter all tables with the word "Address" in the table name. Notice that there are five tables from four different schemas: HumanResources, Person, Purchasing, and Sales. The idea is that in the AdventureWorks application database, the schemas are used to group together all tables related to a specific focus area such as sales or human resources.

To help visualize this, Figure 2-5 shows the relationships of instance to database to schema for both Oracle and SQL Server.

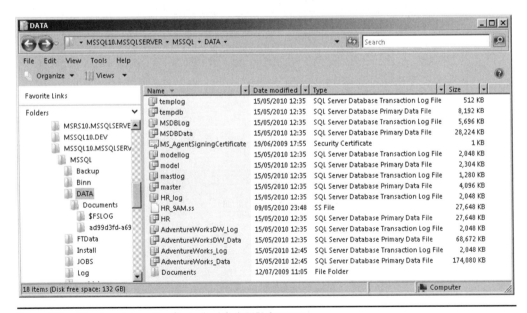

Figure 2-3   *Database data and log files in the default DATA directory*

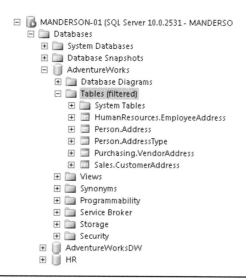

Figure 2-4   *Schemas inside a database*

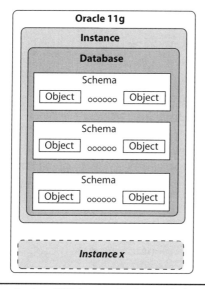
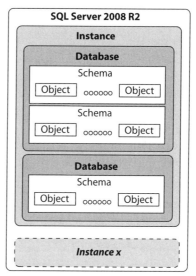

Figure 2-5   *Oracle and SQL: instance, database, and schema comparison*

ON THE JOB

When teaching SQL Server architecture to Oracle DBAs, one key confusing issue is the aforementioned fundamental difference in the implementation of schemas in each platform. As we have explained, in Oracle, a schema is a collection of objects owned by a user and the schema has the same name as the user, whereas in SQL Server, a schema is a namespace for a collection of objects within a database not tied to a user (although schemas do have owners). This highlights one area where prior knowledge of Oracle can be a potential hindrance.

Schemas are covered in more detail in Chapter 4.

Database Architecture

Previously, we described a database in SQL Server as being analogous to a schema in Oracle. This was to enforce the point that a database in SQL Server can be thought of as a container of data and objects related to one specific application or function. For example, the HR sample schema in Oracle would translate to being an HR database in SQL Server. The analogy between Oracle schemas and SQL Server databases makes sense on the surface (that is, a container of objects related to an application), but the analogy becomes less appropriate when you look deeper into the SQL Server implementation of a database in comparison to an Oracle schema.

Each database in SQL Server is an autonomous unit in that each has its own set of data files for objects in addition to maintaining its own transaction log for recovery purposes (that is, its own version of redo log/undo tablespace). As a result, each database within an instance can use different recovery models and is backed up independently of other databases. This is the equivalent of having some databases in ARCHIVELOG mode and others in NOARCHIVELOG mode, each with its own backup strategy. This level of isolation makes moving databases between instances and servers fairly simple; you will see examples of how to do this in later chapters.

Database Storage Model

As an Oracle DBA you already understand the concept of separating the logical presentation of storage from the physical implementation through the use of tablespaces and data files; that is, when users place objects in tablespaces, they do not need to understand or even be aware of the underlying physical data file implementation. The placement of objects within tablespaces removes the user's need to be aware of physical data file locations by creating a logical layer over the underlying storage.

Oracle DBA Q&A

Q: In Oracle, when I do a full database backup, I back up not only all of my user data, but also my system tablespace containing my critical data dictionary information. If you are saying that in SQL Server all databases are separate entities, what happens when I do a full database backup? Does my SQL equivalent of the system tablespace also get backed up?

A: First, it should be noted that although there is a system database in SQL Server known as the master database, it does not hold exactly the same information. The master database in SQL Server holds information about the instance-level objects such as logins and the databases connected to it. Each database, regardless of whether it is a user or system database, contains its own data dictionary; that is, objects such as tables, procedures, permissions, and so forth. Therefore, making a change to a procedure in a user database does not require that you back up the master. Making system-level changes (adding logins and so on) does require that you back up the master. More detail on what needs to be backed up and how to back up is covered in Chapter 7.

Q: What is the limit to the number of databases you can have in a single SQL Server instance? And how many would you typically put in the same instance?

A: It depends. The physical limit is 32,767 databases per instance, but in practice it is much lower than this. The limit is really a practical one. That is to say, how many can you efficiently manage in one instance? With regard to how many you would put in an instance, this very much depends on the type of database you are hosting. For small, departmental-type databases that are up to a few gigabytes in size, you can normally consolidate many of these together in a single instance (subject to available system resources). In general, corporate customers tend to group these small databases together up to a maximum of around 150 in a single instance. At the other end of the scale, if you are looking at a mission-critical application such as the corporate SAP implementation, you would place this database (or set of application databases) in an instance of its own.

Figure 2-6 shows the Oracle and SQL Server logical and physical models side by side. First, let's remind ourselves of the Oracle storage model. At the top level we have tablespaces where objects are logically placed. Tablespaces contain segments such as table and index segments, which are the tables and indexes. Segments consist of one

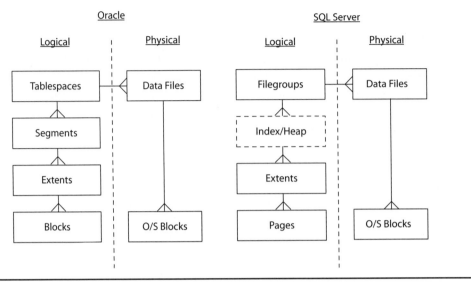

Figure 2-6 *Oracle and SQL Server database storage models*

or more allocated extents, and extents are made up of blocks. At a physical level, a tablespace consists of one or more data files.

In SQL Server the model is similar but with a few exceptions. Filegroups are at the top level and can be thought of as comparable to tablespaces in Oracle, as this is the level at which users place objects. Moving a level down, there is no equivalent concept to a segment within SQL Server. Tables and indexes are allocated space directly from extents. Extents are made up of pages, which are the SQL Server equivalent of Oracle blocks, and finally, a filegroup is physically made up of one or more data files.

If we move a little deeper, this time starting from the bottom of the storage model working our way up, the lowest level of storage in SQL Server is the page, which is the equivalent of a block in Oracle. In SQL Server, pages are always a fixed size of 8K (8192 bytes), whereas in Oracle you can choose to set your database block size from a range of different sizes. Pages are then grouped together to create extents, and in SQL Server, extents are always made up of eight pages, making an extent 64K (8×8K). Each page that is assigned to an extent is physically consecutive in the data file.

Moving up the logical storage model, we are now at the point where in Oracle we would be at segments, but in SQL Server there is no equivalent structure to a segment. Tables and indexes are allocated space directly from extents. As previously mentioned, extents in SQL Server are always 64K in size, but there are two different types of extent, which means that extents are not always a one-for-one mapping with an object (or segment) as in Oracle. The two different types of extent in SQL Server are known as *mixed* and *uniform*. When an object such as a table is initially created, it is allocated a single 8K page of storage from a mixed extent and, up until its ninth single page allocation, all pages come from mixed extents. This is to ensure that small objects do not take up entire extents of 64K. Several different tables and indexes can be allocated pages from the same mixed extent. Once it is time for the ninth page allocation for an object, SQL Server then allocates space to it from that point on using only uniform extents. A uniform extent is an extent that is entirely dedicated to only one object.

ON THE JOB

Although we have said that extent sizes and allocation are fixed, there are some advanced ways to control extents such as allocating a larger number of extents from each file in a filegroup (useful for data warehousing scenarios) and removing the single-page allocation behavior. These types of options are implemented using special startup parameters and are considered to be advanced options for use in very specific scenarios.

Filegroups are at the top level of the logical storage model and are where objects are logically placed. Every SQL Server database will always consist of at least one filegroup, known as the primary filegroup. It is possible to create additional filegroups within a database to create logical (and physical) separation of objects. For example, you may create a filegroup to contain all your data and create another one to hold binary large object data. Another common usage is to use filegroups to create logical separation of data that may be partitioned; for example, creating a filegroup per archive year (2010, 2009, and so on). It is possible for a database to consist of just the primary filegroup and for all user objects to be placed within it. As your databases become more complex and you have different performance and backup/recovery requirements, filegroups play a greater role in the design of your database. Chapter 4 demonstrates the use of filegroups in conjunction with table partitioning strategies, and Chapter 7 shows how spreading data among different filegroups can be used to devise more advanced backup and restore approaches.

One filegroup within a database will always be marked as the default, which means that any objects that are created without explicitly specifying the destination filegroup as part of the CREATE syntax will automatically be created in the default filegroup. When you initially create the database, the primary filegroup will have the DEFAULT attribute, but this can be changed to a user-created filegroup. It is also possible to mark user-created filegroups as read-only to prevent accidental modification of data.

At the physical level, filegroups are made up of data files. A filegroup can consist of one of more data files, which can be on the same disk or in different disk locations. To understand how SQL Server allocates space to objects and keeps track of free space using data files, we need to look in more detail at how a data file works.

When data files are added to a database, you specify information such as the logical file name, physical location and details of the initial size, growth settings, maximum size, and the filegroup with which it will be associated. At the point of creation, the file is assigned a unique file ID. Within each data file, the space is divided up into 8K pages, which are numbered contiguously from 0 to *x*, where *x* is the last page in the file.

Figure 2-7 graphically depicts two data files: the primary data file with a file ID of 01 and pages numbered up to 511, and a secondary data file with a file ID of 03 and pages numbered up to 1279. As a point of interest, notice the correlation between file size and the last page number; the primary file is 4MB, which is 8K×512 pages = 4096K.

The 8K pages are not just used to store user data such as tables and indexes; they are also used to store system information such as page free space and extent allocation. There are also system pages, which are used to keep track of extents that have changed since the last backup or minimally logged operation. Table 2-1 lists some of the different page types that are used in data files.

Figure 2-8 represents the start of a data file and notes the first few system pages. Page 0 in every file is always the File Header, which stores various file attributes. The page following the File Header is page 1, which is the Page Free Space (PFS) page. The PFS page is used to track page allocation and free space information. Page free space is only tracked and maintained for Data and Text/Image pages and is used by SQL Server when it needs to find a page to hold a newly inserted piece of data. A PFS page uses 1 byte of storage per page it is tracking and records if the page is allocated. This is followed by tracking percentage full values of 1–50, 51–80, 81–95, and finally 96–100. Using 1 byte per page means that a single PFS page tracks 8000 pages within the file; therefore, there is a PFS page for every 8000 pages in a data file.

Pages 2 and 3 contain the Global Allocation Map (GAM) and Shared Global Allocation Map (SGAM) pages. GAM pages are used to track which extents are

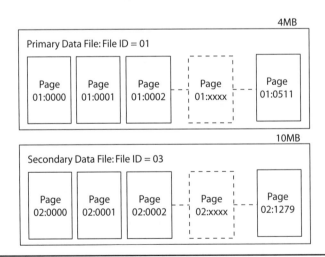

Figure 2-7 *Data files and pages*

Page Type	Description
Data	Data rows with all data, except: text, ntext, image, nvarchar(max), varchar(max), varbinary(max), and xml data, when text in row is set to ON.
Index	Index entries
Text/Image	Large object data types: text, ntext, image, nvarchar(max), varchar(max), varbinary(max), and xml data. Variable-length columns when the data row exceeds 8K: varchar, nvarchar, varbinary, and sql_variant.
Page Free Space (PFS)	Information about page allocation and available free space on pages.
Global Allocation Map (GAM) Shared Global Allocation Map (SGAM)	Information about extent allocation.
Bulk Change Map (BCM)	Information about extents modified using a bulk operation since the last BACKUP LOG statement.
Differential Change Map (DCM)	Information about extents that have changed since the last BACKUP DATABASE command was issued.

Table 2-1   *Page Types Used in Data Files*

currently free or allocated. Each extent is represented in the GAM page with a bit value of 0 for *in use* or 1 for *free*. SGAM pages track mixed extents. If an extent is currently being used as a mixed extent and has at least one free page, it is marked with a bit value of 1; if the extent is not being used as a mixed extent or has no free pages, then it has a value of 0. Both GAM and SGAM pages cover 64,000 extents per page and appear at every 511,230-page interval, which is approximately at every 4GB of a file.

When an object needs to be allocated more space, SQL Server uses the GAM pages to quickly identify an unused extent. In the case of the allocation needing to come from a mixed extent, SQL Server can review SGAM pages to look for a mixed extent that has a free page that can be allocated. If no free mixed extents can be found on the SGAM page, SQL Server will find a free extent within the GAM page and allocate it

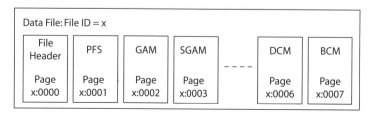

Figure 2-8   *System pages within a data file*

as a mixed extent. If SQL Server cannot find any free space in the GAM and SGAM pages, then the file is full.

The Differential Change Map (DCM) and Bulk Change Map (BCM) pages are not used to track space, unlike the PFS, GAM, and SGAM pages. Their purpose is to track extents that have changed over time.

The first DCM page of a file is located on page 6 and tracks all extents that have changed since the last BACKUP DATABASE command was issued. The DCM page can be thought of as similar to the block change tracking feature in Oracle in that it is used to quickly identify areas of the file that have changed, for backup, without having to read the entire file. The DCM page is different from block change tracking in that it is always on; tracking is internal to the file, and it tracks extents as opposed to blocks or pages. When a differential backup command is issued, the backup reads all the DCM pages (1 for every 64,000 extents) and if an extent is represented with a bit value of 1 then it has changed since the last backup; a value of 0 indicates no change.

The BCM page is only applicable when the database is using the BULK_LOGGED recovery model. Full details behind how this recovery model works and when to use it are covered in Chapter 7. Without going into detail of BULK_LOGGED recovery but to help explain why BCM pages are used, we need to briefly cover what a bulk-logged operation is. When an operation is carried out that is bulk (minimally) logged, the transaction log file (redo file) only tracks which extents have been allocated to the operation, not the data. Therefore, to fully recover the database using transaction log backups, the backup must also contain the data images. BCM pages keep track of any extents that have been allocated or modified as part of a bulk-logged operation. When a BACKUP LOG command is issued, it checks the BCM pages for extents that have been modified and includes them in the log backup. As per the DCM page, there is 1 BCM page for every 64,000 extents.

Finally, if the data file is the primary data file, then one of the system pages also contains the boot page for the database, and this boot page contains all the information about the database.

Physical Implementation

The physical implementation of a database consists of three types of file: primary and secondary data files, and log files. A database always consists of at least two files: a primary data file and a log file. There is only one primary data file per database and it is part of the primary filegroup. Its main function is to hold the system tables containing the database catalog and boot information. The primary data file can, and in many cases does, also contain user data. The log file is the database transaction log that holds all information required to recover the database and is analogous to the redo log/undo tablespace (more details on the transaction log later in this section).

By default, primary data files have an .mdf file extension and log files have an .ldf extension. Any additional data files that are added to a database are known as secondary data files and by default have an .ndf file extension. Secondary files can be added to the primary filegroup as well as any user-created secondary filegroups. A data file only ever belongs to one filegroup.

ON THE JOB

The naming convention of .mdf, .ndf, and .ldf for file extensions for primary, secondary, and log files, respectively, is not enforced or required by SQL Server. It is a good idea to follow this convention for two reasons: first, it makes it easy when browsing the files on the file system to work out what type of file it is; second, many of the dialog boxes in SSMS filter based on using these extensions. Therefore, if you don't use the naming conventions, you are just making life more difficult for yourself and others who may inherit your system. In addition, when running antivirus software on machines running SQL Server, you should add the SQL Server data files to the exception list so that they are not being constantly scanned. Therefore, using the standard extensions means that you only need to add *.mdf, *.ndf, and *.ldf files to the exception list. I have still to come up with a good reason not to follow this.

Figure 2-9 shows an example of a database called HR; the HR database has a single primary data file and a single log file. It also contains a secondary filegroup, which is made up of three data files.

Table 2-2 summarizes the limitations of a SQL Server database with regard to the number of files and filegroups, and the sizes of the files. Note that these figures place the largest theoretical size of a SQL Server database at 524,272TB (524PB).

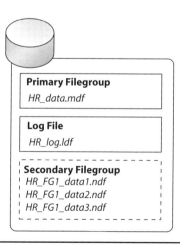

Figure 2-9   *A user database with a secondary filegroup and additional data files*

Object	Number of/Size
Files per database	32,767
Filegroups per database	32,767
Maximum data file size	16TB
Maximum log file size	2TB

Table 2-2   *Database Limits*

Just as in Oracle, where you would use multiple data files for a tablespace to spread disk I/O across multiple disks, or use tablespaces as a unit of grouping for objects and also as a unit of backup and restore, the same principles apply to files and filegroups in SQL Server.

ON THE JOB

If you are working with small databases (up to several gigabytes), it is highly likely the database will consist of just the primary filegroup containing only the primary data file and a single transaction log file. Don't worry, you have not inherited a badly designed database! For databases of this size, there is nothing wrong with this approach. It actually makes administration of the database much easier. There is no need to introduce multiple files and filegroups to the setup unless you need to start distributing the database across disks for performance, storage, or backup and recovery reasons.

As with data files in Oracle, a file in SQL Server can have an automatic growth increment and maximum file size specified. If there are multiple files in a filegroup, then autogrow will not take place until all files are full, at which point the files will be increased in size in a round-robin approach.

Although we are focusing on data and log files in this section, when you are using features such as full text indexing (similar to Oracle Text) and FILESTREAM (similar to BFILE), there are other files and configuration options to be aware of. Both of these features are outside the scope of this book, but you can find more details in SQL Server Books Online.

Transaction Log Files

The roles of undo and redo with respect to transaction logging and recovery in Oracle are treated as separate entities through redo log files and undo tablespaces. In SQL Server, both of these roles are performed by the transaction log file. The transaction log is responsible for tracking all activity in the database such that it can be recovered in the event of system failure (crash recovery). This therefore includes tracking operations such as the start and end of every transaction, DDL operations, page and extent allocation/deallocation, as well as other activities. The other role that the transaction log provides in SQL Server is its transaction rollback capability for any transaction that is aborted or rolled back; SQL Server uses the transaction log to follow the chain of events associated with a transaction, allowing it to undo any work that the transaction had created up to the point of a rollback being issued.

Every database has its own transaction log file, which means that each database is responsible for its own recovery. This also allows each database within an instance to operate using different recovery models (that is, the SQL Server equivalent of ARCHIVELOG and NOARCHIVELOG mode).

Logically, the transaction log operates as a sequential string of incrementing log records identified by log sequence numbers (LSNs), which are similar to System Change Numbers (SCNs) in Oracle. Each record contains the transaction ID to which it is associated. To facilitate rollback operations, all log records that are associated with a particular transaction are individually linked backward to provide a chain of pointers to allow SQL Server to quickly follow a chain of actions to undo.

In Oracle we must always have at least two redo log files, but in many cases a system will have more than this. In SQL Server only one transaction log file is required. The internals of a SQL Server transaction log file are analogous to having multiple redo log files in Oracle, where log files are used in a circular fashion. In Oracle the redo log currently in use is marked as CURRENT, any redo logs that are still required for recovery are marked as ACTIVE, and if the redo log is no longer required for instance recovery, it is marked as INACTIVE and can be reused. In SQL Server the approach is similar, except SQL Server uses a single transaction log file (multiple log files can be used; more on this later) and logically divides the log file internally into a series of smaller virtual log files (VLFs), the size and number of which is controlled by SQL Server dynamically when it creates or extends log files. See Figure 2-10.

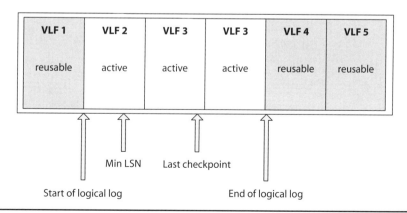

Figure 2-10 *Transaction log file with virtual log files*

As operations occur, SQL Server adds the log records sequentially, appending each record at the end of the logical log. Remembering that transaction log files in SQL Server are required for transaction rollback as well as recovery, the min LSN represents the oldest open transaction in the log that is still required to perform any rollback operations. The last checkpoint indicates when the last database checkpoint took place to secure dirty buffer pages to the data files. As the min LSN moves forward by older transactions completing, VLFs become candidates for truncation and reuse. Upon a checkpoint operation, SQL Server is able to truncate the VLFs that are no longer required for database recovery or transaction rollback and can mark them as reusable.

When the end of the logical log file reaches the end of the physical log, SQL Server wraps back around to the start of the log, as shown in Figure 2-11. In this example, once VLF 5 was full, SQL Server wrapped back around to VLF 1.

Provided the end of the logical log does not meet the start of the logical log, then SQL Server has enough log space to continually log in a circular fashion. If the two points do meet, then either the log file will automatically grow as per the growth settings you specified for the log file (provided there is enough physical space on disk) or the database will generate an error indicating it can no longer continue.

The explanation of transaction log file reuse just given assumes that the database was using the SIMPLE recovery model, which is akin to operating in NOARCHIVELOG mode in Oracle. It should be noted that how the log file is truncated depends upon the recovery model being used. If the database is using the SIMPLE recovery model and a database checkpoint is issued, or if the log file itself gets to 70 percent full (at which point it triggers a database checkpoint), then the log file will truncate the inactive portion of the log, making the log file self-maintaining. If the database is running in the FULL

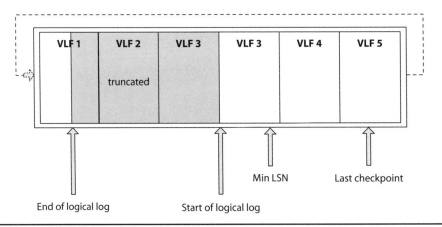

Figure 2-11 *Transaction log file used in a circular fashion*

(or BULK_LOGGED) recovery model, which is similar to ARCHIVELOG mode, then the transaction log file is unable to truncate the inactive portion of the log until a log file backup has taken place. If a truncation was to take place before the log file was backed up, this would break the chain of log records, which would prevent point-in-time recovery in the same way that reusing a redo log file marked as INACTIVE before it was archived would also break the log sequence. When running in a recovery model other than SIMPLE, only a BACKUP LOG command can truncate and clear down the log. Therefore, if you were to never back up your log file, it would continue to grow until you ran out of space.

ON THE JOB

Although the previous text mentioned that the SIMPLE recovery model is "self-maintaining" when it comes to the transaction log, this is only true to a point. If the log were to have a long-running transaction that remained open, then the log would be unable to truncate. The default growth settings for the log file are to grow by 10 percent with unrestricted growth, which means that the log file will continue to grow until it runs out of disk space. Also, even if your log file that normally is 5MB were to grow to, say, 250MB because of an open transaction that you subsequently spotted and rolled back or committed, the log file would physically remain at 250MB, although it would be logically truncated internally. To get the log file back down to size, you would have to issue a command to physically shrink it back down. On another point, autogrowth operations are bad: every time an autogrow takes place, all transactions are halted while the file expands. See this Microsoft Support knowledge base article for more details: http://support.microsoft.com/kb/315512.

SQL Server allows you to have more than one log file per database, and log files are used in a sequential manner. That is to say, in a database that has two log files, SQL Server will only move to the second log file when the first log file is full. Due to the internal circular nature of a transaction log file, it is possible that SQL Server never moves to the second log file if the VLFs in the first log file are cleared and made available.

ON THE JOB

It is rare to see a SQL Server database with more than one transaction log file as there is no great advantage (such as performance or resilience) to having additional files. The only scenario that springs to mind is if you were going to perform an operation that you knew would grow the log to a point that is greater than the disk volume it resides on. If you were to create an additional log file on another drive this would allow the transaction to continue once it had filled the initial log file by moving onto the second file. In this scenario, you probably should look at other potential alternatives, such as changing the recovery model (which can be done online in SQL Server), if possible, to a model that minimally logs the operation.

Oracle DBA Q&A

Q: Can you multiplex your log files as you can with redo log files in Oracle?

A: SQL Server does not have the ability to multiplex transaction log files. To protect your transaction log files from physical disk failure, you should place them on resilient storage, such as RAID 1. If the database is critical, such that you need to protect against complete loss of the transaction log file, then you should have your database configured to use a high-availability feature such as database mirroring. High availability is covered in Chapter 9.

Q: In write-intensive systems, can the log file in SQL Server suffer the same way redo logs do in Oracle in that they can become a bottleneck since all transactions must be secured to the log?

A: Yes, it's exactly the same. Therefore, for databases in which you expect there to be a lot of Insert, Update, and Delete operations, it is important to ensure that your log file resides on a disk array that can provide the required performance. Ideally, this would be a separate volume from your data files.

System Databases

By this point it should be ingrained that, logically, an Oracle schema tends to map onto a SQL Server database. This also applies to system-related schemas and tablespaces. In Oracle, the data dictionary is stored in the SYS schema in the SYSTEM tablespace and operations that require temporary space use the temporary tablespaces. In SQL Server these functions are moved into system databases, described next.

master/Resource

As with the System tablespace in Oracle, the master and Resource databases are essential to SQL Server operation. The function of the System tablespace with regard to maintaining system catalog information and holding all system-related objects (system procedures and packages etc.) in SQL Server are split between the master and Resource databases. In SQL Server, the master database is responsible for holding all instance-wide settings, including information such as the databases currently attached to the instance, login accounts, file allocation and usage, and other system settings; the Resource database holds all of the system objects, such as system stored procedures and so forth. The master database does not hold the catalog information for each database, such as the tables and so forth contained within each database; this is stored at the database level, where each database has its own catalog. This is an important point to note because one of its consequences is that it allows SQL Server to perform DDL operations inside a transaction, which Oracle prohibits because of the shared nature of the catalog.

Unlike the master database, which appears within the SSMS tools alongside other system databases, the Resource database is not visible or accessible. Prior to SQL Server 2005, the master database held all of the system configuration and objects. In SQL Server 2005, Microsoft split the executable system objects into the Resource database. This allowed for quicker and easier upgrades, because to update executable system objects, you simply needed to replace the Resource database rather than make modifications to the master database. Although the Resource database is actually a real database with a data and log file, it resides in the Binn directory alongside all other libraries and executables, not with the other system and user databases, which hints toward its contained functionality; that is, it's more like a library of functions and procedures.

tempdb

The tempdb database performs the same function as the temporary tablespace in Oracle: it is used as temporary workspace. Operations that require temporary storage, such as those that use temporary tables, row versioning and sorting operations for queries, and so forth, all use tempdb. It is important to note that tempdb is re-created every time SQL Server is restarted; therefore, any objects you place in tempdb will not survive a restart of the instance.

ON THE JOB

Configuring tempdb correctly is an important task. The performance of tempdb can and will impact the operation of your SQL Server instance, especially if you make heavy use of features such as temporary tables and row versioning. If you search the Microsoft TechNet website (http://technet.microsoft.com), you'll find whitepapers and best practice articles for working with tempdb. A recent trend is to also use solid-state drives (SSDs) or RAM drives to host tempdb for maximum performance.

msdb

The msdb database does not have a directly equivalent Oracle tablespace. The msdb database is predominately used by SQL Server Agent (SQL Server's scheduling and automation capability, covered more fully in Chapter 10) for storing job and alert definitions, and is also used by features such as Database Mail (for sending e-mail) and Service Broker (the SQL Server version of Oracle Advanced Queuing). All database backup and restore history information is also stored in msdb. In addition, if you are using SQL Server Integration Services (SSIS) and maintenance plans, they can also be stored in msdb.

model

The model database, as with msdb, does not have a direct Oracle equivalent. The model database, as the name suggests, is used as a template or model for all new databases that get created within the instance. Therefore, if you have a common set of objects or settings that you want all new databases to inherit, then you place or set them in the model database.

distribution

The distribution database is a special case. It is only present on the system when the instance is (or was at some time) performing the Distributor role in a SQL Server Data Replication setup. SQL Server Replication is a technology used for publishing and subscribing to data. It is introduced in Chapter 11.

Database Snapshots

A database snapshot is a way to provide a static, read-only, point-in-time view of an existing user database. Database snapshots appear as normal databases from the point of view of being able to query them with SELECT statements and so forth. A database snapshot, when created, consists of a sparse file, which is, over time, populated with pages from the source database when they are updated for the first time since the snapshot was created. A database snapshot is dependent upon its source database as it only contains the changed pages and not the full original source.

From a management perspective, database snapshots appear in SSMS under the Database Snapshots subfolder, as shown in Figure 2-12.

Database snapshots are primarily used for reporting, as they allow a consistent view of a database at a particular point in time. They can also be used to revert a database to an earlier state by restoring the snapshot over the source database. It is also possible to create multiple snapshots of the same database representing different points in time.

Figure 2-13 shows what happens when you query a snapshot database (Step 1), when a page in the source data is updated (Step 2), and then finally when you reissue the same query (Step 3). In Step 1 a query is issued against the HR_9AM snapshot database. At this point there has been no change to the data in the source HR database,

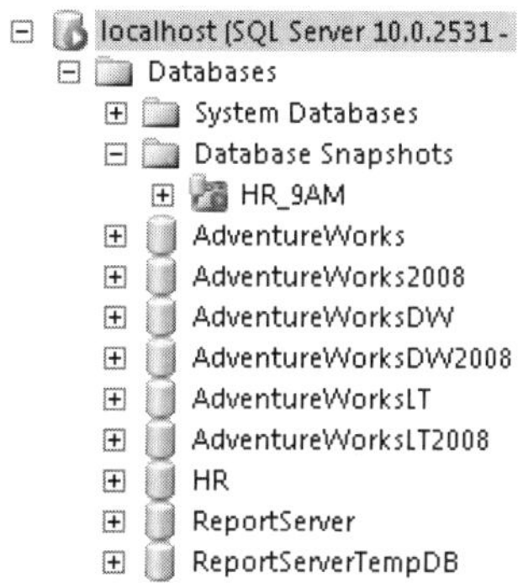

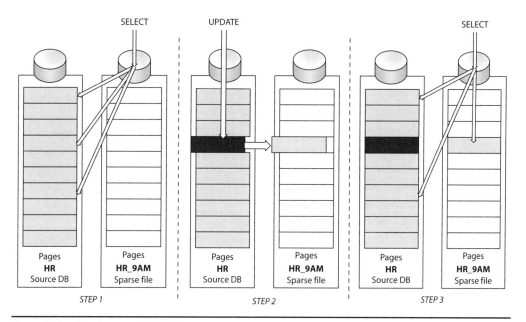

Figure 2-12   *Database snapshots in SSMS*

so the query passes through to the HR source. In Step 2 an update is issued to the HR source database, causing the before image of the updated page to be copied over to the HR_9AM snapshot. In Step 3 the same query that was issued in Step 1 is once again issued against the snapshot. This time the query uses both the source and the snapshot database to create the point-in-time view of the database.

Figure 2-13   *Querying a snapshot database*

ON THE JOB

It is possible to revert a database to a point in time using a database snapshot, but this should not be substituted for database backups. A snapshot only contains pages that have changed since the snapshot was created, and not the entire database. Reverting to a database snapshot is most useful to provide a quick way to undo an upgrade or a test scenario.

Instances

As previously stated, SQL Server and Oracle instances are identical in concept, in that they are responsible for servicing client requests by interacting with the database data files. By this point it should be clear that, unlike Oracle, where an instance is associated with only one database, in SQL Server the instance is associated with multiple system and user databases.

Like Oracle, SQL Server supports multiple instances hosted on the same physical machine. Unlike Oracle, which gives you the option to have instances that can share the same binaries, each SQL Server instance is always an independent installation. Each instance is installed as a separate Windows service and, when started, has its own process, threads, and memory allocation independent of any other instances running on the same machine. This level of isolation allows instances of different versions (SQL Server 2005/2008/R2), editions (Enterprise, Standard, and so on), and Service Pack levels to run alongside each other.

NOTE

Some binaries are shared between the installations, such as the client tools. Installing instances is covered in detail in Chapter 3.

When installing SQL Server instances onto a machine, there is the concept of a "default" instance and a "named" instance. A server can have only one default instance but multiple named instances. Default and named instances are identical with regard to the artifacts that get installed, such as binaries, registry keys, and so forth. The only thing that makes a default instance special is that it can be addressed from a client using only the server name, whereas a named instance must be addressed with the server and instance name. For example, if your server is called SVR-PROD-01, you can connect to the default SQL Server instance by specifying only SVR-PROD-01 in your client tools, whereas to connect to a named instance called DEV on the same server, you would address the server with SVR-PROD-01\DEV. Client connectivity is covered in more detail later in this chapter.

ON THE JOB

Default instances are by far the most popular type of installation on stand-alone servers, and in the majority of cases, the default server port of 1433 is also used. This means that to connect to a SQL Server, you only need to specify the machine name (and the relevant credentials). As you move to more consolidated environments where multiple instances are running on the same machine and in clusters, named instances are essential since you can only have one default instance. Even with multiple instances, you can configure multiple IP addresses on a server and configure each instance to listen on port 1433 on its own IP address.

The resources that an instance can consume on a server can be managed by setting limits for the individual instance or they can be set to allow access to all available resources. Each running instance can be left to share and contend for the same available resources, such as CPU and memory. Setting boundaries for CPUs is done through setting an affinity mask, which instructs SQL Server as to which of the available CPUs in the server it can use. Memory settings are controlled by setting a minimum and maximum memory limit that the instance can use.

Unlike Oracle, where automatic memory-management features have been introduced only within the past few releases, the SQL Server platform has always used automatic management of memory and, as such, has only a small number of configurable parameters that can be set to control memory allocation. Allocation of memory to the various caches is dynamically controlled by SQL Server based on demand. The most notable of the available settings are the Min Server Memory and Max Server Memory parameters. A default out-of-the-box installation sets the SQL Server Min and Max Server Memory settings to allow SQL Server as much memory as it requires without creating problems for the OS it is running on. This is achieved by SQL Server receiving notifications from the Windows OS when it is starting to experience memory-pressure issues. When a notification is received, SQL Server reviews its memory allocation and releases memory back to the OS when it can do so.

Inside the Instance

Internally, SQL Server is broken down into four main components: the protocol layer, the relational engine, the storage engine, and SQLOS. Figure 2-14 shows the four layers and the components found at each layer. The diagram is by no means an exhaustive list of all the components but it does highlight the major elements found at each layer.

Protocol Layer

At the top of the stack, the protocol layer is responsible for receiving the client requests over the various protocols such as TCP/IP; it also unpacks the request (or T-SQL language event, as it is known) and passes it to the relational engine for processing. (Client connectivity is covered later in this chapter.)

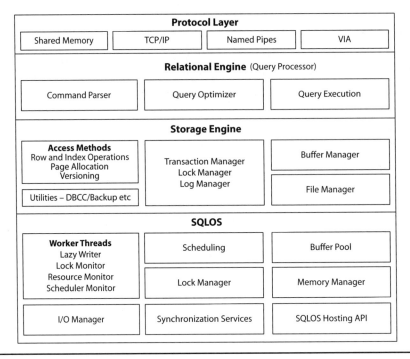

Figure 2-14 *SQL Server Engine*

Relational Engine

The relational engine (also known as the query processor) is the layer that takes the T-SQL language event from the protocol layer and interprets, optimizes, and executes the command. The components at this stage are similar to the components found in Oracle, where SQL statements are processed using a parser, optimizer, row source generator, and, finally, SQL execution engine. The command parser component initially checks the command for syntax errors. Assuming the command passes this check, it then breaks down the command into its constituent parts, which produces a query tree. Once the command parser has completed, it then passes the query tree to the query optimizer for processing. The query optimizer in both Oracle and SQL Server is cost-based. The job of the optimizer component is to determine the optimum plan to execute the command. The plan itself is based on the evaluation of elements such as table and index statistics and how much CPU and I/O the query will take to complete. The resultant output of the query optimizer is an execution plan that is then passed to the Query Executor.

ON THE JOB

The query optimizer is the most complex part of SQL Server. Understanding how it works is the key to optimal query performance. There are several good books on this subject; one of our favorite authors is Itzik Ben-Gan, who has a series of books on T-SQL querying and programming.

The query executor is the final component at this layer and, as the name suggests, it is responsible for stepping through and executing the plan. In the majority of cases, the command will involve interacting with the storage engine to read or manage data and to manage functions such as transactions and locking. Interaction between the relational and storage engines is done using an OLE DB interface.

Other components at the relational engine layer that are not shown on the diagram include the components that are responsible for caching query plans. Also, the components that interact with the databases for metadata that is required for query compilation are also handled at this layer.

Storage Engine

The next layer down is the storage engine. It is at this layer that SQL Server interacts with the database files. When data needs to be located, the access methods component is responsible for returning OLE DB row sets (the results) to the relational engine. Likewise, when the relational engine needs to insert or update data, it passes the access methods component an OLE DB row set for processing. The access methods component does not fetch the actual data or index pages requested; it does this via the buffer manager. The buffer manager is responsible for the data cache (SQL Server's version of the buffer cache). The buffer manager first checks to see if the requested page is available in the data cache. If it's not, then it performs the relevant I/O operation to retrieve the page from disk and place it in the data cache. The access methods component is also responsible for page allocation and row versioning operations.

As a DBA you should already understand the basic principles of ACID and transactions: all transactions must be atomic, consistent, isolated, and durable. The transaction manager is the part of the storage engine responsible for ensuring ACID is implemented. The transaction manager consists of two main components: the lock manager and the log manager. When a transaction needs to work with a piece of data, it needs to know that another transaction is not going to change the data that it is currently working with. Since it is highly likely your database will have more than one user and, therefore, multiple transactions taking place, the locking of resources is essential to maintain consistency of data and results. The lock manager is the component responsible for controlling these locks. Coordination, escalation of locks (such as from a row lock to a table lock), and deadlock resolution are all services of the lock manager. In addition to just locking data, it is essential that data can be recovered in the event of a system failure. SQL Server uses write-ahead logging to ensure that modifications to the database are first stored in the transaction log before the data is stored in a data file. This is the same principle as with redo log files in Oracle. Write-ahead logging is the responsibility of the log manager.

Other components that reside at the storage engine layer include utilities such as the backup and restore functionality, bulk loading, and DBCC commands. DBCC commands are Database Console Commands that Microsoft provides to perform tasks such as database maintenance, validation, and display of system information. For example, DBCC CHECKDB checks the logical and physical integrity of a database and its objects.

SQLOS

The final layer is the SQLOS layer. The role of SQLOS is to provide operating system services to SQL Server such as scheduling, memory management, exception handling, and deadlock detection. It also provides a hosting layer for components such as the common language runtime (CLR). The CLR provides the ability to use the .NET programming language within the database, similar to the Java functionality in Oracle.

SQLOS creates a powerful API that all other components of the SQL Server engine can consume. Therefore, the SQL Server developers within Microsoft, who look after the other components within the engine, write their code to consume resources via SQLOS. SQLOS then takes care of any optimizations that are required for running on different hardware architectures, such as taking advantage of servers that use non-uniform memory access (NUMA, more information on which can be found at http://msdn.microsoft.com/en-us/library/ms178144.aspx). An added benefit of using this layer to access resources is that it creates a common point from which resources can be monitored.

Two of the main functions of SQLOS are scheduling and memory management. The approach that the Windows OS takes to scheduling and execution of work is to provide each request with a fixed time slice within which to execute on a CPU. This time slice is called a *quantum*, and each request will be scheduled to have one or more quantums in which to run, after which they will be stopped to allow something else to run. This allocation of time slices is necessary to provide the illusion of multitasking because a single CPU can only ever do one thing at a time.

The way in which Windows manages the scheduling of work is referred to as preemptive scheduling. In the early versions of SQL Server, the SQL Server development team soon found that a general-purpose preemptive scheduler was not going to provide the level of performance required, so they decided to build a scheduler within SQL Server itself. This was introduced into the product in SQL Server 6.5 and later became part of SQLOS. The scheduler type employed by SQLOS is cooperative as opposed to preemptive. In the cooperative scheduler model, threads voluntarily yield when they are at an appropriate point, whereas in the preemptive model they are removed from the scheduler when their quantum is finished. This does create an onus on the Microsoft developers to write efficient code that does not allow the thread to monopolize the scheduler on which it is running, but the benefit of this approach provides greater scalability than does the generic Windows scheduler. Using the cooperative model, a thread can run until it hits a point where it is waiting for a resource such as a network or disk I/O. As soon as it hits a point where it needs to wait for a resource, it will be put aside while another thread that is waiting for time on the scheduler can run. This approach to scheduling ensures efficient CPU utilization by ensuring that no threads sit idle, tying up CPU time while simply waiting for something else. Monitoring SQL Server waiting for an operation to complete is a great way to troubleshoot performance problems and is covered in detail in Chapter 8.

Execution of work is accomplished in SQL Server using schedulers and worker threads. When SQL Server starts up, a scheduler is created for each logical CPU that is presented to the Windows OS. The scheduler is set to be either ONLINE or OFFLINE depending upon the affinity mask settings for the instance. For each scheduler, a set of worker threads is created that is bound to that scheduler. Worker threads, as the name suggests, are the threads that perform tasks such as queries, DML statements, and so forth. A task is tied to a worker thread until it is completed. The number of worker threads that exist at any one time is dynamically controlled by SQL Server based on system load. If the current number of worker threads is not able to cope with the demand, then the scheduler is able to create more until it hits its limit. Likewise, when the workload is low and schedulers sit idle for greater than 15 minutes, the worker may be closed down to recover system resources. Although the number of worker threads available is dynamically handled by SQL Server based on system load and processor architecture (more worker threads can be created on 64-bit systems), it is possible to limit the number of worker threads that it can create. As a result, when the number of query requests is less than the maximum worker threads value, then each request is handled by just one thread. When the number of query requests exceeds the limit of worker threads, then SQL Server will pool the worker threads to service the workload.

Background Processes   Whereas in Oracle there are background processes such as SMON, PMON, RECO, CKPT, DBWn, and other monitoring and task-oriented processes, in SQL Server the equivalent processes run as background threads. One of the main differences between SQL Server and Oracle is the amount of control you have over these threads. In SQL Server there is very little that you need to set because the engine is dynamic and self-managing. Examples of parameters that you do have control over in SQL Server include the checkpoint process and the maximum number of worker threads (the equivalent of shared server processes).

There are many background tasks that run in SQL Server, but the following are some of the most common ones that you should be aware of:

▶ **Lazywriter**   Data and Index pages can only be accessed after they have been retrieved into the data cache. Ensuring that the data cache always has a list of available buffers into which the pages can be read is important to performance. With no list of free buffers, the data cache would need to be constantly scanned to locate one. The lazywriter is responsible for periodically checking the free buffer list and, if the value is below a predetermined threshold (which SQL Server has dynamically set), scanning the data cache to check the usage history of each page. If the usage history of the page indicates that it is a candidate for removal, it will be placed on the free buffer list. If the page happens to be dirty (that is, it has been modified but not yet written to the data file), the lazywriter will also write the page to disk. This could be compared to the database writer (DBWn) processes in Oracle.

▶ **Checkpoint**   The checkpoint process, as in Oracle, is the process responsible for performing checkpoint operations, which consist of scanning the data cache looking for dirty pages to flush to disk. Checkpoints can be issued manually with a CHECKPOINT statement or they can be triggered by certain operations, such as a clean shutdown of SQL Server, performing a database backup, or issuing an ALTER DATABASE statement. Automatic checkpoints also occur when the database transaction log reaches 70 percent full or the database engine estimates that reprocessing the number of records in the transaction log following a crash is going to take longer than the time specified in the Recovery Interval setting. The Recovery Interval is the equivalent of the MTTR setting in Oracle.

▶ **Log writer**   The same concept as the log writer (LGWR) in Oracle, the log writer thread is responsible for writing data to the transaction logs.

▶ **Deadlock/Lock monitor**   When two threads are deadlocked—that is, neither can progress because they are both trying to lock a resource that the other thread already has locked—something needs to intervene to resolve the situation. The lock monitor thread is responsible for detecting deadlocks and resolving them. The lock monitor will wake up every five seconds to check the system for deadlock situations. Upon finding a deadlock, the lock monitor chooses a deadlock victim and terminates it, rolling back any work carried out by the victim. The victim is chosen based on which thread has the least estimated cost to roll back the work already carried out. A record of the deadlock is recorded in the SQL Server error log. After a deadlock has been detected and dealt with, deadlock searches are immediately triggered for the first few lock wait events in the system following the previous deadlock. This is to ensure that if another deadlock occurs in quick succession, the system does not have to wait for the five-second standard wait interval before being able to deal with it.

▶ **Scheduler monitor**   The Scheduler monitor is a task that runs continuously, checking the health state of all schedulers. Its responsibilities include ensuring that the number of worker threads is balanced across all of the available schedulers. It also ensures that work is evenly distributed between the schedulers. By keeping track of the workload across all of the schedulers, it is able to update system information that allows new tasks to be routed to the schedulers with the least load.

▶ **Resource monitor**   As previously mentioned, when SQL Server is left to dynamically use as much memory as it needs on a machine, it can receive notifications from the Windows OS when it is starting to experience memory pressure. The Resource Monitor thread is responsible for receiving these notifications, as well as internal notifications when cache areas are under pressure. The Resource Monitor is responsible for sending notifications to the various caches to instruct them to review the amount of memory they require and to reduce the memory usage where possible.

Other system threads include the network thread responsible for network communication and threads that control background tasks such as automatic shrinking of databases (when enabled), which can be loosely compared to the system monitor process (SMON).

SQL Server also has services that are external to the SQL Server engine that in Oracle would normally be background processes. Two of the most common ones are SQL Server Agent and the Microsoft Distributed Transaction Coordinator (MSDTC). SQL Server Agent is an external service (which is dependent on the SQL Server service) responsible for automation and alerting. One of its main functions is the running of jobs, which in Oracle would be done using the job queue (CJQ0) and job processor (J000) processes. MSDTC is a Windows service that SQL Server uses for distributed transactions, which in Oracle would be handled by the recoverer process (RECO).

Although you don't have much control over the behavior of most of the background threads in SQL Server, you can see how they are performing by using dynamic management views (DMVs, the equivalent of V$ views) and performance counters. Using DMVs and performance counters for performance monitoring and tuning is covered in Chapter 8.

Memory   Before looking at how SQL Server uses memory, it is important to understand how Windows works with memory and how that can differ between 32-bit and 64-bit platforms, as this can have an effect on how SQL Server operates.

ON THE JOB

With 64-bit hardware now prevalent, the use of 32-bit is quickly diminishing. Windows Server 2008 was the last 32-bit server-based OS from Microsoft. Windows Server 2008 R2 and beyond are now only available as 64-bit, although SQL Server is still available in both 32- and 64-bit versions. In our experience, for the past few years it has been very rare to find anyone deploying new SQL Servers on anything other than 64-bit Windows and SQL Server. This section of the chapter describing the behavior of 32-bit systems is included for completeness and for those who are managing older SQL Server solutions. 64-bit really does simplify and release some of the shackles the 32-bit version imposed on SQL Server.

In Windows, as with other operating systems, when a process is started it is assigned a Virtual Address Space (VAS). The VAS provides the process with a range of virtual memory addresses within which it can operate. The size of the VAS is dictated by the processor architecture (32-bit or 64-bit). 32-bit CPUs can only directly address up to 4GB of RAM. With an out-of-the-box installation of Windows, the top 2GB of this 4GB is reserved for the OS, leaving only 2GB for an application, as shown on the left side of Figure 2-15. It is possible to adjust this balance such that the OS reserves only 1GB of RAM and the application, such as SQL Server (or Oracle), can have the remaining 3GB. This is achieved by setting an OS boot parameter switch known as the /3GB switch.

It is possible for a 32-bit machine to have greater than 4GB of RAM installed, in which case it needs a way to address this additional RAM. Physical Address Extensions (PAE) is a technology introduced by the processor manufacturers to increase the address bus from 32 bits to 36 bits, allowing for access of up to 64GB of RAM.

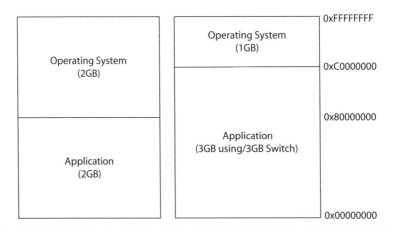

Figure 2-15   *32-bit 4GB address space is divided between OS and application*

Windows can take advantage of PAE through the setting of a /PAE boot switch. Although, setting /PAE only allows Windows to use greater than 4GB of physical RAM; it does not affect the size of the VAS, so processes are still restricted to 4GB of VAS. To bypass this, Microsoft introduced Addressing Windows Extensions (AWE), a set of programming interfaces that allows developers to write programs that can address more memory than the standard 4GB.

For 64-bit CPUs the story is much simpler, as the VAS address space has a theoretical size in the exabyte range, though it is currently limited by Windows at 8TB. The 3GB and PAE options no longer play a part in using this additional RAM.

Now that you have an understanding of how Windows uses memory, let's look at how SQL Server uses its VAS. When SQL Server is first started, the VAS for the SQL Server process is divided into two areas, one for the buffer pool and the other as Reserved Address Space. Most of the memory allocations that reside in the SGA and PGA in Oracle are controlled by the buffer pool in SQL Server. The buffer pool is almost akin to a combined SGA and PGA where allocation for caches such as the SQL Server equivalents of the buffer cache and library cache and the workspace for queries all use memory allocated from the buffer pool. The buffer pool itself consists of 8KB buffers and is the provider for all SQL Server memory allocations that require less than an 8KB contiguous page of memory. This includes but is not limited to data cache, plan cache, connections, locks, and query workspace. If an allocation of greater than 8KB is required, or memory is being requested by a component that is unable to interact with the buffer pool, then this is found in the VAS outside of what is allocated to the buffer pool.

How the VAS is used by SQL Server differs between the 32-bit and 64-bit platforms. Figure 2-16 graphically depicts memory usage by SQL Server on a 32-bit platform with 4GB VAS.

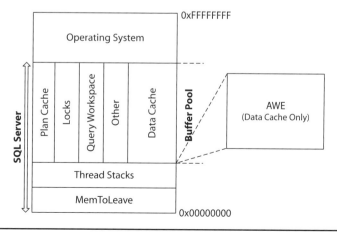

Figure 2-16 *SQL Server memory usage on 32-bit platforms*

Because VAS on a 32-bit machine is limited to either 2GB or 3GB (depending on whether the /3GB switch is used), SQL Server ensures at startup that it reserves areas of memory before the buffer pool is allocated, as shown in Figure 2-16. Under the default memory-management settings for SQL Server, the buffer pool will continue to dynamically grow until it uses all of the available VAS. This will not leave any space for objects that require an allocation of memory from outside of the buffer pool, such as a linked server (the SQL Server version of Oracle database links) or an extended stored procedure (external DLL called from within SQL Server). Due to this behavior, SQL Server has to ensure it has memory available for non–buffer pool allocations. It does this by initially reserving an area of memory called Reserved Address Space (more commonly known as MemToLeave) at startup. Once this area has been reserved and the buffer pool has been allocated, the MemToLeave area is released by SQL Server so that it can be used by any non–buffer pool memory allocations. The MemToLeave area is 256MB plus the amount of memory required by the worker threads.

The Thread Stacks area of memory is used by the worker threads in SQL Server. Each worker thread on a 32-bit system uses 0.5MB of memory. The maximum number of worker threads that can be spawned is calculated based on the number of logical CPUs available. For less than or equal to four logical CPUs, the maximum number of worker threads is 256, making the maximum amount of memory used by the thread stacks 128MB. As the number of logical CPUs increases, the maximum number of worker threads also increases. Using the formula MaxWorkerThreads = 256 + [(# of logical CPUs − 4)×8], you can work out the maximum amount of thread stack space required. Therefore, if the maximum number of worker threads has been set to 256, then the Reserved Address Space will be 256MB in addition to the maximum number of worker threads multiplied by their size, that is, (256×512KB = 128MB), which in total equals 384MB of Reserved Address Space.

Figure 2-16 also shows the use of AWE. As previously mentioned, AWE is a programming interface for Windows that allows application developers to access memory outside of the 4GB VAS restriction. SQL Server has been written such that it can use AWE, but it is restricted to only using it for the data cache area of the buffer pool. Other caches, such as connections and query plans, and other areas, such as thread stacks, are unable to use this additional memory made available via AWE.

When using 64-bit SQL Server, the concept of the Reserved Address Space no longer exists because the VAS for 64-bit is 8TB. Therefore, there is no need to reserve such a small amount of memory. The thread stacks on 64-bit also slightly differ in that each thread stack uses 2MB and the maximum thread value is double that of the 32-bit equivalent—that is, less than or equal to four processors has a maximum of 512 threads. The 8TB VAS on 64-bit also means that there is no need for AWE and that all data caches and external components can take advantage of the extra memory beyond the

4GB barrier, allowing for a greater number of connections, cache plans, and other non-AWE-capable components.

Although you can set SQL Server minimum Min Server Memory and Max Server Memory settings, it is important to note that it is not actually possible to completely control the amount of memory that SQL Server will use. The minimum and maximum memory settings only control the size of the buffer pool and have no effect on other areas such as thread stacks or other allocations made outside of the buffer pool.

Setting Min Server Memory sets the minimum amount of memory that an instance should allocate to the buffer pool, although when an instance first starts up, SQL Server dynamically determines how much memory it requires. Therefore, it is possible that the amount of memory that is allocated is less than the Min Server Memory. As the system is used, the buffer pool will dynamically grow. Once the buffer pool allocation has surpassed the Min Server Memory value, SQL Server will not drop below the Min Server Memory setting from that point on. The Max Server Memory value represents the maximum amount of memory that can be allocated to the SQL Server buffer pool.

Inside the Buffer Pool   Figure 2-16 provided a view of the types of memory consumers that reside in the buffer pool. Let's drill into them in a little more detail.

The data cache performs the same function as the buffer cache in Oracle and is where the mass majority of memory is allocated. It is where pages that are retrieved from disk are placed in memory to be worked with by the engine. The plan cache (also known as the procedure cache) in SQL Server maps to the library cache in Oracle. This cache is responsible for storing all execution plans for SQL statements, stored procedures, and so forth. The memory used by the plan cache is dynamically controlled by SQL Server. The locks cache is responsible for keeping track of all locks acquired within the instance. There are no configurable options for the amount of memory that the locks cache can use, although you can influence how much is used by changing the default locking behavior of SQL Server; note, however, that this could have knock-on effects on concurrency, taking out page locks where row locks would have sufficed.

Although it's not explicitly shown in Figure 2-16 because it falls into the Other category, there is an equivalent of the Oracle redo buffers known as the log cache. Each database within SQL Server has its own log cache. There are no user-configurable options for the log cache in SQL Server, although you can monitor its performance.

So far, the various pools and caches we have compared map onto the SGA in Oracle; we have not covered where the equivalent function of the PGA fits in. The PGA in Oracle, which is responsible for performing operations such as sorting and hash joins on user queries, is known as query memory or workspace memory in SQL Server. Query memory is allocated out of the buffer pool and is dynamically managed by SQL Server. It can consume between 25 percent and 75 percent of the buffer pool.

It is possible to configure the "minimum memory per query" option, which sets the minimum amount of memory a query will be allocated. By default, this value is set to 1024KB, although in most queries that have hash and sort operations, the amount of memory required will exceed this. Setting a value too high for this option can also lead to unnecessary memory pressure because wasted amounts of memory are allocated.

ON THE JOB

In general, for most "every day" departmental systems, the DBA normally only sets the Min Server Memory and Max Server Memory settings for SQL Server. It is also possible to leave those settings at their defaults, in which case SQL Server will work with whatever memory is available in the machine. One complaint from both inexperienced DBAs and Windows administrators when looking at the SQL Server process running on a machine is something along the lines of, "This SQL Server is using 500MB of RAM and it's not even doing anything!" This behavior is by design—if SQL Server has acquired that memory and nothing else on the same machine needs it, then why release it? The SQL Server process has mapped out that chunk of memory, which is now ready for immediate use. If it were to keep releasing that memory, it would have to go through the acquisition process every time it needed more RAM. Therefore, don't just rely on looking at the top-level counters you see in utilities such as Task Manager; you need to understand what is going on inside that block of 500MB, or whatever has been mapped, to see how much is actually being used. Then if you know it only uses 300MB and you don't want it to grab 500MB, simply set the Max Memory limit.

Client/Server Communication

When working with an Oracle database, communication between client and server is provided through the use of Oracle Net Services and the Listener Service. Oracle Net provides the capabilities to establish and maintain a connection between the client and server and then allows exchange of information between these endpoints.

Connecting to an Oracle database requires Oracle Net client software to be installed at the client and server. The Oracle Net foundation layer packages the requests from a client application (such as a SELECT query or command) into a proprietary Oracle format ready to be sent to the server. In order to send the request across to the server, the request must be encapsulated by the Oracle Protocol Support layer into a standard communications protocol provided by the platform such as TCP/IP or Named Pipes. The same process is repeated in reverse for returning information to the client.

At the server side, connections are initially established by first reaching the listener service, which is responsible for setting up the connection to the RDBMS. Once a connection has been established, the listener plays no further part in the conversation. Figure 2-17 depicts the communications stack from application through to RDBMS on both the client and server, including the listener service used for initial connection.

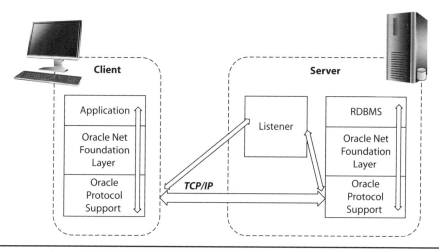

Figure 2-17 · *Oracle network communication*

Client requests within Oracle can be handled using either dedicated or shared server processes. In dedicated mode, each client connection has its own dedicated server process that is responsible for servicing its requests. In the shared server architecture, clients connect to a dispatcher that is responsible for placing the request in a work queue from which a pooled set of server processes picks up work items. Once the work item is completed, the results are then returned to the client.

The equivalent of Oracle Client is SQL Server Native Client (SNAC), which allows connection to SQL Server using OLE DB and ODBC programming interfaces. SNAC comes with the SQL Server installation and is also available for separate download from the Microsoft website. It was created and is maintained by the SQL Server development team, ensuring that it supports all the latest features and functionality. We will assume that you are using this method, although it is important to note that there are other ways to connect to SQL Server without using SNAC. In particular, Microsoft provides two other client libraries: the .NET SqlClient for use in Microsoft .NET programming languages, and the Microsoft SQL Server JDBC Driver.

It does not matter if your application is using OLE DB, ODBC, or ADO.NET as the data access programming method, because ultimately any command or query that is sent to SQL Server will be formatted into a Microsoft request format known as a TDS (Tabular Data Stream) packet. TDS packets themselves must be encapsulated inside some form of communications protocol to allow transmission to an endpoint. This functionality is provided by the SQL Server Network Interface (SNI) protocol layer. The SNI is used by both SNAC at the client side and SQL Server at the server side to pack and unpack the requests into TDS packets. It is also responsible for

Oracle DBA Q&A

Q: Is SNAC available on other platforms such as Linux/Unix? If not, then how do you connect to SQL Server from non-Windows platforms?

A: At present Microsoft only provides the JDBC Driver for connectivity from non-Windows platforms. There are third-party organizations such as DataDirect that have developed ODBC drivers for non-Windows platforms connecting to SQL Server. In addition, there is also an open source project known as FreeTDS (www.freetds.org) that provides a set of libraries for Unix and Linux to talk directly to Microsoft SQL Server.

encapsulating the packets for transmission across the network using protocols such as TCP/IP (see Figure 2-18).

At the server side, SQL Server does not have a separate service that compares to the listener in Oracle; instead, SQL Server has TDS endpoints. The TDS endpoints are configured to listen over different protocols for incoming client requests. There are different types of endpoints available for different types of operations. Connections to the instance for standard database services such as SQL queries and commands are done through TSQL TDS endpoints. For services such as database mirroring

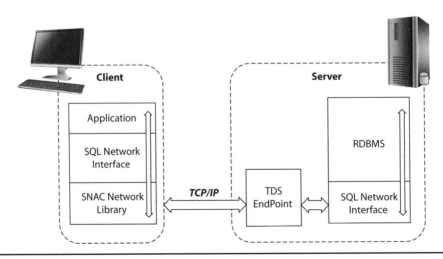

Figure 2-18 *SQL Server network communication*

(high-availability feature) and Service Broker (SQL Server version of Oracle Advanced Queuing), there are special endpoint types known as Database Mirroring and Service Broker endpoints, respectively. When SQL Server is installed, a set of system endpoints is created for the four protocols that are supported, including a special type of endpoint known as the Dedicated Administrator Connection (DAC, covered in Chapter 3). Figure 2-19 shows the system endpoints listed in SSMS. It is also possible to review the available endpoints by querying the sys.endpoints system catalog view. By default, all users have permissions to access the TSQL endpoints unless they have had their permissions revoked or have been denied permission.

NOTE

Figure 2-19 also shows a type listed as a SOAP endpoint. SOAP endpoints enable SOAP over HTTP access to SQL Server, which allows administrators to expose functionality within SQL Server as web services. This functionality has now been marked as deprecated from SQL Server and will be removed in a future version. Therefore, it should be avoided in any new development.

For TSQL endpoints, connection to SQL Server can be made using four different types of protocol: Shared Memory, TCP/IP, Named Pipes, and Virtual Interface Adapter (VIA). TCP/IP and Named Pipes will be familiar to you as they are also supported by Oracle. Shared Memory is only applicable when you are working on the same machine that SQL Server is installed on, as it does not require any networking since all communication uses shared memory segments to communicate between

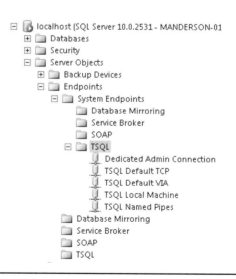

Figure 2-19 *Endpoints in SSMS*

the client process and SQL Server. VIA is a protocol used by specific hardware that supports the VIA specification, and is used in specialized scenarios to create a dedicated high-performance link between SQL Server and a client.

In order to connect to these endpoints, the protocol associated with the endpoint must first be enabled. For example, to use the TSQL Default TCP endpoint shown in Figure 2-19, you must first configure and enable the TCP/IP protocol using SQL Server Configuration Manager. Note that we are assuming that TCP/IP is already installed and configured at the Windows Server OS level.

The default instance of SQL Server is configured to use TCP port 1433 or named pipe \sql\query if either of these protocols is enabled. Because these are well-known values that the client-side libraries are aware of, you do not have to specify them when connecting to the server. When you have multiple instances of SQL Server installed on the same machine, each instance must use a unique TCP/IP address or a unique port number and a uniquely named pipe. Although these values can be manually set, it is possible to have dynamic assignment of these values upon startup of SQL Server. In order to connect to SQL Server, the client must know the full details of where to connect (for example, in the case of TCP/IP, the client must know the IP address and port number). If the port number assignment is dynamic, then this value may change during each service restart.

The SQL Server Browser service is a Windows service that runs on port 1434 and is aware of all the SQL Server instances installed on the machine, including full details of how to connect to them. Therefore, when a client tries to connect to the server using only the server name and instance name, the client-side network library sends a message using UDP to port number 1434 of the server requesting the port or pipe details for the specific instance. The SQL Server Browser service responds with the relevant details, and the client then connects and continues with its operation. It is possible to use SQL Server with multiple instances without the SQL Server Browser service, but each client must know the full connection details of how to reach the specific instance (connection methods are covered in more detail in Chapter 3).

Now that you understand how to establish a connection and communicate between client and server, the next step is to understand how the client requests are processed within SQL Server. As mentioned at the start of this section, Oracle has two methods of servicing client requests using either dedicated or shared server mode where OS-level processes (or threads on Windows) are created, which carry out the work.

The way in which SQL Server fulfills client requests is similar to the shared server model in Oracle. As we discussed in the SQLOS section, SQL Server uses a cooperative scheduling model where SQL Server creates a scheduler for each available CPU. For each scheduler, SQL Server creates a set of worker threads. These worker threads are used to carry out a client request or task such as a query or command.

Connections to SQL Server are identified by session IDs (SPIDs), as shown in Figure 2-20. When a SPID is created by a user connection, it is assigned a preferred scheduler, which is calculated based on current system workload. As a request is received by SQL Server over that SPID, the task is then bound to a worker thread from the associated scheduler to complete the required task. The task remains bound to that worker thread until it is completed. Once the task is complete, the worker thread is released. Provided the system load characteristics remain the same, any new requests on the same SPID will continue to use a worker thread from the pool available to its preferred scheduler. In the case where system load changes (for example, another schedule has a lower workload factor than its preferred scheduler), the request can be routed to a worker thread from that scheduler for execution.

Although the number of worker threads available is dynamically handled by SQL Server based on system load and processor architecture, it is possible to limit the number of worker threads that it can create. As a result, when the number of query requests is less than the maximum worker threads value, each request is handled by just one thread. When the number of query requests exceeds the limit of worker threads, SQL Server will pool the worker threads to service the workload.

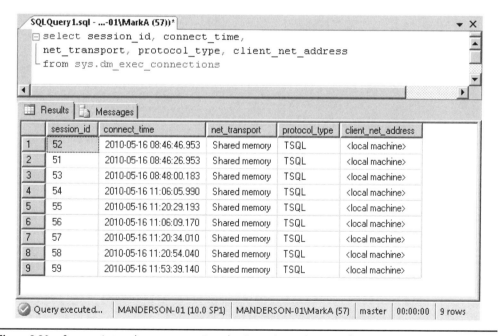

Figure 2-20 *Query against sys.dm_exec_connections, showing sessions and connect information*

Chapter 3

Installing and Configuring SQL Server

In This Chapter

▶ **Installing SQL Server**
▶ **Configuring SQL Server**

This chapter covers installing the SQL Server software and client tools and then identifies the utilities and commands available to perform basic administrative tasks against a SQL Server instance and to make server configuration changes. Whereas Chapter 2 identified the different components of SQL Server and how these components consume and manage operating system resources, this chapter shows administrators how to create a SQL Server instance and then implement changes that alter the behavior of its components.

Installing SQL Server

Although installing SQL Server is a largely automated process that can be carried out without a large degree of product knowledge, it is still important to understand the choices that are available to an administrator when installing SQL Server and how these choices influence the resulting system.

Media and Licensing

Oracle software and manuals are available for download without any restrictions, such as license keys, from the Oracle Technology Network (OTN) website. It is an individual's or company's responsibility to ensure that they purchase appropriate licenses for the Oracle software that they use.

It is possible to purchase SQL Server through Microsoft resellers or, in many countries, directly from Microsoft via the http://store.microsoft.com website, although many organizations have in place a Volume Licensing agreement or similar agreement that makes it possible to download licensed copies of Microsoft software, including SQL Server, as and when they are needed.

Whether SQL Server has been bought in a physical or digital format, the resulting set of files (see Figure 3-1) will be referred to here as the SQL Server installation media.

Oracle DBA Q&A

Q: Can I download and install the SQL Server software without restrictions in the same way that I can download and install the Oracle database software?

A: Microsoft makes freely available a 180-day evaluation of SQL Server Enterprise Edition, which can be downloaded from either the TechNet or MSDN website. In addition, an unrestricted copy of SQL Server Express Edition can also be freely downloaded from the same locations. For all other SQL Server editions, the appropriate license must be purchased prior to the installation of the software—at which point a license key must be provided.

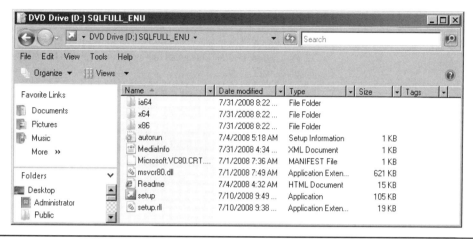

Figure 3-1 *SQL Server installation media*

Software Prerequisites

SQL Server requires only a few software components to be installed on the machine prior to installation (see Chapter 1 for details). The SQL Server Installation Center, discussed later in the chapter, can download and install these prerequisite components on an administrator's behalf if required (see Figure 3-2).

SQL Server Components

When installing SQL Server, several additional products are available on the same set of installation media as the Database Engine. These components are listed and described in Table 3-1. It is a key point to note that each of these components is available in each edition (excluding Express).

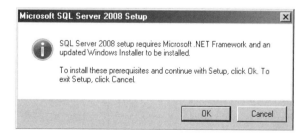

Figure 3-2 *Prerequisites can be automatically installed.*

Server Component	Description
SQL Server Database Engine	Includes the Database Engine, the core service for storing, processing, and securing data, Replication, Integrated Full-Text Search, and tools for managing relational and XML data.
SQL Server Analysis Services (SSAS)	Includes the tools for creating and managing multidimensional online analytical processing (OLAP) and data mining applications.
SQL Server Reporting Services (SSRS)	Includes server and client components for creating, managing, and deploying tabular, matrix, graphical, and free-form reports. Reporting Services is also an extensible platform that you can use to develop report applications.
SQL Server Integration Services (SSIS)	A set of graphical tools and programmable objects for moving, copying, and transforming data.

Table 3-1   *SQL Server Products on Installation Media*

For a fuller description of these components, see Chapter 1.

This chapter makes no further reference to Analysis Services, Reporting Services, or Integration Services other than how they influence the naming of instance objects. Please see TechNet for further details on installing these products.

The SQL Server product itself is made up of various components, all available to install from the installation media. Some of these components support the work of a SQL Server instance and can be installed multiple times on the same computer to create multi-instance installations, whereas others are shared between instances of the same version of SQL Server and so can be installed only once on a given computer.

The shared tools and libraries available for installation from the SQL Server installation media are listed and described in Table 3-2.

Also available for installation are the following documentation sets:

SQL Server Books Online	Core documentation for SQL Server. This is also available at http://technet.microsoft.com/en-gb/library/ms130214.aspx.
Programming Reference	Programming reference material for SQL Server developers.

NOTE

Samples are no longer supplied with the installation of SQL Server. Samples and Community Projects can be found at http://sqlserversamples.codeplex.com/.

Client Components	Description
Connectivity Components	Components for communication between clients and servers, including SQL Native Client (SNAC) and network libraries for ODBC, and OLE DB (and DB Library, although Microsoft has stated that a future version of the Database Engine will drop support for connections from DB Library).
Management Tools	
SQL Server Management Studio	An integrated environment for accessing, configuring, managing, administering, and developing all components of SQL Server.
SQL Server Configuration Manager	Provides basic configuration management for SQL Server services, server network protocols, client network protocols, and client network aliases.
SQL Server Profiler	Provides a graphical user interface (GUI) for monitoring an instance of the Database Engine or an instance of Analysis Services.
Database Engine Tuning Advisor (DTA)	Helps create optimal sets of indexes, indexed views, and partitions.
Services	
SQL Server Browser service	See Chapter 2 for a detailed description.

Table 3-2   *Shared Components and Management Tools on Installation Media*

The installation options that include or omit some or all of the preceding components are described later in this chapter. These client tools and documentation sets can be installed independently of the Database Engine and are well suited to running on a separate client machine.

SQL Server Version Identifiers

Versions of SQL Server following SQL Server 7.0 have all been identified by a year (2000, 2005, 2008, and 2008 R2). However, within these later versions, reference is still made to a numbering that has continued from 7.0. Hence, 2000 is identified as 8.0, 2005 as 9.0, 2008 as 10.0, and 2008 R2 as 10.5.

These numeric identifiers can be found in various places in a SQL Server installation, including in file and folder names. Often the decimal point is omitted, so you will see labels such as 80, 90, 100, and 10_50 used to denote the particular versions.

Although shared features cannot be installed multiple times for a given version of SQL Server, they may be present at each version level, if required. For example, SQL Server 2000 Management Studio may reside on the same computer as SQL Server 2008 Management Studio. See Chapter 12 for a discussion of how SQL Server 2008 and SQL Server 2008 R2 are something of a special case in this respect.

Instance Objects

SQL Server allows the installation of multiple instances of the Database Engine on the same machine. There can be one instance that is not given an explicit name at installation time (the "default instance") but the rest must be named instances.

In terms of the installed artifacts, both named and default instances are identical; both result in files, registry keys, and Windows services being created on the host server, and to support the side-by-side installation of multiple instances, both use an instance identifier to differentiate these items. For named instances, a label denoting the server component that the instance represents is prefixed to the given instance name to create the instance identifier. These labels are

▶ **For the Database Engine**   MSSQL followed by the major version number and a period

▶ **For Analysis Services**   MSAS followed by the major version number and a period

▶ **For Reporting Services**   MSRS followed by the major version number and a period

For the default instance, the alias MSSQLSERVER is added to the preceding label to form the instance identifier. Examples of instance identifiers can be found in the registry key examples given next. The MSRS and MSAS labels are introduced only to help administrators identify directories and other artifacts that might relate to this product in existing installations.

Registry Keys

For each SQL Server Database Engine instance, a registry hive is created under HKLM\Software\Microsoft\Microsoft SQL Server\MSSQL10_50.*inst* for instance-aware components. For example:

▶ HKLM\Software\Microsoft\Microsoft SQL Server\MSSQL10_50.INST01

▶ HKLM\Software\Microsoft\Microsoft SQL Server\MSSQL10_50.INST02

▶ HKLM\Software\Microsoft\Microsoft SQL Server\MSSQL10_50 .MSSQLSERVER

NOTE

These registry keys can yield useful information with regard to a SQL Server installation, such as the location of installed components. However, it is not common practice for administrators to make any system change through amending registry information.

Database Engine Services

The SQL Server Database Engine itself comprises the following Windows services, which combine to provide the functionality associated with the core SQL Server database product.

Component	Service Name	Description
SQL Server	MSSQLSERVER	The service for the SQL Server relational database.
SQL Server Agent	SQLSERVERAGENT	The service that executes scheduled administrative tasks and other user-defined tasks against a SQL Server instance (for example, backups and integrity checks). For each instance of SQL Server, there is a dedicated instance of the SQL Server Agent service.
Full-Text Engine	MSSQLFDLauncher	The service that provides the functionality needed to issue full-text queries against plain character-based data in SQL Server tables. Full-text queries can include words and phrases, or multiple forms of a word or phrase. For each instance of SQL Server, there is a dedicated instance of the Full-Text Engine, including dedicated components such as word breakers and filters, resources such as memory, and configuration such as service-level settings at the instance level.
SQL Server Browser	SQLBrowser	The SQL Server Browser service lets users connect to instances of the Database Engine that are not listening on the default port, without knowing the port number.

These services can be viewed like any others, in Service Control Manager (see Figure 3-3). You'll recall that MSSQLSERVER denotes the default instance, so the first three services in the preceding table relate to that instance on the server. Also, remember that the SQL Server Browser service is a shared feature.

Directory Structures

The directory structures that are created during instance installation are discussed in detail in the following sections. However, it is important to note that in SQL Server, instances can never share binaries; they are always executed as a unique set of binaries

Name ▲	Description	Status	Startup Type	Log On As
SQL Active Directory Helper Service	Enables int...		Disabled	Network S...
SQL Full-text Filter Daemon Launcher (...	Service to l...	Started	Manual	Local Servi...
SQL Server (MSSQLSERVER)	Provides st...	Started	Automatic	.\sqlexec
SQL Server Agent (MSSQLSERVER)	Executes jo...		Manual	.\sqlagent
SQL Server Browser	Provides S...		Disabled	Local Servi...
SQL Server VSS Writer	Provides th...	Started	Automatic	Local System

Figure 3-3   *SQL Server services in Service Control Manager*

under a discrete root directory known as the instance directory. For implications regarding updating instances, see the section "Service Packs and Hotfixes" later in the chapter. The directory into which shared features are installed is referred to as the shared feature directory and it can be completely separate from any instance directory, but all shared features for a version of SQL Server must reside under this root.

NOTE

Where utilities can be installed per-instance and multiple instances have been installed, the version of the utility launched from the program group in the Start menu is from the first instance of SQL Server installed on the computer.

When installing SQL Server the five system databases, master, model, msdb, tempdb, and resource, are always automatically created. However, user and application databases can only be created post-installation.

Installation Locations and Conventions

Oracle administrators are often experienced in implementing the Optimal Flexible Architecture (OFA) standard. To summarize the aims of the standard, OFA is designed to

- ▶ Organize large amounts of complicated software and data on disk, to avoid device bottlenecks and poor performance.

- ▶ Facilitate routine administrative tasks such as software and data backup, which are often vulnerable to data corruption.

- ▶ Facilitate administrators switching between multiple Oracle databases.

- ▶ Adequately manage and administer database growth.

- ▶ Help eliminate fragmentation of free space in the data dictionary, isolate other fragmentation, and minimize resource contention.

Oracle DBA Q&A

Q: Is there an OFA for SQL Server?

A: There are many reference architectures for SQL Server but nothing that seeks to work at the level of detail of OFA. However, many aspects of a SQL Server installation are in keeping with the aims of OFA.

Oracle promotes OFA as a set of guidelines that you should adopt when organizing Oracle directories and files on your computer. All Oracle components on the installation media are compliant with OFA. This means that Oracle Universal Installer places Oracle Database components in directory locations that follow OFA guidelines. In doing this, the goal is to maintain good database health as your database grows in size or you expand to have multiple databases.

A detailed treatment of the OFA standard is outside the scope of this book, but key recommendations are

▶ Database files are named so that they are easy to distinguish from other files.

▶ Files belonging to one database are easy to distinguish from files that belong to another database.

▶ Control files, redo log files, and data files can be identified as such.

▶ The association of data file to tablespace is clearly indicated.

▶ Tablespace contents are separated to minimize tablespace free space fragmentation and minimize I/O request contention.

▶ I/O loads are tuned across all drives.

SQL Server has not traditionally been aligned with efforts such as OFA to standardize deployed artifacts. There are probably many reasons for this but they include the fact that SQL Server has only ever been available for the Windows operating system and that, historically, there have been relatively few options available to those installing SQL Server with regard to system component location and naming. This meant that either the defaults were accepted or that administrators put in some considerable effort post-installation to move and rename SQL Server files and components to adhere to a required design or corporate standard.

Fortunately, SQL Server now provides a great deal of flexibility to those looking to establish non-default configurations, and these options are specified at install time. The result of these choices (discussed later, in the section "The Installation Center") is that independent subdirectories and files are separated by categories and instances to minimize effects upon each other and to ease navigation. Table 3-3 identifies for each SQL Server component the default path and whether that path is fixed or configurable.

In Table 3-3, *inst* stands for the name of the SQL Server instance. For any instance, the MSSQL10_50.*inst* folder may be placed in any available location, and elsewhere we will refer to the MSSQL10_50.*inst* folder (wherever it has been installed) as the instance directory. Note that both SQL Server 2008 and SQL Server 2008 R2 install

Component	Default Path	Configurable or Fixed Path
Database Engine server components	\Program Files\Microsoft SQL Server\MSSQL10_50.*inst*\MSSQL\Binn\	Configurable
Database Engine data files	\Program Files\Microsoft SQL Server\MSSQL10_50.*inst*\MSSQL\Data\	Configurable
Client Components	Program Files\Microsoft SQL Server\100\Tools\	Configurable
Replication and server-side COM objects	Program Files\Microsoft SQL Server\100\COM\	Fixed path
SQL Server Browser service, WMI providers	\Program Files\Microsoft SQL Server\100\Shared\	Fixed path
Other components that are shared between all instances of SQL Server	\Program Files\Microsoft SQL Server\100\Shared\	Fixed path

Table 3-3 *Default Installation Paths for SQL Server Components*

shared components to a directory called 100 and the location of this directory can be set once only (when the first shared component is installed). Wherever installed, this is the shared feature directory for these versions of SQL Server.

SQL Server supports the aims of OFA in the following additional areas:

▶ **Integrity of home directories** SQL Server keeps the software separate from the data files, which allows the software to be moved, deleted, and so on without affecting the application.

▶ **Separation of administrative information for each database** System data is stored in the master and resource databases separate from other data.

▶ **Separation of tablespace (or filegroup content)** Every instance of SQL Server is installed with the system databases master, model, msdb, tempdb, and resource. Unlike the other system databases, the resource database is not visible.

▶ **Tuning I/O load across all disks** SQL Server implements filegroups, each with potentially multiple data files that provide identical advantages to Oracle tablespaces. In addition, storage allocated to an object is distributed relatively evenly across all data files belonging to a filegroup.

Security Considerations

An installation that is secure—that is, one that is not vulnerable to malicious usage or likely to cause loss or damage through unintended operations—should be a key consideration of any database installation, and the decisions that should be taken to maximize security when installing SQL Server are not unique to SQL Server.

As well as physical security (ensuring that physical access to the server is granted only to those who require it and that the server is protected from physical damage), the main areas for consideration at installation time are securing networking via firewalls and assigning service identifiers to services.

Firewalls

Firewalls play an important part in helping to secure the SQL Server installation. The recommended firewall guidelines for SQL Server installations are

▶ Install databases in the secure zone of the corporate intranet and do not connect your SQL Servers directly to the Internet.

▶ Put a firewall between the server and the Internet. Enable your firewall. If your firewall is turned off, turn it on. If your firewall is turned on, do not turn it off.

▶ Divide the network into security zones separated by firewalls. Block all traffic, and then selectively admit only what is required.

▶ In a multitier environment, use multiple firewalls to create screened subnets.

For a complete list of firewall requirements for the principal SQL Server components, see the Books Online article "Configuring the Windows Firewall to Allow SQL Server Access."

Windows authentication is an authentication model commonly used in SQL Server installations. It is discussed in detail in Chapter 5. It functions in the same way as Oracle External Authentication (ops$) in that it allows database users to be authenticated using their Windows identity (logon). When installing SQL Server to use Windows authentication, interior firewalls (those between clients, servers, and Windows domain controllers with which they are both communicating) must be configured to allow Windows authentication. Fortunately, enabling Windows authentication is an area that is well understood by Windows server and network administrators and one for which there is built-in support within Windows itself.

Using dynamic ports complicates connecting SQL Server through a firewall because the port number may change when SQL Server is restarted, requiring changes to the firewall settings. To avoid connection problems through a firewall, configure each SQL Server instance to use a static port, and ensure that clients are aware of the correct port numbers.

Services and Identities

As previously discussed, the various SQL Server components are installed to run as a set of Windows services, which in itself reduces the risk that one compromised service could be used to compromise others. Furthermore, this also gives an administrator the opportunity to assign an individual Windows identity to each of these services and for these identities to have only the least privileges required for them to function correctly.

Service identities may be defined either locally or at a domain level, and when they are specified at install time, the SQL Server installer grants those rights and access permissions required for the given service to run under that identity. Therefore, making SQL Server service identities high-privilege users or groups is not required (and is actively discouraged). However service identities are defined, they should be created with passwords that comply with accepted practice with regard to password strength.

Windows Server 2008 and later creates a special per-service security account for these service identities, called a Service ID (SID). This SID is derived from the service name and is unique to that service. Privileges granted to a SID are available only to that service and are active regardless of what account started the service. SQL Server 2008 and later assign the privileges necessary to run SQL Server to its SID instead of the account used to start the service. During installation, SQL Server Setup creates a service group for each component of SQL Server, and on Windows Server 2008 and later, it is the SID that is added to the local security group instead of the SQL Server service account. Table 3-4 details the operating system permissions granted to SQL Server services, and Table 3-5 details the file system permissions.

Service	Permissions
SQL Server	Log on as a service (SeServiceLogonRight)
	Replace a process-level token (SeAssignPrimaryTokenPrivilege)
	Bypass traverse checking (SeChangeNotifyPrivilege)
	Adjust memory quotas for a process (SeIncreaseQuotaPrivilege)
	Start SQL Server Active Directory Helper
	Start SQL Writer
	Read the Event Log service
	Read the Remote Procedure Call service
SQL Server Agent	Log on as a service (SeServiceLogonRight)
	Replace a process-level token (SeAssignPrimaryTokenPrivilege)
	Bypass traverse checking (SeChangeNotifyPrivilege)
	Adjust memory quotas for a process (SeIncreaseQuotaPrivilege)
Full-Text Search	Log on as a service (SeServiceLogonRight)
SQL Server Browser service	Log on as a service (SeServiceLogonRight)

Table 3-4   *Permissions Granted to SQL Server Services*

Service	Location	Access
SQL Server	*instance directory*\MSSQL\backup	Full Control
	instance directory\MSSQL\binn	Read, Execute
	instance directory\MSSQL\data	Full Control
	instance directory\MSSQL\FTData	Full Control
	instance directory\MSSQL\Install	Read, Execute
	instance directory\MSSQL\Log	Full Control
	instance directory\MSSQL\Repldata	Full Control
	shared feature directory\100\shared	Read, Execute
SQL Server Agent	*instance root*\MSSQL\binn	Full Control
	instance root\MSSQL\Log	Read, Write, Delete, Execute
	shared feature directory\100\com	Read, Execute
	shared feature directory\100\shared	Read, Execute
	shared feature directory\100\shared\Errordumps	Read, Write
Full-Text Search	*instance directory*\MSSQL\FTData	Full Control
	instance directory\MSSQL\FTRef	Read, Execute
	shared feature directory\100\shared	Read, Execute
	shared feature directory\100\shared\Errordumps	Read, Write
	instance directory\MSSQL\Install	Read, Execute
	instance directory\MSSQL\jobs	Read, Write
SQL Server Browser	*shared feature directory*\100\shared\ASConfig	Read
	shared feature directory\100\shared	Read, Execute
	shared feature directory\100\shared\Errordumps	Read, Write

Table 3-5   *File System Access Granted to SQL Server Services*

In order for these access permissions to be evaluated, the target disk subsystem must use the NTFS file system (NTFS). During installation, SQL Server will set appropriate ACLs on registry keys and files if it detects NTFS. These permissions should not be changed. Although the FAT file system is currently still supported, future releases of SQL Server will likely not support it.

It should be noted that if a SQL Server service cannot access the SQL Server portion of the Windows Registry, the service might not start properly.

Software Installation

SQL Server can be installed in either of two ways: interactively and unattended. To create an unattended installation, you must provide all of the required information as parameters to the executable setup.exe found on the SQL Server installation media. For example:

```
Setup.exe /q /ACTION=Install /FEATURES=SQL,AS,RS,IS,Tools,BIDS,BOL
/INSTANCENAME=MSSQLSERVER /SECURITYMODE=SQL /SQLSYSADMINACCOUNTS="Builtin\
Administrators" /SAPWD="StrongPassword" /SQLSVCACCOUNT="DomainName\
UserName" /SQLSVCPASSWORD="StrongPassword" /AGTSVCACCOUNT="DomainName\
UserName" /AGTSVCPASSWORD="StrongPassword" /ASSYSADMINACCOUNTS="Builtin\
Administrators" /ASSVCACCOUNT="DomainName\UserName"
/ASSVCPASSWORD="StrongPassword" /RSSVCACCOUNT="DomainName\UserName"
/RSSVCPASSWORD="StrongPassword" /SQLBROWSERACCOUNT="DomainName\UserName"
/SQLBROWSERPASSWORD="StrongPassword" /ISSVCACCOUNT="NT Authority\Network
Service"
```

This chapter discusses interactive installation only; however, the options that must be specified for either installation method are identical and it is only the means by which this information is gathered that changes. Therefore, an administrator with a good understanding of the purpose of the installation options will find that building unattended installations is a simple task. For further information, see "How to: Install SQL Server 2008 R2 from the Command Prompt" at http://technet.microsoft.com/en-gb/library/ms144259.aspx.

The Installation Center

Administrators who are familiar with Oracle's Universal Installer will find immediate similarities in the SQL Server Installation Center, shown in Figure 3-4. As with its Oracle counterpart, the Installation Center can assess a target environment with regard to its suitability for hosting SQL Server; it can automatically detect dependencies among components, drive complex installation logic that carries out consistency checks throughout the install, and roll back in the case of failure. This chapter concentrates on using the Installation Center to perform a new installation of SQL Server; however, it can also be used to

▶ Add features to an existing installation.

▶ Upgrade a SQL Server 2000 or SQL Server 2005 instance to SQL Server 2008 or SQL Server 2008 R2.

▶ Add or remove a node to/from a high-availability cluster (see Chapter 9).

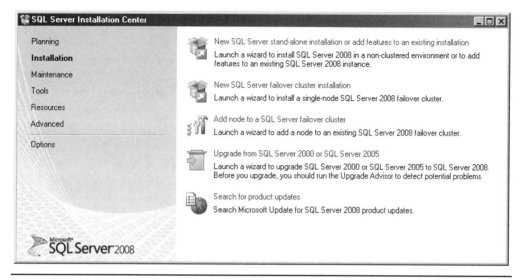

Figure 3-4   *The SQL Server Installation Center*

▶   Repair a damaged installation.

▶   Upgrade an edition of a SQL Server instance (where permitted—for example, from Developer to Enterprise).

Selecting the first option, New SQL Server Stand-alone Installation or Add Features to an Existing Installation, launches the SQL Server Setup program, shown in Figure 3-5, which is a wizard that performs the prerequisite checks on the target system and gathers the information required to complete the installation. This section details the options available to you at installation time.

As previously discussed, for all editions of SQL Server, with the exception of the free and trial editions, a product key must be specified at installation time. The product key provided must represent the edition you wish to install. If a key is not provided at this point, you can proceed using the trial edition and provide the system with a key at any time during the trial period. After you enter the product key, click Next.

The following screen asks you to accept SQL Server license terms. These terms are copied to the local computer when SQL Server is installed. When multiple instances of the same SQL Server edition and language are installed on the same computer, a single copy of the license terms is deemed to apply to all instances of that edition and language.

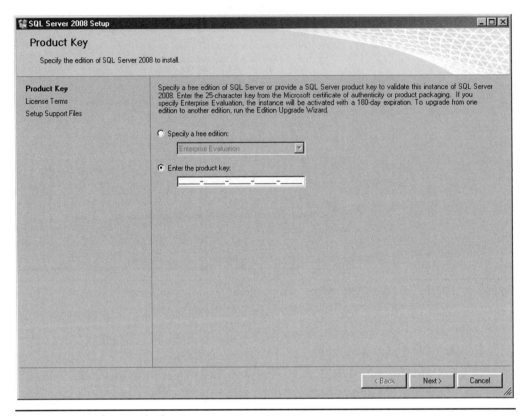

Figure 3-5 *Specifying a product key*

After you click Next, a set of supporting files is then loaded and the system prerequisite checks are carried out. Each individual check can result in a pass, a breaking failure, or a warning (see Figure 3-6). If no corrections are required, click Next.

The Feature Selection page, shown in Figure 3-7, allows you to select the required components for the installation. A description for each component group appears in the right pane after you select the feature name. You can select any combination of check boxes during the first SQL Server installation on a given server.

The Features box is organized into Instance Features, Shared Features, and Redistributable Features.

Everything listed under Instance Features can be installed multiple times on a single server, with the proviso that every instance must be installed to a unique instance root. To install multiple instances of SQL Server components, you return to the installation

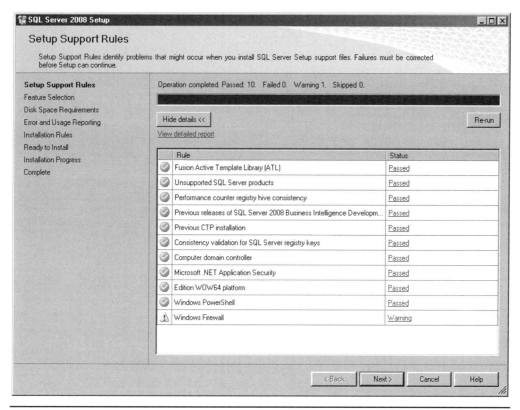

Figure 3-6   *Setup Support Rules page*

media and run setup.exe to launch the Installation Center exactly as you did for the first installation, specifying the options detailed in the following pages as required for that instance. As with the Management Tools, instances of SQL Server 2000, SQL Server 2005, and later versions can be installed on the same hardware, although it is recommended (for both instance and shared components) that previous versions are installed before any later versions to avoid any forward-compatibility issues.

You can specify the directory for shared components using the Shared Feature Directory field at the bottom of the page. To change the installation path for shared components, update the path name in the field manually or click the browse button (three dots) to navigate to an installation directory. The default installation path is C:\ Program Files\Microsoft SQL Server\, and this can only be changed the first time that a shared feature is installed. Click Next after you have specified the directory.

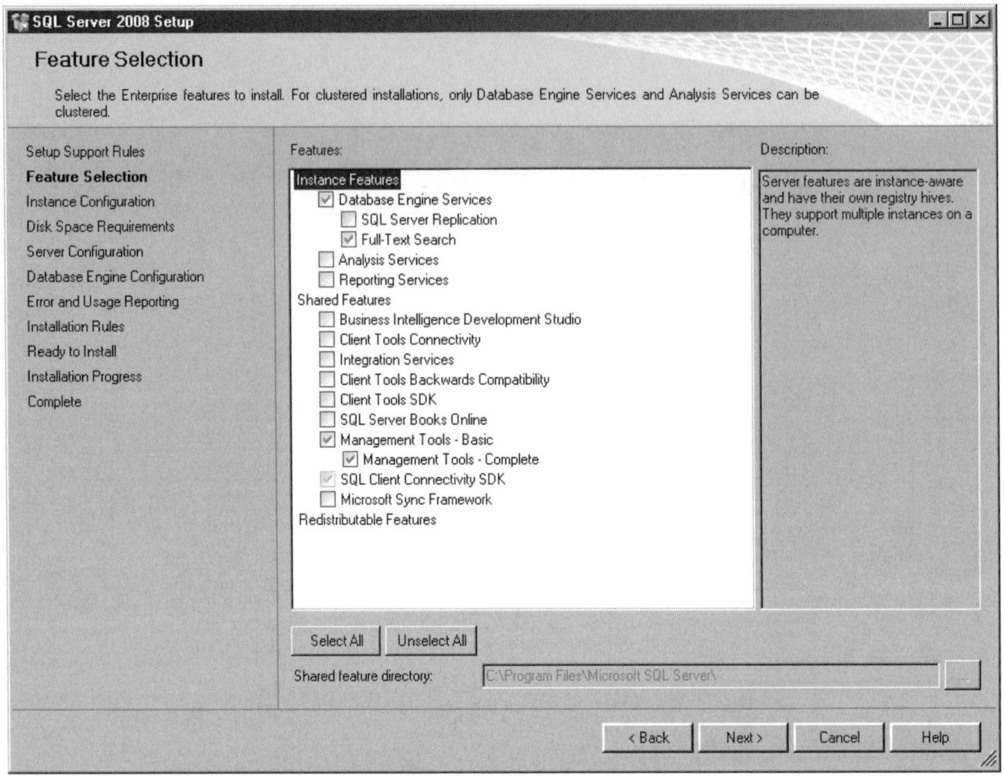

Figure 3-7 *Feature Selection page*

On the Instance Configuration page, shown in Figure 3-8, specify whether to install a default or a named instance. For more information on the exact nature of named and default instances, see Chapter 2.

Whether you choose to install a named or default instance, there are some additional options that determine how the instance will be identified and where components are installed. These are:

▶ **Instance ID** By default, the instance name is used as the instance ID suffix. This is used to identify installation directories and registry keys for your instance of SQL Server. As shown in Figure 3-8, for a default instance, the instance name and instance ID suffix become MSSQLSERVER. To use a non-default instance ID suffix, enter a value in the Instance ID field.

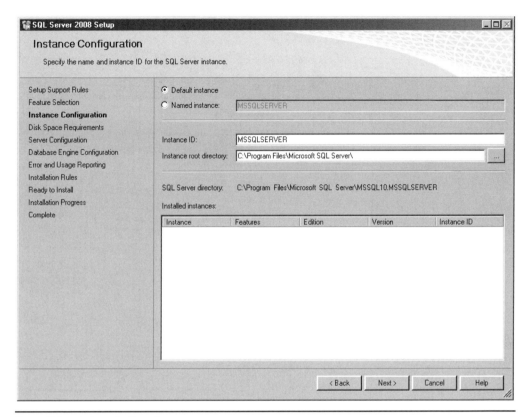

Figure 3-8   *Instance Configuration page*

▶ **Instance root directory**   By default, the instance root directory (the instance directory) is C:\Program Files\Microsoft SQL Server\. To specify a non-default instance directory, use the field provided or click the browse button (three dots) to locate an installation folder.

▶ **Installed instances**   Shows instances of SQL Server that are already installed on this server.

After you have configured the instance, click Next to move to the Disk Space Requirements page, shown in Figure 3-9, which calculates the required disk space for the features you specify. It then compares requirements to the available disk space. Click Next.

On the Server Configuration page, shown in Figure 3-10 with the Service Accounts tab displayed, specify login accounts for SQL Server services. The actual services that are configured on this page depend on the features you selected to install.

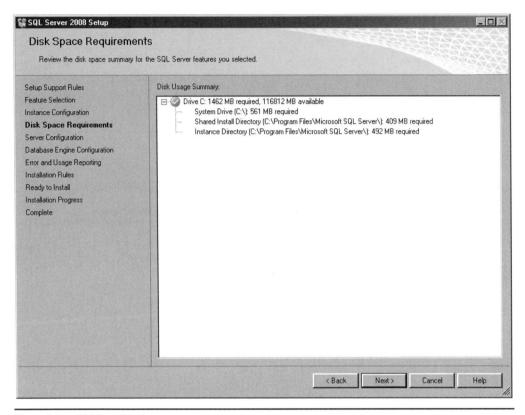

Figure 3-9 *Disk Space Requirements page*

You can assign the same login account to all SQL Server services, although it is recommended that you configure each service account individually, as previously discussed in the section "Security Considerations." By default, services are installed to run under the built-in Local System identity. You can also specify whether services start automatically, are started manually, or are disabled.

The Collation tab allows you to specify non-default collations for the Database Engine. Collations in SQL Server provide sorting rules and case- and accent-sensitivity properties for its data and can be specified at a database, table, and even column level. By specifying a collation at this point, you are assigning the default for new database objects (including databases) and also specifying the rules that will be enforced for the system catalog.

After you click Next, the Database Engine Configuration page, shown in Figure 3-11, allows you to specify engine configuration relating to data directories, the security model, and FILESTREAM access.

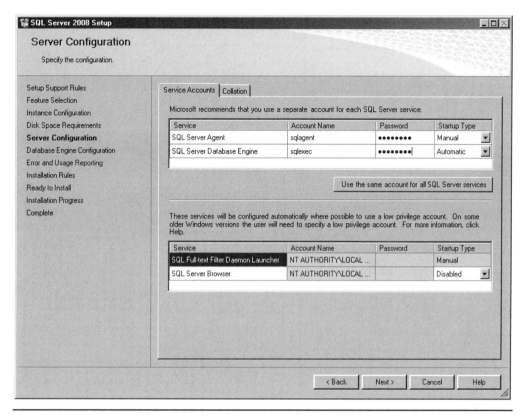

Figure 3-10   *Server Configuration page*

The following are the options on the Account Provisioning tab:

▶ **Authentication Mode**   Select Windows Authentication Mode or Mixed Mode for your instance of SQL Server. These modes are described in detail in Chapter 5; review the section "Security Considerations" earlier in this chapter for the installation implications of this selection.

▶ **Specify SQL Server Administrators**   You must specify at least one system administrator for the instance of SQL Server. In versions of SQL Server previous to 2008, the account under which setup was run was always granted sysadmin privileges; now another account can be specified. To add the account under which SQL Server Setup is running, click Add Current User. To add or remove accounts from the list of system administrators, click Add or Remove, and then edit the list of users, groups, or computers that will have administrator privileges for the instance of SQL Server.

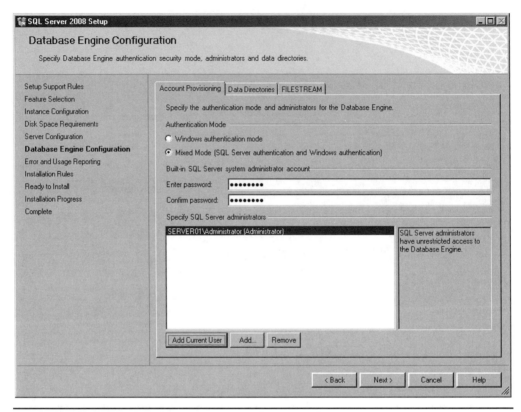

Figure 3-11 *Database Engine Configuration page, Account Provisioning tab*

The Data Directories tab options are as follows (see Figure 3-12):

▶ **Data root directory**   A directory to be used as the root directory for all instance-specific data files (as opposed to product binaries) for this installation. The locations specified in the following options are set to be subfolders of an instance directory at this location unless otherwise specified. Changing this location from the default is common in larger installations where it is a requirement to separate binaries and data files.

▶ **System database directory**   The directory in which system database (excluding tempdb) data and log files are created.

▶ **User database directory**   The default directory in which user or application database data files are created unless otherwise specified at database creation time.

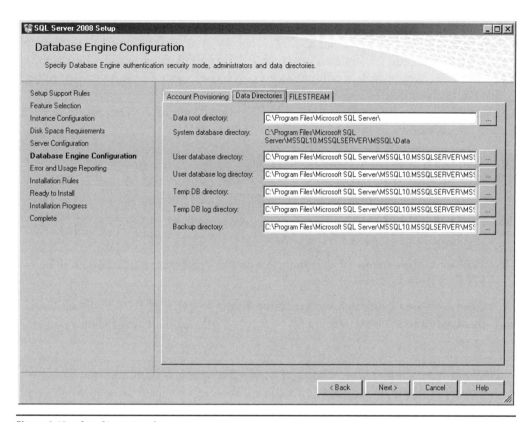

Figure 3-12   *Data Directories tab*

▶ **User database log directory**   The default directory in which user or application database log files are created unless otherwise specified at database creation time.

▶ **Temp DB directory**   The directory in which the tempdb system database data files are created. Special consideration is often given to the location of tempdb for performance reasons—see Chapter 8 for details.

▶ **Temp DB log directory**   The directory in which the tempdb system database log files are created.

▶ **Backup directory**   The default directory for SQL Server database backups.

CAUTION

If you specify non-default installation directories, you must ensure that the installation folders are unique to this instance of SQL Server. None of the directories specified on this tab should be shared with directories from other instances of SQL Server.

FILESTREAM integrates the SQL Server Database Engine with an NTFS file system by storing binary object data as files on the file system. Transact-SQL statements can insert, update, query, search, and back up FILESTREAM data while the Win32 file system interfaces provide streaming access to the data. FILESTREAM needs to be enabled only if you plan to access data in this fashion.

The following are the options on the FILESTREAM tab of the Database Engine Configuration page:

- ▶ **Enable FILESTREAM for Transact-SQL access**   Select to enable FILESTREAM for Transact-SQL access. This control must be checked before the other control options will be available.

- ▶ **Enable FILESTREAM for file I/O streaming access**   Select to enable Win32 streaming access for FILESTREAM.

- ▶ **Windows share name**   Enter the name of the Windows share in which the FILESTREAM data will be stored.

- ▶ **Allow remote clients to have streaming access to FILESTREAM data**   Select this control to allow remote clients to access this FILESTREAM data on this server.

Clicking Next presents the Error and Usage Reporting page, where you have the option to allow information regarding your installation experience to be sent to Microsoft. Clicking Next again presents the Installation Rules page, where the System Configuration Checker will run one more set of rules to validate your computer configuration against the SQL Server features you have specified, as shown in Figure 3-13. Click Next.

The Ready to Install page displays a tree view of installation options that were specified during Setup. Click Next.

During installation, the Installation Progress page provides status so you can monitor installation progress as Setup proceeds. For local installations, you must run Setup as an administrator. If you install SQL Server from a remote share, you must use a domain account that has Read and Execute permissions on the remote share.

Each execution of SQL Server Setup creates log files with a new time-stamped log folder at *shared feature directory*\Microsoft SQL Server\100\Setup Bootstrap\Log\. When Setup is run in an unattended mode, the logs are created at *temp*\sqlsetup*.log.

Service Packs and Hotfixes

Because instances of all SQL Server components are executed as entirely isolated sets of binaries, individual instances of SQL Server of the same major version (for example, SQL Server or SQL Server 2005) may have Service Packs applied independently

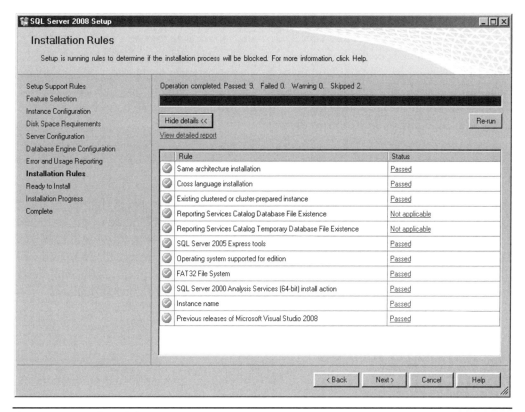

Figure 3-13   *Installation Rules page*

of other instances on the same server. The Service Pack installer will prompt the administrator to choose the instance that is to be upgraded by this execution of the installer.

ON THE JOB

Service Packs may contain updates to shared components. These updates can be applied only once because only one copy of these shared components exists. Because incompatibilities might be created between, say, Management Tools and Database Engine instances if these two sets of components exist at different minor version (Service Pack) levels, it is common for installations that comprise both client and server components to have all server components instances upgraded together.

Since SQL Server 2008 Service Pack 1, it has been possible to uninstall the Service Pack separately from the database release. It is also possible to slipstream Service Packs and cumulative updates into the SQL Server install media; see the Microsoft Support article "How to Update or Slipstream an Installation of SQL Server 2008" (Article ID: 955392).

While it is good practice to maintain SQL Server instances at the most recent Service Pack or hotfix level, remember that client applications may require thorough testing before the upgrade is put into production. Where applications are supplied by third parties, the vendor should be consulted prior to implementing the change.

Configuring SQL Server

Having installed the SQL Server software the job of creating a system that meets the business requirements has only just begun. Changes will likely be made to the instance and databases through the life of the system and some need to be made immediately to allow users and applications to begin interacting with their databases. The remainder of this chapter looks at these initial configuration tasks and then introduces the commands and built-in features that SQL Server administrators use to configure SQL Server instances.

Networking Overview

Unlike Oracle, SQL Server does not store client configuration information in operating system files. In fact, such configuration files are not used by any component of a SQL Server installation. This information is stored in the registry keys (described earlier in the "Registry Keys" section) and in the system catalog. However, as an administrator, it is expected that the only way you will interact with this configuration information is by using the tools described in the section "Network Configuration."

For SQL Server Express or Developer Edition, after installation the SQL Server instance is configured to listen only to Shared Memory, for security protection. Therefore, the SQL Server system is not exposed in any way to the network environment. In providing this functionality, TDS endpoints exhibit some similarity with Listeners; however, there are a couple of key differences: endpoints cannot be added to or removed from an instance—they are only enabled or disabled—and endpoints cannot be started and stopped independently of the instance itself.

SQL Server Configuration Manager (described a bit later in the chapter) is used to configure SQL Server instances and clients to use these networking protocols correctly.

Oracle DBA Q&A

Q: **If there is no Listener, what should I do if I want to disallow client connections but connect myself to administer a database?**

A: Start the instance in single-user mode (see the section "Basic Administration Tasks" later in the chapter), or disable the TCP/IP or Named Pipes connections in SQL Server Configuration Manager.

Network Configuration

Once SQL Server has been installed, the first configuration task is usually to make sure that clients can effectively communicate with the new instance. This section looks at the tools and options available to allow the correct network configuration to be created.

Client Network Configuration

Oracle uses an alias (also called a net service name) to refer to an instance of a database. Resolving the service name can be accomplished by several methods, the most common of which is to use a tnsnames.ora file on every client to provide the required information. The other methods include directory naming (central directory), Oracle Names (centralized server), host naming (host file), external naming (NIS, CDS, and so on), and EZCONNECT.

Clients connecting to SQL Server must specify exactly the same kind of information as Oracle clients, and the most verbose format for this is

```
Protocol:ComputerName\InstanceName,Port
```

In certain circumstances, the protocol, instance name, and port can be omitted. The port need not be specified if communication occurs on the default port, or if a named instance is being addressed and it is configured to use dynamic ports. The instance name can be omitted when it is the default instance that is being addressed or a named instance configured to listen on the default port of 1433. So, the following are all correct forms of address:

▶ **SERVER01** Connecting to the default or named instance on SERVER01 over port 1433

▶ **SERVER01, 8888** Connecting to the default or named instance on SERVER01 over port 8888

▶ **SERVER01\INST01**   Connecting to a named instance on SERVER01 over port 1433 (or where INST01 is using dynamic ports)

▶ **SERVER01\INST01,8888**   Connecting to a named instance on SERVER01 over port 8888

Where a client cannot provide this information directly, the SQL Native Client Configuration tools in SQL Server Configuration Manager (see Figure 3-14) can be used to set up for SQL Server alias names that can be resolved to an IP address (and port) or a Named Pipes address.

SQL Server Configuration Manager can also be used to enable or disable and configure network protocols for connections from remote clients.

Client protocols are given an order of precedence, and communication is first attempted using the lowest-numbered protocol, followed by the other enabled protocols in the order in which they are specified, until a connection is established or all protocols have been tried. Also, you can force the protocol within the connection string; for example, tcp:ServerName for TCP and np:ServerName for Named Pipes.

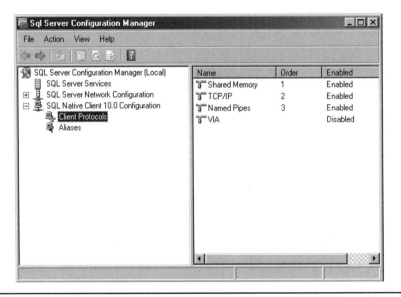

Figure 3-14   *SQL Server Configuration Manager—Client Protocols*

For the TCP/IP protocol, the available client properties (accessed by right-clicking TCP/IP in the list of client protocols and selecting Properties) are shown in Figure 3-15 and described here:

▶ **Default Port**   Specifies the port that the TCP/IP libraries will use to attempt to connect to the target instance of SQL Server. When connecting to a named instance of the Database Engine, the client will attempt to obtain the port number from the SQL Server Browser service running on the server computer. If the SQL Server Browser service is not running, the port number must be provided through this setting, or as part of the connection string.

▶ **Enabled**   Specifies whether the TCP/IP protocol is available to clients when communicating with SQL Server.

▶ **Keep Alive**   This parameter (in milliseconds) controls how often TCP attempts to verify that an idle connection is still intact by sending a keep-alive packet. The default is 30000 milliseconds.

▶ **Keep Alive Interval**   This parameter (in milliseconds) determines the interval separating keep-alive retransmissions until a response is received. The default is 1000 milliseconds.

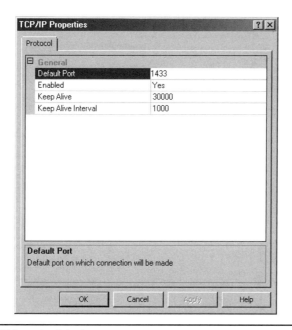

Figure 3-15   *Client TCP/IP Properties dialog box*

Creating SQL Aliases   Right-clicking the Aliases entry and selecting New Alias… in Configuration Manager opens the Alias – New dialog box, which allows you to specify the required information to create a server alias in SQL Server. The available options are shown in Figure 3-16 and described here:

▶ **Alias Name**   The name (alias) that you want to use to refer to this connection.

▶ **Pipe Name/Port No/VIA Parameters**   In this example, we are creating a TCP/IP alias, so the Port No option is presented. If this alias was to use any of the other protocols, then options specific to those protocols would be presented here. Providing a port number results in that TCP port being used whenever a client uses the alias to address the SQL Server instance.

▶ **Protocol**   The protocol used for the connection.

▶ **Server**   The name of the Microsoft SQL Server instance being connected to. Remember the rules previously discussed for whether an instance name must be specified as well as the computer name.

Using aliases requires that the SQL Server client components are installed on each client computer and that the alias configuration is set for each client.

Figure 3-16   *Creating a new SQL Server alias*

The Dedicated Administrator Connection

If an administrator requires access to a running instance of the SQL Server Database Engine to troubleshoot and resolve problems even when the server is unresponsive to other client connections, SQL Server has available the Dedicated Administrator Connection (DAC).

The DAC is available through the sqlcmd utility and SQL Server Management Studio (both are described a bit later in the chapter) and, by default, the connection is only allowed from a client running on the server. Network connections are not permitted unless they are configured by using the sp_configure stored procedure with the 'remote admin connections' option.

To use the DAC, the server is addressed in a fashion similar to that described in the preceding section "Client Network Configuration," but the label ADMIN: is prefixed to the server instance. For example:

```
ADMIN:SERVER01\INST01
```

To guarantee that there are resources available for the connection, only one DAC is allowed per instance of SQL Server. If a DAC connection is already active, any new request to connect through the DAC is denied with an error.

NOTE

Connecting via the DAC to a named instance, or to the default instance if you're not using TCP/IP port 1433, will not work without the SQL Server Browser service.

Server Network Configuration

SQL Server Configuration Manager also allows administrators to configure TDS endpoints for server communications. Server protocols have no order of precedence—they are simply enabled (listening) or disabled (see Figure 3-17). For TCP/IP connections, the configuration options are organized into Protocol and IP Address.

The Protocol options are as follows:

- ▶ **Enabled**   Possible values are Yes and No.

- ▶ **Keep Alive**   Specify the interval (milliseconds) in which keep-alive packets are transmitted to verify that the computer at the remote end of a connection is still available.

- ▶ **Listen All**   Specify whether SQL Server will listen on all the IP addresses that are bound to network cards on the computer. If set to No, configure each IP address separately using the Properties dialog box for each IP address. If set to Yes, the settings of the IPAll Properties dialog box will apply to all IP addresses. The default value is Yes.

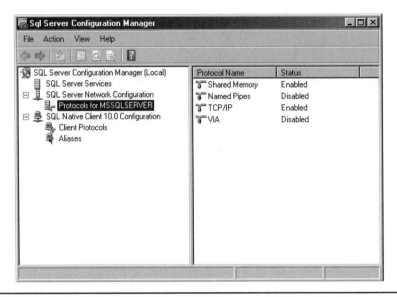

Figure 3-17   *SQL Server Configuration Manager—server protocols*

It is possible to create different configurations for each and every network adapter present on the host computer or to have configuration options apply across all adapters. SQL Server Configuration Manager uses the term IPAll to refer to the configuration for all adapters.

Following are the options on the IP Addresses tab (see Figure 3-18):

▶ **Active**   Indicates that the IP address is active on the computer.

▶ **Enabled**   If the Listen All property in the Protocol tab is set to No, this property indicates whether SQL Server is listening on this particular IP address. If the Listen All property on the TCP/IP Properties dialog box (Protocol tab) is set to Yes, this property is disregarded.

▶ **IP Address**   View or change the IP address used by this connection. The IP address can be in either IPv4 or IPv6 format.

▶ **TCP Dynamic Ports**   Blank, if dynamic ports are not enabled. To use dynamic ports, set to 0.

▶ **TCP Port**   View or change the port on which SQL Server listens (if dynamic ports are enabled, this displays the port currently assigned).

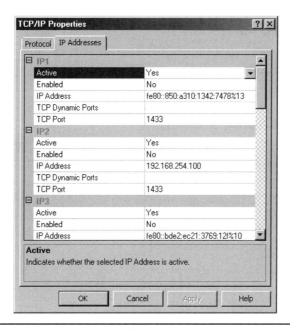

Figure 3-18   *Server TCP/IP Properties dialog box—IP Addresses tab*

Following are the IPAll options:

► **TCP Dynamic Ports**   Blank, if dynamic ports are not enabled. To use dynamic ports, set to 0.

► **TCP Port**   View or change the port on which SQL Server listens (if dynamic ports are enabled, this displays the port currently assigned).

A SQL Server instance can listen on multiple ports on the same IP address. To configure this, list the ports, separated by commas, in the format 1433, 8888, 8889. To configure a single IP address to listen on multiple ports, the Listen All parameter must also be set to No.

SQL Server Configuration Manager displays the IP addresses that were available at the time SQL Server was installed. The available IP addresses can change when network cards are added or removed, when a dynamically assigned IP address expires, when the network structure is reconfigured, or when the computer changes its physical location. To change an IP address, edit the IP Address field, and then restart SQL Server.

Basic Administration Tasks

In addition to being used to configure SQL Server networking, SQL Server Configuration Manager is also used to carry out fundamental administration tasks against a SQL Server instance.

Starting and Stopping Services

As previously discussed, the SQL Server Database Engine is implemented as a collection of Windows services, which can be viewed in Windows Service Manager. SQL Server Configuration Manager also provides a view of these services (in fact, it displays only the SQL Server services present on the target computer). Hence, the service state (start, pause, or stop) can be set using any of the following options:

- ▶ Service Manager
- ▶ SQL Server Configuration Manager
- ▶ Management Studio
- ▶ Net commands such as

```
net start mssqlserver
```

However, there are properties regarding SQL Server services that are only available in SQL Server Configuration Manager, as shown in Figure 3-19. These are discussed next.

Changing Service Logins

Within SQL Server Configuration Manager, the Properties dialog box for a given service allows you to change the account used by the service, or to change the provided password for the account. When this is carried out using Configuration Manager, in addition to changing the account name, Configuration Manager also performs configuration such as setting permissions in the Windows Registry so that the new account can read the SQL Server settings. Other tools such as Windows Service Manager can change the account name but do not change the other associated settings; therefore, you should only use Configuration Manager for this task.

Setting Startup Parameters

When SQL Server is installed, Setup writes a set of default startup options for SQL Server to the Windows Registry. You can use these startup options to specify an alternate master database data file, master database log file, or error log file. These default startup

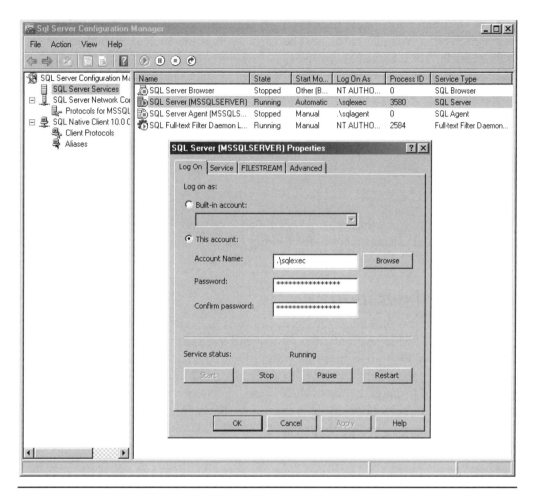

Figure 3-19   *SQL Server Configuration Manager—service properties*

options can be changed if required using SQL Server Configuration Manager by selecting the Startup Parameters option on the Advanced tab of the service's Properties dialog box.

Under normal operation, these three parameters are the only ones passed to the SQL Server instance as it starts. However, in addition to these defaults, there are a number of parameter options available to an administrator to alter the behavior of a SQL Server instance on startup. Examples of these behaviors are starting an instance in single-user mode or overriding a setting such the amount of available memory used by the instance. See http://technet.microsoft.com/en-us/library/ms190737.aspx for a complete list of additional startup parameters.

Also, SQL Server uses trace flags to temporarily set specific server characteristics or to switch off a particular behavior. These flags, which are detailed in the Books Online article "Trace Flags (Transact-SQL)," are not normally applied to SQL Server instances, but they can be useful in diagnosing performance issues and are often used by Microsoft Support when resolving customer problems.

If you are going to use a startup parameter temporarily (usually as part of a troubleshooting exercise), it is recommended that you start the service from the command prompt. For example, the following starts the default instance in single-user mode:

```
net start mssqlserver -m
```

If you expect one or more startup parameters to remain in use permanently, it is recommended that you add them to the Startup Parameters option within Configuration Manager.

Server Configuration

Having established communications between the SQL Server instance and its clients, there will usually be further configuration required to ensure that the instance behaves exactly as required and can support the workload expected of it. In reality, configuring an instance is not something carried out once, post-installation, but instead may take place many times through the life of the instance. Therefore, an understanding of the options that represent optimal SQL Server configuration in a given environment can take years to gain. This section provides a brief look at the tools and commands available to an administrator when configuring SQL Server instances and databases.

SQL Server Management Studio

SQL Server Management Studio is an integrated environment for accessing, configuring, managing, administering, and developing all components of SQL Server and is the environment in which most SQL Server administrators carry out the majority of their tasks. Administrators familiar with current and past Oracle tools such as Database Control, Enterprise Manager, and PL/SQL Developer will find elements of all these utilities combined in a single environment.

Functionality within Management Studio for carrying out each specific administration task will be highlighted in the corresponding chapter that discusses the given task. This section introduces the basic Management Studio functionality to connect to an instance and carry out simple interactions.

Although Management Studio allows you to construct queries without first establishing a connection to a data source, most other tasks require you to first connect to

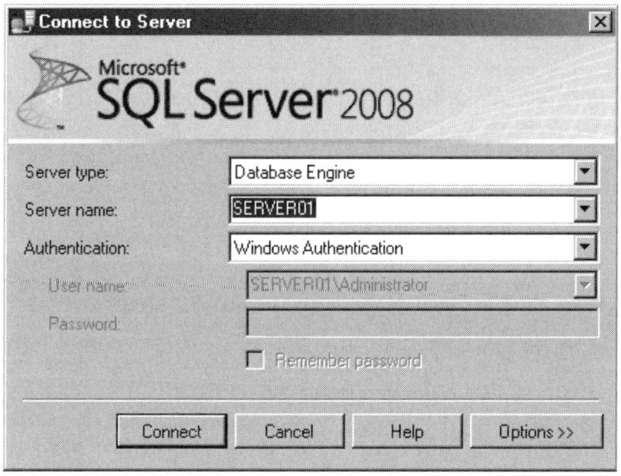

Figure 3-20   *Connecting to a SQL Server instance*

a SQL Server instance. When Management Studio starts, it opens the Connect to Server dialog box and prompts you to connect to a server, as shown in Figure 3-20. The Connect to Server dialog box retains the connection settings from the last time it was used.

Again, bear in mind the rules discussed earlier in the chapter regarding specifying instance names and port numbers when supplying the Server Name information.

Object Explorer (see Figure 3-21), a component of SQL Server Management Studio, connects to SQL Server instances and provides a view of all the objects in the server and presents a user interface to manage them.

You can use the Connect button on the Object Explorer toolbar to connect to additional instances, in which case each instance is represented as a separate top-level node in the Object Explorer tree. Object Explorer can also connect to instances of SQL Server 2000 and SQL Server 2005; however, not all Management Studio functionality will be accessible when working with older versions.

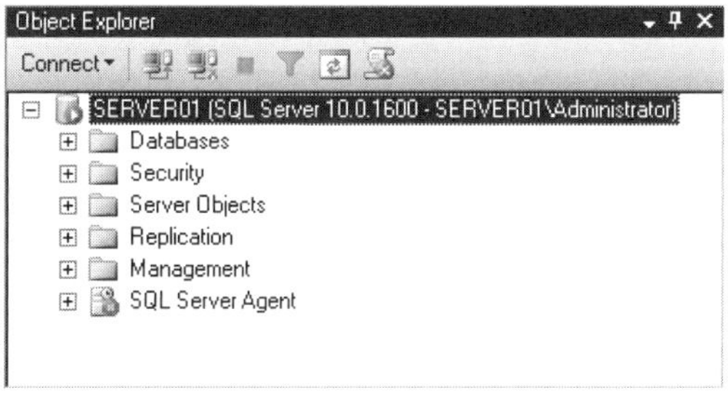

Figure 3-21   *Object Explorer*

NOTE

Object Explorer does not update automatically. If you add or delete databases or database objects, you need to click the Refresh button on the Object Explorer toolbar to see the result of this change in Object Explorer.

The high-level information given by the label of the top-level node for an instance in Object Explorer includes the following:

► Server and instance name (omitting the instance name if it is the default instance).

► The version of SQL Server. The last part of this (the build number) denotes the Service Pack or hotfix level of the instance.

► The credentials used to connect.

ON THE JOB

From an administrative point of view, it is worth knowing that Object Explorer maintains its own connection to the target SQL Server instance, independent of any connection subsequently used to execute queries. This is despite connection information being only collected once. This can cause issues for the unaware when attempting to work with an instance in single-user mode (because Object Explorer will be using the only available connection, leaving none free for queries). In situations where you need to pay particular attention to the number of connections in use, consider using the sqlcmd utility, described at the end of the chapter.

Executing SQL Commands and Scripts

Within SQL Server Management Studio, selecting New Query, either from the Management Studio toolbar or from the context menu (right-click) of the top-level instance node in Object Explorer, opens a new query window in which SQL commands can be constructed. Using Management Studio to build and execute SQL commands is discussed in detail in later chapters; at this point, it is sufficient to note that the contents of a query window are executed against the currently connected instance when you click Execute from the Management Studio toolbar (see Figure 3-22).

Management Studio Server Reports

SQL Server provides graphical reports for monitoring system health and performance. While there have always been various means, such as queries and stored procedures, to gather system statistics, none brought this information together in a single graphical report as we now have available (see Figure 3-23).

NOTE

The Management Studio reports are built using SQL Server Reporting Services (SSRS), but SSRS is not required to be installed to run and view them.

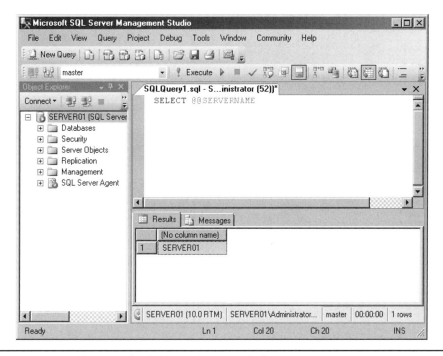

Figure 3-22   *Executing SQL commands in SQL Server Management Studio*

Server reports are accessed from the context menu (right-click) of the instance node in Object Explorer, under a submenu called Reports.

The built-in server reports include the following:

- ▶ Server Dashboard (shown in Figure 3-23)
- ▶ Configuration Changes History
- ▶ Schema Changes History
- ▶ Scheduler Health
- ▶ Memory Consumption
- ▶ All Blocking Transactions
- ▶ Batch Execution Statistics
- ▶ Top Queries by Average CPU Time

The built-in reports cover a range of types of static and dynamic information. However, it is also possible to use SSRS to construct custom reports and have these installed within Management Studio.

Server Dashboard

on SERVER01 at 2/3/2010 3:58:12 PM

This report provides overview data about the SQL Server instance, its configuration, and activity on it.

⊟ Configuration Details:

Server Startup Time	Feb 3 2010 3:40PM
Server Instance Name	SERVER01
Product Version	10.0.1600.22
Edition	Enterprise Edition
Windows ProcessID	3580
Scheduled Agent Jobs	1

Server Collation	SQL_Latin1_General_CP1_CI_AS
Is Clustered	No
Is FullText Installed	Yes
Is Integrated Security Only	No
Is AWE Enabled	No
# Processors (used by instance)	1

⊞ Non Default Configuration Options:

⊟ Activity Details:

Active Sessions	1
Active Transactions	9
Active Databases	4
Total Server Memory (KB)	57088

Idle Sessions	2
Blocked Transactions	0
Distinct Connected Logins on Sessions	1
Traces Running	1

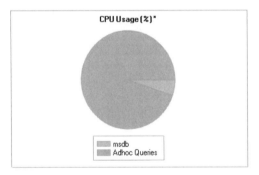

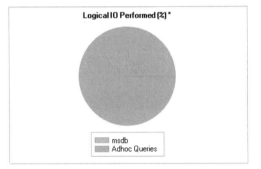

* : "CPU Usage" and "IO Performed" charts show the cumulative share of all objects by databases.

Figure 3-23 *The Server Dashboard report*

Setting Server Options

In Oracle, the initialization parameter file (init.ora or spfile) is used to store values for the various parameters that characterize the instance and the database. SQL Server provides equivalent functionality, though not an equivalent to every initialization parameter, through its configuration options. These options can be configured as server properties using SQL Server Management Studio or using the sp_configure system stored procedure. As mentioned previously, you should not expect to amend any configuration files when working with SQL Server.

The functionality of sp_configure is similar to Oracle's ALTER SYSTEM and ALTER DATABASE commands. The syntax of sp_configure is

```
sp_configure [option, [value]]
```

For example:

```
sp_configure 'show advanced options', 1
GO
RECONFIGURE
GO
```

In the preceding example, the RECONFIGURE statement allows an administrator to call sp_configure repeatedly to make multiple configuration changes and to have all of these configuration changes applied as a single batch when RECONFIGURE is issued.

Depending upon the option set, configuration options take effect either immediately after setting the option and issuing the RECONFIGURE statement, or after performing the preceding actions and restarting the instance of SQL Server.

Of SQL Server's configuration options, a subset is considered user configurable and an additional set is considered advanced. Advanced options, which are similar to Oracle's hidden parameters, are either self-configuring or should be manipulated only by experienced administrators (Microsoft recommends a certified SQL Server technician). Parameters such as Max Server Memory and Min Server Memory are good examples of self-configuring advanced options. SQL Server configures these parameters dynamically based on factors such as available system memory and demand.

Any option deemed to be advanced is not available for configuration using sp_configure until the 'show advanced options' option has itself been set to 1 (the default is 0) as shown in the previous example (setting this option will also list those options deemed to be advanced). For example, simply issuing

```
sp_configure 'fill factor', 100;
GO
RECONFIGURE;
GO
```

results in the following error if 'show advanced options' has not been previously set:

```
Msg 15123, Level 16, State 1, Procedure sp_configure, Line 51
The configuration option 'fill factor' does not exist, or it may be an
advanced option.
```

All server options can be configured using sp_configure, and a subset of these options is also presented to an administrator in the Server Properties dialog box, shown in Figure 3-24, which is accessible by right-clicking the instance node in Object Explorer and selecting Properties.

As Figure 3-24 shows, the Server Properties dialog box is organized into pages. However, somewhat confusingly, options deemed advanced for sp_configure are located on these pages and not just on the Advanced page! There is no requirement for setting the 'show advanced options' option when working with the Server Properties dialog box. For example, from the Database Settings page, it is possible to make a change to the 'fill factor' option, which was shown to give an error when set using sp_configure—the configuration is accepted with no warning other than that this change will not take

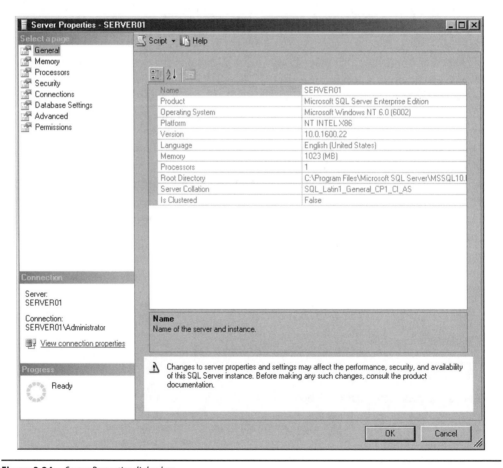

Figure 3-24 *Server Properties dialog box*

effect until the instance is restarted. In the Server Properties dialog box, clicking OK has the effect of issuing the RECONFIGURE statement.

On each page of the Server Properties dialog box, it is possible to use the radio buttons Configured Values and Running Values to inspect whether there are any pending changes—that is, configuration changes that will come into effect following the next instance restart. Any option that has a pending change will show a different value when Running Values is selected rather than Configured Values. These radio buttons can be seen in Figure 3-25, which shows the memory properties for an instance.

A list of the available SQL Server configuration options is available at http://msdn .microsoft.com/en-us/library/ms189631.aspx.

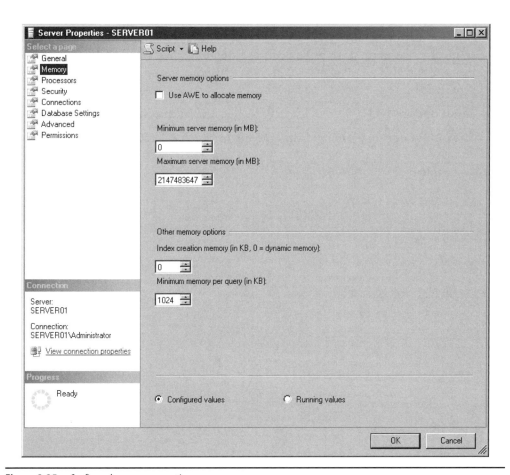

Figure 3-25 *Configured memory properties*

NOTE

A useful element of the Server Dashboard Management Studio report shown in Figure 3-23 is the Non Default Configuration Options section, which lists all changes to server options (whether from sp_configure or server property changes) since instance installation. The default value and the currently running value are reported.

The sqlcmd Utility

Chapter 1 introduced the sqlcmd utility. This section highlights some of the parameters that are most useful to administrators when running the tool:

▶ **The server option (-S)**   Identifies the instance of SQL Server to which sqlcmd connects.

▶ **Authentication options (-E, -U, -P)**   Specify the credentials that sqlcmd uses to connect to the instance of SQL Server. -E requests that Windows authentication be used, and -U and -P allow a SQL Server username and password to be supplied.

▶ **Input options (-Q , -q, -i)**   Identify the location of the input to sqlcmd.

▶ **The output option (-o)**   Specifies the file in which sqlcmd is to put its output.

For example:

```
sqlcmd -S SERVER01\INST01
```

or

```
sqlcmd -i C:\Scripts\MyScript.sql -o C:\Scripts\MyOutput.txt
```

Chapter 4

Database Objects

In This Chapter

- ► **Schemas**
- ► **Schema Objects**
- ► **Working with Data Objects**
- ► **Filegroups and Partitioning**

I n larger organizations, often the lines between those building database applications and those ensuring the day-to-day smooth running of those applications are very clearly defined—usually to the point where these individuals belong to different departments. Even in smaller organizations, many database administrators encounter databases only after they have been designed, built, and tested by someone else. In the past, SQL Server's heritage as a database that tended to support smaller applications perhaps led this line between application developers and professional administrators to be less clearly defined. In more recent versions, the fact that SQL Server Management Studio is a powerful tool for both those carrying out development and those in charge of administration may have continued this trend despite the fact that SQL Server now commonly supports enterprise-level workloads.

SQL Server now resides in the data center, and many new SQL Server administrators will be less concerned with building database objects than with enforcing security, ensuring high performance, and maximizing availability. However, an understanding of the objects that manage data and those that facilitate access to it is important for any database, so, with this in mind, this chapter looks at the principal objects available within SQL Server databases and the operations that administrators will commonly perform on those objects. It is not a complete reference—especially when it comes to the programmatic objects—but it should serve as a good foundation for working with SQL Server database objects.

Schemas

While we've already seen that in SQL Server many of the characteristics of the Oracle schema are exhibited by the database itself, SQL Server does still implement a schema object. Schemas provide security and administrative functions (both described in Chapter 5); however, the way most administrators first encounter them is as a way of creating logical groupings of database objects.

Database objects such as tables and views (and programmatic objects such as stored procedures and functions) all belong to a schema. In the AdventureWorks sample databases, schemas such as Human Resources and Sales have been created, and you can immediately see how adding an object to such a schema imparts information as to the intent or purpose of the object, aiding future maintenance. However, there are more concrete implications to objects belonging to schemas:

- ▶ Object names within a given schema must be unique (but may be duplicated across more than one schema).

- ▶ Because of the preceding rule, the schema name must be provided when referencing the object (although there are exceptions to this, described later in this section).

When you create an object in a SQL Server database, it is good practice to add the object to a previously created schema that groups this object with other related objects. However, if you choose not to do this, your object will be assigned to your default schema, which if you are the database owner or in a role of sysadmin will typically be dbo. Exactly how default schemas are used is also explained later in this section.

ON THE JOB

Before SQL 2005, there was a one-to-one mapping between database users and schemas, much like in Oracle. User-schema separation and the ability to assign a User's default schema were introduced to SQL Server in version 2005, so many SQL Server administrators and developers are still not used to working with them. It is therefore not uncommon to see SQL Server databases where all of the objects reside in the dbo schema. These databases are not "wrong" and will function perfectly correctly.

The full syntax for addressing a database object (from a connection to the instance or from any other object within that instance) is

```
[database].[schema].[object]
```

For example:

```
[AdventureWorks2008].[HumanResources].[Employee]
```

Notes on Object Naming

The square bracket notation allows us to specify SQL Server identifiers that are themselves reserved words (such as a column called "Index") or contain characters such as spaces. However, there is no penalty in using them when not required, (indeed, the brackets can help SQL Server in recognizing a word as an identifier) so many examples and the output of scripting tools will include them as a matter of course. Having said this, you should adhere to commonly-held best practice and avoid using reserved identifiers. Whether or not SQL Server object names are case sensitive is dependent upon the collation order of the database in which the object resides. If you choose a case-sensitive collation order, you have a case-sensitive catalog; otherwise, object names are not case sensitive. See the section "Character Data" later in the chapter for more information on collation in SQL Server. In Oracle, object names not specified in double quotes are automatically converted to all capital letters. SQL Server doesn't do this because it natively supports case-insensitive collations.

Furthermore, SQL Server allows us to create linked servers (equivalent to an Oracle database link), which allow us to address objects in other SQL Server instances and, indeed, other providers such as Oracle, Excel, or flat files, as if they were local objects. (Linked servers are discussed in detail in Chapter 11.) In this case, the syntax becomes

```
[server].[database].[schema].[object]
```

For example:

```
[REMOTEINSTANCE].[ManufacturingDB].[UK].[Products]
```

SQL Server provides the USE directive, which can be issued in the format

```
USE AdventureWorks2008
```

This instructs SQL Server to connect to the given database and resolve object names relative to that database if no database name is specified when addressing an object; this directive persists for the life of the user session or until another USE directive is issued. The same functionality can be achieved in SQL Server Management Studio using the Available Databases drop-down box (shown in Figure 4-1), and is also known as "setting the database context."

As a last note on addressing databases, each SQL Server login is assigned a default database (master if none is specified), and SQL Server will work against this database where no database name is given and no USE directive is issued. (See Chapter 5 for a detailed look at logins and Users.)

So, a database name need only be provided when addressing SQL Server objects when no USE directive has been issued and the object does not reside in the User's default database.

ON THE JOB

Pay particular attention to database context when executing DDL statements. There is nothing to stop you from creating or editing objects in the system databases (assuming you have the appropriate permissions). It is not uncommon to find non-system objects in the Master database because a script has been run without setting the appropriate application database context. Be sure to test before removing such objects from a production database, as Users with a default database of Master may be using them without realizing it.

Figure 4-1 *The Available Databases drop-down box*

A similar approach is taken to providing a schema name when addressing objects. Database Users have default schemas assigned to them, and if none is specified, dbo is assigned as their default. If an object is addressed without giving a schema name, SQL Server first attempts to find the object within the User's default schema, and then, if unsuccessful, looks in dbo; it will only return an error if the object still can't be found.

So, if we consider the objects

▶   AdventureWorks2008.dbo.ErrorLog

▶   AdventureWorks2008.HumanResources.Employee

and the Users

▶   Support (default Schema: dbo)

▶   HRAdmin (default Schema: HumanResources)

we can see how various object calls would succeed or fail (in all cases, the database context has already been set to AdventureWorks2008). This is set out in Table 4-1.

NOTE
The built-in schemas that are created when you install SQL Server are identified in Chapter 3.

User	Call	Result
HRAdmin	SELECT * FROM HumanResources.Employee	Succeed
HRAdmin	SELECT * FROM Employee	Succeed (default schema)
Support	SELECT * FROM dbo.ErrorLog	Succeed
Support	SELECT * FROM ErrorLog	Succeed (default schema)
HRAdmin	SELECT * FROM ErrorLog	Succeed (dbo schema)
Support	SELECT * FROM Employee	Fail (no schema name and not in default schema or dbo)
HRAdmin	SELECT * FROM HumanResources.ErrorLog	Fail (object isn't in this schema!)

Table 4-1   *Addressing Schema Objects*

To talk briefly about how other applications may connect to a SQL Server database, applications can specify what database to connect to as part of their connection string. It is a best practice for applications to explicitly connect to their target database, and to only specify three-part object names when accessing objects in a different database.

Working with Schemas

Creating a schema is simply a case of specifying a schema name and the schema owner (if none is specified, then the owner will default to the dbo User). You can do this from the Schema – New dialog box (see Figure 4-2), which you can access either from

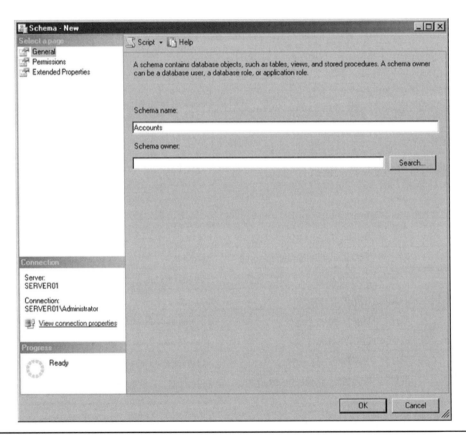

Figure 4-2   *The Schema – New dialog box*

the context menu of the Schemas node in Object Explorer or by using the CREATE SCHEMA statement. For example:

```
CREATE SCHEMA Accounts AUTHORIZATION AccountsAdmin
```

Moving Objects Between Schemas

Objects may be moved between schemas in SQL Server, but doing so causes any permissions explicitly set on that object (see Chapter 5) to be dropped. The object's schema can be reassigned from the object's designer pages in Management Studio (see the section Working with Data Objects for examples covering multiple object types) or by using the following script:

```
USE AdventureWorks2008
GO
ALTER SCHEMA HumanResources TRANSFER Person.Person
GO
```

Synonyms

Another SQL Server object that is likely to catch the eye of the Oracle administrator, but is far from commonly used by SQL Server administrators, is the synonym.

As with Oracle, synonyms are aliases or alternative names by which tables, views, stored procedures, and other programmatic objects can be addressed. Synonyms can refer to remote objects, making them appear local, and can make objects in one schema appear as if they reside in another. While SQL Server DBAs have not traditionally used synonyms to support addressing objects outside of schemas or databases (like schemas, synonyms were introduced in version 2005), they can be very useful in abstracting changes to the location of underlying objects from clients. In this scenario, the moved object is replaced by a synonym in the old location that references the object in the new location. Figure 4-3 shows creating a synonym that would allow the failing call by HRAdmin described in Table 4-1 to succeed.

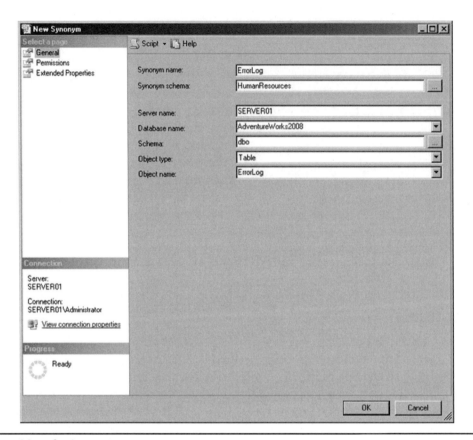

Figure 4-3   *Creating a new synonym*

Schema Objects

As you can see in the following table, the objects that are found in SQL Server databases will be very familiar to Oracle administrators, with the majority of the principal object types having exact counterparts in SQL Server.

Oracle	SQL Server
Table	Table
Index	Index
View	View
Synonym	Synonym
Sequence	N/A*
Procedure	Stored procedure
Function	Function
Package	N/A

*The SQL Server objects that provide some of the capabilities of Oracle sequences are described in the section "Identity Columns and Sequences" later in the chapter.

The fact that SQL Server does not implement anything that acts as an Oracle package will mostly be of interest to those who are familiar with this functionality in Oracle and are now looking to build applications in SQL Server. As demonstrated above, SQL Server schemas give application developers a means of creating logical groupings of objects, and while this does not provide a way of passing application state between objects in the same way as package-scoped variables, there are means available to SQL Server developers to achieve the same end. A common solution is to use temporary tables, which are discussed later in the chapter.

After we take a brief look at the programmatic objects available in SQL Server, the remainder of this section looks at those objects that allow developers and administrators to effectively store data in a SQL Server database, namely the types of tables and indexes available and how views can be used to aid data retrieval and modification. The next section looks at some common administrative tasks associated with these objects.

Programmatic Objects

SQL Server provides many types of objects to allow complex business functionality to be built into the database. In Object Explorer, these objects can be found under the Programmability node, as shown in Figure 4-4.

Stored Procedures

SQL Server store procedures are very similar to equivalent constructs in other databases and other programming languages. They are written in the Transact-SQL (T-SQL) language; some of the high-level concepts of this language are covered in Chapter 6.

Figure 4-4 *Programmatic objects*

Briefly, SQL Server stored procedures can

► Query and modify data in the database, call system functions and procedures, and call other procedures. Sets of data rows may be passed back to the calling procedure or query directly.

► Accept parameters. These may be input, output, or both. Additionally, an optional single return status value is passed back from a stored procedure (this is additional to any output parameters and any data rows).

To differentiate them from system stored procedures, user-defined stored procedures are termed *user procedures*. Following is an example of creating a user procedure in the Accounts schema to return invoices for a given customer:

```
CREATE PROCEDURE [Accounts].[uspGetCustomerInvoices]
     -- Parameters
     @CustomerID int,
     @InvoiceDateStart datetime2,
     @InvoiceDateEnd datetime2
AS
BEGIN
     -- Execute the query, directly returning the results
     --  as a Result Set
     SELECT InvoiceNo, CustomerID, InvoiceDate,
          InvoiceDueDate, CustomerRefNo, HeaderText
```

```
      FROM Accounts.Invoice
      WHERE (CustomerID = @CustomerID AND (InvoiceDate
            BETWEEN @InvoiceDateStart AND @InvoiceDateEnd))
END
GO
```

This procedure can then be executed using the EXECUTE statement:

```
EXECUTE [AdventureWorks2008].[Accounts].[uspGetCustomerInvoices]
  1,
  '2010-02-01',
  '2010-02-28'
GO
```

CLR Procedures   In previous versions of SQL Server, the term extended procedure (or XP) was used to describe stored procedures written outside of SQL Server in C or C++. These procedures allowed access to the additional features of these programming languages and could interact with objects outside of SQL Server, such as the file system. The extended procedure APIs will be removed in a future version of SQL Server and have been replaced by common language runtime (CLR) procedures. CLR procedures are written in a Microsoft .NET language such as C# or VB.NET, compiled into assemblies, and registered with the SQL Server database. They can then be accessed in queries exactly as with user procedures.

Functions

Two types of user-defined functions can be created in SQL Server, scalar and table-valued. Scalar functions return a single value and table-valued functions return a set of rows as a user-defined data type. Scalar functions can be executed directly in SQL statements, for example,

```
DECLARE @ReturnValue varchar(8)
EXECUTE @ReturnValue = dbo.ufnLeadingZeros @Value = 99
```

Both scalar and table-valued functions can be executed inline within SELECT, INSERT, UPDATE, and DELETE statements and also within views. Table-valued functions are referenced in the FROM clause of these queries. To use an example from the AdventureWorks sample database:

```
SELECT ContactID, FirstName, LastName, JobTitle, ContactType
FROM dbo.GetContactInformation(2200);
GO
```

It should be noted that SQL Server places greater restrictions on the actions permitted within functions than it does with stored procedures (and greater restrictions than Oracle places on function). The actions carried out within a function must not change the state of objects outside of the function and this includes database tables. Furthermore, schema objects cannot be created or modified by functions and functions cannot execute stored procedures (although they may consume other functions).

Functions may also be defined within CLR assemblies and registered with the database.

Triggers

SQL Server provides two types of trigger that may be executed as a result of Data Manipulation Language (DML) operations: the AFTER trigger and the INSTEAD OF trigger. The INSTEAD OF trigger is not a direct equivalent of Oracle's BEFORE trigger in that it genuinely replaces the functionality of the operation that fired the trigger.

Other key characteristics of SQL Server AFTER triggers include the following:

► They can only be applied to tables.

► Multiple triggers can be associated with each DML operation (INSERT, UPDATE, and DELETE), in which case the order of execution can be enforced only so far as the first and last to fire can be specified.

INSTEAD OF triggers have these other key characteristics:

► They can be applied to tables and views.

► Only one trigger may be associated with each DML operation.

► They are not allowed on tables that are the targets of cascading referential integrity constraints.

NOTE

In Figure 4-4, the Database Triggers node shown in Object Explorer would contain database triggers, which may be fired by Data Definition Language (DDL) operations at a database level such as changing user permissions or dropping a table. DML triggers are found under the table or view to which they belong.

Tables, Indexes, and Views

The following table lists the types of tables available in Oracle and their direct equivalents in SQL Server, where they exist.

Oracle	SQL Server
Heap-organized table	Heap table
Clustered table	N/A
Partitioned table	Partitioned table
Nested table	N/A
Temporary table	Temporary table
External table	N/A*
Object table	N/A
Index-organized table	Clustered index

*The linked server feature in SQL Server can be used to implement functionality similar to that offered by the external table feature in Oracle insomuch as the referenced server need not be another relational database—it could be a spreadsheet or a text file or anything else for which the appropriate provider exists. Chapter 11 gives more details.

Partitioning, including how it can be applied to tables, is discussed at the end of this chapter.

Heap Tables

As with Oracle, SQL Server can store table data in an unordered manner, with rows being placed within data pages wherever there is free space. Although it is less commonly used than with Oracle databases, the term *heap* still accurately describes these unordered SQL Server tables. Queries against heap tables do not return data in the order in which the rows were inserted and, as you would expect, can be very inefficient to execute if only a subset of the table data is to be returned or if the results need to be ordered.

Temporary Tables

SQL Server allows those writing queries to create and use temporary tables that can be either local or global in scope. The scope of a temporary table (and the fact that it is a temporary table at all) is governed by a naming convention: local temporary tables have their names prefixed with the pound or hash character (#) and are visible only to the session that creates the table. Local temporary tables are dropped from the database when the session disconnects. Global temporary tables are prefixed with a double pound or hash (##) and may be referenced by other sessions. Global temporary tables are not dropped until all sessions referencing the table have disconnected. In all cases, temporary table data is stored in the tempdb system database.

The syntax for creating temporary tables is exactly the same as for a regular table (an example of which is given later in this chapter), with the addition of the appropriate prefix to the table name.

Identity Columns and Sequences

Oracle sequences are a powerful feature for application developers, allowing automatically generated numbers to be managed in a flexible way across multiple tables and other objects; there is no exact equivalent in SQL Server.

What SQL Server does allow us to do is apply the Identity property to a column (such a column is commonly referred to as an identity column) and, in doing so, specify a seed value and an increment. Having done this, for new rows in the table, an automatically generated number will be applied to the identity column with the sequence of numbers starting with the seed and increasing by the increment value. There can be only one identity column per table, and the values are always specific to that table.

The seed and increment values must be integers but can be negative or positive depending on the data type of the column.

Programmatic access to identity values is limited (we cannot, for example, inspect the next available value in a trigger), but the IDENT_CURRENT('table_name') function can be used to return the last-used identity value for a given table across all sessions, or the SCOPE_IDENTITY() function can be used to return the last-inserted identity value for the session, which is useful for retrieving the key value of a row you have just inserted.

Ordinarily you can't insert values into an identity column (or update them), but the command SET IDENTITY_INSERT (ON | OFF) can be used to disable automatic number generation and allow rows with this column already populated to be inserted into the table. An example of using an identity column is given later in the chapter, in the section "Working with Data Objects."

Clustered Indexes

The equivalent of the index-organized table in SQL Server is the clustered index. Both clustered and nonclustered indexes are implemented as balanced trees (b-trees). In a clustered index, nodes at the leaf level contain the actual data pages of the underlying table. A clustered index specifies the order in which the actual rows are stored in the table and, because of this, there can be only one clustered index for a table.

Clustered indexes do not need to be defined based on a primary key in SQL Server; they can be defined on any column (including those that accept null values), but adding a primary key to a table automatically creates a clustered index by default. Clustered indexes are recommended for situations where column values increase by fixed amounts row-by-row, are unique and comprise small data types which stay static over the life of a row; thus, SQL Server tables can often be seen with a primary key defined on an identity column. This is certainly the approach displayed by many SQL Server samples and learning materials.

However it is defined, it is recommended that every table should have a clustered index in the following scenarios:

▶ Queries regularly use ORDER BY or GROUP BY on key columns.

▶ Queries regularly return a range of values using clauses like BETWEEN, >, and <.

▶ Queries are expected to return large result sets.

Nonclustered Indexes

A nonclustered index is a stand-alone storage structure with each row in the leaf level of the b-tree containing a key value and a row locator. This locator points to the data row in the clustered index or heap having the key value. The rows in the index are stored in the order of the index key values, but the data rows to which they point are not guaranteed to be in any particular order unless a clustered index is also created on the table. Up to 1000 nonclustered indexes may be applied to a table (or 999 if a nonclustered index is also present).

Both clustered and nonclustered indexes in SQL Server can exhibit the following qualities:

▶ Composite—can contain more than one column in the index key

▶ Can be unique or nonunique

▶ Can be sorted in either ascending or descending order on the key columns

Clustered and nonclustered indexes are visited again later in the chapter, in the section "Working with Data Objects."

Functional Indexes

Oracle enables you to build indexes on the results of applying some function to the column in question (a common example would be indexing on UPPER(LastName)). SQL Server does not support this capability exactly, but it is possible to index computed (or derived) columns in SQL Server. Therefore, we could add to our table a column called ULastName whose default value was specified as the result of UPPER(LastName) and then use this as a key column in an index. Examples of defining tables and indexes and specifying default constraints are given in the section "Working with Data Objects."

Views

All aspects of SQL Server views will be familiar to Oracle administrators, so we only need to note a few general points here before visiting them from a practical standpoint later in this chapter.

Views can be updated (that is, we can INSERT, UPDATE, and DELETE against the base tables by referencing the view), although certain rules apply:

▶ Modifying statements must reference columns from only one base table. Where more complex modifications are required, INSTEAD OF triggers on views can be used.

▶ The columns that are being modified in the view must reference the underlying data in the table columns directly. They cannot be derived in any other way, such as through an aggregate function (for example, AVG or MAX) or being computed based on other columns.

As with Oracle, the WITH CHECK option can be specified when a view is created, the result being that the view will not allow any modifications that cause data that previously met the criteria of the view to now not be returned by the view. For example, if the WHERE clause of a view specified InvoiceDate < '2010-12-31', then attempting to use the view to update the InvoiceDate value for a row to '2011-01-01' would fail. TOP cannot be used anywhere in the SELECT statement of the view when WITH CHECK OPTION is also specified.

SQL Server views can be indexed and, as such, function in exactly the same way as Oracle's materialized views. Indexed views are created by applying a clustered index to the view and using this to store the view's result set as if it were a table. There are a couple of benefits from doing this: First, for a standard view, the overhead of dynamically building the result set for each query that references a view can be significant if the view involves complex processing of large numbers of rows or joining many tables. This overhead is avoided when the view is indexed, although there is a new cost in updating the clustered index as the underlying data changes. The second benefit is that the SQL Server query optimizer will consider an indexed view for inclusion in an execution plan as if it were any other index, i.e., even when the view is not specifically named in the FROM clause. This can potentially benefit existing queries without having to re-write them (although this automatically considering indexed views is an Enterprise Edition feature). See Chapter 6 for more details on the query optimizer.

Data Types

SQL Server provides native data types that allow us to efficiently store and effectively work with the wide range of data required by modern business applications. Although recent versions of SQL Server have added types such as those required by applications working with geospatial data and XML, this section concentrates on the "traditional" categories of database data type: character, numeric, date, and binary.

In-Row and Out-of-Row Data

As earlier chapters have covered, the smallest unit of logical storage within a SQL Server data file is the fixed 8KB page. With the exception of special circumstances described later in this section, SQL Server does not allow row chaining (that is, all row data must fit into a single page) and, taking into account the overhead required for header and directory information within the page, this means the maximum size of any row of data is 8060 bytes.

This can be demonstrated by attempting to execute the following:

```
CREATE TABLE [Accounts].[BigData]
(
     Col1 char(2500),
     Col2 char(2500),
     Col3 char(2500),
     Col4 char(2500)
) ON [PRIMARY]
```

The resulting error is

```
Msg 1701, Level 16, State 1, Line 1
Creating or altering table 'BigData' failed because the minimum row size
would be 10007, including 7 bytes of internal overhead. This exceeds the
maximum allowable table row size of 8060 bytes.
```

While this restriction might seem like a severe limitation, subsequent to very early versions of SQL Server, changes have been made that, in practice, enable you to easily avoid this row size restriction. The first of these is that SQL Server provides dedicated large object (LOB) data types (and LOB variants of other data types that are properly known as large-value data types) that store columns using these types outside of the regular data page on their own LOB pages. In these cases, a 16-byte pointer is stored in the data row, indicating the location of the actual LOB data.

ON THE JOB

These LOB data types are identified in the individual sections that follow and should always be used for any single column that might be required to store more than 8000 bytes. The default for the newer LOB types is to store data in-row when it is smaller than 8000 bytes and out-of-row when larger. If required, the default behavior can be changed to force LOB data to be stored out-of-row even if it is small.

The second enhancement to SQL Server in this area is to allow columns defined with regular variable-width data types (those whose size is determined by the amount of data stored, rather than the column definition) to behave in a similar fashion to LOB types and overflow onto separate pages if the 8060-byte row limit is encountered. When inserting a row that would not fit into a regular data page, SQL Server moves variable-width columns (starting with the largest) onto row-overflow pages. These are separate from LOB pages and, unlike LOB columns, variable-width columns are always stored in-row until they need to overflow. Additionally, if space is freed within a row, SQL Server will move data from a row-overflow page back to the original data page to help optimize performance. Again, the variable-width types are identified in the following sections.

Character Data

In storing and working with character data, SQL Server stores each character as either 1 or 2 bytes depending on whether it is non-Unicode or Unicode data. In each case, the byte or bytes represent a single character as defined in a code page. SQL Server supports a number of different code pages that map Latin (Western), Cyrillic, Arabic, and Asian characters, among others, and the code page that SQL Server uses when reading and writing character data is dependent upon the collation order in place.

Collation Orders   Collations specify the rules for how strings of character data are sorted and compared, based on the norms of particular languages and locales. These rules are used by SQL Server in ordering query results and in building and organizing indexes. Collation orders can be specified at different levels, from the instance to the database and column or statement, and the order most specific to the data being evaluated will be used. The instance collation order is specified when the instance is installed, and this becomes the default for new databases; the collation order for the database (either the instance default or a collation order specified when the database was created) will be used as a default for columns in new tables.

When a collation is specified for non-Unicode character data, a particular code page is associated with the collation. For example, if a char column in a table is defined with the Latin1_General collation, the data in that column is interpreted and displayed by SQL Server using the 1252 Latin 1 (ANSI) code page.

The full list of collation orders and code pages supported by SQL Server can be found in Books Online.

The details of SQL Server's character data types are shown in Table 4-2. Unicode types have the "n" prefix before their names and use 2 bytes to store each character.

NOTE

The ntext and text data types will be removed in a future version of Microsoft SQL Server. Avoid using these data types in new development work, and plan to modify applications that currently use them. Use nvarchar(max) and varchar(max) instead.

Numeric Types

At first glance, SQL Server seems to provide a large number of different data types for storing numeric data. These are, in fact, variations on three categories of data type: those that store varying sizes of exact integer data, those that store exact versions of decimal values at varying sizes and precisions, and those that store floating-point approximations of numbers. A summary of these data types is given in Table 4-3.

Data Type	Size	Storage	Can Overflow
char	1 to 8000 bytes (fixed; but variable when nullable)	In-row	No
nchar	1 to 4000 bytes (fixed; but variable when nullable)	In-row	No
varchar	1 to 8000 bytes (variable)	In-row	Yes
varchar(max)	1 to $(2^{31}) - 1$ bytes (variable)	In-row or out-of-row (large value)	N/A
nvarchar	1 to 4000 bytes (variable)	In-row	Yes
nvarchar(max)	1 to $(2^{31}) - 1$ bytes (variable)	In-row or out-of-row (large value)	N/A
text	1 to $(2^{31}) - 1$ bytes (variable)	In-row or out-of-row (LOB)	N/A
ntext	1 to $(2^{30}) - 1$ bytes (variable)	In-row or out-of-row (LOB)	N/A

Table 4-2 *SQL Server Character Data Types*

Data Type	Range	Storage Size	Notes
bigint	-2^{63} to $2^{63}-1$	8 bytes	
int	-2^{31} to $2^{31}-1$	4 bytes	
smallint	-2^{15} to $2^{15}-1$	2 bytes	
tinyint	0 to 255	1 byte	
decimal (precision, scale)	$10^{38}+1$ to $10^{38}-1$	Between 5 and 17 bytes depending upon the precision	Use the decimal data type to store numbers with decimals when the data values must be stored exactly as specified.
numeric			The numeric data type is functionally equivalent to the decimal data type.
float	$-1.79*10^{308}$ to $-2.23*10^{-308}$; 0; $2.23*10^{308}$ to $1.79*10^{308}$	Between 4 and 8 bytes depending upon the precision	The float and real data types are approximate numeric data types and do not store the exact values specified for many numbers. In many cases, the tiny difference between the specified value and the stored approximation is not noticeable. Be aware, however, that at times the difference becomes noticeable.
real	$-3.40*10^{38}$ to $-1.18*10^{-38}$; 0; $1.18*10^{-38}$ to $3.40*10^{38}$	4 bytes	
money	$-922,337,203,685,477.5808$ to $922,337,203,685,477.5807$	8 bytes	Values can be inserted into Money and Smallmoney columns, including a recognized currency symbol (e.g., \$), without the need to enclose the value in quotes. However, the currency symbol is not stored, only the numeric value. Money and Smallmoney are limited to four decimal points. Use the decimal data type if more decimal points are required.
smallmoney	$-214,748.3648$ to $214,748.3647$	4 bytes	
bit	0 to 1	1 bit	Storage can be shared between bit columns; that is, up to eight 1-bit columns can share a single byte of storage.

Table 4-3   *SQL Server Numeric Data Types*

All numeric storage is fixed (even for numeric data types whose maximum storage size is dependent upon their precision) and is stored in-row. You may see reference to a SQL Server data type called vardecimal offering variable-length numeric storage, but be aware that this has always been referred to as a storage format rather than a data type and has been marked for deprecation.

In SQL Server 2008 a data compression option called ROW COMPRESSION can be used to convert all column data into variable-width storage. For large and wide tables, this can reduce storage size significantly and provide similar storage characteristics to Oracle, where all numeric types are stored in a variable-width format.

Date and Time Types

For older SQL Server databases, the stock data type for storing date and time information was called datetime. This type is equivalent to Oracle's timestamp time insomuch as it stores both date and time data in a single structure (two 4-byte integers, the first to store the number of days before or after January 1, 1900, represented by the date element and the second to store the number of milliseconds after midnight that corresponds to any time part). Alongside this we have the smalldatetime type, which uses two 2-byte integers to store dates in a much smaller range and with lower precision in storing time data.

datetime has been considered limited for some time, not least for the reason that the earliest date that can be stored using this type is January 1, 1753, making it acceptable for, say, an HR system, but not so good for cataloging historic monuments. For this reason, SQL Server now has the datetime2 type, which can be considered as an extension of the existing datetime type and should be used for all new applications as it has a larger date range and a greater (and user-defined) precision.

The characteristics of SQL Server's date and time data types are shown in Table 4-4.

Data Type	Range	Storage Size	Notes
datetime	January 1, 1753 to December 31, 9999	8 bytes	Precise to one three-hundredth of a second
datetime2(n)	January 1, 0001 to December 31, 9999	Between 6 and 8 bytes depending upon the precision	User-defined precision up to a maximum of 100 nanoseconds
datetimeoffset	January 1, 0001 to December 31, 9999	10 bytes	As above and adds time zone awareness (although it has no daylight saving awareness). By this we mean that a time zone offset (−14 to 14) can be stored with the date and time data.
smalldatetime	January 1, 1900 to June 6, 2079	4 bytes	Precise to one minute
date	January 1, 0001 to December 31, 9999	3 bytes	Precise to one day (stores no time information)
time	00:00:00.0000000 to 23:59:59.9999999	5 bytes	User-defined precision up to a maximum of 100 nanoseconds

Table 4-4 *SQL Server Date and Time Data Types*

Oracle DBA Q&A

Q: I've seen reference to a timestamp data type in SQL Server; how does this relate to Oracle's timestamp type?

A: It does not relate at all. SQL Server's timestamp data type is now deprecated and has been replaced by rowversion. Even so, neither of these types is related to the SQL-92 timestamp as implemented by Oracle; they are binary types that are used to version-stamp table rows. Another common misconception is that timestamp can be used to create a human-readable record of when a row was created. To create such a timestamp, you would use your required date data type from Table 4-4 and the GETDATE() function in conjunction with a default constraint (an example of this is given later in this chapter).

Binary Types

As with character data, binary data types in SQL Server can be either fixed or variable in length and may be stored either in-row or out-of-row depending upon the data type chosen and table options. SQL Server's binary data types are summarized in Table 4-5.

NOTE

The image data type will be removed in a future version of Microsoft SQL Server. Use varbinary(max) instead.

Data Type	Size	Storage	Can Overflow
binary	1 to 8000 bytes (fixed)	In-row	No
varbinary	1 to 8000 bytes (variable)	In-row	Yes
varbinary(max)	1 to $(2^{31}) - 1$ bytes (variable)	In-row or out-of-row (large value)	N/A
image	1 to $(2^{31}) - 1$ bytes (variable)	In-row or out-of-row (LOB)	N/A

Table 4-5 *SQL Server Binary Data Types*

Other Data Types

Other data types of note that don't fit into any of the preceding categories are

▶ **uniqueidentifier**   A data type that can store a Globally Unique Identifier (GUID), a 16-byte binary value that is guaranteed to be unique across all computers. The NEWID() and NEWSEQUENTIALID() functions generate such an identifier. NEWSEQUENTIALID() generates monotonically increasing values and can only be specified in a column default.

▶ **sql_variant**   A data type that can store values of multiple different SQL Server data types, including character, numeric, date, and binary types. It cannot store, however, LOB or large-value data types, timestamp, sql_variant itself, or user-defined data types.

User-Defined Data Types

SQL Server allows administrators and developers to create three kinds of user-defined data types:

▶ **User-defined data types**   Take system types and specialize them to create new types. To take an example from the AdventureWorks2008 sample database, the syntax for creating such a type is

```
CREATE TYPE [dbo].[Phone] FROM [nvarchar](25) NULL
```

▶ **User-defined table types**   Allow us to define in-memory table structures that can be used to work with sets of data in a similar fashion to cursors but, crucially, also allow these structures to be passed between programmatic elements such as stored procedures and functions. For example:

```
CREATE TYPE dbo.ContactInformation AS TABLE
(
    [PersonID] int NOT NULL,
    [FirstName] [nvarchar](50) NULL,
    [LastName] [nvarchar](50) NULL,
    [JobTitle] [nvarchar](50) NULL,
    [BusinessEntityType] [nvarchar](50) NULL
)
GO
```

▶ **User-defined types (as opposed to user-defined data types)**   Defined outside of SQL Server using a CLR programming language such as C# or VB.NET; they may contain multiple elements and may even encapsulate behaviors that then become available in queries.

Querying the System Catalog

As discussed earlier, SQL Server provides a large number of system catalog views to enable administrators to inspect all aspects of the objects within a database. Following is a selection of those views that would prove useful in querying for the objects described in this chapter:

sys.objects	sys.tables
sys.columns	sys.views
sys.computed_columns	sys.default_constraints
sys.check_constraints	sys.filegroups
sys.foreign_keys	sys.foreign_key_columns
sys.identity_columns	sys.indexes
sys.index_columns	sys.key_constraints
sys.synonyms	sys.partitions
sys.partition_schemes	sys.sql_dependencies

ON THE JOB

A very useful resource to guide administrators as to how to construct queries across these various views is the SQL Server System Views Map, which is a poster showing the key system views included in SQL Server and, perhaps more importantly, the relationships between them. You can find the map by searching for "SQL Server 2008 System Views Map" using your favorite search engine.

Working with Data Objects

SQL Server Management Studio provides a great deal of support for administrators working with data objects. Several specific tasks are described through the course of this section and we will take a quick look at some others here:

▶ **Read and update tables** From the right-click context menu of any table or view, you can choose Select Top 1000 Rows or Edit Top 200 Rows, either of which opens a grid that allows you to read or update the contents. The actual number of rows in each case can be customized through setting Management Studio options.

▶ **Script DDL and DML for objects** The options vary depending upon the type of object, but the context menu of each SQL Server object allows you to create scripts for the object's CREATE, DROP, and (potentially) ALTER DDL statements. Additionally, DML scripts representing the actions relevant for that object type (for example, INSERT, SELECT, UPDATE, and DELETE for tables and EXECUTE for stored procedures) can also be scripted. The scripts can be sent to file, the clipboard, or to a new query window in Management Studio.

▶ **View dependencies**   From the context menu of any SQL Server object, you can select View Dependencies and either list those objects that depend on the selected object or vice versa. The output is shown in Figure 4-5.

▶ **Rename and drop objects**   From the context menu of any SQL Server object, you can drop the object from the database by selecting Delete or, where appropriate, you can rename the option by selecting Rename.

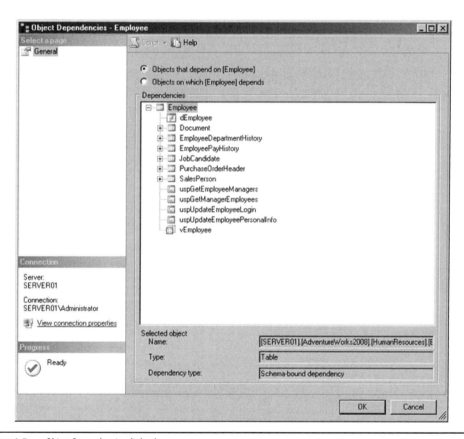

Figure 4-5   *Object Dependencies dialog box*

Creating Tables

This section describes using SQL Server Management Studio to create tables.

Selecting New Table from the context menu of the Tables node of Object Explorer opens the Table Designer, shown in Figure 4-6. From here, you can add columns to the table, specifying for each a name, a data type, and some additional properties.

However, while the Column Properties pane is always visible, the right-hand pane showing properties for the table itself may not be. If this is closed, make sure you have focus on the Table Designer and then select View | Properties Window from the Management Studio menu bar.

From the Properties window, you can

▶   Set the table name (if you don't specify a name at this point, you will be prompted to name the table at the point you apply your changes).

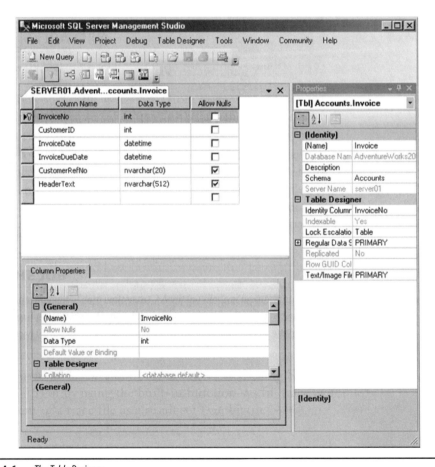

Figure 4-6   *The Table Designer*

▶ Add a description for the table.

▶ Set the schema for the table.

▶ Specify the filegroup to which this table will belong (both for "regular" data and for out-of-row large-value types).

The remaining property, Lock Escalation, is discussed in Chapter 6.

In this example, the InvoiceNo column is an identity column seeded at 1 and increasing in increments of 1. This is set from the Column Properties pane for the column, as shown in Figure 4-7.

To create the table, or to apply any subsequent changes made in the Table Designer, you need to click the Save button on the Table Designer toolbar (see Figure 4-8) or press CTRL-S.

However, before saving a change, it is worth knowing that you can script the proposed changes out to a file, perhaps for review or approval before applying them. In this case, click the Generate Change Script button on the toolbar, shown in Figure 4-9.

The following is the script generated from creating the table shown in Figure 4-6 using the Table Designer:

```
BEGIN TRANSACTION
GO
CREATE TABLE Accounts.Invoice
      (
      InvoiceNo int NOT NULL IDENTITY (1, 1),
      CustomerID int NOT NULL,
      InvoiceDate datetime NOT NULL,
      InvoiceDueDate datetime NOT NULL,
      HeaderText nvarchar(512) NULL
      )  ON [PRIMARY]
GO
ALTER TABLE Accounts.Invoice SET (LOCK_ESCALATION = TABLE)
GO
COMMIT
```

Note that, unlike Oracle, SQL Server supports running a DDL statement in a transaction, which enables the DBA to write more reliable change scripts.

Whenever you're creating a new object in SQL Server, you may need to refresh Object Explorer to see the new object in the tree. The location of the Refresh button is shown in Figure 4-10.

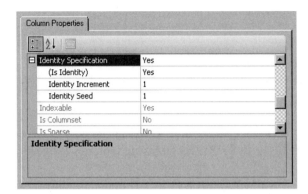

Figure 4-7 *Column Properties pane*

Figure 4-8 *Saving in the Table Designer*

Figure 4-9 *Generate Change Script button*

Figure 4-10 *The Object Explorer Refresh button*

Figure 4-11   *The Table Designer Check Constraints button*

Once you have applied changes and closed the Table Designer, you can reopen it for an existing object by selecting Design from the context menu for the table in Object Explorer.

Creating Constraints

The Table Designer makes applying a certain kind of constraint—whether or not a column may accept NULL values—extremely simple by providing the Allow Nulls check box, as seen in Figure 4-6. Other constraints, such as key constraints and unique constraints, are implemented as indexes and are discussed in the next section. Here, we will look at creating check constraints using the Table Designer.

Clicking the Check Constraints button on the Table Designer toolbar (see Figure 4-11) opens the Check Constraints dialog box (see Figure 4-12).

For a new check constraint, you need to specify an expression to describe the constraint and you need to allow or prevent the following rules:

▶ Check Existing Data On Creation Or Re-Enabling

▶ Enforce For INSERTs And UPDATEs

▶ Enforce For Replication

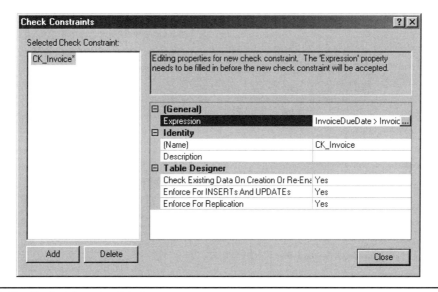

Figure 4-12   *The Check Constraints dialog box*

In this example, the expression specified is

```
InvoiceDueDate > InvoiceDate
```

By way of a test, executing the following query gives the error that this constraint has been violated:

```
INSERT INTO [AdventureWorks2008].[Accounts].[Invoice]
           ([CustomerID]
           ,[InvoiceDate]
           ,[InvoiceDueDate])
    VALUES
           (2
           ,'2010-02-11'
           ,'2010-02-10')
GO
Msg 547, Level 16, State 0, Line 1
The INSERT statement conflicted with the CHECK constraint "CK_Invoice".
The conflict occurred in database "AdventureWorks2008", table "Accounts.
Invoice".
The statement has been terminated.
```

Although not always thought of as constraints, you can also add default value specifications to your columns in the Table Designer. This time the default value or the expression used to compute it is specified in the Column Properties pane for the column in question. Figure 4-13 shows the GETDATE() function being used to write

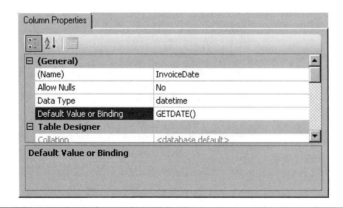

Figure 4-13   *Using a function in a default value*

Figure 4-14   *Constraints in Object Explorer*

today's date to the InvoiceDate column by default. Default constraints are applied only when no value is provided for the column upon insert and will not be applied if NULL is specified for the column (this is not considered the same as not providing a value).

Figure 4-14 shows both of the items created as constraints in this section in Object Explorer (DF_Invoice_InvoiceDate is the name of the default value definition).

Creating Indexes

As mentioned in the previous section, key constraints are implemented as indexes; in fact, the most common way that clustered indexes are applied to SQL Server tables is by creating a primary key on the table. You should remember that you can apply a clustered index to a table without creating a primary key, but, however it is created, there can be only one clustered index for a given table.

In the Table Designer, you can select a column (or use the CTRL key to select more than one column) and click the Add Primary Key button on the Table Designer toolbar, shown selected in Figure 4-15.

The key symbol should appear next to the required column, as shown in Figure 4-16.

After you have done this, Object Explorer displays the new object as both a key and an index, as shown in Figure 4-17. The script for this new primary key is given at the end of this section.

Figure 4-15   *The Table Designer Add Primary Key button*

	Column Name	Data Type	Allow Nulls
🔑	InvoiceNo	int	☐
	CustomerID	int	☐
	InvoiceDate	datetime	☐
	InvoiceDueDate	datetime	☐
	CustomerRefNo	nvarchar(20)	☑
	HeaderText	nvarchar(512)	☑
			☐

Figure 4-16 *A Primary Key column in the Table Designer*

To create a nonclustered index or to create a clustered index without a primary key, you can use the Indexes/Keys dialog box, which you open by clicking the Manage Indexes and Keys button on the Table Designer toolbar (selected in Figure 4-18).

However, it is simpler to select New Index from the context menu of the Indexes node of Object Explorer to open the New Index dialog box. The same dialog box is also used to edit an existing index and in this case it is called the Index Properties dialog box, as shown in Figure 4-19.

Figure 4-19 shows the General page of the Index Properties dialog box during the process of creating a nonclustered index named IX_Invoice_InvoiceDueDate on the table [Accounts].[Invoice]. This index is being created with the following example query in mind:

```
SELECT CustomerRefNo FROM Accounts.Invoice WHERE
    (CustomerID = 1 AND InvoiceDueDate = '2010-02-21')
```

```
☐ 📁 Tables
   ⊞ 📁 System Tables
   ☐ 📁 Accounts.Invoice
      ⊞ 📁 Columns
      ☐ 📁 Keys
         🔑 PK_Invoice
      ⊞ 📁 Constraints
      ⊞ 📁 Triggers
      ☐ 📁 Indexes
         ⬚ PK_Invoice (Clustered)
      ⊞ 📁 Statistics
```

Figure 4-17 *A Primary Key in Object Explorer*

Figure 4-18   *The Table Designer Manage Indexes and Keys button*

From the General page, you can specify

▶   Table name

▶   Index name

▶   Index type—Clustered or Nonclustered

▶   Unique—whether the index is to be used to create a Unique constraint

▶   A list of index key columns (up to 16)

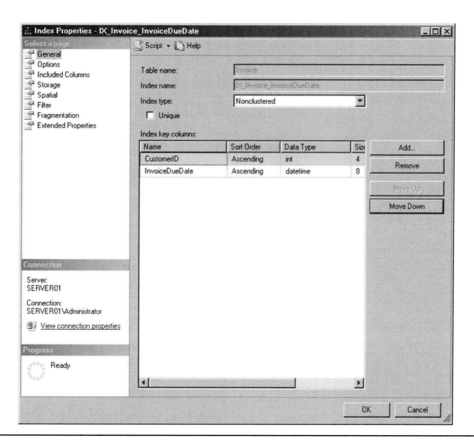

Figure 4-19   *The Index Properties dialog box*

The Options page offers the following options:

Option	Description
Automatically recompute statistics	Specifies whether distribution statistics are automatically recomputed for the index. The default value is ON.
Use row locks when accessing the index	Allows SQL Server to acquire row locks on the index when accessing it. The default is ON.
Use page locks when accessing the index	Allows SQL Server to acquire page locks across the index when accessing it. The default is ON.
Store intermediate sort results in tempdb	Specifies whether the intermediate sort results that are used to build the index are stored in the tempdb system database. This may reduce the time required to create an index if tempdb is on a different set of disks from the user database. However, this increases the amount of disk space that is used during the index build. The default is OFF.
Set fill factor	Determines the percentage of space on each leaf-level page to be filled with data, reserving the remainder on each page as free space for future growth. The default is 0, which SQL Server interprets as "fill each leaf-level page to capacity."
Allow online processing of DML statement while creating the index	Specifies whether data in the underlying table is available for modification while the index is created or rebuilt. See the upcoming section "Rebuilding and Reorganizing Indexes" for more information.
Set maximum degree of parallelism	Can be used to override the instance-wide setting governing the number of processors that SQL Server will use to process queries using this index when the execution plan allows for parallel operations. The default is 0, which instructs SQL Server to use the instance option or to determine the degree of parallelism depending upon the instance workload. A value of 1 suppresses parallel plan generation, and any other value specifies the number of processors to be used.
Use index	Allows an index to be disabled. A disabled index is not considered by the optimizer when generating execution plans, and the index is not maintained. If the index is a clustered index, then data in the underlying table becomes unavailable.

Chapter 6 describes concepts such as execution plans, statistics, and locks in more detail.

Included Columns

SQL Server allows columns to be used by the index without being key columns. These columns, called included columns, are added only to the leaf level of the index. This has the benefit of giving administrators and developers the best chance of covering their queries (ensuring that all of the columns referenced in the query are part of an index) while optimizing index size by making sure that the intermediate level of the index is not "bloated" with columns that are not part of the search criteria. Furthermore, included columns overcome the 16-column limit applied to key columns since the maximum number of included non-key columns for an index is 1023. Included columns can be used with nonclustered indexes only.

The Included Columns page of the Index Properties dialog box allows the list of included columns to be specified. In our example index, the column CustomerRefNo has been included.

The Storage page of the Index Properties dialog box allows you to associate this new index with a Filegroup.

Filtered Indexes

A filtered index is a nonclustered index that uses a filter expression to index only a portion of rows in a table. This could be a range of values, such as a date range. However, filtered indexes are perhaps best suited to queries that select from tables that contain a smaller subset of data. For example, when the values in a column are mostly NULL and the query selects only from the non-NULL values, you can create a filtered index for the non-NULL data rows. The resulting index will be smaller and cost less to maintain than a nonclustered index on the same key columns. Or, a "sliding" index might be created that indexes only rows relating to the previous month or year.

The Filter page of the Index Properties dialog box allows you to specify a filter expression for an index. This expression cannot reference a computed column or use the LIKE operator.

Like the majority of dialog boxes in the SQL Server Management Studio, the Index Properties dialog box has a Script menu, as shown in Figure 4-20, which allows an administrator to script the action about to be applied to various destinations.

Figure 4-20 *The Script menu in the Index Properties dialog box*

The resulting script for our example index is

```
CREATE NONCLUSTERED INDEX [IX_Invoice_InvoiceDueDate]
      ON [Accounts].[Invoice]
(
      [CustomerID] ASC,
      [InvoiceDueDate] ASC
)
INCLUDE ([CustomerRefNo])
WITH (PAD_INDEX   = OFF, STATISTICS_NORECOMPUTE   = OFF,
      SORT_IN_TEMPDB = OFF, IGNORE_DUP_KEY = OFF,
      DROP_EXISTING = OFF, ONLINE = OFF,
      ALLOW_ROW_LOCKS  = ON, ALLOW_PAGE_LOCKS  = ON)
ON [PRIMARY]
GO
```

This index with a filter expression might look like this:

```
CREATE NONCLUSTERED INDEX [IX_Invoice_InvoiceDueDate]
      ON [Accounts].[Invoice]
(
      [CustomerID] ASC,
      [InvoiceDueDate] ASC
)
INCLUDE ([CustomerRefNo])
WHERE ([InvoiceDueDate] >'2010-01-01')
WITH (PAD_INDEX   = OFF, STATISTICS_NORECOMPUTE   = OFF,
      SORT_IN_TEMPDB = OFF, IGNORE_DUP_KEY = OFF,
      DROP_EXISTING = OFF, ONLINE = OFF,
      ALLOW_ROW_LOCKS  = ON, ALLOW_PAGE_LOCKS  = ON)
ON [PRIMARY]
GO
```

As a final point, it is interesting to compare the syntax for creating a Primary Key and a clustered index on the same columns:

```
CREATE UNIQUE CLUSTERED INDEX [IX_Invoice]
      ON [Accounts].[Invoice]
(
      [InvoiceNo] ASC
)
WITH (STATISTICS_NORECOMPUTE   = OFF,
      SORT_IN_TEMPDB = OFF, IGNORE_DUP_KEY = OFF,
      DROP_EXISTING = OFF, ONLINE = OFF,
      ALLOW_ROW_LOCKS  = ON, ALLOW_PAGE_LOCKS  = ON)
```

```
ON [PRIMARY]
GO
ALTER TABLE [Accounts].[Invoice]
     ADD CONSTRAINT [PK_Invoice] PRIMARY KEY CLUSTERED
(
     [InvoiceNo] ASC
)
WITH (PAD_INDEX  = OFF, STATISTICS_NORECOMPUTE  = OFF,
     SORT_IN_TEMPDB = OFF, IGNORE_DUP_KEY = OFF,
     ONLINE = OFF, ALLOW_ROW_LOCKS  = ON,
     ALLOW_PAGE_LOCKS  = ON)
ON [PRIMARY]
GO
```

This should confirm that creating a Primary Key is equivalent to a CREATE UNIQUE CLUSTERED INDEX statement within an ALTER TABLE statement.

Rebuilding and Reorganizing Indexes

Indexes can be either rebuilt or reorganized to improve query performance by reducing fragmentation—that is, where the logical ordering of the index does not match the physical ordering within the data file.

These two techniques can be described as follows:

- ▶ **Reorganizing**   The physical reordering of leaf-level pages to match the logical order.

- ▶ **Rebuilding**   Dropping the index and creating a new one. The physical ordering of this new index matches the logical ordering, and the index rows are positioned in contiguous pages. This has the additional benefit of acting to reduce the number of page reads required to return the required index data.

The system function sys.dm_db_index_physical_stats can be used to return information that is useful in determining which of the preceding methods is most appropriate in defragmenting a particular index (or indexes, including indexed view, which are discussed later in the chapter).

The result set returned by the sys.dm_db_index_physical_stats function includes the following columns:

Column	Description
avg_fragmentation_in_percent	The percent of logical fragmentation (out-of-order pages in the index)
fragment_count	The number of fragments (physically consecutive leaf pages) in the index
avg_fragment_size_in_pages	Average number of pages in one fragment in an index

Based on the value returned in the avg_fragmentation_in_percent column, the recommendation is that where fragmentation is between 5 percent and 30 percent, the index should be reorganized, and where fragmentation is greater than 30 percent, the index should be rebuilt. Where fragmentation is less than 5 percent, the cost of either rebuilding or reorganizing the index almost always outweighs the benefits.

From SQL Server Management Studio, you can rebuild or reorganize an index from the context menu of that index in Object Explorer, as shown in Figure 4-21.

The following are the equivalent scripts for rebuilding and reorganizing the table [Accounts].[Invoice].

Rebuild:

```
ALTER INDEX [IX_Invoice_InvoiceDueDate] ON
      [Accounts].[Invoice] REBUILD PARTITION = ALL
WITH (PAD_INDEX = OFF, STATISTICS_NORECOMPUTE = OFF,
      ALLOW_ROW_LOCKS = ON, ALLOW_PAGE_LOCKS = ON,
      ONLINE = OFF, SORT_IN_TEMPDB = OFF,
      DATA_COMPRESSION = NONE)
GO
```

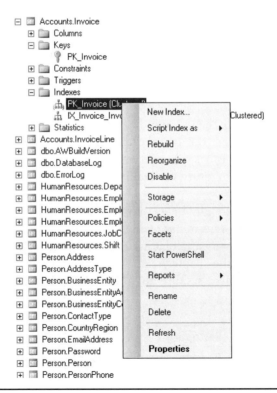

Figure 4-21 *The index context menu*

Reorganize:

```
ALTER INDEX [IX_Invoice_InvoiceDueDate] ON
      [Accounts].[Invoice] REORGANIZE
WITH (LOB_COMPACTION = ON)
GO
```

ON THE JOB

Reorganizing indexes is always an online operation (that is, one that can be performed while the database processes queries against the index's underlying table). Rebuilding an index can potentially be performed either online or offline, with the default being offline. To rebuild an index online, you need to specify the ONLINE = ON option as part of the WITH clause and, crucially, you need SQL Server Enterprise Edition because this is considered a high-availability feature and is not present in other editions.

Modifying Indexes

Only a few changes can be made to an existing index. The ALTER INDEX statement allows for certain options to be set, but not for any changes to the structure of the index. To modify an index in this way, you need to drop and re-create the index, although the CREATE INDEX statement does, at least, allow you to carry this out in one step using the WITH DROP EXISTING = ON option. For example:

```
CREATE NONCLUSTERED INDEX [IX_Invoice_InvoiceDueDate]
      ON [Accounts].[Invoice]
(
      [CustomerID] ASC,
      [InvoiceDueDate] ASC
)
INCLUDE ([CustomerRefNo])
WITH (DROP_EXISTING = ON, PAD_INDEX = OFF,
      STATISTICS_NORECOMPUTE = OFF,
      SORT_IN_TEMPDB = OFF, IGNORE_DUP_KEY = OFF,
      ONLINE = OFF, ALLOW_ROW_LOCKS = ON,
      ALLOW_PAGE_LOCKS = ON)
ON [PRIMARY]
GO
```

Creating Relationships

Let's imagine that we want to create a Foreign Key relationship between the [Accounts]. [Invoice] table and a new table described in the following CREATE TABLE statement:

```
CREATE TABLE Accounts.InvoiceLine
      (
      InvoiceNo int NOT NULL,
```

```
InvoiceLineNo int NOT NULL,
ProductID int NOT NULL,
Quantity int NOT NULL,
UnitPrice money NOT NULL,
InvoiceLineDesc nvarchar(50) NULL
)  ON [PRIMARY]
```
GO

Having created this table, we can click the Relationships button on the Table Designer toolbar (highlighted in Figure 4-22) to open the Foreign Key Relationships dialog box.

NOTE

Make sure that the relationship is created from the "child" table.

In the Foreign Key Relationships dialog box (shown in Figure 4-23), we can specify a name for the relationship and, by clicking the ellipsis (...) button next to the Tables And Columns Specification label, use the Tables and Columns dialog box to define on which columns the relationship between [Accounts].[Invoice] and [Accounts].[InvoiceLine] will be built.

As shown in Figure 4-24, for our example we can use the Tables and Columns dialog box to give the relationship a name, pick the Invoice table as the Primary Key table, and identify the InvoiceNo column in both tables as the key column.

You can now see the relationship in Object Explorer, as shown in Figure 4-25.

The equivalent script for this Foreign Key is

```
ALTER TABLE [Accounts].[InvoiceLine]  WITH CHECK ADD  CONSTRAINT
[FK_InvoiceLine_Invoice] FOREIGN KEY([InvoiceNo])

REFERENCES [Accounts].[Invoice] ([InvoiceNo])

GO
```

If we want to inspect relationships within a SQL Server database, we can use Management Studio to view dependencies between objects, as described earlier in

Figure 4-22 *The Table Designer Relationships button*

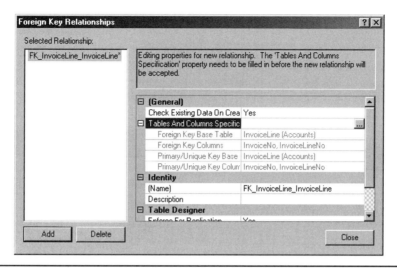

Figure 4-23   *The Foreign Key Relationships dialog box*

this chapter, or we can use the following system catalog and dynamic management views:

▶   sys.sq_dependencies

▶   sys.sql_expression_dependencies

▶   sys.dm_sql_referenced_entities

▶   sys.dm_sql_referencing_entities

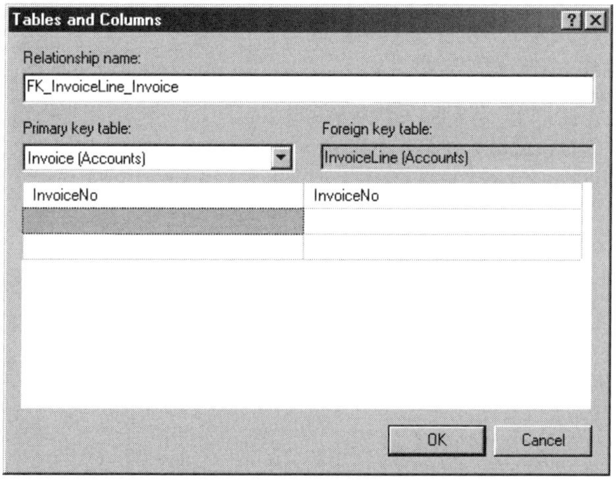

Figure 4-24   *The Tables and Columns dialog box*

Figure 4-25 *A Foreign Key relationship in Object Explorer*

We can also use a SQL Server Management Studio feature called database diagrams. These provide a graphical representation of the relationships between some or all of the tables in a database and can be created by selecting New Database Diagram from the context menu of the Database Diagrams node in Object Explorer. Working with database diagrams also allows us to edit the table definitions and relationships.

The Add Table dialog box (see Figure 4-26) allows us to select the tables we require in our diagram, the resulting output of which is shown in Figure 4-27. In this case, additional relationships have been created between the Invoice and Customer tables and between the InvoiceLine and Product tables.

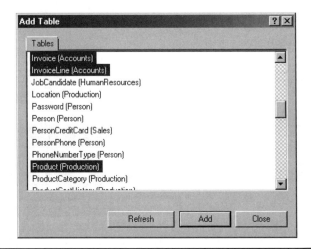

Figure 4-26 *The Add Table dialog box for creating database diagrams*

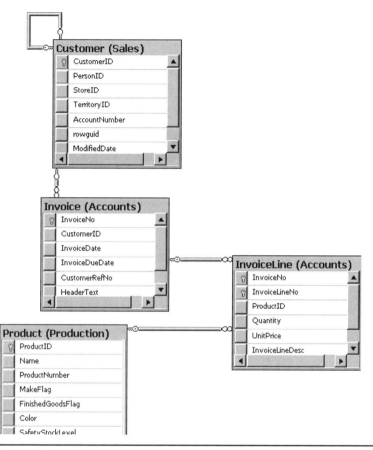

Figure 4-27   *A Database Diagram*

Be aware that when you're creating a database diagram for the first time within a SQL Server database, you are prompted to create some required objects. The objects that SQL Server automatically creates within the database are listed here:

Object Type	Name
Function	fn_diagramobjects
Stored procedure	sp_alterdiagram
Stored procedure	sp_creatediagram
Stored procedure	sp_dropdiagram
Stored procedure	sp_helpdiagramdefinition
Stored procedure	sp_renamediagram
Stored procedure	sp_upgradediagrams

All of these objects are created in the dbo schema.

Creating Views

The syntax for creating a view in SQL Server is almost identical to that in Oracle (an example of which is given later in this section). However, SQL Server Management Studio provides a graphical designer (which is in certain ways similar to the Database Diagram functionality described previously) that can be used as an alternative to "handcrafting" the scripts to create and modify views.

The View Designer is similar to the Table Designer in that it is accessed by selecting New View from the Views node in Object Explorer or by selecting Design from the context menu of an existing view. For a new view, the Add Table dialog box is opened automatically as when constructing a Database Diagram, although in this case you can select views, functions (table-valued), and synonyms as well as tables. With tables selected, the View Designer is shown, and it will look similar to Figure 4-28.

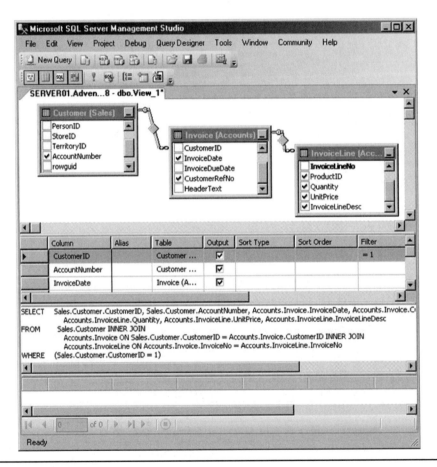

Figure 4-28 *The View Designer*

In the View Designer, you can check columns to include them in the view, and you can use the center grid to specify filter expressions and aliases for columns and include them in the ORDER BY clause. The SELECT statement on which the view is based is generated and updated automatically. Clicking Execute from the View Designer toolbar causes this statement to be executed and the results to be returned in the lower pane of the View Designer.

As with tables, you need to ensure that the Properties pane for the view is visible by selecting View | Properties Window from Management Studio, so that you can specify properties such as the schema in which the view will be created. You must click Save for changes to be applied.

This same graphical view can be used when creating ad hoc SELECT queries in Management Studio. Right-clicking in any white space in a query window allows you to select Design Query in Editor. This opens the Add Table dialog box, in which you select base tables and then select columns and specify filter expressions, causing the SELECT statement to be built automatically.

```
CREATE VIEW [Accounts].[CustomerInvoices]
AS
SELECT      Sales.Customer.CustomerID, Sales.Customer.AccountNumber,
 Accounts.Invoice.InvoiceDate, Accounts.Invoice.CustomerRefNo,
 Accounts.InvoiceLine.ProductID,
                     Accounts.InvoiceLine.Quantity,
 Accounts.InvoiceLine.UnitPrice, Accounts.InvoiceLine.InvoiceLineDesc
FROM        Sales.Customer INNER JOIN
                     Accounts.Invoice ON Sales.Customer.CustomerID =
 Accounts.Invoice.CustomerID INNER JOIN
                     Accounts.InvoiceLine ON Accounts.Invoice.InvoiceNo =
 Accounts.InvoiceLine.InvoiceNo
WHERE       (Sales.Customer.CustomerID = 1)
GO
```

Creating Indexed Views

To create an indexed view, the view definition must include the WITH SCHEMABINDING option, as follows, which instructs SQL Server to check any modifications to objects on which the view depends (such as the underlying tables) and disallow modifications that would render the view invalid:

```
CREATE VIEW [Accounts].[CustomerInvoices]
WITH SCHEMABINDING
AS
...
```

Once this has been done, an index may be applied to the view in the same way that it would be for the table, either using SQL Server Management Studio or in script—although only unique clustered indexes are allowed for views. For example:

```
CREATE UNIQUE CLUSTERED INDEX [IX_CustomerInvoices] ON
[Accounts].[CustomerInvoices]
(
       [CustomerID] ASC,
       [InvoiceDate] ASC
ON [PRIMARY]
GO
```

Indexed Views vs. Filtered Indexes

Given that a fundamental characteristic of views is that they can use a predicate to return a subset of the underlying data, an indexed view and a filtered index have a large amount of functional equivalence. However, filtered indexes have a number of performance advantages over indexed views, namely that they require fewer CPU resources when updated and are more likely to be considered by the optimizer when building query plans (see Chapter 6). Also, filtered indexes can be rebuilt as an online operation, whereas indexed views cannot. Finally, filtered indexes offer the flexibility of using non-unique indexes, which is not possible with indexed views.

Having said this, there will be circumstances in which only a view gives you the required functionality, such as when you want to reference more than one underlying table or want to use computed columns, or when the predicate expression (the WHERE clause) is more complex than could be applied to a filtered index.

Filegroups and Partitioning

As described in Chapter 2, filegroups provide an interface between objects that store data and SQL Server's data files, and if you want to implement a physical data design that separates sets of data across more than one physical file location, you need to create additional files and filegroups within your databases.

Creating Files and Filegroups

Files and filegroups can both be created from the Database Properties dialog box. Because data files must always belong to a filegroup, it is necessary to create the new filegroup before creating the files that it will manage. The Filegroups page of the Database Properties dialog box is shown in Figure 4-29.

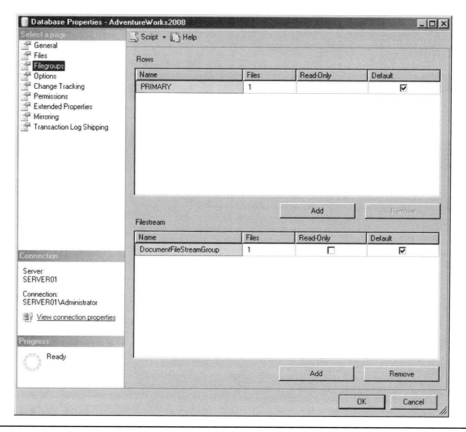

Figure 4-29   *Filegroups in the Database Properties dialog box*

As the dialog box indicates, two types of filegroup exist, Rows and Filestream. Rows filegroups manage data in tables and indexes. Filestream filegroups are a means of presenting an interface to binary data (varbinary(max)) objects stored outside of SQL Server, directly on the NTFS file system. Filestream filegroups are not described here; we will look only at Rows filegroups.

Clicking Add on the Filegroups page creates a new blank row in the list of filegroups, allowing you to specify a name for the new filegroup. It is created when you click OK. Having done this, you can use the Files page of the Database Properties dialog box (see Figure 4-30) to add data files to this filegroup. Again, clicking Add

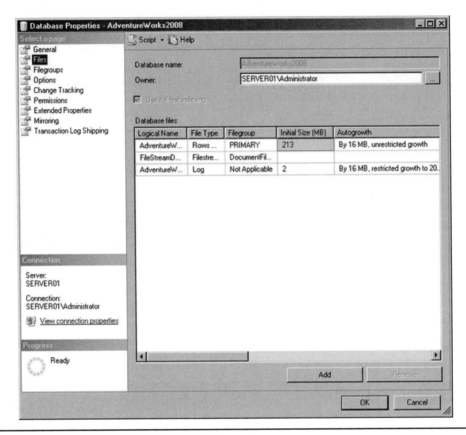

Figure 4-30 *Files in the Database Properties dialog box*

creates a new row in the list of files but this time, you need to specify slightly more information, namely:

▶ **Logical Name** The name used by SQL Server to refer to the file.

▶ **Physical Name** This will default to a combination of the default data directory, the logical name, and the file extension .ndf.

▶ **Initial Size** The initial size of the new file.

▶ **Autogrowth** Whether the file may auto-grow as it becomes full, the increment by which it will grow if autogrowth is enabled and, optionally, a maximum file size.

The script for creating a new filegroup named IndexData and adding three new data files to it would look like this:

```
USE [master]
GO
ALTER DATABASE [AdventureWorks2008]
      ADD FILEGROUP [IndexData]
GO
ALTER DATABASE [AdventureWorks2008]
      ADD FILE ( NAME = N'IndexData1',
      FILENAME = N'C:\Program Files\Microsoft SQL
Server\MSSQL10.MSSQLSERVER\MSSQL\DATA\IndexData1.ndf',
      SIZE = 2048KB , FILEGROWTH = 1024KB ) TO FILEGROUP [IndexData]
GO
ALTER DATABASE [AdventureWorks2008]
      ADD FILE ( NAME = N'IndexData2',
      FILENAME = N'C:\Program Files\Microsoft SQL
Server\MSSQL10.MSSQLSERVER\MSSQL\DATA\IndexData2.ndf',
      SIZE = 2048KB , FILEGROWTH = 1024KB ) TO FILEGROUP [IndexData]
GO
ALTER DATABASE [AdventureWorks2008]
      ADD FILE ( NAME = N'IndexData3',
      FILENAME = N'C:\Program Files\Microsoft SQL
Server\MSSQL10.MSSQLSERVER\MSSQL\DATA\IndexData3.ndf',
      SIZE = 2048KB , FILEGROWTH = 1024KB ) TO FILEGROUP [IndexData]
GO
```

Having done this, you can add tables or indexes to this filegroup in accordance with your data design. Existing tables cannot be moved between filegroups and, strictly speaking, neither can indexes; however, by using the DROP_EXISTING =ON option, you can re-create an index on your new filegroup like so:

```
CREATE NONCLUSTERED INDEX [IX_Invoice_InvoiceDueDate]
      ON [Accounts].[Invoice]
(
      [CustomerID] ASC,
      [InvoiceDueDate] ASC
)
INCLUDE ([CustomerRefNo])
ON [IndexData]
GO
```

Keep in mind that if the index is a clustered index then recreating it on a new filegroup will, in effect, move the table to which the index belongs to the new filegroup. For a new table, the CREATE TABLE statement would simply reference the new filegroup just as the preceding example does.

Partitioning

Tables, indexes, and indexed views can have their storage partitioned across multiple filegroups. This can provide several benefits, including improved performance because the SQL Server optimizer is partition-aware and will design data access plans accordingly when partitions are found. Furthermore, various maintenance operations can be carried out at the partition level, including recovery from backup.

Much like in Oracle, tables and indexes are partitioned "horizontally," meaning that all partitions contain the same columns (and, in the case of tables, the same constraints) but rows are divided between partitions based upon a set of rules known as a partition scheme.

In this example, the index IX_Invoice_InvoiceDueDate will be partitioned across four filegroups, each containing data belonging to a calendar quarter of the year 2010. The first step is to create the filegroups and data files:

```
ALTER DATABASE [AdventureWorks2008]
      ADD FILEGROUP [2010Q1]
GO
ALTER DATABASE [AdventureWorks2008]
      ADD FILEGROUP [2010Q2]
GO
ALTER DATABASE [AdventureWorks2008]
      ADD FILEGROUP [2010Q3]
GO
ALTER DATABASE [AdventureWorks2008]
      ADD FILEGROUP [2010Q4]
GO
ALTER DATABASE [AdventureWorks2008]
      ADD FILE ( NAME = N'2010Q1',
      FILENAME = N'C:\Program Files\Microsoft SQL
Server\MSSQL10.MSSQLSERVER\MSSQL\DATA\2010Q1.ndf',
      SIZE = 2048KB , FILEGROWTH = 1024KB ) TO FILEGROUP [2010Q1]
GO
ALTER DATABASE [AdventureWorks2008]
      ADD FILE ( NAME = N'2010Q2',
      FILENAME = N'C:\Program Files\Microsoft SQL
Server\MSSQL10.MSSQLSERVER\MSSQL\DATA\2010Q2.ndf',
```

```
        SIZE = 2048KB , FILEGROWTH = 1024KB ) TO FILEGROUP [2010Q2]
GO
ALTER DATABASE [AdventureWorks2008]
        ADD FILE ( NAME = N'2010Q3',
        FILENAME = N'C:\Program Files\Microsoft SQL
Server\MSSQL10.MSSQLSERVER\MSSQL\DATA\2010Q3.ndf',
        SIZE = 2048KB , FILEGROWTH = 1024KB ) TO FILEGROUP [2010Q3]
GO
ALTER DATABASE [AdventureWorks2008]
        ADD FILE ( NAME = N'2010Q4',
        FILENAME = N'C:\Program Files\Microsoft SQL
Server\MSSQL10.MSSQLSERVER\MSSQL\DATA\2010Q4.ndf',
        SIZE = 2048KB , FILEGROWTH = 1024KB ) TO FILEGROUP [2010Q4]
```

We now need to define the rules that determine how rows are divided among the filegroups:

```
CREATE PARTITION FUNCTION PF_InvoiceInvoiceDueDate(datetime2)
AS
RANGE RIGHT FOR VALUES
('20100101','20100301','20100601','20100901')
GO
```

This partition function object states that when the column in question is inspected, rows will be placed in either the first, second, third, or fourth partition based on whether the column value is greater or less than the specified boundary values. The RANGE RIGHT option instructs SQL Server that each boundary value belongs to the partition on its right, so values from Midnight, March 1, 2010, and less than Midnight, June 1, 2010, will belong to partition number 3. Note that all values earlier than 20100101 (January 1, 2010) will belong to the first partition.

A partition scheme object can now be created to tie our partition function ranges to the filegroups that we created earlier:

```
CREATE PARTITION SCHEME PS_InvoiceInvoiceDueDate
AS
PARTITION PF_InvoiceInvoiceDueDate
TO ([PRIMARY],
 [2010Q1],[2010Q2],[2010Q3],[2010Q4])
GO
```

Multiple tables can share the same partition scheme or partition function. And a table's indexes can be located on the same partition scheme as the table, in which case they are called "partition aligned," or the indexes can be unpartitioned or stored on a different partition scheme. In SQL Server, a table can only be partitioned on a single column, and cannot be subpartitioned.

There is also a wizard in the GUI to partition an existing table, available in the context menu for the table under Storage | Create Partition. Existing partition schemes and partition functions can be viewed in Object Explorer, as shown in Figure 4-31.

Tables and indexes can now be assigned to this partition scheme in exactly the same way as specifying a standard filegroup. In doing this, we need to specify which column will provide the values that will be evaluated as rows are placed in partitions:

```
CREATE NONCLUSTERED INDEX [IX_Invoice_InvoiceDueDate]
     ON [Accounts].[Invoice]
(
     [CustomerID] ASC,
     [InvoiceDueDate] ASC
)
INCLUDE ([CustomerRefNo])
ON [PS_InvoiceInvoiceDueDate] ([InvoiceDueDate])
GO
```

To give an example of a common operation performed against a single partition, we can now rebuild only the latest partition of this index. To do this we need to determine

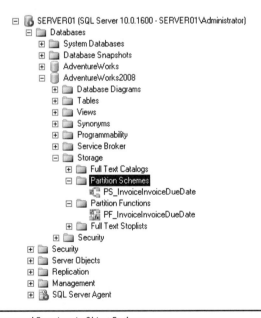

Figure 4-31 *Partition Schemes and Functions in Object Explorer*

a value known as the destination_id for the partition, for which we can use the following query (which aliases this column as Partition No.):

```
SELECT
     ds.name AS [Filegroup],
     dds.destination_id AS [Partition No],
     ps.name AS [Scheme]
FROM
     sys.data_spaces ds
     JOIN
     sys.destination_data_spaces dds
     ON
     (ds.data_space_id = dds.data_space_id)
          JOIN
          sys.partition_schemes ps
          ON
          (ps.data_space_id = dds.partition_scheme_id)
ORDER BY ds.name, ps.name ASC
```

The result of running this query is shown in Figure 4-32.
We can now use this value when rebuilding the index:

```
ALTER INDEX IX_Invoice_InvoiceDueDate
    ON [Accounts].[Invoice]
    REBUILD PARTITION = 5
GO
```

The $PARTITION function can also be very useful when working with partitions or when testing new partition functions, as it can return the partition number for a given value or set of values. For example:

```
ALTER INDEX IX_Invoice_InvoiceDueDate
    ON [Accounts].[Invoice]
    REBUILD PARTITION = $partition.PF_InvoiceInvoiceDueDate('20100901')
GO
```

	Filegroup	Partition No	Scheme
1	2010Q1	2	PS_InvoiceInvoiceDueDate
2	2010Q2	3	PS_InvoiceInvoiceDueDate
3	2010Q3	4	PS_InvoiceInvoiceDueDate
4	2010Q4	5	PS_InvoiceInvoiceDueDate
5	PRIMARY	1	PS_InvoiceInvoiceDueDate

Figure 4-32 *Identifying partitions*

Chapter 5

Security

In This Chapter

- ▶ Security Objects
- ▶ Protecting SQL Server Databases

T his chapter describes the features available in SQL Server that allow administrators to effectively control access to database objects and data. It also describes the database features that can further enhance security within a SQL Server installation. Where there are security implications for administrators in carrying out tasks that are described elsewhere in this book, those implications are discussed in the relevant chapters.

This chapter does not attempt to highlight every aspect of SQL Server that, through misconfiguration or improper deployment, can act to create security vulnerabilities, nor does it try to list every tool or technique for addressing these vulnerabilities. Put simply, there are so many factors outside of any database system that can influence its operational security, from physical access through to operating system and network configuration, that becoming an expert in this field takes many years and is beyond the scope of this book.

NOTE

The chapter introduces a SQL Server object called a User. To differentiate this object from a person initiating a database request, the SQL Server object is always capitalized ("User") and the more general term is written in lowercase ("user").

Security Objects

The model for controlling access to a SQL Server database is built from a combination of many types of objects, from those working at a very high level, representing people or applications, to very fine-grained objects that allow us to associate the granting or denying of individual privileges (permissions) with objects such as tables and columns. The way these objects come together will be very familiar to Oracle administrators, with possibly two subtle differences to keep in mind:

▶ To control access to SQL Server database objects, a combination of security objects at both the instance and database level is required.

▶ There is no logical 1:1 relationship between SQL Server Users and schemas (or the functional equivalent of the Oracle schema, the SQL Server database).

Server Security

In security terms, the SQL Server instance acts as the "front door"—without the granting of some degree of access at this point, no request will be fulfilled (and the user or application will certainly not get as far as their intended database). So we will first take a look at the instance-level objects that control user access: principals, logins, roles and permissions.

Principals

The term *principal* is applied to an entity that can request access to SQL Server. Very often, these relate directly to individual users or applications and can also represent groups of users. Instance-level principals are called logins, while database-level principals are called Users. These two levels of principals are necessary because a SQL Server instance can have any number of databases, each of which can have a completely separate security model.

There are two types of instance-level principals:

► Windows principals:
  ► Domain or Local Users
  ► Domain or Local Group
► SQL Server principals:
  ► SQL Server login

These two types of principals are the result of two different authentication models that can be used in SQL Server: Windows authentication and SQL Server authentication. In SQL Server authentication, a login object is defined along with a password, which is stored in the master database (the password is hashed), and this login name and password are passed to SQL Server for evaluation at the point the client connection is requested. SQL Server authenticates the user (establishes that they are who they say they are, in this case by hashing the provided password and matching it against the stored hash). In Windows authentication, a login object is also created and stored in the master database; however, no password is supplied and the login is associated with a preexisting Windows principal. Now, it is Windows that authenticates the user prior to the client request being made, and evidence of this authentication (a Kerberos ticket) is passed to SQL Server as the connection is requested to allow SQL Server to carry out authorization. Note that in both cases, a login object represents the instance-level permissions granted to the principal; the difference is only whether the login is mapped to a Windows principal or whether it represents a SQL Server principal in its own right. To keep things simple, we'll refer to these two types of login as Windows logins and SQL Server logins, respectively.

SQL Server authentication can be enabled and disabled for an instance, whereas Windows authentication is always enabled.

NOTE

Even if SQL Server authentication is not enabled, SQL Server logins can still be created; however, they will not be able to connect.

Logins

As previously stated, a login object is required in all cases to connect to a SQL Server instance. Certain logins are automatically created when the SQL Server instance is installed (as shown in Figure 5-1) and are added to groups that give certain privileges; these groups are detailed later in this section.

Earlier versions of SQL Server created logins associated directly with the Windows accounts under which the instance service and the SQL Server Agent service were configured to run. As discussed in Chapter 3, the SQL Server installer now creates per-service identities (SIDs) and adds them to the appropriate SQL Server service groups in Windows. Remember that there are two different Windows identities associated with any Windows service: the service account and the per-service SID. The service account is the user who starts the service and owns the service process. The per-service SID is a special account that represents the service itself. It has no password, and can be used to assign privileges to a service directly, instead of having to assign them to the service account. Per-service SIDs are referred to with a name of the form NT SERVICE*SERVICE NAME*, where *SERVICE NAME* is the name of the service. The groups created to support the database engine are

- **SQLServerMSSQLUser$*Server Name*$*Instance Name***   The group of SIDs representing the SQL Server instance services on a given server
- **SQLServerSQLAgentUser$*Server Name*$*Instance Name***   The group of SIDs representing the SQL Server Agent services on a given server

NOTE

Remember that the default instance will have the name MSSQLSERVER.

The logins that are created to map to these principals (the Windows groups) are named slightly differently from the groups themselves (presumably to aid readability):

- NT SERVICE\MSSQLSERVER for a default instance
- NT SERVICE\MSSQL$*INSTANCE NAME* for a named instance
- NT SERVICE\SQLSERVERAGENT for a default instance
- NT SERVICE\SQLAGENT$*INSTANCE NAME* for a named instance

Regardless of whether SQL Server authentication is enabled or not, a SQL Server login called sa is created by the installer. This login can be thought of as literally the "system administrator" and is a member of the sysadmin group. The sa login cannot

Figure 5-1   *Automatically created Logins*

be dropped but it can be disabled, and usually should be. When sa is disabled, it can't be used to connect to SQL Server, but it can still own objects such as databases and SQL Agent jobs. It's often better to have sa own these objects than to have them owned by the Windows login of a particular administrator. It is possible to rename the sa login and this is advisable for security reasons unless a particular application is dependent on it being named sa.

When installing SQL Server, you must specify at least one account to act as an administrator of the instance, and Windows logins are created for each of these accounts (in Figure 5-1 this is the login SERVER01\Administrator, meaning that the local Administrator account was the only one specified during installation). These logins can be modified or dropped, but be careful to ensure that doing either of them doesn't render the instance inaccessible to everyone.

Oracle DBA Q&A

Q: **Should I use this sa login to manage SQL Server? Is there some way I can connect 'AS' this user?**

A: No on both counts. Even if SQL Server authentication is enabled, the recommendation is still to create Windows logins for those users who need to act as database administrators and then to add these logins to the sysadmin group. See the section "Creating Logins" for instructions on how to carry out these actions.

ON THE JOB

Okay, suppose that even after reading the preceding warning, you've deleted the only login with permissions to administer the instance. What can you do? Fortunately, all members of the Windows Administrators local group have access to SQL Server when SQL Server is started in single-user mode. After specifying the -m startup parameter (see Chapter 3), a member of this group can use sqlcmd.exe to connect to the instance. From there, the member can re-create logins and add logins to groups to restore normal access. See the upcoming sections "Creating Logins" and "Managing Logins" for details of how to carry out these actions.

A number of logins are created for a SQL Server instance with names enclosed in double hashes (##). These logins are for internal system use only. Those present will vary depending upon the features installed, and they are created from certificates when the instance is installed. The full list is

▶ ##MS_SQLResourceSigningCertificate##

▶ ##MS_SQLReplicationSigningCertificate##

▶ ##MS_SQLAuthenticatorCertificate##

▶ ##MS_AgentSigningCertificate##

▶ ##MS_PolicyEventProcessingLogin##

▶ ##MS_PolicySigningCertificate##

▶ ##MS_PolicyTsqlExecutionLogin##

These logins cannot be used to connect to SQL Server and should not be modified or deleted.

Finally, the NT AUTHORITY\SYSTEM built-in Windows group is granted a login with and added to the sysadmin group. It is used by Service Packs and hotfixes (among other things) and should not be modified or deleted.

Creating Logins   You can create a new SQL Server login using the Login – New dialog box (see Figure 5-2), accessed from the context menu of the Logins node (under Security) for the instance in Object Explorer.

Before specifying a name for the login, you need to determine whether this will be a Windows login or a SQL Server login. For a Windows login, you need to provide the name of an existing Windows account in the format DOMAIN\USERNAME. Instead of typing the name in the Login Name field, you can click the Search button to search either locally or in Active Directory for the required account.

For a SQL Server login, you specify the new login name at this point and provide a password. If there is a password policy defined for your organization (either locally on

Option	Description
Enforce password policy	Specifies whether SQL Server should enforce the password policy. If this is enabled, new passwords will be evaluated to ensure they meet complexity requirements.
Enforce password expiration	Password expiration as defined in the password policy will be enforced for this login.
User must change password at next login	SQL Server will prompt the user for a new password the first time the new login is used. Note that the SQL Server management tools will present a dialog box that allows the user to change their password—other applications will need to capture the particular error returned by SQL Server and respond accordingly.

Table 5-1   *SQL Server Login Password Policy Options*

the machine on which SQL Server is installed or at a domain level), then this can be enforced by SQL Server for SQL Server logins. The available options are seen in Table 5-1.

NOTE

Windows password policies are managed outside of SQL Server using the Security Policy tool (SecPol.msc).

As you can see in Figure 5-2, as well as creating Windows logins and SQL Server logins, you also have the option to create logins mapped to other kinds of principals, namely certificates and asymmetric keys; however, although you can create these logins, they cannot be used to connect to SQL Server. Logins created from certificates or asymmetric keys are used only for code signing and won't be discussed here.

The option Map to Credential allows you to associate credentials managed outside of SQL Server (typically a username and password) with your new login. These credentials can then be passed to some external system when bespoke functionality in your database calls that system within a session started by this login.

The final two dialog box options allow you to provide defaults to be used for this Login. The Default Database drop-down list box specifies how the database context will be set if this login opens a connection without specifying an "initial catalog" (or similar) value and does not issue any USE directive. This option can be useful in ensuring that users and applications do not inadvertently issue commands against inappropriate databases. The Default Language drop-down list box guides the database engine as to how to apply locale-specific formatting (for example, for dates and numbers) in the absence of any other directive.

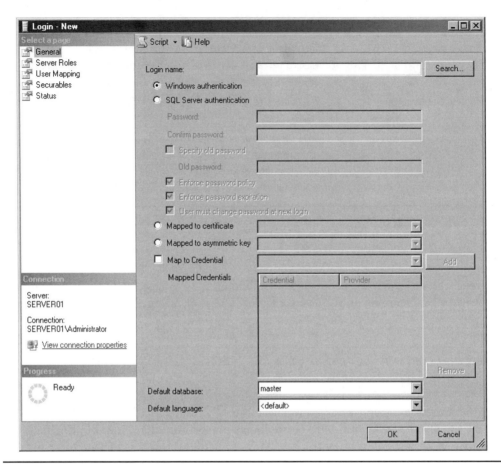

Figure 5-2 *The Login – New dialog box*

Managing Logins   Because SQL Server doesn't manage any authentication information (passwords) for Windows logins, it is very simple to move or copy logins between instances. They can be scripted using SQL Server Management Studio as follows, for example:

```
CREATE LOGIN [SERVER01\Administrator] FROM WINDOWS WITH
    DEFAULT_DATABASE=[master], DEFAULT_LANGUAGE=[us_english]
```

This script can then be run on the target instance. However, if you attempt to have SQL Server script a SQL Server login in the same way, it will create a script containing a random password (and a disabled login), for obvious security reasons. If you want to move a SQL Server login between instances without having to reset passwords, there are two options available. You can use either the Copy Database Wizard from within Management Studio or use SQL Server Integration Services and the Transfer Logins task. See Chapter 11 for further details on these tools.

The Login Properties dialog box for an existing login is identical to the Login – New dialog box shown in Figure 5-2. From the Status page, you can make a number of security settings for a login, including these two:

- ▶ **Permission to connect to database engine**   Can be set to Grant or Deny
- ▶ **Login**   Can be set to Enabled or Disabled

Setting either of these options to Deny or Disabled, respectively, effectively renders that user unable to connect to the instance. However, enabling or disabling a login is an action that is reflected in both Object Explorer and in the catalog views listed in the section Viewing Login Details making this a much more manageable option. Choosing Deny for Permission to Connect to the Database Engine acts to deny a permission called CONNECT SQL, and this can be harder to trace after the option has been set.

If a SQL Server login has been expired due to the password policy in force, the Status page will display this through the Login Is Locked Out check box, but it cannot be reset from within the property pages. Instead, you have to issue an ALTER LOGIN statement. For example, to unlock the account by specifying a new password (recommended), use

```
ALTER LOGIN [NewLogin] WITH PASSWORD='NewPassword01' UNLOCK
```

To unlock the account without specifying a new password, use

```
ALTER LOGIN [NewLogin] WITH CHECK_POLICY = OFF
GO
ALTER LOGIN [NewLogin] WITH CHECK_POLICY = ON
GO
```

Note that with the second approach, you will lose any password history for the login. See the full syntax of the ALTER LOGIN statement in SQL Server Books Online for full details of the operations that can be performed on a login.

The following catalog views can be used to return details of logins created for an instance:

- ▶ **sys.server_principals**   Returns general information, including that specified when the login was created, as previously described
- ▶ **sys.sql_logins**   Inherits the columns of sys.server_principals and adds columns specific only to SQL Server logins: is_policy_checked, is_expiration_checked, and password_hash

Fixed Server Roles

A role is a named group of permissions that can represent common tasks or the actions associated with particular jobs. A role can be assigned to users or applications as a single unit, reducing the management overhead of granting commonly used sets of permissions. In SQL Server, roles exist at an instance level and at a database level. If you want to assign a role's permissions to a user or application, you need to make the relevant login a member of the required role.

The prebuilt instance (or server) roles are described in Table 5-2. These roles cannot be modified or dropped, and you cannot create additional server roles. The sysadmin fixed server role has the highest level of privilege and can access any database and carry out any action on any object or any data; as such, logins should only be added to this role after careful consideration.

Every SQL Server login belongs to the public server role. Where a login is required to work with database objects and data only (as is usually the case for applications and non-admin users), the login should remain a member of this role only.

Viewing Role Membership and Permissions   As shown in Figure 5-3, you can view the membership for a server role from the Properties dialog box of the role in question (by clicking Properties in the context menu of the Roles node in Object Explorer).

Fixed Server Role	Role Name	Description
sysadmin	System Administrator	Can perform any activity in SQL Server. The permissions of this role span all of the other fixed server roles.
serveradmin	Server Administrator	Can configure instance-wide settings.
setupadmin	Setup Administrator	Can add and remove linked servers and execute some system stored procedures.
securityadmin	Security Administrator	Can create and manage logins.
processadmin	Process Administrator	Can manage processes running in an instance of SQL Server.
dbcreator	Database Administrator	Can create and alter databases.
diskadmin	Disk Administrator	Can manage physical database files.
bulkadmin	Bulk Insert Administrator	Can execute the BULK INSERT statement.
public	Public	No elevated instance-level permissions.

Table 5-2   *Fixed Server Roles*

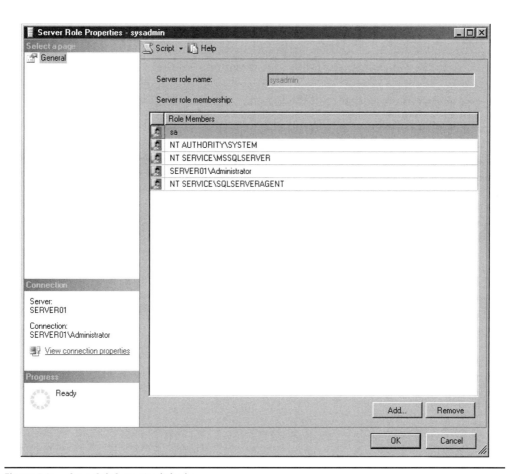

Figure 5-3   *Server Role Properties dialog box*

Additionally, the following system stored procedures, functions, and views can also be used to view the membership of fixed server roles in SQL Server and to inspect the permissions held by those roles:

Name	Type	Description
sp_helpsrvrole	System procedure	Displays a list of server roles
sp_srvrolepermission	System procedure	Displays the permissions assigned to a server role
sp_helpsrvrolemember	System procedure	Displays a list of members of a fixed server role
is_srvrolemember	System function	Indicates whether a login is part of a role
sys.server_role_members	Catalog view	Returns one row for each member of each server role

Adding Logins to Roles   To add a login to a built-in server role, access the Login Properties pages and select the Server Roles page, as shown in Figure 5-4.

Alternatively, you can use the following system procedures:

- ▶ **sp_addsrvrolemember**   Adds a login account to a fixed server role
- ▶ **sp_dropsrvrolemember**   Removes a login account from a fixed server role

Logins may belong to many roles and may be added to or removed from roles at any time.

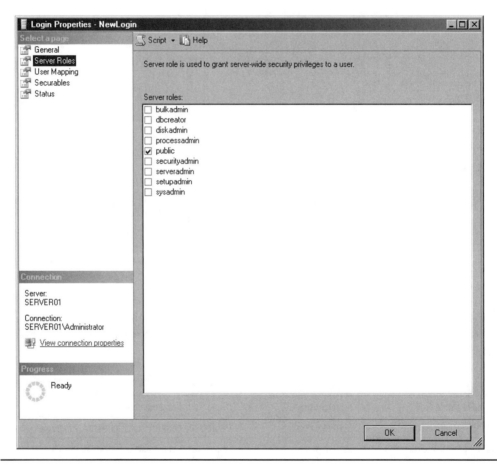

Figure 5-4   *The Server Roles page*

Server Permissions

Although you cannot modify the prebuilt server roles, for a given login, you can add or (effectively) remove permissions from the list that makes up each of the server roles to fine-tune a role to better suit that login. Or, you can avoid using roles altogether and assign instance permissions directly to logins.

Working with Server Permissions   From the Securables page of the Login Properties pages (see Figure 5-5), you can grant, revoke, or deny any of the individual instance permissions to a login. At this point, you need to be aware of how doing this may impact the permissions already held by the login as a result of belonging to one or more groups. Throughout SQL Server (not just relating to server roles) the rules are as follows:

▶ Permissions granted are combined. A login receives the sum of all the permissions granted through role membership or directly.

▶ Denying a permission always takes precedence over granting it. If role membership grants a permission but either another role or an explicit Deny elsewhere denies it, then the login is denied that permission.

NOTE

An exception to the preceding rule is that you cannot deny any permission from a login belonging to the sysadmin role.

To use the Securables page to grant or deny permissions, click the Search button to find the objects you wish to grant or deny permission—for server roles, this is likely to be the current instance (the other options are endpoints and logins). As shown in Figure 5-5, there are a large number of individual permissions on an instance that can be granted or denied for a login; see Books Online for a full list. Any permission assigned With Grant, as shown in Figure 5-5 will allow that login to grant the permission to other logins.

The catalog view sys.server_permissions can be used to return details as to exactly which server permissions have been directly granted or denied to which logins. You can check the effective permissions for the current user with the fn_my_permissions function. But how do you check for the effective permissions for another user? A sysadmin can impersonate any login or database User and run queries as that user. So if you want to check the effective server permissions for a Windows login, you could use a query like this:

```
EXECUTE AS LOGIN='SERVER01\AnotherLogin'
  SELECT * FROM sys.fn_my_permissions(null,'SERVER')
REVERT
GO
```

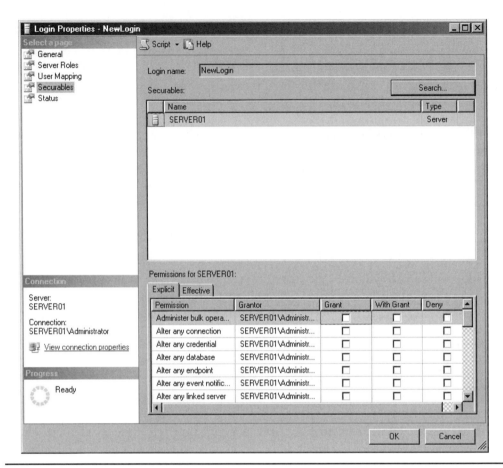

Figure 5-5 *The Login Securables page*

Database Security

All of the objects described in the previous section are used to control access to a SQL Server instance only. If a user or application needs to work with a database (as is usually the case), then you use another set of objects at the database level to represent the database permissions you wish to associate with the user. Inbound requests are not authenticated by the database (this only happens at the instance level or outside of the instance), but there is another authorization stage because (with the exception of logins that belong to the sysadmin role) instance permissions held by logins do not imply any database permissions—even the ability to connect to the database.

SQL Server database-level principals that are used to control access are

▶ Database User

▶ Database role

▶ Application role

Users

Users are database-level objects that act as an identifier and as a permissions container for logins within a particular database. A User usually is associated with a login (as orphaned Users would serve no useful purpose), and this association is called a *mapping*. There are a few exceptions to this rule: you can get orphaned Users when you restore a database to an instance with different logins; you can explicitly create database Users without an associated login; and you can have multiple logins associated with a single User, called an alias. But orphaned Users are a problem that needs correcting, Users without logins are rarely used, and aliases are deprecated and will be removed from a future version of SQL Server. So the basic rule is that each User is associated with one login.

However, logins need not be mapped to any User if the intention is for that login to work only with the instance—for example, a login belonging to the securityadmin role that allows an administrator to create and manage other logins. In the most common case, a login is mapped to a User of the same name defined in a database, and where the login requires access to more than one database, the login will be mapped to Users defined in each of these databases, each User having the same name.

A number of Users are created automatically for a new SQL Server database:

▶ **dbo**   A User called dbo (Database Owner) is present in every SQL Server database and has the permissions to perform any activity and grant any permission inside the database. This User is mapped either to the login that created the database or to another login that was specified at the time of creation. The login mapped to dbo is also referred to as the owner of the database. However, a member of the sysadmin group can still connect to any database and will always connect as dbo, regardless of which login is the database owner.

▶ **INFORMATION_SCHEMA and sys**   These Users are used internally by SQL Server and are, in fact, not database principals at all. They cannot be modified or dropped.

▶ **Guest**   If the Guest User is enabled in a database, then all logins that do not have associated users in the database become mapped to this User and can access the database. Enabling the Guest User is not recommended for security reasons.

Creating Users   You have two options for creating new database Users using Management Studio, both of which achieve exactly the same results. The first is to return to the Properties pages for a login and select the User Mapping page (see Figure 5-6). Selecting one or more databases from here and optionally requesting role membership within those databases will cause User objects to be created in the specified databases. The created User(s) will have the same name as the login.

Alternatively, you can create new database Users from the Database User – New dialog box, accessed from the context menu of the Users node (under Security) of the database in Object Explorer (see Figure 5-7). The only mandatory settings are a name for the User and the login to which it maps. In this case, the User name doesn't

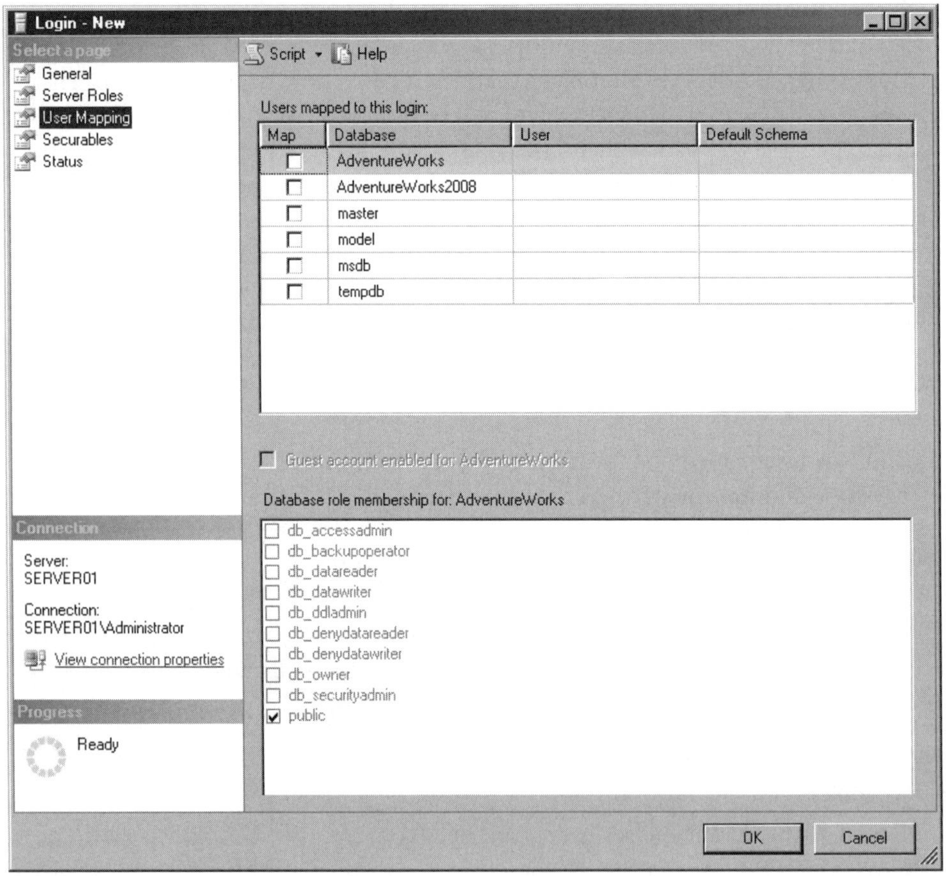

Figure 5-6   *The User Mapping page*

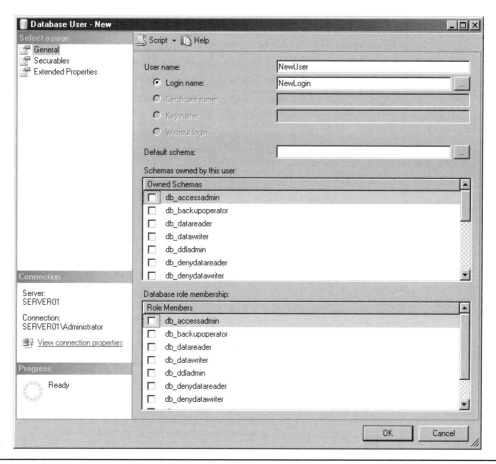

Figure 5-7   *The Database User – New dialog box*

have to be the same as that of the login, but from the point of view of simplifying administration, keeping them the same is recommended. The ellipsis (...) button next to the Login Name text box allows you to search for existing instance logins to map to the User.

You also can use the CREATE USER statement to create a new User. For example:

```
CREATE USER NewUser FOR LOGIN NewLogin
```

A list of database Users can be returned using the sys.database_principals catalog view.

Fixed and User-Defined Database Roles

As with the prebuilt server roles, a number of fixed database roles exist in each SQL Server database and their scope is limited to that database only. As before, these roles serve to represent common database user functions. However, at a database level we can create new roles to represent the activities of users or applications specific to our own organizations.

Table 5-3 shows the fixed database roles. Note that many Users may belong to the db_owner fixed role and act as if they were the database owner; this does not change the fact that the database can only ever be genuinely owned by one login (mapped to the dbo User).

As with server roles, every database User is added to the public role. However, it is not usual for Users to remain a member of this role only, because without any further role membership or additional permissions, they will not be able to carry out any useful task within the database.

Privileges that are dynamically added to or dropped from a role will dynamically take effect for Users belonging to that role.

Fixed Database Role	Name	Description
db_owner	Owner	Can perform all maintenance and configuration activities in the database. The permissions of this role span all the other fixed database roles.
db_accessadmin	Access Admin	Can add or remove access for logins for a database.
db_datareader	Data Reader	Can read all data from all user tables in the database.
db_datawriter	Data Writer	Can insert, update, or delete data from all user tables in the database.
db_ddladmin	DDL Admin	Can add, modify, or drop objects in the database.
db_securityadmin	Security Admin	Can manage database roles and role members and manage statement and object permissions in the database.
db_backupoperator	Backup Operator	Has permission to back up the database.
db_denydatareader	Deny Data Reader	Cannot read data from user tables in the database.
db_denydatawriter	Deny Data Writer	Cannot insert, delete, or change data of user tables in the database.
public	Public	Every database user belongs to the public database role. When a user has not been granted or denied specific permissions on a securable, the user inherits the permissions granted to public on that securable.

Table 5-3   *The Fixed Database Roles*

Oracle DBA Q&A

Q: Why would I ever use a role like Deny Data Writer? Wouldn't I just not grant any write permissions in that case?

A: Be aware that, unlike the sysadmin server role, you can deny permissions from the db_owner database role and any user-defined roles (and remember that a Deny always overrides a Grant). A user might be made a member of a privileged role in order to carry out administration and maintenance on a database, but the organization might wish to ensure that, in this particular instance, the user doesn't modify any data. Adding the user to db_denydatawriter as well as the privileged role would achieve this. Note that db_denydatareader can be used in the same way, but this will cause many actions performed using Object Explorer to fail because the User will not have permission to select from the system catalog. Note also that while it is possible to deny permissions from the db_owner role, anyone who belongs to this role can manage their own role membership and permissions and so could just grant themselves whatever they liked.

Q: Can roles be password protected, like in Oracle databases?

A: In SQL Server, database roles cannot be password protected, and all of a User's roles are always active. For password-protected roles that can be activated on demand, SQL Server has application roles.

Application Roles

Application roles are a special case of database role that allow you to separate the permissions given to an application that connects to SQL Server from those belonging to the User that connects to the database.

Once an application role has been created, the process for authorizing an application request would be as follows:

1. The application connects to SQL Server using the appropriate login, which is mapped to a User in the target database.
2. The application sets (requests) the Application role, specifying a password that was set when the role was created.
3. For the life of the current session, the application now has the privileges associated with the Application role, not with the login and User used to connect.

The syntax for creating an application role is:

```
CREATE APPLICATION ROLE application_role_name
    WITH PASSWORD = 'password'
```

The system stored procedure sp_setapprole can be used to set an application role in a particular user session:

```
EXEC sp_setapprole 'SalesApprole', 'AsDeF00MbXX';
GO
```

Adding Users to Roles   Users can be added to one or more database roles at the time that they are created (see the Database Role – New dialog box, shown in Figure 5-8)

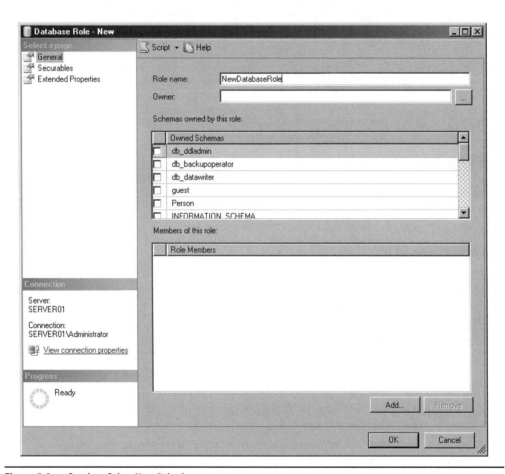

Figure 5-8   *Database Role – New dialog box*

or subsequently. To add an existing User to a role, simply open the Database User Properties pages and select the required Role(s), as shown in Figure 5-8.

Alternatively, you can use the system procedure sys.sp_addrolemember to add a database User to a database role.

For a list of Users belonging to database roles, you can use the catalog view sys.database_role_members.

Creating Database Roles   To create a new database role, you need to specify a name and an owner (if none is provided, it will default to the dbo User). You do this in the Database Role – New dialog box (see Figure 5-8), which you access from the context menu of the Schemas node for the database in Object Explorer.

Alternatively, you can pass exactly the same information to the CREATE ROLE statement. For example:

```
CREATE ROLE NewDatabaseRole AUTHORIZATION dbo
```

The process for assigning permissions and schema ownership to database roles and to Users is identical and is detailed next.

Database and Object Permissions

The Properties pages for both Users and database roles have identical Securables pages (the page for a User is shown in Figure 5-9). From here you can follow exactly the same process as described in the previous section "Server Permissions" to grant or deny individual permissions to a User or role. The rules governing the precedence of Deny over Grant are also exactly as described in that section.

There are, however, a larger number of object categories that you can choose from when searching for the objects to which you wish to grant or deny user permissions.

Figure 5-9 shows the results of searching across tables, views, and stored procedures in the AdventureWorks sample database; the full list of object types is much larger than this, as it includes every type of object available in a SQL Server database, including schemas and the database itself. The permissions that may be set on an object vary depending upon the object type. See Books Online for a complete list of object and permission types.

The syntax for granting, revoking, and denying permissions is practically identical:

```
GRANT ALTER ON [dbo].[ErrorLog] TO [NewUser]
```

or

```
REVOKE ALTER ON [dbo].[ErrorLog] TO [NewUser]
```

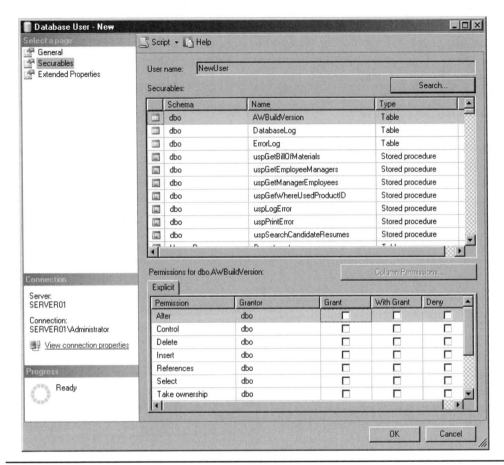

Figure 5-9 *The User Securables page*

or

```
DENY ALTER ON [dbo].[ErrorLog] TO [NewUser]
```

The catalog view sys.database_permissions returns all permissions granted to all Users in a database.

Schemas

Schemas are very much a primary object in Oracle and represent a number of "hard" logical and functional boundaries. As described in Chapter 4, things are slightly different in SQL Server. As well as the benefits of using schemas in SQL Server described in earlier chapters, two of the most compelling drivers behind using schemas in SQL Server are both security related. The first of these is to solve a problem faced by administrators of previous versions of SQL Server (and, as such, we won't dwell on it too long here), and that is that database objects used to be owned by Users. The problem would arise when it became time to drop a User that owned objects—the ownership would need to be reassigned before the User could be dropped, and when a large number of objects were involved, this was a very time-consuming task. Furthermore, these named Users would be referenced in queries as part of the object name (for example, James. Employee), meaning that many additional references would also need to be changed. Now, objects aren't owned by Users; instead they belong to schemas, which, in turn, have owners. So, if the HumanResources schema is owned by the User James and it is time to drop that User, all that is required is to reassign ownership of the schema and the User can be dropped.

The second driver is that schemas can be used to create dynamic security "zones" within SQL Server databases. At the simplest level, the owner of a schema automatically receives dbo permissions for that schema's objects. However, a more sophisticated model can be built by assigning object-level permissions (as described in the section Database and Object Permissions) to schemas themselves. While slightly more involved than using database roles alone, you can fine-tune these roles at a schema level or assign permissions at this level directly. For example, the User James may have the database role db_datareader but may then be issued Insert, Update, and Delete permissions for the schema Human Resources, meaning he can read from all database objects but has full DML permissions for objects in the Human Resources schema. Crucially, this would continue to be the case as new objects were created in the databases—no further management would be required to assign permissions to these new objects. So in the same way that roles are containers of permissions for Users, schemas are containers for objects, and a permission granted at the schema level applies to all objects in that schema.

See Chapter 4 for details on creating schemas, assigning ownership, and moving objects between schemas.

Protecting SQL Server Databases

Having looked at the objects that allow administrators to design and implement databases that effectively control user access to data, the rest of this chapter looks at other features available in SQL Server that can be used to further enhance database security.

Proxy Accounts

The Windows identities under which the SQL Server instance service and the SQL Server Agent service run require sufficient privileges to carry out the tasks required of them. In the case of the instance service, the required privileges are ordinarily relatively low (see Chapter 3 for details); however, SQL Server provides a facility for executing command-line statements from within database procedures, and this suggests the granting of a much wider set of permissions. Fortunately, these permissions do not need to be granted to the identity running SQL Server because you can specify a server proxy account for use in this case, meaning that your least-privileges approach toward the SQL Server's service accounts can be preserved.

Specifying a Server Proxy Account

The procedure xp_cmdshell is used to execute Windows command-line statements from within procedures; it is disabled after installation and must be enabled before it can be used. You can specify an account for use by xp_cmdshell by providing an account name and password on the Security page of the Server Properties dialog box (accessible by selecting Properties from the context menu of the instance in Object Explorer), as shown in Figure 5-10. Setting this property causes SQL Server to impersonate the specified account when calling xp_cmdshell.

Alternatively, the procedure sp_xp_cmdshell_proxy_account can be used to set up a proxy account. The syntax is

```
sp_xp_cmdshell_proxy_account [ NULL | { 'account_name' , 'password' } ]
```

NOTE

Passing the NULL parameter causes the proxy account to be deleted.

SQL Agent Proxy Accounts

A more common use for proxy accounts in SQL Server is to use them in conjunction with the SQL Server Agent. Tasks defined as SQL Server Agent jobs or as part of maintenance plans are often required to access network resources or external systems (for example, when copying backup files or importing and exporting data) or carry out

> Server proxy account
> ☑ Enable server proxy account
> Proxy account: SERVER01\PrivAct
> Password: ********

Figure 5-10 *Server proxy account details*

other activities that suggest a high level of privilege. If you don't want to grant the sum of all of these permissions to the SQL Server Agent service simply so that a few tasks can succeed, you can specify proxy accounts for use by those tasks only. Additionally, the SQL Server Agent service account (or per-service SID) always belongs to the sysadmin group, and there may be cases where you may want an Agent job to connect to the SQL instance as a non-sysadmin login.

See Chapter 10 for details of creating SQL Server Agent jobs using proxy accounts.

Encryption

As well as making sure that permissions are correctly managed and that system access is protected both physically and using firewalls, you should consider encrypting sensitive data within the database. SQL Server provides encryption features that help you to protect against three types of attack or vulnerability:

- ▶ **The "wiretap"** You can encrypt the traffic that passes between SQL Server and its users and applications so that if somebody manages to capture these network packets, they won't be able to inspect them to reveal data.

- ▶ **A snooping user** If you can't deny overly curious users access to a particular resource but would rather they didn't take notice of its contents, you can encrypt the contents.

- ▶ **Lost media** If either a database's data files or its backups fall into the wrong hands, a malicious party can attach or restore the database and browse it at their leisure. If these files are encrypted, then this isn't possible.

While we have a lot of out-of-the box functionality at our disposal, this kind of protection must be planned in advance. To discuss encryption (and decryption), we first need to establish how the following terms are used in SQL Server. These definitions are taken from SQL Server Books Online.

- ▶ **Symmetric keys** A symmetric key is one key that is used for both encryption and decryption. Encryption and decryption by using a symmetric key is fast, and suitable for routine use with sensitive data in the database.

- ▶ **Asymmetric keys** An asymmetric key is made up of a private key and the corresponding public key. The public key can be used to encrypt data that can only be decrypted by the private key. Asymmetric encryption and decryption are relatively resource-intensive, but they provide a higher level of security than symmetric encryption. An asymmetric key can be used to encrypt a symmetric key for storage in a database.

► **Certificates** A public key certificate, usually just called a certificate, is a digitally-signed statement that binds the value of a public key to the identity of the person, device, or service that holds the corresponding private key. Certificates are issued and signed by a certification authority (CA). The entity that receives a certificate from a CA is the subject of that certificate…This signature attests to the validity of the binding between the public key and the identifier information of the subject. (The process of digitally signing information entails transforming the information, as well as some secret information held by the sender, into a tag called a signature.) A primary benefit of certificates is that they relieve hosts of the need to maintain a set of passwords for individual subjects. Instead, the host merely establishes trust in a certificate issuer, which may then sign an unlimited number of certificates.

Encrypted Connections

SQL Server can be configured to use Secure Sockets Layer (SSL) to encrypt the data that is sent between an instance and a client user or application and, additionally, to validate the identity of a server to the client.

If the instance of SQL Server is running on a computer that has been assigned a certificate from a public CA, the identities of that computer and the instance of SQL Server are vouched for by the chain of certificates that leads to the trusted root authority. Such server validation requires that the computer on which the client application is running be configured to trust the root authority of the certificate that is used by the server.

Enabling SSL encryption increases the security of data transmitted across networks between instances of SQL Server and applications. However, enabling encryption does slow performance. When all traffic between SQL Server and a client application is encrypted using SSL, the following additional processing is required, namely that an extra network roundtrip is required as the connection is established, and that the client and server network libraries must carry out the encryption and decryption of packets. On Windows Server 2008 and later operating systems, the level of encryption is 128 bit.

The following procedure describes how to configure SSL for SQL Server:

1. Install a certificate in the Windows certificate store of the server computer.
2. In SQL Server Configuration Manager, right-click the Protocols for... node for the required instance and select Properties to open the Protocols for *Instance* Properties dialog box (see Figure 5-11).

Figure 5-11   *The Protocols for* Instance *Properties dialog box*

3. On the Flags tab, you can force the instance to always use SSL by setting the Force Encryption option to Yes. If this option is set, all client/server communication is encrypted and clients that cannot support encryption are denied access. If the option is set to No (the default), encryption can be requested by the client application but is not required. The Flags tab also allows you to specify that this particular instance will not allow users to discover its port number using the SQL Server Browser Service, by setting Hide Instance to Yes.

4. On the Certificate tab, you can associate this instance with the certificate that you installed in step 1.

Regardless of any networking configuration, the credentials that are transmitted when a client connects to SQL Server are always encrypted. SQL Server will use an installed certificate from a trusted CA if available, and if a trusted certificate is not installed, SQL Server will generate a self-signed certificate when the instance is started and use the self-signed certificate to encrypt the credentials. This self-signed certificate helps increase security but it does not provide protection against identity spoofing by the server. If no trusted certificate is installed and the Force Encryption option is set to Yes, all data transmitted across a network between SQL Server and the client application will be encrypted using the self-signed certificate.

Encryption Functions

If you're looking to encrypt data within your SQL Server databases rather than just the traffic that is sent between the server and its clients, then you need to be aware of two types of symmetric key used by SQL Server to enable this encryption and decryption:

► The Service Master Key (SMK) is automatically created the first time that an instance is started. This key is itself encrypted by Windows APIs on the local computer using a key derived from the local computer's credentials (binding the key to that machine) and the SQL Server service account. The SMK can only be decrypted by the service account under which it was created or by a principal that has access to the machine's credentials.

► Database Master Keys are used to protect the private keys of certificates and asymmetric keys that are present in a given database. When it is created, the Database Master Key is encrypted by using the Triple DES algorithm and a user-supplied password. To enable the automatic decryption of the Database Master Key, a copy of the key is encrypted by using the SMK. It is stored in both the database where it is used and in the master system database.

While you cannot simply enable the encryption of particular data columns in SQL Server, you can use built-in functions to encrypt values as they are inserted or updated and then decrypt these values as they are read.

Encrypting Columns   The steps you need to follow to encrypt data in this way are

1. Create a Database Master Key (if one hasn't been created already).
2. Create a certificate.
3. Create a symmetric key, encrypted using the certificate.
4. "Open" the key (make it available for use by SQL Server).
5. Encrypt the value and write it to the column (this could be in a stored procedure or trigger).

The following code shows how to encrypt a column by using a symmetric key:

```
--If there is no master key, create one now.
Step 1
IF NOT EXISTS
    (SELECT * FROM sys.symmetric_keys WHERE symmetric_key_id = 101)
    CREATE MASTER KEY ENCRYPTION BY
    PASSWORD = '<password>'
```

```
GO
Step 2
CREATE CERTIFICATE HumanResources037
   WITH SUBJECT = 'Employee Social Security Numbers';
GO
Step 3
CREATE SYMMETRIC KEY SSN_Key_01
    WITH ALGORITHM = AES_256
    ENCRYPTION BY CERTIFICATE HumanResources037;
GO
Step 4
-- Open the symmetric key with which to decrypt the data.
OPEN SYMMETRIC KEY SSN_Key_01
   DECRYPTION BY CERTIFICATE HumanResources037;
Step 5
UPDATE HumanResources.Employee
SET EncryptedNationalIDNumber = EncryptByKey(Key_GUID('SSN_Key_01'),
 NationalIDNumber);
GO
```

To decrypt the value, you need to

1. Ensure that the key used to encrypt the data is open.
2. Decrypt the value and return it (for example, in a stored procedure or view):

```
-- Now list the original ID, the encrypted ID, and the
-- decrypted ciphertext. If the decryption worked, the original
-- and the decrypted ID will match.
Step 1
-- We will assume that the key is already open
Step 2
SELECT NationalIDNumber, EncryptedNationalIDNumber
    AS 'Encrypted ID Number',
    CONVERT(nvarchar, DecryptByKey(EncryptedNationalIDNumber))
    AS 'Decrypted ID Number'
    FROM HumanResources.Employee;
GO
```

ON THE JOB

As soon as you have completed the preceding steps (assuming this is the first time that encryption has been employed within this instance), you should back up the Service Master Key. Without this key, you won't be able to decrypt your encrypted data if you have to restore your database to a new instance. See the upcoming section "Managing Keys and Encrypted Data."

The cryptographic functions used in the preceding procedure can also be provided with an optional "authenticator" value to make the process even more secure. This value would likely be a GUID or Identity value for the row being written or read and would act to bind the encrypted value to that particular row, meaning that decryption would fail if someone with access to the encrypted data were to simply update one encrypted value with another from another row.

There are variations on this approach available: the functions EncryptByPassPhrase and DecryptByPassPhrase allow for temporary encryption and decryption keys to be created and used based on a pass phrase provided as the data is written or read. However, this approach suggests that application builders or users are responsible for keeping pass phrases private, so unless the requirement is for system administrators to not be able to decrypt application data (since this is another implication of this approach), the recommendation would be to use the functions given in the examples.

Database Encryption

Transparent Data Encryption is a term well known to many Oracle administrators because it is the name given to Oracle's facilities for encrypting some or all of the data in a database within an easy-to-manage encryption infrastructure. Fortunately, the same term is used to describe SQL Server's implementation of the same features; however, we will see that there are some key differences to be aware of.

Transparent data encryption (TDE) in SQL Server is a special case of encryption that uses a symmetric key and allows us to avoid having to build any of the encryption/decryption functionality described in the previous section. TDE encrypts an entire database using a symmetric key, called the database encryption key (DEK), which is secured using a certificate stored in the master database and protects data "at rest." This mean there is page-level encryption and decryption of data and log files as they are written to disk or read into memory, ensuring that even if these files (or backups of these files) fall into the wrong hands, the database cannot be attached or restored without the appropriate certificate.

Oracle DBA Q&A

Q: In an Oracle database, if you want to encrypt only a certain set of tables, you put them in a tablespace and only encrypt that tablespace. Can you do something similar using filegroups in SQL Server to just select certain tables for encryption?

A: No, when TDE is enabled in SQL Server, it affects the entire database; there is no way to select individual tables within a database.

ON THE JOB

After enabling TDE, you should immediately back up the certificate and the private key associated with the certificate (assuming that you've already backed up your SMK). Also, the encrypting certificate should be retained even if TDE is no longer enabled on the database, because it may need to be accessed for some operations (such as restoring an encrypted backup).

The code to back up a certificate is

```
BACKUP CERTIFICATE <certname> TO FILE = '<path_to_file>'
   [ WITH PRIVATE KEY
     (
       FILE = '<path_to_private_key_file>' ,
       ENCRYPTION BY PASSWORD = '<password>'
     )
   ]
```

The <password> value is used to encrypt the key as it is written to the file. To use TDE, follow these steps:

1. Create a Database Master Key (if one doesn't already exist).
2. Create a certificate protected by the Database Master Key.
3. Create a Database Encryption Key, encrypted using the certificate.
4. Enable database encryption.

The following code details how to carry out these steps:

```
--Step 1
USE master;
GO
CREATE MASTER KEY ENCRYPTION BY PASSWORD = '<password>';
GO
--Step 2
CREATE CERTIFICATE MyServerCert WITH SUBJECT = 'My DEK Certificate'
GO
--Step 3
USE AdventureWorks
GO
CREATE DATABASE ENCRYPTION KEY
WITH ALGORITHM = AES_128
ENCRYPTION BY SERVER CERTIFICATE MyServerCert
GO
--Step 4
```

```
ALTER DATABASE AdventureWorks
SET ENCRYPTION ON
GO
```

Enabling database encryption can also be carried out from the Options page of the database property pages, as shown in Figure 5-12.

Managing Keys and Encrypted Data

In order to recover an instance where TDE has been used, you will need a copy of the SMK. This copy can be created by generating a backup to file like so:

```
BACKUP SERVICE MASTER KEY TO FILE = '<path_to_file>'
ENCRYPTION BY PASSWORD = '<password>'
```

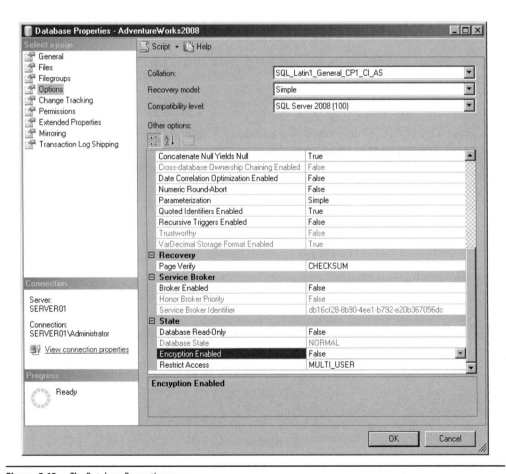

Figure 5-12   *The Database Properties page*

In this case the supplied password is used to encrypt the key in the resulting file. To restore this key into a new instance, you can use

```
RESTORE SERVICE MASTER KEY FROM FILE = '<path_to_file>'
DECRYPTION BY PASSWORD = '<password>'
```

Restoring or Attaching an Encrypted Database   If you are restoring an encrypted database to the same instance from which the backup was taken (or if the instance has been recovered and the original SMK restored, as in the preceding example), then there are no additional considerations beyond those you would normally take into account. The same is true of reattaching an encrypted database to its original instance. However, if the database is being restored or attached to a new instance, that instance must have access to the certificate used to encrypt the DEK. You can use the following code to import this certificate from a backup:

```
CREATE CERTIFICATE <certname>
        FROM FILE = '<path_to_file>'
        WITH PRIVATE KEY (
                FILE = '<path_to_private_key_file>'
                , DECRYPTION BY PASSWORD = '<password>'
                )
```

A final point to note is that the tempdb system database will be automatically encrypted if any other database on the instance of SQL Server is encrypted by using TDE. This might have a performance effect for unencrypted databases on the same instance of SQL Server.

Auditing

Another key element to operating secure systems is the ability to record the activities that take place within those systems. Often we're interested in this information because we want to improve performance or enhance functionality. The act of recording this data is often referred to as tracing. The term *auditing* is used in many industries to refer to reviewing past activities or transactions to ensure that some behavior has been in keeping with the mandated regulations or standards. SQL Server provides several features that enable us to audit database activity against both predefined standards relating to information systems security and other standards that we might adopt or develop within our own organizations.

While Oracle's auditing support allows for audit records to be stored in the database audit trail or in files on the operating system, the recommendation is that the audit trail be written to the operating system files, as this configuration imposes the least amount of overhead on the source database system. This is also the approach taken with SQL Server's prebuilt auditing features, which, as administrators, provides us the best chance that audit information will be available to us even after some catastrophic database failure.

Login Auditing

The simplest, or most lightweight, SQL Server auditing option is Login auditing. As the reference to logins (as opposed to Users) should suggest, this is configured at an instance level and allows us to record who has connected to SQL Server and, perhaps more importantly, who has tried to connect and failed.

Login auditing is available from the Server Properties dialog box, on the Security page, as shown in Figure 5-13. Note that it is also from this page that SQL Server authentication can be enabled or disabled as described at the beginning of this chapter.

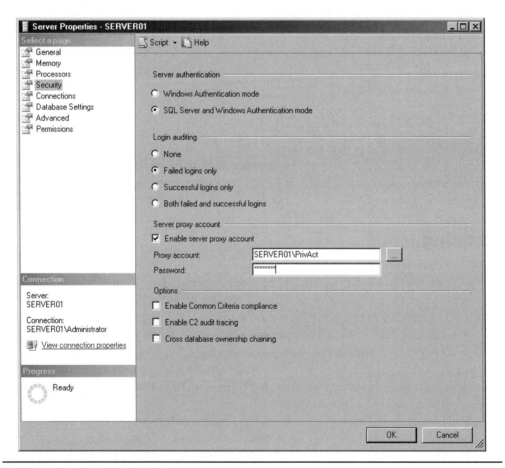

Figure 5-13 *Server Properties dialog box*

The options under Login Auditing are

▶ **None**   Turns off login auditing.

▶ **Failed logins only**   Audits unsuccessful logins only.

▶ **Successful logins only**   Audits successful logins only.

▶ **Both failed and successful logins**   Audits all login attempts.

The default setting is Failed Logins Only; changing the audit level requires restarting the service. Login audit records are stored in the Windows application log, an example of which is given in Figure 5-14.

C2 Audit and Common Criteria

Without reference to any particular system or vendor, the U.S. Department of Defense (DoD) has established a set of ratings for the security levels of computer systems, based on their ability to govern and audit usage and access. These ratings range from D (Minimum Protection) through to A1 (the most secure, Verified Design, which requires features such as labeled data and the passing of formal functional analysis procedures).

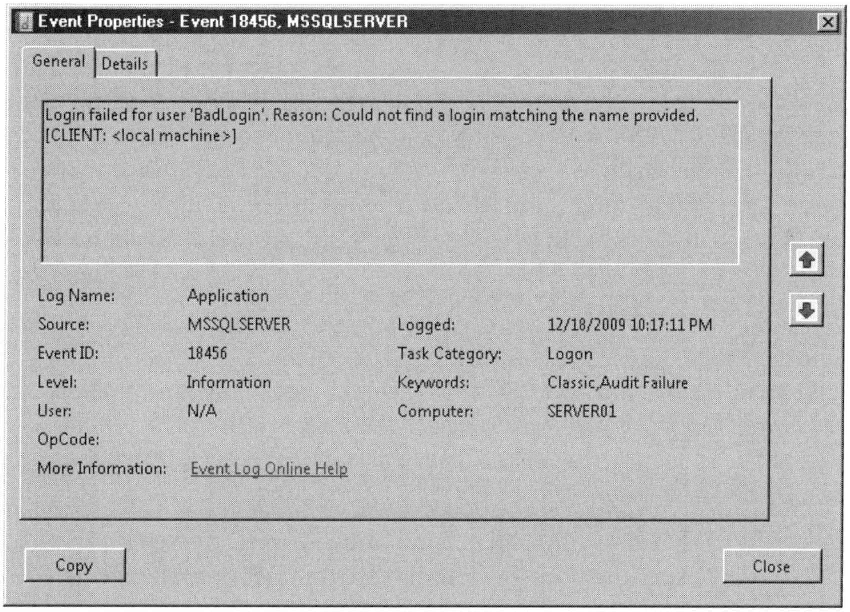

Figure 5-14   *A SQL Server event*

A C2 rating, Controlled Access Protection, is an absolute security minimum required for implementation in U.S. government agencies. It is awarded to systems that pass the DoD's Trusted Computer System Evaluation Criteria (TCSEC) tests and requires that auditing goes beyond successful and failed login attempts, extending it to successful and failed use of permissions when accessing individual database objects and executing all SQL statements. SQL Server has held a C2 rating since version 2000.

As not all organizations have a requirement to adhere to the U.S. government security standards, C2-level auditing is not enabled by default in SQL Server. C2 Audit is enabled or disabled from the Security page of the Server Properties dialog box (refer to Figure 5-13) or by using the "c2 audit mode" option with sp_configure.

C2 Audit records contain the following:

- A timestamp
- The login that raised the event
- The server name
- The event type
- An indication of the result (success or failure)
- Application name (if present)
- The SQL Server process ID of the user request

Audit logs are stored in the Data folder under the instance Root and are named AuditTrace_yyyymmddhhmmss.trc, with the timestamp part of the name indicating the date and time the log file was created. C2 Audit log files are limited to 200MB, and new files are generated automatically when the previous one is full. If the audit log can't be written (potentially because there is insufficient disk space), the instance will shut down.

ON THE JOB

Because the amount of data written to C2 Audit log files can be substantial, running out of disk space is a real possibility if there is no process in place for archiving older files. If SQL Server cannot start because no space can be freed for new log files, you can use the startup parameter -f, which causes SQL Server to disregard audit settings.

The contents of the audit files can be viewed using SQL Server Profiler (see Figure 5-15) or by using the built-in function sys.fn_trace_gettable, which displays the content of a trace file as a result set (see Figure 5-16).

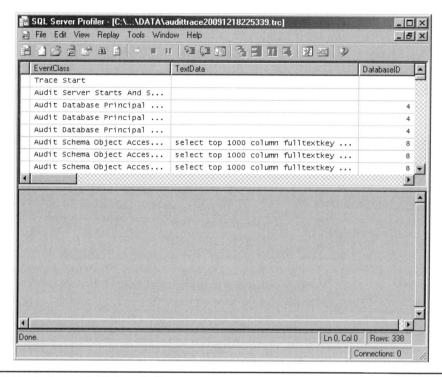

Figure 5-15   *Audit records in SQL Server Profiler*

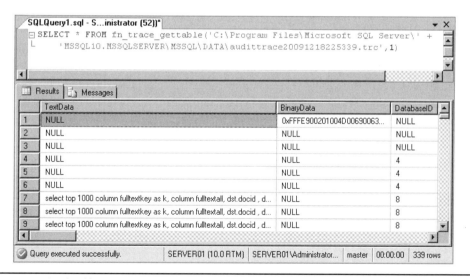

Figure 5-16   *Results of fn_trace_gettable*

As well as support for the C2 security standard, SQL Server also provides a built-in implementation of another set of standards known as the Common Criteria for Information Technology Security Evaluation (usually shortened to just Common Criteria). Common Criteria is managed by a membership that includes government agencies and industry bodies from around the world, and the requirements go beyond auditing. With this in mind, Common Criteria has come to effectively supersede the C2 standard.

Common Criteria compliance is also disabled by default in SQL Server and can be enabled from the Security page of the Server Properties dialog box (refer to Figure 5-13) or by using the "common criteria compliance enabled" option with sp_configure. Changing this value requires an instance restart.

The "common criteria compliance enabled" option changes the following aspects of SQL Server:

Criteria	Description
Residual Information Protection (RIP)	RIP requires a memory allocation to be overwritten with a known pattern of bits before memory is reallocated to a new resource. Meeting the RIP standard can contribute to improved security; however, overwriting the memory allocation can slow performance.
The ability to view login statistics	Each time a user successfully logs into SQL Server, information about the last successful login time, the last unsuccessful login time, and the number of attempts between the last successful and current login times is made available. These login statistics can be viewed by querying the sys.dm_exec_sessions dynamic management view (DMV).
That column GRANT should not override table DENY	After the common criteria compliance enabled option is enabled, a table-level DENY takes precedence over a column-level GRANT. When the option is not enabled, a column-level GRANT takes precedence over a table-level DENY.

Common Criteria compliance in SQL Server does not log audit records outside of SQL Server; it simply causes additional login information to be captured, which can then be viewed using the DMV referenced in the preceding table. Figure 5-17 shows a call to sys.dm_exec_sessions shortly after enabling Common Criteria compliance.

SQL Server Instance and Database Audit

For organizations that have different audit requirements from those met by the previous options, bespoke, fine-grained auditing can be created in SQL Server. In older versions of SQL Server, using DML and DDL triggers was a recommended approach for building this kind of functionality, but now SQL Server Audit gives administrators the tools to define, enable, store, and view audits on various server and database objects.

NOTE

Unlike the other auditing features previously described, SQL Server Audit is an Enterprise Edition feature.

Figure 5-17 *Viewing sys.dm_exec_sessions*

The objects that require configuration in order for SQL Server Audit to produce the required output are

▶ **Audit**   Defines general audit properties such as the output location and the required behavior if the output can't be written. You can define multiple Audit objects for a given SQL Server instance.

▶ **Audit Specification**   Defined either at an instance or database level and bound to an Audit. There can be only one Audit Specification per Audit at the instance level and one Audit Specification per database per Audit at the database level. Audit Specification acts as a container for multiple Audit Actions.

▶ **Audit Action**   Depending upon whether the Audit Specification is for an instance or database, the Audit Action type specifies the instance or database events to include in the audit.

A new Audit is created in a disabled state, and does not automatically produce any output. After the Audit is enabled, the audit destination receives the defined events.

Creating SQL Server Audit Objects   You can create an Audit by selecting New Audit from the context menu of the Audits node of the instance in Object Explorer, which opens the Create Audit dialog box (see Figure 5-18).

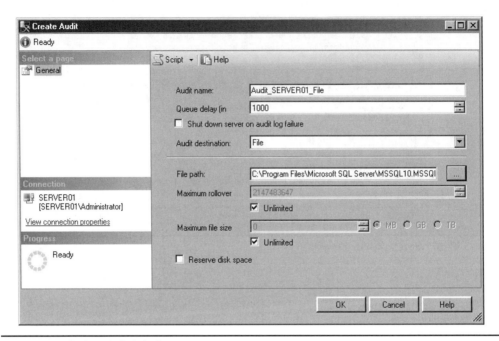

Figure 5-18 *The Create Audit dialog box*

The required settings are listed and described in Table 5-4.

No additional configuration is required when the Audit Destination field is set to the Windows application log because any authenticated user can read and write to this log (however, keep in mind that this makes the application log intrinsically less secure than the Windows Security event log). When the Audit Destination field is set to the Windows Security log, you need to additionally configure two Windows Security settings:

► Enable the "Audit object access security" policy for both Success and Failure. In Windows Server 2008 and later, this is achieved by using the Audit Policy utility (AuditPol.exe). For more information about the AuditPol.exe program, see Knowledge Base article 921469, "How to Use Group Policy to Configure Detailed Security Auditing."

► Configure the local or domain security policy to add the account that SQL Server is running under to the "Generate security audits" policy (by default, Local System, Local Service, and Network Service are already part of this policy). This setting can be configured by using the Security Policy snap-in (SecPol.msc).

Settings	Description
Audit name	The name by which you will refer to this Audit object.
Queue Delay (in milliseconds)	Allows for audit records to be written either synchronously or asynchronously by specifying the amount of time in milliseconds that can elapse before audit actions are forced to be processed. A value of 0 indicates synchronous delivery. The default minimum value is 1000 (1 second).
Shut down server on audit log failure	When enabled, forces instance shutdown if audit events cannot be written to their destination.
Audit destination	The destination to which audit events will be written. The options are as follows: ▶ File (binary) ▶ Security log ▶ Application log Further details on using the Windows Security and application logs are given in the text accompanying this table.
The remaining settings apply only when the Audit Destination field is set to File.	
File path	Specifies the location of the folder where audit data is written. The audit log filename is automatically constructed using the following elements: ▶ **AuditName** The name of the audit provided when the audit is created ▶ **AuditGUID** The GUID that identifies the audit that is stored in the metadata ▶ **PartitionNumber** A number generated by SQL Server Extended Events to partition file sets ▶ **TimeStamp** A 64-bit integer generated by converting the UTC time when the audit file is created ▶ **File extension** .sqlaudit
Maximum rollover	By default there is no restriction on the number of audit files kept in the audit destination (where the Audit Destination field is File). By removing the check from the Unlimited check box and specifying a value, you can enforce a maximum number of files to be retained.
Maximum file size	By default there is no restriction placed on the maximum size for an audit file. By removing the check from the Unlimited check box, you can enforce a maximum size. When this size is reached, new files are created in accordance with the Maximum Rollover settings.
Reserve disk space	Can only be used when the Maximum file size option is set and causes SQL Server to reserve space in the audit destination equivalent to the specified Maximum File Size when creating a new audit file.

Table 5-4   *Create Audit Dialog Box Settings*

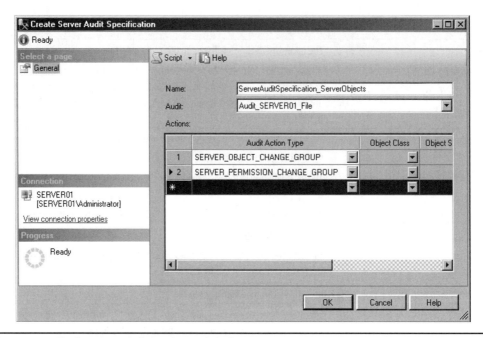

Figure 5-19 *The Create Server Audit Specification dialog box*

Having created an Audit, you can create an Audit Specification by selecting New Audit Specification from the context menu of the Audit Specifications node of either the instance or a database in Object Explorer, which opens the Create Server Audit Specification dialog box (see Figure 5-19).

You specify a previously created Audit and can then add multiple Actions to define those events that will be included in the Audit. Actions are built from Audit Action Type items that can refer to either a group of actions, such as Server_Object_Change_ Group (which, for example, includes CREATE, ALTER, and DROP for any server object), or individual actions, such as SELECT operations on a table.

The elements that make up an Audit Specification Action are outlined in Table 5-5.

Once created, an Audit can be enabled (and disabled) from the context menu of the audit object, as shown in Figure 5-20.

From the same menu, you can view the contents of an Audit log. Selecting View Audit Logs opens Log File Viewer, shown in Figure 5-21, allowing you to browse the contents of either a log file, the Windows application log, or the Windows Security log. Naturally, the two Windows logs can also be viewed using other Windows tools such as Event Viewer.

Column Name	Description
Audit Action Type	The class of event or group of events to capture. For a full list of the available instance and database-level events, see the SQL Server Books Online article "SQL Server Audit Action Groups and Actions."
Object Class	For individual events (such as SELECT), you can set the scope of the event to one of the following: ▶ Database ▶ Object ▶ Schema This field is not available when the Audit Action Type is a group.
Object Name	For individual events, the name of the object to be audited. This field is not available when the Audit Action Type is a group.
Object Schema	This field is automatically completed to give the schema in which the object specified in the preceding row resides.
Principal Name	Allows the audit to be filtered to include only the actions of a specified principal (User, database role, or application role).

Table 5-5   *Audit Specification Action Elements*

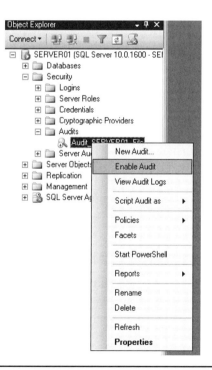

Figure 5-20   *Enabling auditing*

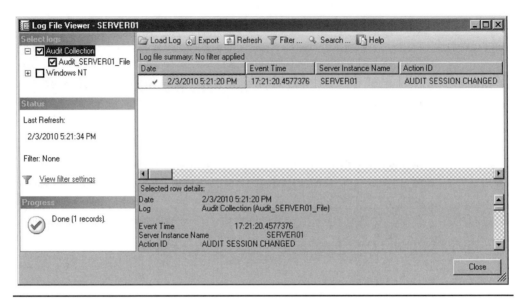

Figure 5-21 *Audit records in Log File Viewer*

As with C2 Audit, the -f startup parameter can be used to disable auditing and allow an instance to start in the case where audit failure is forcing a shutdown. Additionally, an administrator can bypass any audit-induced shutdown by starting SQL Server in single-user mode using the -m startup parameter. Starting in single-user mode downgrades any audit where "Shutdown server on audit log failure" is enabled so that it runs in that session with the setting disabled. If a failure to write the Audit event does not trigger the SQL Server instance to shut down, Audit events are buffered in memory until they can be written to the target. If the records fill the memory buffer and still cannot be written to the Audit log, the instance will block any new activity that would result in an Audit event being written until the buffer space is freed up or the audit is disabled.

Policy-Based Management and Security

SQL Server's Policy-Based Management allows administrators to create and enforce policies governing many aspects of SQL Server usage at a database or instance level or even across many instances (see Chapter 10 for a more-detailed look at Policy-Based Management).

Policies that act to increase SQL Server security can

▶ Test for security-related configuration options. For example, you can use the Login facet to test whether the password policy is enforced, or use the Database facet to detect whether all databases are owned by sa. Other facets can be used to test the properties of user connections or whether Common Criteria compliance or C2 auditing are enabled.

▶ Test for and enable or disable features that increase the attack surface area of a SQL Server instance, such as Ad Hoc Remote Queries, xp_cmdshell, and Database Mail.

▶ Enforce segregation of duties. For example, a policy might state that members of the dbcreator role may not also be part of the diskadmin role.

▶ Be automatically evaluated and re-evaluated as the server estate grows and changes, generating alerts where noncompliance is detected or even automatically reconfiguring instances that breach the policy.

Oracle DBA Q&A

Q: **Can Policy-Based Management be used to "lock down" a SQL Server estate?**

A: No. In most cases policies can be bypassed or violated by users with the appropriate permissions, and these users will be able to reconfigure options set as part of a security policy. Policy-Based Management should be treated as a useful tool to help evaluate security and detect potential vulnerabilities, not as a security enforcement feature.

Chapter 6

Data Access and Transaction Control

In This Chapter

This chapter details the activities carried out by the SQL Server Database Engine in executing user queries and ensuring that SQL Server can support applications that require the highest levels of concurrent access while ensuring that the actions of any user attempting to work with the same data as another user do not cause application errors by allowing these user actions to unduly interfere with each other. We will look at the SQL Server features that allow administrators to ensure that SQL Server databases manage data access as efficiently as possible, and we will give insight into exactly what the Database Engine is doing on behalf of users.

Underpinning SQL Server data access is the programmatic language that allows administrators and developers to create potentially complex queries and even express application logic. A detailed look at this language is outside the scope of this book; however, we will take the opportunity to introduce this language and describe some high-level concepts.

The T-SQL Language

Like all commonly implemented relational database management systems, SQL Server allows users to access and manipulate data and modify database objects and behavior using the Structured Query Language (SQL). The SQL language defines several categories of statements, including Data Manipulation Language (DML) statements, Data Definition Language (DDL) statements, and transaction control statements.

DML statements are used to retrieve and manipulate data. As in Oracle, these statements are

Action	Statement
Create	INSERT
Read	SELECT
Update	UPDATE
Delete	DELETE

In addition, both SQL Server and Oracle provide the MERGE statement to query the database and insert, update, or delete data depending upon the result of the query. All relational data access and manipulation in SQL Server, however complex the query, is carried out as a combination of these DML statements; how the Database

Engine acts to manage this statement execution forms the bulk of the remainder of this section.

DDL statements, listed next, are used to modify database objects such as tables, views, and stored procedures:

Action	Statement
Create object	CREATE
Modify object	ALTER
Drop object	DROP

Oracle DBA Q&A

Q: In Oracle, when creating objects it is possible to specify CREATE OR REPLACE, which will overwrite an object if it already exists or create it afresh if it doesn't. Does SQL Server have the same functionality?

A: No, SQL Server does not have a CREATE OR REPLACE statement. Instead, the same result is achieved (albeit not as gracefully) by checking whether the object exists and, if so, then dropping it, and if not, then continuing with the CREATE statement. The following example shows the code that is used to do an IF EXISTS check, followed by a DROP PROCEDURE if it does exist, followed by the creation. Keep in mind, though, that for changing existing tables, views, stored procedures, and functions, the T-SQL ALTER statement is the usual approach.

```
IF  EXISTS (SELECT * FROM sys.objects WHERE object_id =
OBJECT_ID(N'[dbo].[MyTestProc]') AND type in (N'P', N'PC'))
DROP PROCEDURE [dbo].[MyTestProc]
GO
CREATE PROCEDURE [dbo].[MyTestProc]
AS
BEGIN
    SELECT @@VERSION
END;
```

Transaction control statements, listed next, give greater control over the work done by batches of DML statements. They are discussed in greater detail later in this chapter.

Type	Oracle	SQL Server
System control	ALTER SYSTEM	EXEC sp_configure
	ALTER DATABASE	ALTER DATABASE
		EXEC sp_dboption
Session control	ALTER SESSION	SET

Refer to Chapter 3 for more details on configuring SQL Server instances using sp_configure. Refer to SQL Server Books Online for details on using SET to govern session settings in SQL Server (settings that persist only for the lifetime of a given connection).

While the statements just described allow administrators, developers, and users to carry out powerful set-based data manipulation, they do not provide for other functionality more commonly associated with procedural programming languages:

▶ Defining stored procedures, triggers, scalar-valued user-defined functions, and table-valued user-defined functions.

▶ Control-flow constructs such as loops and conditional branches (IF, THEN, ELSE).

▶ The ability to pass state between programmatic elements using variables, parameters, and subprocedures.

▶ Exception handling. Older SQL Server functionality based upon inspecting the value of a built-in function to determine whether an operation returned an error has been superseded by the ability to use TRY…CATCH blocks more commonly found in languages such as Java and C#.

▶ The ability to inspect and work with individual rows within a set of results using cursors.

SQL Server provides these capabilities (and many others) by implementing a set of statements in addition to the SQL statements previously described. This superset of programming functionality is known as the Transact-SQL, or T-SQL, language. To put this another way, instead of having two separate but interoperable languages (as with SQL and PL/SQL), SQL Server has a single server-side programming language. Clients always communicate with SQL Server by sending T-SQL batches. A T-SQL batch is similar to a PL/SQL anonymous block in that it can contain multiple statements, embedded SQL, and parameters to pass data back and forth, but it can also return one or more result sets to the client and error and information messages.

To make a brief point about cursors, they can be used in SQL Server in exactly the same way as they can in Oracle—to navigate through sets of rows, inspecting and potentially modifying them. However, one area in which cursors cannot be used in SQL Server is in returning sets of results to clients (or procedures further up the call stack). Result sets are passed directly out of SQL Server procedures without the need to define a parameter of type Cursor and direction Out; hence, it is very common to see SQL Server procedures such as

```
CREATE PROCEDURE [HumanResources].[uspUpdateEmployeeHireInfo]
    @EmployeeID [int],
    @Title [nvarchar](50),
    @HireDate [datetime],
    @RateChangeDate [datetime],
    @Rate [money],
    @PayFrequency [tinyint],
    @CurrentFlag [dbo].[Flag]
AS
BEGIN
    BEGIN TRY
        BEGIN TRANSACTION
        UPDATE HumanResources.Employee
        SET Title = @Title
            ,HireDate = @HireDate
            ,CurrentFlag = @CurrentFlag
        WHERE EmployeeID = @EmployeeID
        INSERT INTO HumanResources.EmployeePayHistory
            (EmployeeID
            ,RateChangeDate
            ,Rate
            ,PayFrequency)
        VALUES (@EmployeeID, @RateChangeDate, @Rate, @PayFrequency)
            SELECT HumanResources.Employee.EmployeeID,
                HumanResources.Employee.NationalIDNumber,
                HumanResources.EmployeePayHistory.RateChangeDate,
                HumanResources.EmployeePayHistory.Rate,
                HumanResources.EmployeePayHistory.PayFrequency,
                HumanResources.EmployeePayHistory.ModifiedDate
            FROM HumanResources.Employee INNER JOIN
                HumanResources.EmployeePayHistory ON
                HumanResources.Employee.EmployeeID =
```

```
                        HumanResources.EmployeePayHistory.EmployeeID
            WHERE HumanResources.Employee.EmployeeID = @EmployeeID
        COMMIT TRANSACTION
    END TRY
    BEGIN CATCH
        -- Roll back any active or uncommittable transactions before
        -- inserting information in the ErrorLog
        IF @@TRANCOUNT > 0
        BEGIN
            ROLLBACK TRANSACTION
        END
        EXECUTE [dbo].[uspLogError]
    END CATCH
END
```

In this example in which multiple DML statements are grouped together to form a single transaction, TRY and CATCH statements are used to detect and handle exceptions, and (in the successful case) the procedure ends by simply SELECT-ing a set of results to the caller.

Query Execution

The tasks that the Database Engine carries out as users submit queries and results are (potentially) returned can be divided into four categories:

▶ Parsing

▶ Optimization

▶ Execution

▶ Fetching

Parsing

During this phase, the SQL statements issued by the user or application are checked for syntactic and semantic correctness and then broken down into logical elements such as keywords, identifiers, operators, and parameters. Security checks such as the validation of access rights are also performed at this stage.

Optimization

During optimization, the Database Engine determines the most efficient sequence of operations to access the data required by the query; this sequence is called an execution plan. SQL Server analyzes the different index and join strategies available to it, taking into account statistics describing the distribution of column data where they are available, to establish an execution plan with the lowest cost, where cost is generally a measure of response time. While the query optimizer will take into account CPU usage and memory pressure, the optimizer mostly tries to minimize the amount of logical I/O required to process the query. Logical I/O is a main consumer of CPU time, and minimizing logical I/O also minimizes physical I/O. As a rule of thumb, the optimizer will also try to find the plan that completes the query execution soonest.

Notes on Statistics

SQL Server maintains statistical information about the distribution of the key values in each index; however, administrators can create statistics on non-indexed columns by using the CREATE STATISTICS statement.

By default, the AUTO_UPDATE_STATISTICS database option is set to ON, meaning that the Database Engine will automatically update statistics information as the data changes. A random sample across data pages is used to evaluate whether the statistical information still accurately represents the nature of the data, and this (instead of analyzing all the data) minimizes the cost of automatic statistical updates. Having said this, it is still possible for an administrator to disable AUTO_ UPDATE_STATISTICS, with the recommendation being that statistics updates should be built into a regular maintenance plan (see Chapter 10).

Unlike Oracle's now-deprecated rules-based optimization, SQL Server has never offered a facility to assign priorities to indexes in order to guide optimizer choices; however, it is possible for administrators and developers to instruct the optimizer using hints or plan guides (see "Plan Guides" later in the chapter).

As optimization can require some complex processing on the part of the Database Engine, SQL Server attempts to minimize the need to optimize queries by caching execution plans once they have been created. The goal for a well-performing database is for as many queries to be executed against plans retrieved from the procedure cache as possible, compared with those for which an optimized plan needs to be created afresh. For a cached plan to be used, the SQL statement must match exactly the one that generated the plan. Also, as the data in a database changes over time and the statistics fail a test as to their accuracy, new optimizations will be performed for previously cached plans (note that this failure will cause a recomputation of the statistics in question).

Execution

Whether the execution plan was cached or not, during execution the Database Engine steps through the logical operations defined in the plan, carrying out each one.

Fetching

Where queries contain SELECT statements, execution is followed by a fetch phase, which actually returns the results of the query to the user or application. Any formatting required for values such as dates and times and certain numeric values is carried out during this phase.

Execution Plans

SQL Server execution plans are a representation of the data access paths chosen by the query optimizer and show the sequence of data access operations and the cost associated with them in various formats. Being able to see the choices made by the optimizer is vital to administrators looking to understand where performance issues are occurring or where performance can be further improved.

You can generate execution plans for the queries you execute using the following syntax:

SET SHOWPLAN_TEXT {ON|OFF}	Produces a textual representation of the execution plan as a set of rows that forms a hierarchical tree representing the steps taken by the SQL Server query processor as it executes each statement. The format is similar to Oracle's EXPLAIN PLAN.
SET SHOWPLAN_ALL {ON|OFF}	Produces a more verbose version of the preceding syntax, designed for applications able to handle this output not for readability.
SET SHOWPLAN_XML {ON|OFF}	Produces an XML document describing the execution plan, which can be used by the Management Studio and other applications to provide a graphical representation of the plan. See the following example.

NOTE

In all cases, the execution plan is returned for the query without actually executing the query.

Example Execution Plan

```
SET   SHOWPLAN_TEXT ON
GO
USE AdventureWorks2008
```

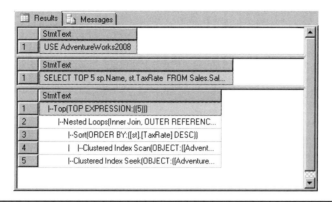

Figure 6-1   *SHOWPLAN_TEXT results*

```
GO
SELECT TOP 5sp.Name, st.TaxRate
FROM Sales.SalesTaxRate st
JOIN Person.StateProvince sp
     ON st.StateProvinceID = sp.StateProvinceID
WHERE sp.CountryRegionCode = 'US'
ORDER BY st.TaxRate desc
```

Executing the preceding example produces the results shown in Figure 6-1.

Viewing the output at this level of detail, the results using SHOWPLAN_ALL will be very similar to those shown in Figure 6-1.

XML Showplans

Perhaps the most useful Showplan format for administrators (and the one that is recommended for use going forward in SQL Server) is the XML Showplan. The XML created by this Showplan can be interpreted by SQL Server Management Studio so that the execution plan is displayed using icons rather than the tabular representation produced by the SET SHOWPLAN_ALL and SET SHOWPLAN_TEXT statements. This graphical approach is very useful for understanding the performance characteristics of a query.

XML Showplans can be created using the syntax shown in the preceding example or by using the SQL Server Management Studio features highlighted in Figure 6-2.

Figure 6-2   *Management Studio support for execution plans*

In Figure 6-2, the toolbar button marked 1 is Display Estimated Execution Plan and the button marked 2 is Display Actual Execution Plan. Display Estimated Execution Plan works in the same fashion as the SET SHOWPLAN_ statements in that it causes an execution plan to be returned without executing the query. If Display Actual Execution Plan is clicked, the query is executed prior to the execution plan being returned.

Whether the Showplan is created using SET SHOWPLAN_XML or by selecting either of the Management Studio toolbar options, the output generated for a sample query is shown in Figure 6-3.

The individual data access operations are displayed as icons, with the operational sequence represented as a flow and each icon accompanied by summary information detailing

▶ The type of operation

▶ The object name, where applicable

▶ The cost of the operation, relative to the other operations within the batch

If a batch contains multiple queries, the execution plan is returned in multiple rows (the example in Figure 6-3 contains one query and shows one such row). In this case, the relative overall cost for each query within the batch is displayed.

Each icon in an XML Showplan can be made to reveal much more information with regard to the operation than initially displayed in the execution plan window. To do this, right-click the icon and select Properties; this opens the Properties dialog box for the operation, an example of which is shown in Figure 6-4.

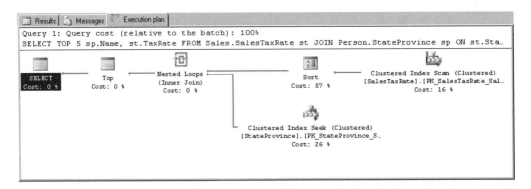

Figure 6-3 *SHOWPLAN_XML results*

Figure 6-4   *Properties for a Clustered Index Seek operation*

ON THE JOB

Comparing the estimated properties for an execution plan with the actual properties can be a useful exercise. For example, if the Estimated Number of Rows property is very different from the Actual Number of Rows property, this is a good indicator that statistics are out of date.

XML Showplans can be saved in their entirety by right-clicking any white space in the execution plan window and selecting Save Execution Plan As. A saved execution plan can be opened in any instance of SQL Server Management Studio by selecting File | Open; doing so re-creates all of this rich, graphical information exactly as it was originally displayed, making XML Showplans very useful when execution information needs to be shared between administrators or between administrators and application developers.

As a final point, it is also possible to retrieve XML Showplans for queries already executed by querying the plan column of the sys.dm_exec_query_plan dynamic management view (DMV). For example:

```
select  st.text,
        qs.execution_count,
        qs.total_logical_reads,
        qs.total_worker_time/1024 total_cpu_ms,
        qp.query_plan
from sys.dm_exec_query_stats qs
cross apply sys.dm_exec_sql_text(qs.sql_handle) st
cross apply sys.dm_exec_query_plan(qs.plan_handle) qp
order by total_logical_reads desc
```

Optimizer Hints

SQL queries can include directives that limit the access paths that will be considered by the optimizer. This can force the optimization phase to choose particular indexes or access table data in accordance with a particular locking model, and also has the effect that changes in the statistical information regarding the data in the tables and their indexes will be disregarded.

There are different types of hints, which fall into the following categories:

▶ Table hints

▶ Join hints

▶ Query hints

The SQL Server syntax is

```
{SELECT|INSERT|DELETE|UPDATE} statement ::=
    <query_expression>
    [OPTION( <query_hint> [ ,...n ]) ]
```

A detailed discussion of all the available hints is outside the scope of this book, but the Books Online article "Hints (Transact-SQL)" gives a full description of them.

In all cases, it is recommended that you thoroughly test any use of optimizer hints prior to putting them into production, as the execution path chosen by the query optimizer will be the best in most cases, and using hints can, in fact, degrade rather than improve performance. Additionally, you should monitor and periodically reevaluate your use of hints to ensure that the hints remain valid as your data changes.

Plan Guides

Although optimizer hints give administrators a great deal of control over the exact way in which the Database Engine executes particular queries, not all queries can be modified with optimizer hints. For example, administrators often can't make direct changes to queries generated by a third-party application or during a database upgrade. In such cases, though, optimizer hints can still be used to direct the chosen execution plan. This is achieved using plan guides.

Plan guides are database objects that allow optimizer hints or a fixed query plan to be associated with a query. They can be used to apply query hints to a query, control query plan compilation, or specify the exact plan that a query will use. They are useful in database upgrades to redress query plan regressions, as a tuning option for third-party applications, and in the scenario where the data environment is highly volatile (large sets of data are being modified, added, or deleted frequently and statistics rapidly become stale) and a set of queries is being reoptimized far more frequently than is desirable. In these situations, you can associate a fixed plan with a query in the hope that any performance penalty of executing a suboptimal plan will be outweighed by saving the cost of repeated recompilation.

Different types of plan guides can be created to match queries that are executed in different contexts:

▶ An OBJECT plan guide matches queries that execute in the context of Transact-SQL stored procedures, certain user-defined functions, and triggers.

▶ A SQL plan guide matches queries that execute in the context of stand-alone Transact-SQL statements and batches that are not part of a database object.

▶ A TEMPLATE plan guide matches stand-alone queries that parameterize to a specified form. These plan guides are used to override the current PARAMETERIZATION database SET option of a database for a class of queries.

Creating a Plan Guide to Use Optimizer Hints

In SQL Server Management Studio, plan guides are found under Programmability. Right-clicking Plan Guides and selecting New Plan Guide opens the New Plan Guide dialog box (see Figure 6-5).

The required values are

▶ **Name**   A name for the Plan Guide.

▶ **Statement**   The SQL statement to which hints should be applied. You must provide this text exactly as the Database Engine will receive the batch.

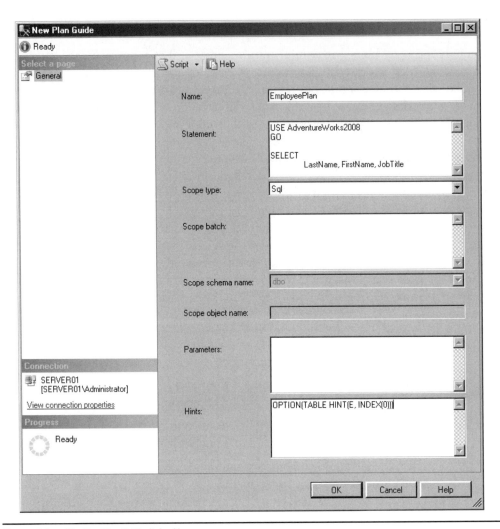

Figure 6-5 *The New Plan Guide dialog box*

- ▶ **Scope type** One of the three query contexts previously described: OBJECT, SQL, or TEMPLATE.

- ▶ **Scope batch** Allows you to specify a larger SQL batch, within which the Statement value is provided. Again, this batch must match exactly, character for character.

- ▶ **Scope schema name** When the Scope Type is OBJECT, the name of the database schema in which the object can be found.

▶ **Scope object name** When the Scope Type is OBJECT, the name of the object.

▶ **Parameters** When the Scope Type is SQL or TEMPLATE, the names and data types of all parameters in the Statement.

▶ **Hints** The optimizer hints to be applied to the statement. In Figure 6-5, a table hint is directing the optimizer to use a particular index whenever the query matches the one specified in the Statement field.

The system procedure sp_create_plan_guide can be called to create a plan guide and you must pass in the preceding information when calling it. See Books Online for the syntax.

Creating a Plan Guide to Use a Fixed Plan

The procedure for creating a plan guide to "pin" a fixed execution plan to a query is identical to that described in the preceding section except that the XML representation of the execution plan is specified in the Hints field (in place of any optimizer hint).

The XML plan representation (the XML Showplan) for the query is obtained by querying the sys.dm_exec_query_stats DMV in conjunction with dm_sec_sql_text and dm_exec_text_query_plan:

```
SELECT query_plan
FROM sys.dm_exec_query_stats AS qs
CROSS APPLY sys.dm_exec_sql_text(qs.sql_handle) AS st
CROSS APPLY sys.dm_exec_text_query_plan(qs.plan_handle, DEFAULT, DEFAULT)
AS qp
WHERE st.text LIKE N'SELECT City, StateProvinceID, PostalCode
FROM Person.Address ORDER BY PostalCode DESC;%')
```

In this example, the XML Showplan for the query referenced in the WHERE clause is returned.

Monitoring Query Execution

The DMV sys.dm_exec_requests returns information about each request that is executing within SQL Server. For the exact structure of this view, see Books Online. Table 6-1 lists and describes the columns most commonly of interest.

In addition, SQL Server Activity Monitor can be used to give an interactive view of the processes that are executing within an instance (see the section "Monitoring Locking" later in this chapter).

Column Name	Description
session_id	ID of the session to which this request is related.
start_time	Timestamp when the request arrived.
status	Status of the request. This can be one of the following: Background Running Runnable Sleeping Suspended
command	Identifies the current type of command that is being processed. Common command types include the following: SELECT INSERT UPDATE DELETE The text of the request can be retrieved by using sys.dm_exec_sql_text with the corresponding sql_handle for the request.
database_id	ID of the database the request is executing against.
user_id	ID of the user who submitted the request.
connection_id	ID of the connection on which the request arrived.
blocking_session_id	ID of the session that is blocking the request. If this column is NULL, the request is not blocked, or the session information of the blocking session is not available (or cannot be identified).
wait_time	If the request is currently blocked, this column returns the duration, in milliseconds, of the current wait.
wait_resource	If the request is currently blocked, this column returns the resource for which the request is currently waiting.
open_transaction_count	Number of transactions that are open for this request.
open_resultset_count	Number of result sets that are open for this request.
cpu_time	CPU time, in milliseconds, that is used by the request.
total_elapsed_time	Total time elapsed, in milliseconds, since the request arrived.
reads	Number of reads performed by this request.
writes	Number of writes performed by this request.
transaction_isolation_level	Isolation level with which the transaction for this request is created.
lock_timeout	Lock time-out period, in milliseconds, for this request.

Table 6-1   *Selected Columns from the DMV sys.dm_exec_requests*

Performance Counters

The Perfmon counters listed and described in Table 6-2 can be useful to administrators looking to understand query execution within a SQL Server database.

Built-in Reports

Among the built-in SQL Server Management Studio reports, the following give insight into query execution:

- ▶ All Sessions
- ▶ Activity – Top Sessions (shown in Figure 6-6)
- ▶ Performance – Top Queries by Average CPU Time
- ▶ Performance – Top Queries by Average IO
- ▶ Performance – Top Queries by Total CPU Time
- ▶ Performance – Top Queries by Total IO

Counter	Description
SQL Server SQL Statistics: Batch Requests/Sec	The number of batch requests that SQL Server receives per second, and is generally a measure of how busy a server's CPUs are.
SQL Server Plan Cache: Cache Hit Ratio	Ratio between cache hits and lookups. Essentially this is the percentage of queries for which a cached plan was executed.
SQL Server SQL Statistics: SQL Compilations/Sec	The number of times per second that the Database Engine is generating new execution plans.
SQL Server Access Methods: Full Scans/sec	Number of unrestricted full scans. These can either be base table or full index scans.
SQL Server SQL Statistics: Guided Executions/sec	Number of plan executions per second in which the query plan has been generated by using a plan guide.
SQL Server Buffer Manager: Page Reads/sec	Number of physical database page reads issued.
SQL Server Buffer Manager: Page Writes/sec	Number of physical database page writes issued.
SQL Server Databases: Transactions/sec	Number of transactions started for the database.

Table 6-2 *Windows Performance Monitor Counters Useful in Analyzing Query Execution*

Activity - Top Sessions

on SERVER01 at 11/1/2009 3:12:14 PM

This report identifies the top user Sessions on the Instance based on age, CPU utilization, memory utilization, and IOs.

⊞   **Top Oldest Sessions**

⊟   **Top CPU Consuming Sessions**

Session ID	Login Time	Last Request End Time	Host Name	Program Name	# Connections	CPU Time (ms.)	Memory Usage (KB)	Total Scheduler Time (ms.)
51	11/1/2009 9:12:10 AM	11/1/2009 1:51:18 PM	SERVER01	Microsoft SQL Server Management Studio	1	2,203.00	16	13,259.00
55	11/1/2009 1:48:29 PM	11/1/2009 1:48:40 PM	SERVER01	Microsoft SQL Server Management Studio	1	1,402.00	16	5,837.00
53	11/1/2009 1:38:24 PM	11/1/2009 2:12:16 PM	SERVER01	Microsoft SQL Server Management Studio - Query	1	120.00	16	1,161.00
54	11/1/2009 1:42:45 PM	11/1/2009 1:42:46 PM	SERVER01	Microsoft SQL Server Management Studio - Query	1	50.00	16	436.00
56	11/1/2009 1:51:18 PM	11/1/2009 1:51:20 PM	SERVER01	Microsoft SQL Server Management Studio - Query	1	30.00	16	861.00

⊞   **Top Memory Consuming Sessions**

⊞   **Top Sessions By # Reads**

⊞   **Top Sessions By # Writes**

Figure 6-6   *The Activity – Top Sessions report*

Transaction Management

A transaction is a logical unit of work that comprises one or more SQL statements executed by a single user. According to the ANSI definition, a transaction begins with the first executable statement and ends when it is explicitly committed or rolled back. Starting with a consistent database state, all modification attempts made by transactions have to complete (commit or roll back), leaving the database in a consistent state regardless of whether the modification attempt was successful or not.

SQL Server transactions exhibit the four qualities that qualify a unit of work as a transaction:

▶   **Atomicity**   A transaction must act as a single block of work; either all of its data modifications are performed or none of them are performed.

▶   **Consistency**   When completed, a transaction must leave all data in a consistent state. In a relational database, all rules must be applied to the transaction's modifications to maintain all data integrity.

▶ **Isolation** Modifications made by transactions must be isolated from the modifications made by any other concurrent transactions.

▶ **Durability** After a transaction has completed, its effects are permanently in place in the system. The modifications persist even in the event of a system failure.

Auto-Commit Transactions

The default behavior of SQL Server is for INSERT, UPDATE, and DELETE statements to be wrapped in a transaction that automatically commits as soon as the statement is executed (unless an explicit transaction is created, as described a bit later). An application or user does not need to do anything to commit the transaction, and the transaction cannot be rolled back.

Implicit Transactions

The Transact-SQL SET IMPLICIT_TRANSACTIONS statement can be used to slightly modify the behavior just described (and bring it closer to that described by the ANSI definition). To Oracle administrators, this transaction management mode is more familiar than auto-commit mode.

For a connection that has issued SET IMPLICIT_TRANSACTIONS ON, the Database Engine still automatically starts a new transaction as with auto-commit transactions; users continue to do nothing to mark the start of a transaction. However, implicit transactions can be committed or rolled back as required using transaction control statements.

When running in implicit transaction mode, the Database Engine automatically starts a transaction when it first executes DML or DDL statements, including

▶ SELECT

▶ INSERT

▶ UPDATE

▶ DELETE

▶ CREATE

▶ ALTER TABLE

▶ DROP

The transaction remains in effect until the user or application issues a COMMIT or ROLLBACK statement. After the first transaction is committed or rolled back, SQL Server automatically starts a new transaction the next time any of these statements is executed by the connection.

Explicit Transactions

In an explicit transaction, the user or application explicitly defines both the start and end of the transaction, either through an API call or by issuing the Transact-SQL transaction control statements. Explicit transactions are the most common method for scoping transactions in SQL Server. The transaction control statements are as follows:

BEGIN TRANSACTION	Marks the starting point of an explicit transaction for a session.
COMMIT TRANSACTION	Used to end a transaction successfully if no errors were encountered. All data modifications made in the transaction become a permanent part of the database. Resources held by the transaction are freed.
ROLLBACK TRANSACTION	Used to erase a transaction. All data modified by the transaction is returned to the state it was in at the start of the transaction. Resources held by the transaction are freed.

In SQL Server, stored procedures do not have any inherent transactional semantics. If you need a multistatement transaction in a stored procedure, you must use implicit or explicit transactions.

Distributed Transactions

SQL Server is able to participate in distributed transactions—that is, transactions that need to govern data updates in two or more systems. These systems may be two instances of SQL Server or they may include another database server such as Oracle or any other system that supports the X/Open XA specification for distributed transaction processing. A transaction involving two different SQL Server databases in the same SQL Server instance is not considered a distributed transaction.

In SQL Server, each instance involved in a distributed transaction is termed a *resource manager*. The coordinator is a Windows component called the Microsoft Distributed Transaction Coordinator (MSDTC) or another transaction manager that supports the X/Open XA specification. MSDTC is managed outside of SQL Server. A "two-phase commit" is used to complete transactions in a distributed system (either commit or rollback) and ensures data integrity and accuracy within the distributed databases through synchronized locking of all pieces of a transaction.

MSDTC manages in-doubt distributed transactions (where one or more participating systems does not return a success or failure notice) by periodically checking to see whether the remote server has become available before eventually instructing resource managers to commit or roll back.

Errors During Transaction Processing

If an error prevents the successful completion of a transaction, SQL Server automatically rolls back the transaction and frees all resources held by the transaction.

Rollback Behavior

If a statement-level run-time error (such as a constraint violation) occurs in a query, the default behavior is for the Database Engine to roll back only the statement that generated the error. Statements following the error will be successfully committed if no further errors occur.

This behavior can be modified by administrators and developers using the XACT_ABORT option, the syntax of which follows:

```
SET XACT_ABORT {ON | OFF}
```

XACT_ABORT is off by default. Issuing SET XACT_ABORT ON causes any run-time statement errors to automatically roll back all of the current transaction.

SQL Server transactions can be nested. This means that within transactions, you may start further transactions, and within those subsequent transactions, you may start still more transactions. You can name transactions to aid readability, or simply let the Database Engine interpret the relationships between transactions on your behalf. Naming multiple transactions in a series of nested transactions with a transaction name has little effect on the transaction. Only the first (outermost) transaction name is registered with the system. A rollback to any other name generates an error. You need to bear this in mind when looking at rollback behavior in nested transactions.

For example:

```
1.   USE AdventureWorks2008
2.  GO
3.   BEGIN TRANSACTION
4.   UPDATE Production.ProductInventory SET
5.     ProductID =  1,
6.     LocationID = 6,
7.     Shelf = 'A',
8.     Quantity = 100
9.     WHERE (ProductID = 1 AND LocationID = 6 AND Shelf = 'A')
10. BEGIN TRANSACTION
11. INSERT INTO Production.TransactionHistory
12.    (ProductID, ReferenceOrderID, TransactionDate,
13.    TransactionType, Quantity, ActualCost)
```

```
14.          VALUES (1, 42000, '2009-10-31', 'S', 2, 241.23)
15. ROLLBACK TRANSACTION
16. COMMIT TRANSACTION
```

In this case the INSERT statement that begins on line 11 executes within a transaction that is nested within the transaction that contains the UPDATE statement that begins on line 4. Line 15 rolls back this inner transaction and line 16 commits the outer transaction.

In SQL Server, with regard to nested transactions, the ROLLBACK TRANSACTION statement rolls back all inner transactions to the outermost BEGIN TRANSACTION statement. Therefore, when line 15 is executed (or if XACT_ABORT were set to ON and some failure occurred between lines 10 and 15), the transaction started on line 3 would also be rolled back, not just the transaction started on line 10.

In fact, in this example, line 16 would raise the following error:

```
The COMMIT TRANSACTION request has no corresponding BEGIN TRANSACTION.
```

If you want to modify this behavior and perform a partial rollback, you need to use the SAVE TRANSACTION statement. If the relevant lines in the preceding example were to read as follows, then you could roll back to a point after the first (UPDATE) statement:

```
10. SAVE TRANSACTION BeforeInsert
15. ROLLBACK TRANSACTION BeforeInsert
```

It is important to understand this behavior when administering SQL Server databases that make use of transactions.

Transaction Isolation

As previously described, users and applications interact with the database using transactions. Consistency becomes an issue when multiple transactions attempt to read and modify the same data concurrently. These potential conflicts can give rise to a number of undesirable outcomes (or phenomena) that SQL Server administrators need to be aware of, outlined in Table 6-3.

If any explicit transaction is employed, the lost update can never be allowed in SQL Server, but the remaining phenomena can be permitted or disallowed, as required, by choosing an appropriate transaction isolation level as is discussed in the upcoming "Isolation Levels" section.

Phenomenon	Occurs When...
Lost updates	Two or more transactions select the same row and then update the row based on the value originally selected. Each transaction is unaware of the other transactions. The last update overwrites updates made by the other transactions, which results in lost data.
Dirty read	A transaction can read data that is written but not yet committed by another transaction. The transaction that wrote the data may roll back the change so that it was never really in the database and was not meant to be read, or it may be that the data is only part of a larger change and the other related changes haven't been made yet, so the data you read is inconsistent. In either case, the data is in an intermediate state and is considered "dirty."
Nonrepeatable (fuzzy) read	A transaction re-reads data at different intervals in the same transaction and sees changes committed by another transaction. The data changes between reads, so it seems that the reads are inconsistent.
Phantom read	An insert or delete action is performed against a row that belongs to a range of rows being read by a transaction. The transaction's first read of the range of rows shows a row that no longer exists in the second or succeeding read as a result of a deletion by a different transaction. Similarly, the transaction's second or succeeding read shows a row that did not exist in the original read as the result of an insertion by a different transaction.

Table 6-3 *Potential Inconsistencies in Concurrently-Modified Databases*

Types of Concurrency Control

Both Oracle and SQL Server offer optimistic and pessimistic methods of concurrency control:

▶   **Optimistic concurrency control**   Users do not lock data when they read it. When a user updates data, the user checks to see if another user changed the data after it was read. If another user updated the data, an error is raised. Typically, the user receiving the error rolls back the transaction and starts over. This is called "optimistic" because it is mainly used in environments where there is low contention for data, and where the cost of occasionally rolling back a transaction is lower than the cost of locking data when read. This model is typically used where end users are selecting and later updating data.

▶   **Pessimistic concurrency control**   A system of locks prevents users from modifying data in a way that affects other users. After a user performs an action that causes a lock to be applied, other users cannot perform actions that would conflict with the lock until the owner releases it. This is called pessimistic control because it is mainly used in environments where there is high contention for data, where the cost of protecting data with locks is less than the cost of rolling back transactions if concurrency conflicts occur. This model is typically used inside short-lived stored procedures on the database server.

In Oracle's READ COMMITTED isolation level, pessimistic locking is achieved by using the FOR UPDATE clause as part of the SELECT query. SQL Server's Transact-SQL does not have a FOR UPDATE clause (although we'll see that the UPDLOCK table hint can be used to accomplish the same thing), and whether a transaction uses optimistic or pessimistic concurrency is generally a product of the transaction isolation level in place. The table in the following section describes when pessimistic locking is the default for SQL Server when using the available transaction isolation levels.

It should be noted that even when pessimistic locking is in place, in SQL Server, readers will still not block other readers, only attempts to write to the same data. For a read operation to block another read, an explicit lock hint must be used (see the section "Locking" later in this chapter).

Isolation Levels

Avoiding all of the phenomena mentioned in Table 6-3 would require that transactions appear to be run sequentially, with each having sole access to the data whenever there could be a conflict—that is, they are serialized. With this in mind, it can be seen that a trade-off must exist between achieving a highly concurrent transactional environment and maintaining data consistency. The higher the level of consistency desired (the level of isolation), the lower the amount of concurrency possible. The SQL-99 standard defines four levels of isolation, giving administrators and developers control over the database behavior that best suits their requirements. SQL Server adds two more to this list. The following table lists these isolation levels, shows which of the three permissible inconsistency phenomena are possible with each, and identifies the concurrency model used when implemented in SQL Server:

Isolation Level	Dirty Read	Nonrepeatable Read	Phantom Read	Concurrency Model
Read Uncommitted	Yes	Yes	Yes	Pessimistic
Read Committed	No	Yes	Yes	Pessimistic
Read Committed (Snapshot)	No	Yes	Yes	Optimistic
Repeatable Read	No	No	Yes	Pessimistic
Snapshot	No	No	No	Optimistic
Serializable	No	No	No	Pessimistic

SQL Server does not have an equivalent to Oracle's Read-Only isolation level. In SQL Server, Read-Only is a state into which an administrator may place an entire database where no updates are allowed, only reads. The equivalent of Oracle's Read Committed isolation level in SQL Server is Read Committed (Snapshot), and the equivalent of Oracle's Serializable isolation level is Snapshot.

Setting the Isolation Level

In SQL Server the default isolation level can be changed at a transaction level by issuing SET TRANSACTION ISOLATION LEVEL before the BEGIN TRANSACTION statement:

```
SET TRANSACTION ISOLATION LEVEL {READ COMMITTED |
            READ UNCOMMITTED | REPEATABLE READ |
            SERIALIZABLE | SNAPSHOT}
```

Snapshot Isolation

Earlier versions of SQL Server provided the four SQL-99 levels of isolation: Read Uncommitted, Repeatable Read, Read Committed, and Serializable.

SQL Server has since added Snapshot and Read Committed Snapshot isolation, which, in effect, provide alternate implementations of Serializable and Read Committed levels of isolation, respectively, and use optimistic locking rather than pessimistic locking to control concurrent access. These two Snapshot isolation levels are implemented on a row versioning model that is built upon having multiple copies of the data. When reading data, the read happens against a copy, and no locks are held. When writing the data, the write happens against the "real" data, and it is protected with a write lock. In this way, we get the real concurrency benefit that writers do not block readers when using Snapshot isolation.

Unlike the other transaction isolation levels, before Snapshot or Read Committed Snapshot isolation can be used, they must be enabled within the SQL Server database. The syntax for these options is

```
ALTER DATABASE databasename SET ALLOW_SNAPSHOT_ISOLATION {ON|OFF}
ALTER DATABASE databasename SET READ_COMMITTED_SNAPSHOT {ON|OFF}
```

Having enabled Snapshot isolation, users and application developers can now request Snapshot isolation when beginning queries using the SET TRANSACTION ISOLATION LEVEL syntax shown in the preceding section. Enabling Read Committed Snapshot is only possible when the database is in single-user mode and is different in that the effect of this setting is to change the default Read Committed isolation level from the traditional pessimistic behavior to the newer optimistic, row versioning implementation. As this is a persistent database change to the isolation level used when no other level is requested, administrators should be aware of the following note before making this change.

Considerations for Snapshot Isolation

While row versioning can increase concurrency, there are also potential drawbacks that administrators need to be aware of. The row versions that are generated whenever a record is updated under Snapshot isolation are stored in the tempdb system database and there is a cost associated with this even if no read operations are executing. Having implemented row versioning for a database, the size of the tempdb database may increase significantly, and if tempdb runs out of space, then uncommitted transactions will fail. Furthermore, in highly concurrent environments, the act of writing to the tempdb database's transaction log can become a performance bottleneck that will cause administrators to, at least, look to move this database and its log onto a separate disk set.

Locking

SQL Server, in common with Oracle, implements the isolation levels described in the previous section (apart from the Snapshot isolation implementations) by managing concurrent access to shared resources using locks. A SQL Server lock is an in-memory structure detailing the object being shared, those transactions using the object, and the type of object usage required by those transactions.

Lock Granularity

Transactions acquire locks on different-sized objects depending upon their requirements, and this size is known as the lock granularity. Whereas in Oracle the available granularities are row and table, in SQL Server the granularities are (in increasing order of size) row or key (a row within an index), page, extent, partition, table, and database. The default lock granted to a transaction is a row lock.

Lock Types

The main types of lock available in SQL Server are

Lock Type	Purpose
Shared (S)	Used for operations that do not change data.
Exclusive (X)	Used for data-modification operations, such as INSERT, UPDATE, or DELETE. Ensures that multiple updates cannot be made to the same resource at the same time.
Update (U)	Prevents a common form of deadlock called a lock conversion deadlock that occurs when multiple sessions are reading, locking, and then potentially updating resources later. Only one session can acquire an update lock on a resource and whilst this lock still needs to be converted to an exclusive (X) lock before any update can take place, the session holding the update lock can be certain that it will receive the X lock as soon as all other locks are released and that no change can have been made to the data that it read before the update takes place.
Intent	Used to establish a lock hierarchy. The types of intent locks are intent shared (IS), intent exclusive (IX), and shared with intent exclusive (SIX).
Schema modification (Sch-M)	Used for performing DDL operations.
Bulk update (BU)	Used for bulk copying data into a table.

SQL Server uses intent locks to protect placing a shared (S) lock or exclusive (X) lock on a resource lower in the lock hierarchy. Intent locks are named intent locks because they signal intent to place locks at a lower level. In doing this they prevent other transactions from modifying the higher-level resource in a way that would invalidate the lock at the lower level.

For example, a shared intent lock is requested at the table level before S locks are requested on pages or rows within that table. Setting an intent lock at the table level prevents another transaction from acquiring an X lock on the table containing that page or rows for the duration of the intent lock. During this time, the other transaction is still likely to be able to acquire the S locks that it needs.

Lock Compatibility

As shown in the Lock Types section, certain locks can be applied to individual database objects in conjunction with other locks granted to other sessions. The following table lists the possible combinations of locking modes in SQL Server. Where the combination is not possible, the session requesting the lock type on the left will have to wait for the lock at the top to be released.

Mode	IS	S	U	IX	SIX	X
IS	Yes	Yes	Yes	No	No	No
S	Yes	Yes	Yes	Yes	Yes	No
U	Yes	Yes	No	No	No	No
IX	Yes	No	No	Yes	No	No
SIX	Yes	No	No	No	No	No
X	No	No	No	No	No	No

In SQL Server, the SET option LOCK_TIMEOUT can be used to govern the way that a transaction will wait for an earlier transaction to release locks or time out.

Both granularity and type of lock impact when transactions will be required to wait for other locks to be released on shared objects. Locks with too large a granularity will cause more objects to be locked than absolutely required, and locks of an inappropriate type can cause transactions to wait unnecessarily before their own locks are granted. With this in mind, ensuring that the required level of protection is achieved using the smallest, most permissive locks possible is a key aim for developers and administrators.

Lock Hints

The choice of isolation level changes the types of locks implicitly acquired by the database and the duration for which they are held, with READ UNCOMMITED being the least restrictive and SERIALIZABLE the most. In addition, the user can explicitly acquire locks above those automatically requested in accordance with the isolation level. The syntax for acquiring such locks is

```
SELECT ... statement ... WITH ({ {NOLOCK | READUNCOMMITTED}
    | ROWLOCK | PAGLOCK | TABLOCK | TABLOCKX | UPDLOCK
    | XLOCK | {HOLDLOCK | SERIALIZABLE} | REPEATABLEREAD })
```

It is recommended that the default locking choices made by the Database Engine should be overridden by use of lock hints in SQL Server only after significant testing, to avoid unforeseen concurrency issues. Table 6-4 provides the types of locking hints that can be used with SQL Server.

Oracle DBA Q&A

Q: If I can't use SELECT...FOR UPDATE, how can I stop other session seeing rows that users or applications have already read?

A: This is not immediately obvious in SQL Server and requires the use of locking hints. The remainder of this section discusses such a scenario.

To better understand how locking hints might be used, consider the following query (Query 1):

```
1. SET TRANSACTION ISOLATION LEVEL REPEATABLE READ
2. BEGIN TRANSACTION
3. SELECT Name FROM TestTable WHERE Id = 1
4. UPDATE TestTable SET Name = 'James' WHERE Id = 1
5. COMMIT
```

Table 6-5 shows that the Repeatable Read isolation level implies pessimistic concurrency control, so you may think that the following query (Query 2) would

Hint	Description
HOLDLOCK	Hold a shared lock until completion of the transaction instead of releasing the lock as soon as the required table, row, or data page is no longer required. HOLDLOCK is equivalent to SERIALIZABLE.
NOLOCK	Do not issue shared locks and do not honor exclusive locks. When this option is in effect, it is possible to read an uncommitted transaction or a set of pages that is rolled back in the middle of a read. Dirty reads are possible. Only applies to the SELECT statement.
PAGLOCK	Use page locks where a single table lock would usually be taken.
READCOMMITTED	Perform a scan with the same locking semantics as a transaction running at the READ COMMITTED isolation level. By default, SQL Server operates at this isolation level but any other isolation level will be overridden for this statement.
READPAST	Skip locked rows. This option causes a transaction to skip rows locked by other transactions that would ordinarily appear in the result set, rather than block the transaction waiting for the other transactions to release their locks on these rows. The READPAST lock hint applies only to transactions operating at READ COMMITTED isolation and will read only past row-level locks. Applies only to the SELECT statement.
READUNCOMMITTED	Equivalent to NOLOCK.
REPEATABLEREAD	Perform a scan with the same locking semantics as a transaction running at the REPEATABLE READ isolation level.
ROWLOCK	Use row-level locks instead of the coarser-grained page- and table-level locks.
SERIALIZABLE	Perform a scan with the same locking semantics as a transaction running at the SERIALIZABLE isolation level. Equivalent to HOLDLOCK.
TABLOCK	Use a table lock instead of the finer-grained row- or page-level locks. SQL Server holds this lock until the end of the statement. However, if you also specify HOLDLOCK, the lock is held until the end of the transaction.
TABLOCKX	Use an exclusive lock on a table. This lock prevents others from reading or updating the table and is held until the end of the statement or transaction.
UPDLOCK	Use update locks instead of shared locks while reading a table, and hold locks until the end of the statement or transaction. UPDLOCK has the advantage of allowing you to read data (without blocking other readers) and update it later with the assurance that the data has not changed since you last read it.
XLOCK	Use an exclusive lock that will be held until the end of the transaction on all data processed by the statement. This lock can be specified with either PAGLOCK or TABLOCK, in which case the exclusive lock applies to the appropriate level of granularity.

Table 6-4   *SQL Server's Locking Hints*

be blocked by the SELECT on line 3 if it were issued before the UPDATE on line 4:

```
SET TRANSACTION ISOLATION LEVEL REPEATABLE READ
BEGIN TRANSACTION
SELECT Name FROM TestTable WHERE Id = 1
COMMIT
```

This is not, in fact, the case. Query 2 is only blocked by the UPDATE on line 4, so if Query 1 performed some long-running task between lines 3 and 4, then Query 2 would still be able to read the row in question during that period. This may be undesirable if your intention is for Query 1 to select and later update the row and for other users to not be able to see old values for the row once this operation has started (in other words, classic SELECT ... FOR UPDATE behavior).

The reason that Query 2 is not blocked after Query 1 executes line 3 is that, at this point, even running under REPEATABLE READ, the SELECT only places a shared lock on the row.

If you want a SELECT to acquire an exclusive lock on an object (such as a row or table), you need to use an explicit hint regardless of what the current transaction isolation level is. So, you might change line 3 of Query 1 to read

```
3.   SELECT Name FROM TestTable WITH (XLOCK) WHERE Id = 1
```

This would have the effect of causing Query 2 to wait for this lock to be released (for the Query 1 transaction to complete) before it could read the required row. However, you now need to make sure that you only have exclusive locks on those objects that you hope to have locked. Imagine Query 2 was amended to read

```
SET TRANSACTION ISOLATION LEVEL REPEATABLE READ
BEGIN TRANSACTION
SELECT Name FROM TestTable WHERE Id = 2
GO
SELECT Name FROM TestTable WHERE Id = 1
GO
COMMIT
```

You would hope that the first SELECT would return and that only the second SELECT would cause the query to wait on the completion of Query 1. In practice, with more complex queries, poor query design or missing indexes can cause more rows or keys to be locked than you expect, and in high-concurrency environments, locks will be escalated (see the next section, "Lock Escalation"). This would likely cause the revised Query 2 to find the row with Id of 2 to be locked as well and cause your application not to perform as expected. See the section "Monitoring Locking" for a discussion on how to track exactly which locks have been granted to objects and transactions and which locks are waiting to be released.

In a similar vein, a common use of explicit lock hints in SQL Server is to allow certain operations to implement pessimistic concurrency when running under SNAPSHOT or READ COMMITTED SNAPSHOT isolation. The following query will not cause any locks to be acquired (as SNAPSHOT causes the row to be versioned instead):

```
SET TRANSACTION ISOLATION LEVEL SNAPSHOT
BEGIN TRANSACTION
SELECT Name FROM TestTable WHERE Id = 1
COMMIT
```

However, you can force a shared lock to be granted if you so desire by changing the query to read

```
SET TRANSACTION ISOLATION LEVEL SNAPSHOT
BEGIN TRANSACTION
SELECT Name FROM TestTable WITH (REPEATABLEREAD) WHERE Id = 1
COMMIT
```

This causes the query to request locks as if the transaction were running under REPEATABLE READ isolation, even though SNAPSHOT is in place.

Lock Escalation

A key point for SQL Server administrators to appreciate is that, in attempting to best manage the memory overhead associated with the locks held for a given transaction, SQL Server can "escalate" a set of small granularity locks into a single larger lock. SQL Server automatically attempts to escalate row locks and page locks into partition locks or table locks when a transaction exceeds a set "escalation threshold." Locks only escalate from row or page to partition or table in SQL Server; it does not attempt to escalate row locks to page locks, for example.

Default lock escalation behavior can be altered using the LOCK_ESCALATION option of the ALTER TABLE statement:

```
SET ( LOCK_ESCALATION = { AUTO | TABLE | DISABLE } )
```

The available options are

AUTO	Allows the Database Engine to select the lock escalation granularity that is appropriate for the table schema. If the table is partitioned, lock escalation will be allowed to partition. After the lock is escalated to the partition level, the lock will not be escalated later to TABLE granularity. If the table is not partitioned, the lock escalation will be done to the TABLE granularity.
TABLE	Lock escalation will be done at table-level granularity regardless of whether the table is partitioned or not partitioned. This behavior is the same as in SQL Server 2005. TABLE is the default value.
DISABLE	Prevents lock escalation in most cases. Table-level locks are not completely disallowed. For example, when you are scanning a table that has no clustered index under the serializable isolation level, the Database Engine must take a table lock to protect data integrity.

For a detailed discussion of the lock escalation thresholds used by a SQL Server database, see the Books Online topic "Lock Escalation (Database Engine)."

Deadlocks

Deadlocking is a situation where two or more users are waiting on locks held by each other—no session can complete without another session completing first. SQL Server automatically detects deadlocks, and acts immediately to resolve the problem by rolling back one of the transactions (be it auto-commit, implicit, or explicit). SQL Server determines the victim transaction based on the cost associated with rolling back the transaction. So a transaction that has updated a small number of rows will likely be chosen over one that has updated a much larger number of rows.

If a deadlock situation is created in SQL Server Management Studio, an error is generated, as shown in Figure 6-7.

The full error message is

```
Msg 1205, Level 13, State 51, Line 11
Transaction (Process ID 66) was deadlocked on lock resources
 with another process and has been chosen as the deadlock victim.
 Rerun the transaction.
```

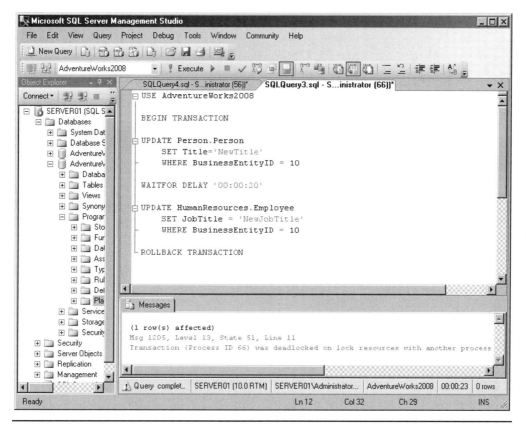

Figure 6-7   *Deadlock in SQL Server Management Studio*

SQL Server Profiler can be used to trace deadlocks and provide information to administrators and developers as to their exact circumstances. An example of this is shown in Figure 6-8.

The available SQL Server Profiler events for reporting deadlocks are

Lock: Deadlock	Indicates that two concurrent transactions have deadlocked each other by trying to obtain incompatible locks on resources that the other transaction owns.
Lock: Deadlock Chain	Produced for each of the events leading up to the deadlock.
Deadlock Graph	Occurs simultaneously with the Lock: Deadlock event class. The deadlock graph event class provides an XML description of the deadlock.

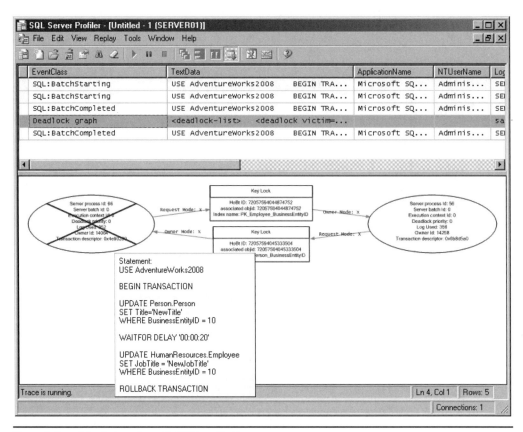

Figure 6-8 *A deadlock graph event in SQL Server Profiler*

The last of these events is potentially the most interesting, as it creates an XML representation of the deadlock event that can be interpreted by SQL Server Profiler to give the graphical representation shown in Figure 6-8, complete with full details as to the processes involved, the locked objects, and the statements issued. This event can be saved as an XML file and then opened in Management Studio, allowing this deadlock information to be effectively communicated, say, between an administrator and an application developer.

Monitoring Locking

An inefficient use of locks is a common cause of poor database application performance. Therefore, database administrators often need to know exactly how locks are being used within a system. There are several options available to SQL Server administrators who need to get this information.

The DMV sys.dm_tran_locks can be queried to return information about currently active lock manager resources. Each row in the view represents a currently active request to the lock manager for a lock that has been granted or is waiting to be granted.

Imagine stepping through the following query to the point just after the SELECT (or place a WAITFOR DELAY statement into the code immediately after the UPDATE to cause execution to pause):

```
SET TRANSACTION ISOLATION LEVEL REPEATABLE READ
BEGIN TRANSACTION
SELECT Name FROM TestTable WITH (XLOCK) WHERE Id = 1
UPDATE TestTable SET Name = 'James' WHERE Id = 1
COMMIT
```

You can then query sys.dm_tran_locks to view the granted locks:

```
SELECT resource_type, request_mode, request_status,
 request_session_id, request_owner_type
FROM sys.dm_tran_locks
```

This gives the results shown in Figure 6-9.

Interestingly, this result set shows that the SELECT has actually caused a lock against each of the rows in the table to be granted to the transaction (there are only three rows, so this is only a very simplistic example), as opposed to only the row with an Id of 1—something that might already be giving you clues to the cause of some performance issue. The result set shown in Figure 6-9 shows only a subset of the columns of the view; see Books Online for a full description of the structure of the view. The columns of particular interest to administrators are listed and described in Table 6-5.

	resource_type	request_mode	request_status	request_session_id	request_owner_type
1	DATABASE	S	GRANT	56	SHARED_TRANSACTION_WORKSPACE
2	PAGE	IX	GRANT	56	TRANSACTION
3	RID	X	GRANT	56	TRANSACTION
4	OBJECT	IX	GRANT	56	TRANSACTION
5	RID	X	GRANT	56	TRANSACTION
6	RID	X	GRANT	56	TRANSACTION

Figure 6-9 *Results of querying sys.dm_tran_locks*

Column Name	Description
resource_type	Represents the resource type. The value can be one of the following: DATABASE, FILE, OBJECT, PAGE, KEY, EXTENT, RID, APPLICATION, METADATA, HOBT, or ALLOCATION_UNIT.
resource_subtype	Represents a subtype of resource_type. Not all resource types have subtypes.
resource_database_id	ID of the database to which the resource belongs.
resource_description	Description of the resource that contains only information that is not available from other resource columns.
resource_associated_entity_id	ID of the entity in a database with which a resource is associated. Depending upon the type of resource, this ID can be used to query the system catalog for details of the entity.
request_mode	Mode of the request. For granted requests, this is the granted mode; for waiting requests, this is the mode being requested.
request_status	Current status of this request. Possible values are GRANTED, CONVERT, or WAIT. A granted request status indicates that a lock has been granted on a resource to the requestor. A waiting request indicates that the request has not yet been granted. A convert request status indicates that the requestor has already been granted a request for the resource and is currently waiting for an upgrade to the initial request to be granted.
request_session_id	Session ID that currently owns this request. The owning session ID can change for distributed and bound transactions. A value of -2 indicates that the request belongs to an orphaned distributed transaction. A value of -3 indicates that the request belongs to a deferred recovery transaction, such as a transaction for which a rollback has been deferred at recovery because the rollback could not be completed successfully.
request_owner_type	Entity type that owns the request. Lock manager requests can be owned by a variety of entities. Possible values are TRANSACTION = The request is owned by a transaction. CURSOR = The request is owned by a cursor. SESSION = The request is owned by a user session. SHARED_TRANSACTION_WORKSPACE = The request is owned by the shared part of the transaction workspace. EXCLUSIVE_TRANSACTION_WORKSPACE = The request is owned by the exclusive part of the transaction workspace.

Table 6-5   *Selected Columns from the DMV sys.dm_tran_locks*

Because the data in this view corresponds to live lock manager state, the data can change at any time and rows are added and removed as locks are acquired and released. The view has no historical information.

Table 6-6 lists the resources that are represented in the resource_associated_entity_id column.

Resource Type	Description
ALLOCATION_UNIT	Represents a set of related pages, such as an index partition.
APPLICATION	Represents an application-specified resource.
DATABASE	Represents a database.
EXTENT	Represents a data file extent.
FILE	Represents a database file. This file can be either a data or a log file.
HOBT	Represents a heap or a B-tree. These are the basic access path structures.
KEY	Represents a row in an index.
METADATA	Represents metadata information.
OBJECT	Represents a database object. This object can be a data table, view, stored procedure, extended stored procedure, or any object that has an object ID.
PAGE	Represents a single page in a data file.
RID	Represents a physical row in a heap.

Table 6-6 *Resources That Can be Locked in SQL Server*

Viewing Session Activity with Activity Monitor

You can use Activity Monitor in SQL Server Management Studio to perform ad hoc monitoring of an instance of SQL Server (see Figure 6-10). This enables you to determine, at a glance, the volume and general types of activity on the system; for example, you can view the following:

▶ Currently blocked and blocking transactions

▶ Currently connected users on an instance of SQL Server, and the last statement executed

▶ Locks that are in effect

From the Processes pane, you can view the sessions (SQL Server processes, denoted by a server process ID, or SPID) currently associated with a SQL Server instance, including both user and background processes and processes in states such as Running and Suspended.

Note that the User Processes column is filtered by default to show only user processes and not background processes. Remove this filter to see all processes.

The Activity Monitor columns that are useful in monitoring lock usage are listed and described in Table 6-7.

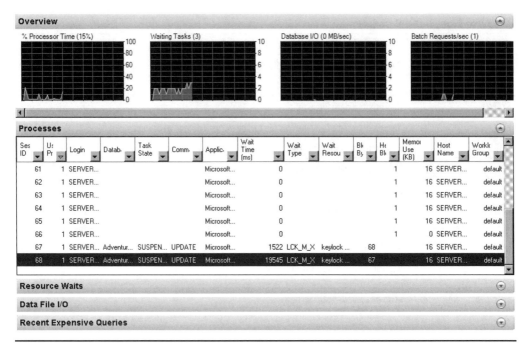

Figure 6-10   *SQL Server Activity Monitor*

Column Name	Description
Session ID	A unique integer (int) that is assigned to each user connection when the connection is made.
Login	The SQL Server login name under which the session is currently executing.
Database	The name of the database that is included in the connection properties of processes that are currently running.
Task State	The state of the task. For tasks in a runnable or sleeping state, the task state is blank. Otherwise, this can be one of the following values: ▶ Background ▶ Running ▶ Suspended
Command	The kind of command that is being processed under the task.
Application	The name of the application program that created the connection.
Wait Time (ms)	The length of time, in milliseconds, that this task has been waiting for a resource. When the task is not waiting, the wait time is 0.
Wait Type	The name of the last or current wait type.
Wait Resource	The name of the resource that is needed.
Blocked By	If there are blocking sessions, the ID of the session that is blocking the task.

Table 6-7   *Session Attributes Relating to Locks Available in the Activity Monitor*

From Activity Monitor, an administrator can terminate a running process (for example, a very long-running process that can be seen to be locking resources upon which other processes are waiting) by right-clicking the process in the Processes pane and selecting Kill Process. This corresponds with issuing the KILL statement.

Performance Counters

The Perfmon counters listed and described in Table 6-8 can be used to trace lock usage in SQL Server.

Built-in Reports

Among the built-in SQL Server Management Studio reports, the following can help give a detailed view as to lock and transaction activity within a SQL Server instance:

- ▶ Top Sessions
- ▶ All Transactions
- ▶ All Blocking Transactions (shown in Figure 6-11)

Counter	Description
SQL Server Locks: Average Wait Time (ms)	The average amount of wait time (milliseconds) for each lock request that resulted in a wait.
SQL Server Locks: Lock Requests/sec	Number of new locks and lock conversions requested from the lock manager.
SQL Server Locks: Lock Timeouts (timeout > 0)/sec	Number of lock requests that timed out. This does not include requests for NOWAIT locks.
SQL Server Locks: Lock Timeouts/sec	Number of lock requests that timed out. This includes requests for NOWAIT locks.
SQL Server Locks: Lock Wait Time (ms)	Total wait time (milliseconds) for locks in the last second.
SQL Server Locks: Lock Waits/sec	Number of lock requests that could not be satisfied immediately and required the caller to wait before being granted the lock.
SQL Server Locks: Number of Deadlocks/sec	Number of lock requests that resulted in a deadlock.
SQL Server Access Methods: Table Lock Escalations/sec	Number of times row or page locks are escalated to table locks.

Table 6-8 *Selected Windows Performance Monitor Counters Useful in Analyzing Locking*

All Blocking Transactions
[AdventureWorks2008]
on SERVER01 at 10/12/2009 8:42:11 PM

This report identifies transactions within the Database that are blocking other transactions and provides details about them.

All Blocking Transactions

The description of transactions which are blocking other transactions.

Transaction ID	# Directly Blocked Transactions	# Indirectly Blocked Transactions	Transaction Name	State	Transaction Type
⊞ 7735 *	1	0	user_transaction	Active	Full Transaction

* The transactions span multiple databases on the same instance.

+ The transactions are distributed transactions.

Figure 6-11 *The All Blocking Transactions report*

The "raw" information that these reports are built upon can also be returned by executing the sp_who system procedure, which returns columns very similar to those presented by the Activity Monitor. The full details for sp_who can be found in Books Online; however, there is an additional, undocumented procedure called sp_who2 that adds in performance information such as CPU time to the sp_who columns.

Automated Alerts

Counters such as Deadlocks/sec are very commonly used to build automated SQL Server Alerts that notify an administrator (usually by e-mail or pager) of some behavior within a database that requires his or her attention. This subject is covered in detail in Chapter 10.

Chapter 7

Backup and Recovery

In This Chapter

- ► **Recovery Models**
- ► **Backup**
- ► **Restore and Recovery**
- ► **Further Reading**

As a DBA, if you do not back up your databases and they experience failure or corruption, you will probably be looking for a new job! It really is fundamental to everything you do.

In Oracle, RMAN is probably the most popular option for backup and recovery of an Oracle system. In SQL Server, backup and recovery is all done within the SQL Server Database Engine using T-SQL and the BACKUP and RESTORE statements; there is no separate tool such as RMAN.

There are many third-party backup and recovery tools and utilities available in the market for SQL Server, each providing its own value-add functionality over the base SQL Server functionality. In the main, most of the tools ultimately make calls to the SQL Server BACKUP and RESTORE commands and the Virtual Device interfaces (VDI), which is why it is important to understand the basics of these commands. The added functionality of these tools tends to focus on centralized administration, scheduling, tape management, and other utilities such as compression and encryption.

It is worth noting that many large or mission-critical databases tend to use some form of storage area network (SAN) to host the SQL Server databases. When this is the case, you will find that many of the main vendors have their own SAN backup utilities that can interoperate with SQL Server through the SQL Server backup APIs. It is worth checking with your SAN vendor.

In this chapter we will cover recovery models, backup, and recovery.

Recovery Models

Before looking at how to back up a database, it is important to understand the different recovery models available in SQL Server. The choice of recovery model can be likened to choosing to use either ARCHIVELOG mode or NOARCHIVELOG mode in Oracle. The choice of recovery model determines how and to what point you can recover a database following media failure or accidental damage. The recovery model will also influence your backup regime and the amount of DBA effort required to maintain the database. It is important to note, as in Oracle, the recovery model does not affect crash recovery.

There are three recovery models in SQL Server:

- FULL
- BULK_LOGGED
- SIMPLE

FULL

The FULL recovery model is akin to ARCHIVELOG mode in Oracle in that it supports granular recovery of the database to a particular point in time. All details of every transaction are fully logged into the database transaction log, enabling complete recovery and redo of any transaction.

When running in ARCHIVELOG mode in Oracle, an archiver process copies the redo log files to an archive location before they can be reused and overwritten. In SQL Server, the backup of the log is a process that the DBA needs to manage. In the FULL recovery model, the database transaction log is not truncated until it has been backed up using a log backup command. Therefore, if the transaction log is never backed up, it will continue to grow as per the file growth settings for the file, which will inevitably stop once the disk it resides on runs out of space.

Even if you do not require granular recovery capabilities for your database, there are some features within SQL Server that require the database to run in the FULL recovery model such as transaction log shipping and database mirroring (covered in Chapter 9). However, unlike in Oracle, FULL recovery is not required to take online database backups. Also, because of SQL Server's multi-database architecture, you can mix and match the recovery models of different databases in an instance.

BULK_LOGGED

The BULK_LOGGED recovery model is intended to be used alongside the FULL recovery model. Large data-loading processes such as BULK INSERT and SELECT INTO or operations such as creating or rebuilding indexes can cause the transaction log to grow significantly in the FULL recovery model. The BULK_LOGGED recovery model is intended for temporary use during these large loading or index maintenance operations. BULK_LOGGED uses a concept called minimal logging. Minimal logging records only the database page allocations for the operation, not the data that makes up the pages, thereby notably reducing the size of the transaction log and increasing the speed of the operation.

Although BULK_LOGGED provides benefits such as reducing the amount of required log space, it does affect the recoverability of the database because only page allocations are recorded. Therefore, your recovery point is your last transaction log backup. Once a log backup is taken following a minimally logged operation, the log backup contains all the altered pages from the minimally logged operation; therefore, even though the transaction log file may be small, the backup may be considerably larger.

For a full list of minimally logged operations, please refer to SQL Server Books Online.

ON THE JOB

Just because you are doing an operation that can be minimally logged does not mean that you must switch to the BULK_LOGGED recovery model. If the additional temporary log growth (until the log is backed up) does not cause you a problem and the total time to execute is acceptable, then it is easier to leave the database in the FULL recovery model. Switching to the BULK_LOGGED recovery model does not always produce a performance improvement for a bulk load operation. At the end of a minimally logged transaction, SQL Server forces a flush of the new data pages to disk to ensure they are secured in the data files, which in turn causes a flood of I/O operations. In comparison, running in FULL recovery does not force a data page flush at the end of the operation as full details of the transaction are already secured in the transaction log and, in the event of a crash, can be recovered from the log.

SIMPLE

The SIMPLE recovery model can be likened to NOARCHIVELOG mode in Oracle. In the SIMPLE recovery model the database is protected to the point of the last full (or differential) database backup; transaction logs are treated in the same way as online redo logs in that they are not backed up or archived.

Even though it is not possible to back up the transaction log in the SIMPLE model, that does not mean you do not need to manage or monitor the transaction log. Whenever a database checkpoint is issued, the transaction log is truncated and the reclaimed log space is then ready for reuse. Because the transaction log will only truncate as far back as the oldest open transaction, a long-running transaction may prevent the log from truncating and cause the log to grow (as per your file growth settings). In addition, once a log file has grown, even if the space is internally reclaimed, the physical file will remain the same size and therefore will need to be manually shrunk by the DBA.

The SIMPLE recovery model also supports minimal logging for bulk-logged operations as per the BULK_LOGGED model.

ON THE JOB

For databases that do not require granular recovery to a point in time or where the work can be redone or replayed, then the SIMPLE recovery model is very useful. For example, a data warehouse may benefit from SIMPLE recovery where the database is backed up on a nightly basis and any data recovery can be replayed by re-importing any data files.

Oracle DBA Q&A

Q: When moving between ARCHIVELOG mode and NOARCHIVELOG mode in Oracle, you need to close the database to change modes. Do you need to do something similar in SQL Server?

A: No, you can change between recovery models while the database is up and running. This can be a good and bad thing. It is good because the system remains online during the operation and users are not affected. It is bad because changing between models breaks backup chains. For example, if a DBA accidentally switches from FULL to SIMPLE and then, upon realizing her mistake, switches back to FULL, she will have caused the log to truncate by switching to SIMPLE, will have broken your log file backup chain, and will need to take new full backup.

Backup

SQL Server contains all the tools you require to back up a database and supports all of the backup methods you would expect, such as online, offline, logical, and physical. This section covers all these elements.

Logical Backups

Logical backups of schema and data in Oracle are normally achieved through the use of Data Pump Export for backup and Data Pump Import for restoring. In SQL Server, the same methods can be applied using utilities such as Bulk Copy Program (BCP), SQL Server Integration Services (SSIS), and the Script Generation Wizards. These are the same tools that are used for general import and export of data between systems and are therefore covered in detail in Chapter 11.

Physical Backups

It is possible to take offline and online (also referred to as cold and hot backups respectively) backups within SQL Server, although all backup types within SQL Server can be performed online regardless of the recovery model being used.

SQL Server database backups are always portable across platforms, and a backup from an older version of SQL Server can be restored on a newer SQL instance. Because of this and because the practice in SQL Server is for applications to have their own databases, SQL Server database backups are also very commonly used to move data from one system to another.

Offline Backups

As with Oracle, an offline backup can be performed by stopping the instance service and taking operating system–level copies of the data and transaction log files. Another approach available within SQL Server, one that does not require the SQL instance to be stopped, is to perform a database detach operation. A database detach operation disconnects the database in question from the instance and closes any file locks it has on the database, leaving the database in a consistent state allowing you to copy the data and log files. Detaching a database affects only the database you are interested in and leaves all others online and operational. It is not possible to use the detach method on system databases. The database detach/attach operation is covered in Chapter 11.

Offline backups are almost never used in SQL Server. If a backup utility wants to take a volume-level backup of SQL Server, such as using a snapshot utility on a SAN, it will typically integrate with the Microsoft Windows Volume Shadow Copy Service, which enables the backup utility to request that SQL Server place all of the files in a consistent state for backup, while remaining online.

Online Backups

Online backups are by far the most common type of backup on the SQL Server platform. There are several types of backup in SQL Server, all of which are online operations regardless of the recovery model:

- ▶ Full
- ▶ Differential
- ▶ Full and differential—partial backup
- ▶ Transaction log (not available in the SIMPLE recovery model)
- ▶ File and filegroup (Note: SIMPLE recovery model only supports read-only files and filegroups)

Full Backup   Full database backups, as the name suggests, back up all the objects within the database and provide a complete copy of the database.

Since a full backup is an online operation and data pages may change during the backup operation, the backup file contains both the data and a portion of the transaction log. The transaction log is used during the restore of the backup to bring the backup to a consistent point in time. A full backup is consistent as of the end of the backup. Therefore, if you start a backup at 2:00 A.M. and it finishes at 3:30 A.M., the backup will restore to a consistent view of the database as it was at 3:30 A.M.

Differential Backup   Differential backups are used in conjunction with full backups. Differential backups are cumulative and copy all changes to the database since the last full backup. Differential backups should not be confused with incremental backups as incremental backups are not available in SQL Server. A differential backup grows over time, whereas an incremental backup only contains changes since the last incremental (or full) backup. If comparing to Oracle, a differential backup is the same concept as a cumulative incremental backup in Oracle.

The advantage of differential backups is that they only back up data that has changed since the last full backup regardless of the number of times the data has changed. This is different from transaction log backups, which would capture every individual update to the same piece of data.

Differential backups are initially smaller and faster than full backups, but as time goes by and data is added or changed, the differential backup becomes larger and will eventually lose its speed and size advantage. At that point, a new full backup should be taken to create a new differential base, and then the process would start again.

As is the case with full backups, differential backups also contain a portion of the transaction log for recovery meaning that they restore to the time of when the backup completed.

Full and Differential—Partial Backup   In databases that contain read-only filegroups (the SQL Server equivalent of read-only tablespaces), such as large data warehouses containing historical data, the data in the read-only filegroups is static and therefore does not need backing up every time a database backup is taken. Partial and differential partial backups allow for the backup of the read-write filegroups while leaving the read-only filegroups out of the backup.

A partial backup covers all the data in the PRIMARY filegroup and the data in all read-write filegroups. Read-only filegroups are excluded unless explicitly specified. A differential partial backup covers the data that has changed since the last partial backup on the same set of filegroups.

If you perform a partial backup on a read-only database, then just the PRIMARY filegroup is backed up. Partial backups are available in all recovery models.

Transaction Log Backup   As discussed in previous chapters, the transaction log is the SQL Server undo/redo log mechanism. The transaction log is a sequential record of all changes to the database (each change is recorded with a log sequence number [LSN], which is comparable to the System Change Number [SCN] in Oracle) and is used to restore a database to any point in time.

A transaction log backup captures all changes since the last transaction log backup and, once complete, truncates the log, allowing reuse of the truncated space. As with archive log backups, transaction log backups are sequential and create what is known as a log chain. If you lose any part of the chain, you can only restore your log backup as far as the backup prior to the missing link in the chain.

Transaction log backups are performed independently of full or differential backups, although log backups are used in conjunction with full and differential backups for "point in time" recovery. For example, for a complete database restore, you would restore the last full backup (and most recent differential if applicable) and then restore all transaction log files in sequence to the point at which you wish to recover.

Transaction log backups are only applicable when operating in the FULL or BULK_ LOGGED recovery model. Transaction log backups take all information in the log up until the point of when the BACKUP LOG statement was issued. This is different from full and differential backups, which are consistent as of the end of the backup process. A final point to note is that it is also possible to back up a transaction log even if the main database has suffered serious media failure and has gone offline. This is called a tail-log backup and allows you to recover a log file up until the point of system failure (provided the log is still accessible) to ensure no work is lost.

Transaction log backups are also used in conjunction with high availability and disaster recovery techniques such as log shipping, where a copy of the most recent log backup is copied to another server and restored to a standby or reporting database (log shipping is covered in further detail in Chapter 9).

File and Filegroup Backup   For larger and more complex databases, SQL Server supports the backup of individual files or filegroups. For example, if you have split a large data warehouse database into multiple filegroups and files, you may rotate which filegroup you back up on a nightly basis.

Implementing individual file and filegroup backup into your backup regime does add complexity to your backup management and therefore should only be used when the other backup approaches do not provide the required flexibility. It is included here for completeness, but we will not go into detail on creating backup plans using this method.

NOTE

You do not need to have done an individual file or filegroup backup to perform an individual file or filegroup restore. These restores can come from a full database backup and will be covered later in the "Restore" section of the chapter.

Performing Backups

As previously mentioned, online backups are the most common method in SQL Server, and therefore we will concentrate on this approach.

Backing up a SQL Server database is done through the T-SQL language and the BACKUP statement. There are several ways to execute a backup, including directly from a script, using the SQL Server Management Studio (SSMS) interface, and via SQL Server Maintenance Plans. Ultimately they all make a call to the BACKUP statement.

The BACKUP statement is quite comprehensive, with several command arguments and options for selection of backup type, location, resilience, media, and monitoring options, to name a few. The full statement syntax is covered in detail in SQL Server Books Online, so instead of repeating all the information here, we will use the rest of this section to demonstrate the use of the BACKUP statement through examples.

The BACKUP statement supports both database and log backups.

Database Backups

Broken down into its most simple form, the syntax for backing up a database is as follows:

```
BACKUP DATABASE database_name
TO backup_location
WITH options
```

The database name and the backup location are the only mandatory parts of the statement. The "WITH options" all have default values, which will be covered shortly. First let's walk through some examples for performing full, differential, and partial backups.

It is possible to make a complete full database backup using just the database name and the filename to which you want to back up; there is no need to specify the backup type, as a full backup is the default action for the statement. The following statement will create a full database backup and will place the backup called AdventureWorks_Full.bak in the default SQL Server backup folder which on a default instance installation would be: \MSSQL10_50.MSSQLSERVER\MSSQL\Backup

NOTE

It is possible to use any file extension for the backup file, but the standard is .bak for database files and .trn for transaction logs. It is a good idea to use these because the SSMS tool uses these as file filters for dialog boxes.

```
BACKUP DATABASE AdventureWorks
TO DISK = 'AdventureWorks_Full.bak'
```

Differential backups are created by using a WITH option. Appending WITH DIFFERENTIAL to the BACKUP statement creates a differential backup that contains all the changes to the data since the last full backup:

```
BACKUP DATABASE AdventureWorks
TO DISK = 'AdventureWorks_Diff.bak'
WITH DIFFERENTIAL
```

Partial backups, which by default include the PRIMARY filegroup and any read-write filegroups, are created by adding the READ_WRITE_FILEGROUPS argument following the database name:

```
BACKUP DATABASE AdventureWorks READ_WRITE_FILEGROUPS
TO DISK = 'AdventureWorks_Partial.bak'
```

As part of a partial backup, you can also optionally specify any read-only filegroups to include in the backup. For example, to include the read-only filegroup FG_2009_ARCHIVE, the statement would look like this:

```
BACKUP DATABASE AdventureWorks READ_WRITE_FILEGROUPS,
FILEGROUP='FG_2009_ARCHIVE'
TO DISK = 'AdventureWorks_Partial.bak'
```

A partial differential backup is created by simply appending WITH DIFFERENTIAL to the statement:

```
BACKUP DATABASE AdventureWorks READ_WRITE_FILEGROUPS
TO DISK = 'AdventureWorks_Partial_Diff.bak'
WITH DIFFERENTIAL
```

ON THE JOB

Partial backups can only be created using your own custom T-SQL scripts, as the SSMS interface and the SQL Server Maintenance Plans features do not give you the option to create partial backups.

Finally, the last type of database backup is the backup of individual files and/or filegroups. As previously mentioned, individual file and filegroup backups can complicate your backup and restore routine and tend to only be used to manage large databases. To perform a full backup of an individual file or filegroup, you specify each one of interest using the FILE and FILEGROUP parameters following the database name. For example:

```
BACKUP DATABASE AdventureWorks
FILEGROUP = 'FG_2009_Archive',
FILEGROUP = 'FG_2008_Archive'
TO DISK = 'AdventureWorks_FG2008_FG2009.bak'
```

When you specify a filegroup, all of the files within the filegroup are backed up. If you are backing up an individual file, you must use the logical filename, not its physical one. Therefore, a file that is part of the FG_2009_Archive filegroup with the logical name of FG_2009_Archive_File1 will be backed up using the following:

```
BACKUP DATABASE AdventureWorks
FILE = 'FG_2009_Archive_File1'
TO DISK = 'AdventureWorks_FG2009_File1.bak'
```

FILE and FILEGROUP backups also support the WITH DIFFERENTIAL option. Also, remember that when running in the SIMPLE recovery model, file and filegroup backups are restricted to secondary read-only files and filegroups only.

Transaction Log Backups

Transaction log backups only apply when using the FULL and BULK_LOGGED recovery models. Backing up the transaction log follows the same basic syntax as the database backup statement with just one difference—the replacement of the argument of DATABASE with LOG:

```
BACKUP LOG database_name
TO backup_location
WITH options
```

Therefore, a simple example of a log backup for AdventureWorks would be

```
BACKUP LOG AdventureWorks
TO DISK = 'AdventureWorks.trn'
```

As with the BACKUP DATABASE statement, there is a series of common WITH options (covered shortly) for specifying options such as media information and whether to use compression or not. BACKUP LOG also has three WITH options, which only apply to LOG backups: NORECOVERY, NO_TRUNCATE, and STANDBY. These options are used in conjunction with a type of backup known as a tail-log backup. A tail-log backup is taken prior to performing a restore operation on your database to capture any transactions that have not yet been backed up by your normal transaction log backup process.

When performing a restore operation on a database that is still online, a tail-log backup is taken using the NORECOVERY option. This option will back up the transaction log and place the database in a RESTORING state, ready for you to start your restore process.

NO_TRUNCATE, as the name suggests, will stop the transaction log from being truncated following the backup. It is also used in the scenario where the database has suffered damage such that it will not start or has missing data files. The NO_TRUNCATE option allows you to back up the tail of the log even without the database being online:

```
BACKUP LOG AdventureWorks
TO DISK = 'AdventureWorks_TailLog.trn'
WITH NO_TRUNCATE
```

ON THE JOB

If you are not sure when to use NORECOVERY or NO_TRUNCATE, think of it like this: NORECOVERY is used when you want to perform a tail-log backup on a database that is still online; NO_TRUNCATE is used when the database is damaged and you need to recover the tail of the log. The CONTINUE_AFTER_ERROR option can also be used in place of NO_TRUNCATE when trying to back up the transaction log of a damaged database.

The final option of STANDBY will perform a tail-log backup and place the database into a standby read-only state. The STANDBY option performs a rollback operation on the open transactions and places this data into a standby file that you specify with the STANDBY option. The WITH STANDBY option is the same as performing a BACKUP LOG WITH NORECOVERY followed by a RESTORE WITH STANDBY. To perform a backup using STANDBY, the statement would look like this:

```
BACKUP LOG AdventureWorks
TO DISK = 'AdventureWorks_TailLog.trn'
WITH STANDBY = 'AdventureWorks_Standby.trn'
```

ON THE JOB

A word of caution here when using BULK_LOGGED as the recovery model. If you are partway through a minimally logged transaction and experience a disaster which means you need to back up the tail of the log, unless the data files are still available, you will not be able to. This applies even when using NO_TRUNCATE as the log would only contain details of the modified extents, not the actual data.

Backup Destinations

In the examples so far, we have used the SQL Server default backup location for the backup files by simply providing a filename. There are three backup destination options available for the BACKUP statement: local disks, remote disk, and tape.

To use a local disk destination other than the default backup location, you must specify the full path and filename of the backup file:

```
BACKUP DATABASE AdventureWorks
TO DISK = 'F:\SQLBackup\AdventureWorks.bak'
```

To use a remote destination, you can use a Windows UNC path. The following example shows the use of a UNC path:

```
BACKUP DATABASE AdventureWorks
TO DISK = '\\FileSvr01\SQLBackup\AdventureWorks.bak'
```

ON THE JOB

It is possible to use a Windows mapped drive as a backup location, such as z:\ mapping to \\Server1\Backups. However, mapped drive settings are not system wide and in some cases may require different credentials to be passed to them. It can be tricky to get a Windows Service (for example, SQL Server) to use mapped drives correctly. Therefore, it is better to steer clear of them and use a full UNC path. If you want to abstract the full backup location from the backup statement, then use a backup device (covered shortly).

Finally, the last option is to back up directly to a tape device:

```
BACKUP DATABASE AdventureWorks
TO TAPE = '\\.\Tape0'
```

The tape option has been included here for completeness; be aware that it has been marked for removal from a future version of SQL Server and therefore should be avoided.

ON THE JOB

Backing up to a local volume is by far the most popular option. SQL DBAs tend to back up the database to a local volume and then rely on the corporate backup software to pick up the backup files as normal files from the volume. Backing up to a network share is probably the second most popular method, but you need to ensure that you have good network connectivity between the two servers.

It is possible to abstract the details of the physical backup device to a logical backup device that can be referenced by name in a backup script, hiding the device type, location, and filename. The logical backup devices are known as backup devices and can be found in SSMS under the Server Objects node. Backup devices can be created graphically in SSMS or in script by calling the sp_addumpdevice stored procedure.

The following example creates a backup device for our AdventureWorks database called AdventureWorksData and is mapped to a local file:

```
EXEC master.dbo.sp_addumpdevice
@devtype = N'disk', @logicalname = N'AdventureWorksData',
@physicalname = N'W:\SQLBackup\AdventureWorksData.bak'
```

To use the backup device, we simply reference it by name as the backup location. For example, to perform a full database backup to the backup device:

```
BACKUP DATABASE AdventureWorks
TO AdventureWorksData
```

The examples shown all reference a database backup as opposed to a log backup, but backup devices can also be used for log backups.

Oracle DBA Q&A

Q: Is the default backup location the same as the Flash Recovery Area?

A: You could compare the two from the point of view that they can be used as default backup storage locations, although the default backup location does not have automatic quota management like the Flash Recovery Area. It is possible to use features such as SQL Maintenance Plans to automatically clean up old and expired backup sets, in addition to writing your own scripts.

Backup Performance

Backup performance is dependent mainly on two factors: how fast SQL Server can read the data from disk, and how fast it can write the data to the backup device.

Although your database data files may be on fast volumes, your backup locations probably do not have the same speed characteristics. Therefore, just as in RMAN where you can set multiple channels and parallelism options, SQL Server provides the option to stripe your backup set across multiple backup devices. The following statement creates a stripe set of the AdventureWorks database backup across three devices, each located on different volumes:

```
BACKUP DATABASE AdventureWorks
TO DISK = 'F:\SQLBackup\AdventureWorks_1.bak',
DISK = 'G:\SQLBackup\AdventureWorks_2.bak',
DISK = 'H:\SQLBackup\AdventureWorks_3.bak'
```

A cautionary note about stripe sets is that although they may help reduce your overall backup times, you must have all the backup files available for the restore. If you lose one, the backup set is useless.

ON THE JOB

If your backups are not performing as you would expect and you are not sure whether it is the reading of the database or the writing of the backup file that is at fault, then a NUL backup destination may assist in the fault-finding process. A NUL destination is specified in place of a backup filename and does not physically write the data out to disk; for example, BACKUP DATABASE AdventureWorks TO DISK = 'NUL'. If you find that this backup completes faster than a normal backup, then the problem lies with the backup destination; if the times are no different, this excludes the writing of the backup file.

Backup Resilience

Losing part of your backup set can affect your ability to restore a database. SQL Server provides the ability to mirror a backup to up to four locations. Although all mirror locations must be present at the time of performing the backup, when restoring a backup if a problem is found with one copy of the media it is possible to select the media from any other mirror backup set.

The following example mirrors the stripe set used in the previous example:

```
BACKUP DATABASE AdventureWorks
TO DISK = 'F:\SQLBackup\AdventureWorks_1.bak',
DISK = 'G:\SQLBackup\AdventureWorks_2.bak',
DISK = 'H:\SQLBackup\AdventureWorks_3.bak'
MIRROR TO DISK = 'I:\SQLBackup\AdventureWorks_1.bak',
DISK = 'J:\SQLBackup\AdventureWorks_2.bak',
DISK = 'K:\SQLBackup\AdventureWorks_3.bak'
```

General WITH Options

We have already seen use of WITH options in a BACKUP statement in some of the previous examples. The options we have used so far have been specific to that particular variation of the statement, such as using WITH DIFFERENTIAL, which only applies to database backups, and WITH NO_TRUNCATE, which only applies to log backups. There are several general options that are used to specify details such as the backup media set, media management options, and the enabling of features such as compression and integrity checking.

Some WITH options are dependent on factors such as the type of physical backup device you are using. For example, when backing up directly to tape, the WITH options include elements such as REWIND and UNLOAD for tape management, which will have no effect when using a disk-based location. In this section we will look at some of the more common options used.

ON THE JOB

Many of the options have default values, although it is usually a good idea to put the values of interest into a statement to ensure you get the behavior you expect. For example, if you do not want a backup to use the compression feature, then ordinarily you do not need to call that out in the statement, as the default value for compression is to not compress the backup. However, if the server-wide setting for compression has been set to always compress and you have not explicitly marked the backup as not to compress, then the backup will pick up the server-wide setting.

Media and Backup Sets Every time you perform a backup, you are creating what is referred to as a "backup set." The backup set either resides on a single file or is striped across multiple files (or tapes), which is referred to as the "media set." A media set can contain many backup sets. In the examples so far, we have been backing up to a single file destination. Using the default WITH options with a BACKUP statement and specifying the same backup filename each time, your backup will result in a media set that contains many backup sets—that is, every time you execute a backup to the same file, it will be appended to the existing file. A media set can contain full, differential, and log file backup sets all in the same media set.

Table 7-1 shows a list of the common media set options for creating and overwriting media information.

Option	Description
NOINIT | INIT	NOINIT appends the backup to the existing media set. INIT overwrites all backup sets but preserves the media set header.
NOSKIP | SKIP	NOSKIP ensures that backup set expiration dates are checked before overwriting existing backups. SKIP disables any checking of backup set expiration dates.
NOFORMAT | FORMAT	FORMAT overwrites all media header and backup set information and creates a new media set.
MEDIANAME	The name of the media set (128 characters max).
MEDIADESCRIPTION	Backup set description (255 characters max).

Table 7-1 *Common Media Set Options*

The following example uses the 'AdventureWorks_Full.bak' file with the INIT option, which specifies it should overwrite all existing backup sets within the file. This is useful if you just want to replace the file with the new backup.

```
BACKUP DATABASE AdventureWorks
TO DISK = 'AdventureWorks_Full.bak'
WITH INIT
```

Each backup set within the media set can also have options set, the most common ones being the name and description, as noted in Table 7-2.

To specify a name for the backup set, use the following:

```
BACKUP DATABASE AdventureWorks
TO DISK = 'AdventureWorks_Full.bak'
WITH INIT, NAME = 'AdventureWorks Full Backup'
```

ON THE JOB

If you were using a tape device as your backup destination, then it is highly likely you will take advantage of the media set features, as you will combine multiple backup sets on one piece of tape media and use the labeling features. However, as mentioned previously, many DBAs these days back up to local files on disk and like to keep one backup per file—that is, each media set contains only one backup set. Combining this with a naming convention for your backup files makes it very quick and easy to see what backups you have available by just browsing the directory. If you look at features such as SQL Server Maintenance Plans that can automate the backup process, these tools also follow the one backup set per file method because it also makes cleaning up old and expired backup sets easier. Figure 7-1 shows the directory where a SQL Server Maintenance Plan produces a daily full backup of msdb, one full backup per file, and then names the file using the database name, date, and time.

Of the backup set options, the Name and Description fields can be especially useful when browsing the backup and restore history tables in msdb. For example, taking an ad hoc backup and naming it 'Ad Hoc Backup' with description 'Backup taken prior to executing price increase script' can make it easy to work out why a full backup was taken outside of the normal backup schedule.

Option	Description
NAME	The name of the backup set (128 characters max)
DESCRIPTION	Backup set description (255 characters max)
PASSWORD	Password to protect the backup set

Table 7-2   *Common Backup Set Options*

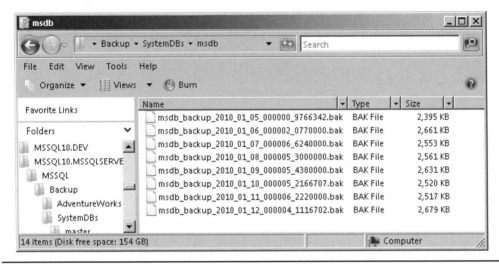

Figure 7-1 *Each backup in its own file*

Copy-Only Backups There are occasions where you may want to take an ad hoc backup of the system outside of the normal backup schedule; for example, a developer might want a copy of the live database to restore to the development system. If you were using the FULL recovery model with a combination of full and differential backups and the developer performs a full backup of the database and takes the backup file with him to the test system, he will have reset the differential base. This means that any differentials you take from that point going forward will be useless since you don't have the last full backup.

Using the WITH COPY_ONLY option on a full database or log backup creates a backup but does not reset any part of the chain and therefore does not affect recovery.

Backup Compression The ability to compress a backup prior to SQL Server 2008 was solely through the use of third-party software. In SQL Server 2008, backup compression was introduced as an Enterprise Edition–only feature, but as of SQL Server 2008 R2, it is now available in the Standard Edition. A compressed backup can be restored to any edition of SQL Server, even if that edition, such as SQL Server Express, does not contain the backup compression feature.

Compression is enabled using the WITH option called COMPRESSION. Conversely, it can be explicitly switched off (to override any global backup compression settings) using NO_COMPRESSION. The following statement enables compression for the backup of the AdventureWorks database:

```
BACKUP DATABASE AdventureWorks
TO DISK = 'AdventureWorks.bak'
WITH COMPRESSION
```

Figure 7-2 shows a simple example of backing up the AdventureWorks database, first with compression off and then with it on. The results show that the standard backup was approximately 122MB and the compressed version was 33MB, which is approximately 3.5 times smaller than the noncompressed version. In addition, since backup duration is often constrained by the speed of the backup destination, compressed backups will often be faster as well as smaller.

The compression rate achieved varies depending upon the type of data in the database. Databases that are encrypted or contain large binary objects don't compress as well as databases that are predominantly character and numerical data.

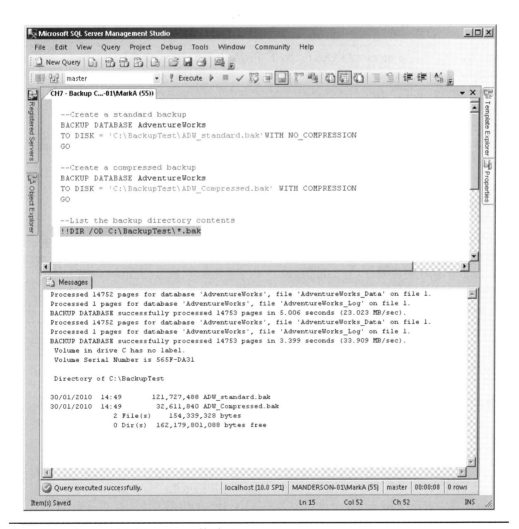

Figure 7-2   *Compressed and noncompressed backups*

Backup compression can be specified as a setting at the server level so that all backups compress by default, but be aware that when performing a compressed backup, the CPU utilization will be greater than for the equivalent noncompressed backup because the system has to perform the compression calculations.

NOTE

A media set cannot contain compressed and noncompressed backup sets. If you try to add a compressed backup to a noncompressed media set, you will get an error explaining that you need to reformat the media set, which will remove all existing backup sets.

ON THE JOB

There is a temptation to just enable backup compression as the default at the server level so that all databases back up with compression (unless explicitly specified not to compress). Although this may seem like a great time saver, it may be a waste of system resources. Certain types of data, such as binary blobs, do not compress very well and, therefore, compressing them will yield little or no gain in reduced disk space—although the server will still have to do the same amount of CPU work to compress the backup regardless of the resultant file size. If the vast majority of your databases do benefit from backup compression, then you may just want to explicitly turn off compression in the BACKUP statement on the databases that are affected using WITH NO_COMPRESSION.

Backup Integrity   The BACKUP syntax contains a WITH option called CHECKSUM. When CHECKSUM is enabled for a backup, the page (block) checksum or torn-page indicator is checked for each page prior to writing the data to the backup media. Secondly, BACKUP creates a checksum over the entire backup that can be used at restore time to ensure the integrity of the backup has not been compromised prior to restore.

The following example shows how to enable CHECKSUM:

```
BACKUP DATABASE AdventureWorks
TO DISK = 'AdventureWorks.bak'
WITH INIT, CHECKSUM
```

Be aware that switching on CHECKSUM will increase the overhead of performing the backup. Also, backing up WITH CHECKSUM is the default behavior when using backup compression.

While performing a backup WITH CHECKSUM, it is also possible to specify what BACKUP should do if it encounters an error such as an invalid checksum or torn page. STOP_ON_ERROR is the default, which will halt the backup upon finding a problem. To ignore any errors, use the CONTINUE_AFTER_ERROR option, which will allow the backup to continue, but be aware that using CONTINUE_AFTER_ERROR means that your backup could contain damaged data.

Backup History

Backup history and the details behind the backup are stored in the msdb system database. The system tables related to backup are listed in Table 7-3. Every time a backup is taken, the details of the backup are stored in these tables. Even if you are using a third-party solution, provided it uses the SQL Server Virtual Device Interface (VDI), details of the backup are recorded.

Although the SSMS tool can be used to surface data from these tables in the GUI, as a DBA you may want to create your own custom scripts that are specific to your way of working. The complete table schema and all the details behind what indicator values mean are available in SQL Server Books Online.

Let's look at a quick example of how to use the backup tables. The following query returns the date of the last full database backup for every database in the instance by joining the sysdatabases table from the master database and the backupset table from the msdb database:

```
SELECT db.name AS [Database], MAX(backup_finish_date) AS [LastBackup]
FROM
  master.dbo.sysdatabases db
    LEFT OUTER JOIN
  msdb.dbo.backupset bks
ON
  bks.database_name = db.name
WHERE bks.type = 'D'
GROUP BY db.name
ORDER BY db.name
```

Table	Description
dbo.backupmediaset	All available media sets.
dbo.backupmediafamily	A record of all media families (backup devices).
dbo.backupset	A record of each successful backup.
dbo.backupfile	Each time the database is backed up, a row for each database file is created describing its configuration at the time of backup, regardless of whether it was included in the backup.
dbo.backupfilegroup	Each time the database is backed up, a row is added for every filegroup present in the database at the time of backup.
dbo.logmarkhistory	A record of every committed marked transaction.

Table 7-3 *Backup-Related System Tables*

Over time, the backup-related system tables will continue to grow with information about every backup that has been performed. Therefore, it is important as a DBA to control the growth of the backup history.

If you want to clear down the backup history tables, there are two stored procedures in msdb that will delete the data from the tables for you:

- ► sp_delete_backuphistory
- ► sp_delete_database_backuphistory

sp_delete_backuphistory will delete history for all databases older than a specified date. sp_delete_database_backuphistory will remove all backup history for a specific database.

Another option is to use the SQL Server Maintenance Plans feature (covered shortly) and create a plan to clear out old backup history information.

Backup Permissions

To back up a database, you must have the BACKUP DATABASE permission, and to backup log files, you must have BACKUP LOG permission. The database owner (dbo) members of the db_owner and db_backupoperator database roles and the sysadmin fixed server role all inherit these permissions.

Securing Backups

Aside from ensuring the physical security of your backup media in safes and offsite storage, for sensitive data, it is important to consider securing the actual data, not just the media on which it resides.

In Oracle, using RMAN, it is possible to encrypt a backup as it is created and then decrypt it as part of the restore process. Creating encrypted backups of nonencrypted databases is not available as a feature within the SQL Server out-of-the-box product, although there are many third-party software vendors that do provide additional backup encryption capabilities for SQL Server.

SQL Server does provide encrypted out-of-the-box backups when the transparent database encryption feature is enabled (TDE is covered in Chapter 5) as the database itself is encrypted. The result of backing up a TDE-enabled database is that the backup file is also encrypted. The database backup cannot be restored without the relevant keys that were used to encrypt the database.

ON THE JOB

There are two very important things to note when using TDE with respect to restore. The first is to ensure that you have backed up your encryption keys. If you lose your keys, you ultimately lose your data (and probably your job!). The second may seem obvious, but do not store or transport your encrypted backups and their associated keys together. That's a bit like writing down your login and password on the lid of your laptop!

You may notice that the T-SQL BACKUP syntax at present allows for a backup to be secured with a password. The protection provided by this feature is weak and the functionality is due to be removed in a future version of SQL Server; therefore, you should avoid using it as your primary means of data protection.

ON THE JOB

The password capability within the BACKUP statement may not be very good at securing the backup from unauthorized access, but some people use it as a safeguard to prevent accidental restore of the wrong database since the password has to be provided to perform the restore.

Backup Scheduling

To schedule a backup script, you would use either SQL Server Agent or an external scheduling tool and make a call to SQLCMD to execute the script. SQL Server Agent and job scheduling are covered in detail in Chapter 10; for now, think of SQL Server Agent as a SQL Server version of DBMS_SCHEDULER.

SQL Server Maintenance Plans

To remove the burden of having to create scripts and to simplify and automate the process of database backup, SQL Server provides a graphical way to describe a backup plan through the use of Maintenance Plans. A Maintenance Plan is a graphical representation of a series of database maintenance tasks that can be organized to run in a workflow style. One of the main tasks available within a Maintenance Plan is a Backup task. Using a Maintenance Plan to describe your backup routine and schedule SQL Server will generate the relevant scheduled jobs and T-SQL code to execute your backup. Maintenance Plans are covered in detail in Chapter 10, including examples on using them for backup.

Back Up Using SSMS

Now that we have looked at using the BACKUP statement in script, let's take a quick look at how to use SSMS to perform a database backup. Within SSMS, right-click the database you wish to back up and select Tasks | Back Up, as shown in Figure 7-3.

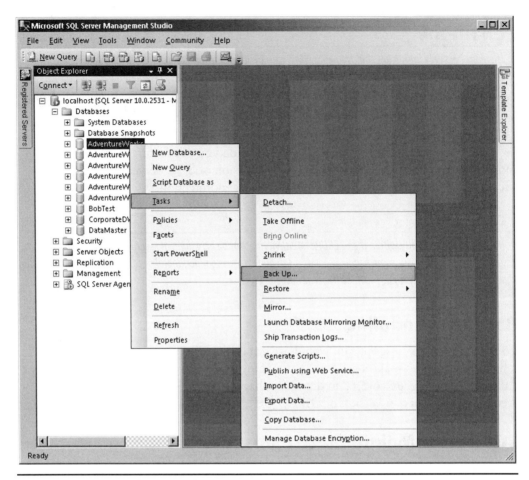

Figure 7-3   *Creating a backup using SSMS*

The Back Up Database dialog box, shown in Figure 7-4, is a way of graphically describing a backup, which, when executed, will convert your selections into a BACKUP statement. The dialog box has two options pages, General and Options, which are accessed by the page selector on the left side of the window. The General page is shown first and allows you to select source database, backup set, and destination information, all of which should be familiar to you by now from the previous examples of using the BACKUP statement.

If you select the Options page, as shown in Figure 7-5, additional backup options are displayed. All the options on here should be familiar to you as they effectively map onto the WITH options for the BACKUP statement, with the exception of one check

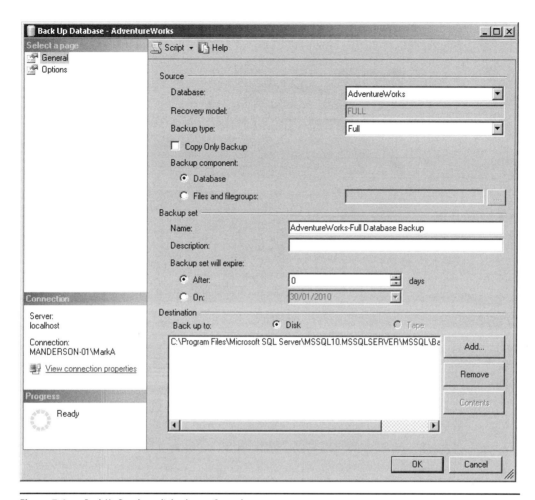

Figure 7-4   *Back Up Database dialog box—General page*

box in the Reliability section, Verify Backup when Finished. When checked, this option will attempt to perform a RESTORE VERIFYONLY statement following a successful backup. We will cover the RESTORE statement in greater detail in the next section of this chapter. For now, just note that the RESTORE VERIFYONLY statement is used to verify that the backup file is usable for a database restore operation without actually performing a full restore.

As with most of the dialog boxes in SSMS, once you have selected and set all your options, you can either click OK, which will execute the action immediately, or use the Script options to have the action scripted out for you.

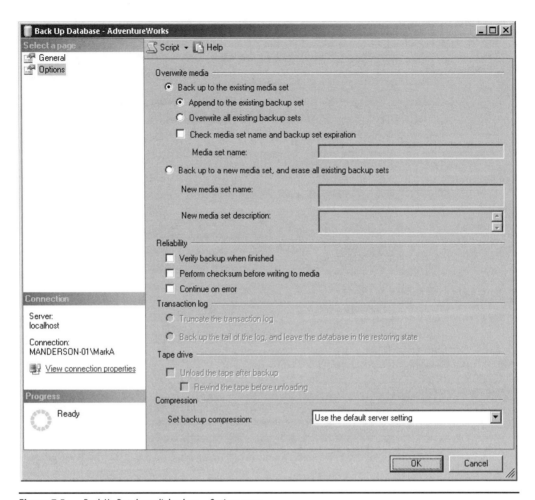

Figure 7-5   *Back Up Database dialog box—Options page*

ON THE JOB

If the world of SQL Server backup is new to you, it is worth taking a look at how the Back Up Database dialog box creates its T-SQL syntax. Select options and click the Script button at the top of the window. If you choose the Verify Backup when Finished option and then review the script, you will see an example of how SQL Server first uses the BACKUP statement, followed by reading data from the backup history tables, and then provides that information to a RESTORE statement. It should provide you with ideas for how you can create your own dynamic backup scripts.

Backup of System Databases

The tools for backing up system databases are no different from those for backing up standard databases; the T-SQL BACKUP and RESTORE methods still apply. What you need to be aware of is how often you need to back up the databases.

The master database is essential to server operation and should be backed up whenever changes are made to the system, such as adding and removing logins or databases or changing server configuration. The master database runs using the SIMPLE recovery model and therefore only supports full database backups. Regular backup of this database is essential.

The msdb database keeps track of all backup and recovery history, job execution details, operators and alert definitions, and potentially SSIS (ETL) packages (if using the msdb storage method). In addition, SQL Server Agent and SSMS both use the msdb database as a storage mechanism for settings and configuration. The default recovery model for msdb is set to SIMPLE, although if you use msdb for tracking backup and restore history and other tasks, it is recommended that you change it to the FULL recovery model and create an appropriate backup regime such as full with transaction log (or full, differential, and transaction log) and take regular backups.

The model database, which is used as a template for all new databases, is only ever updated by you. SQL Server will not make any changes to the model database and therefore you only need to back up the database when you make changes to it.

There is no need to back up tempdb since the database is transient and is re-created every time the instance is started.

The last system database to be aware of is the distribution database, which is created when using the SQL Server Replication feature. Its backup and recovery method can differ depending on which type of replication is being used. For more details on using this feature, see SQL Server Books Online.

ON THE JOB

Backing up the master database should become habitual following any modifications to SQL Server that affect the master database (creating logins, linked servers, databases, and so on). If you do not back up the master database and experience a failure, you will have no option but to rebuild the master database and you will end up with a database server that will look like it did when you first installed it—empty! To compare to Oracle, think losing SYS and SYSAUX!

In contrast to my paranoid approach to master database backup, I remember a conversation with a DBA who told me he never runs a backup of his master database and instead keeps every change he makes as a set of scripts that can be used to restore the master database in the event of failure. Although commendable that he maintained this information, as you should always keep a track of changes you make to the system, I personally find relying on this approach contains potential for errors. All it takes is for another DBA to make a change and not update your scripts library and you have a problem. It also seems very time consuming compared to a simple restore operation.

Chapter 10 shows an example of how to create a SQL Server Maintenance Plan that will automatically back up the core system databases on a regular schedule.

Example Backup Scenarios

Let's walk through a couple of example scenarios on choosing the right recovery model and backup type.

Scenario 1: The Company Data Warehouse

The company uses a central data warehouse for reporting operations within the organization. The warehouse is loaded with data from the line-of-business systems on a nightly basis using SQL Server Integration Services to perform a bulk import.

The agreed recovery point objective (RPO) for the database following a database server problem, such as media failure, is to recover the database to the most recent data import.

Before you look at the type of backup strategy you need, the first step is to think about the recovery model; in this scenario the data is only updated once per evening with a bulk load of data. Following the nightly load, the data is static throughout the day. Therefore, the SIMPLE recovery model seems to best suit your requirements since it uses minimal logging (as per the BULK_LOGGED model), reducing transaction log file overhead for the bulk import operation, and the transaction log file management is simplified through its ability to self-truncate.

Moving to the backup options, the first and simplest approach is to perform a full backup every evening. Although the daily full backup approach may be the simplest to set up, it will also be the approach that uses the most space and takes the most time to execute. Another approach would be to use a combination of full and differential backups.

Figure 7-6 shows a Sunday through Sunday timeline. Using a full database backup at the start of the week establishes a base for the differential backups, and then each evening

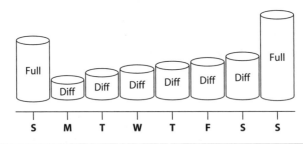

Figure 7-6   *Weekly full backup with daily differential*

a differential backup would be taken following the data load process. Each differential backup would contain all changes since the last full backup (depicted by the increasing size of the differential icon). The following Sunday a full backup would again be taken and the differential base would be reset.

Let's look at one approach to creating this backup regime.

The first step would be to create the weekly full database backup using a SQL Server Agent Job (covered in Chapter 10) that performs a T-SQL step to execute the backup code on a Sunday evening. The following code used to perform the backup dynamically creates the backup filename using the database name, today's date, the word "Full" to identify the backup as a full backup, and the file extension convention of .bak; for example, 'CorporateDW_23012010_Full.bak'. The backup is placed in the default backup location and uses the compression feature.

```
--Full Backup
DECLARE @BackupFile nvarchar(50)
SET @BackupFile = 'CorporateDW_' +
    replace(convert(varchar, getdate(), 103), '/', '') + '_Full.bak'

BACKUP DATABASE CorporateDW
TO DISK = @BackupFile
WITH INIT, COMPRESSION
```

The next step is to create the daily differential backup; the same approach is taken to creating the filename dynamically, with the exception of replacing the word "Full" with "Diff." The code would again run in a SQL Server Agent Job set to run every evening except Sunday.

```
--Differential Backup
DECLARE @BackupFile nvarchar(50)
SET @BackupFile = 'CorporateDW_' +
    replace(convert(varchar, getdate(), 103), '/', '') + '_Diff.bak'

BACKUP DATABASE CorporateDW
TO DISK = @BackupFile
WITH INIT, DIFFERENTIAL, COMPRESSION
```

In this scenario, if the database server were to suffer a failure that required a complete database restore, then a combination of the Sunday full backup and the most recent differential backup would restore to the most recent data load.

ON THE JOB

The scenario and solution described in the previous example is valid for the majority of small data warehouse or data mart implementations. However, if you were implementing a large, multi-terabyte data warehouse, your design would more than likely include data management approaches such as data partitioning that could be spread across multiple filegroups. Other techniques would include marking filegroups read-only, which could lead to the use of partial full and differential backups or individual file and filegroup backups.

Scenario 2: The Line-of-Business Application

The company uses a Customer Relationship Management (CRM) application to record all customer engagement activity. The system is used by agents in the call center and by sales representatives in the stores. Due to the volume of activity on this application, the business leaders have deemed this system to be important to business operation. As such, the recovery point objective following a disaster is to lose no greater than 15 minutes of activity from the point of failure. Speed of recovery is also important to this solution because it is used by customer-facing agents.

To support this level of recovery, the database should use the FULL recovery model. Using the FULL recovery model will make it possible to take frequent transaction log backups to secure data to the granularity of the 15-minute window. Also, depending on the type of disaster, if the transaction log is still available, it will be possible to recover the system to the point of the last committed transaction.

Before looking at the database backup, let's consider the log backup options. To support 15-minute recoverability, the transaction log will need to be backed up every 15 minutes. Over a 24-hour period, that equates to 96 transaction log backups per day, assuming either a full or differential backup is taken nightly. Therefore, as an example, if the system were to fail at 19:30, it would take the restore of the database backup (full or full + differential) and then 76 sequential log file restores, or 77 if you can recover the tail of the log. Not only does this mean you have to deal with a large number of transaction log file backups, but it also increases the chances of losing data because if one of the transaction log file backups was to be corrupted or damaged you would only be able to restore up to the point of the damaged backup. A better approach to this would be to take differential backups at frequent periods throughout the day, as this would then require fewer transaction log restores. Also, there would be no need to retain more than one differential backup since the log chain could be used as a backup for point-in-time restore.

Taking into account all the requirements just described, an appropriate backup regime for this database would consist of a daily full database backup accompanied by differential backups taken every four hours, with the transaction logs being backed up every 15 minutes. This would mean that in the event of a restore, it would take the last full and differential backups and no greater than 16 log backups to recover the system.

ON THE JOB

The purpose of the previous scenario is to highlight how the backup and recovery regime for an important system may be configured to support disaster recovery. Try not to confuse this with its high availability requirements, which such a system is likely to have. In a real-world scenario, this system would probably be running in a cluster or mirroring configuration to provide fast failover and zero data loss capabilities. High availability is covered in Chapter 9.

Oracle DBA Q&A

Q: I am a little confused, if a full backup is only consistent as of when it completes, how can I achieve point-in-time recovery for a time that is during the full backup window? For example, if my full backup starts at 1:00 A.M. and takes one hour to complete, how can I recover to 1:20 A.M.? I assume that I would still continue to run transaction log backups while the full backup is taking place. The reason I am confused is that you said a full backup requires a portion of the transaction log to make it consistent and that a transaction log backup truncates the transaction log. Therefore, how can I run these at the same time?

A: The assumption that log backups can take place while a full backup is taking place is correct. This is how you would still be able to provide the point-in-time recovery to a point during the full backup cycle. SQL Server allows transaction log backups to be taken while a full backup is in progress by deferring the truncation of the log until the end of the full backup. This avoids the issue of not having enough of the log available to complete the full backup. You should always ensure that your log file has sufficient disk space to grow while the full backup is in progress since you will be unable to truncate it until the end of the full backup.

Restore and Recovery

The process of recovering a database from a backup includes restoring the affected parts of the database (putting the files back on disk) and then recovering them to a usable state (rolling forward any completed transactions and rolling back any incomplete ones). Although restore and recovery are separate activities, they are controlled by the same statement.

SQL Server has the ability to perform everything from a full database recovery, through to individual file- and filegroup-level repair, all the way down to very fine page-level (block-level) online repair. Whatever the scope of the recovery, SQL Server always restores the database to a single consistent point in time. You cannot restore just part of a database to a different point in time. However, you can restore a second copy of the database to an earlier point in time and use the data extract and load tools to copy data from the earlier version of the database (Chapter 11 covers data movement tools in detail).

The T-SQL statement used to restore and recover a database is RESTORE. As per the previous "Backup" section of this chapter, we are not going to cover the full range of arguments and options in detail for the statement. Instead we will look at the basics of the statement, review the most common options, and work through several examples of using RESTORE.

Unlike BACKUP, which effectively has just two main arguments, DATABASE and LOG, the RESTORE statement is used not only to restore the database or elements of it but also when you want to inspect the contents of a backup file or check the backup integrity without actually restoring the database to disk.

The arguments available with a RESTORE statement are

▶ RESTORE (DATABASE or LOG)

▶ RESTORE LABELONLY

▶ RESTORE HEADERONLY

▶ RESTORE REWINDONLY

▶ RESTORE FILELISTONLY

▶ RESTORE VERIFYONLY

The first one of the RESTORE arguments is DATABASE or LOG. This is the argument that will perform the actual restore and recovery operations. Before we move into the actual process of restoring a database, let's look at the other arguments that relate to reading the information within the media sets. We need to know what we have before we can restore it!

Even though the backup history tables in msdb keep track of the backup sets that have been taken, the files within them, and the media sets that are contained within, we still need the option to be able to inspect a backup file or tape to work out what it contains. This would be especially useful if the backup history within msdb was lost or accidentally deleted.

Figure 7-7 shows the RESTORE LABELONLY and RESTORE HEADERONLY commands in operation against a single disk-based media set. The detail returned by RESTORE LABELONLY contains information about the backup media, and RESTORE HEADERONLY returns all the backup sets contained on the backup device. Figure 7-7 only shows a subset of the returned fields.

RESTORE REWINDONLY is used only with tape devices and is the equivalent of issuing RESTORE LABELONLY FROM TAPE = *tape_device* WITH REWIND.

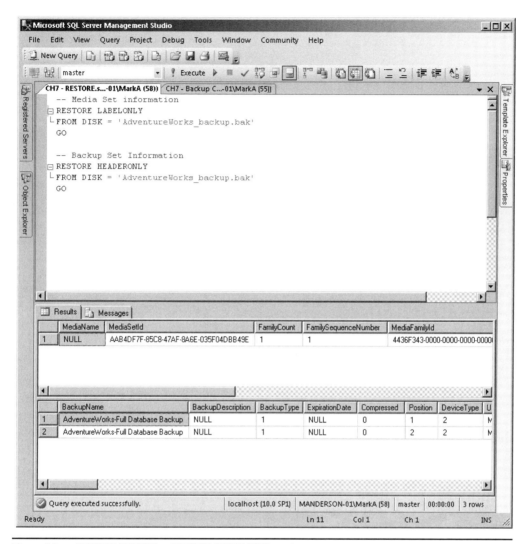

Figure 7-7   *RESTORE LABELONLY and RESTORE HEADERONLY in action*

RESTORE FILELISTONLY returns a list of the database data and log files contained in the backup set and is used alongside the WITH FILE = *n* option, where *n* is the backup set position number in the media set (the Position column is returned in the RESTORE HEADERONLY statement, as shown in Figure 7-7).

Figure 7-8 shows the RESTORE FILELISTONLY statement executed twice to return information about the two backup sets. Notice that backup set 2 contains an

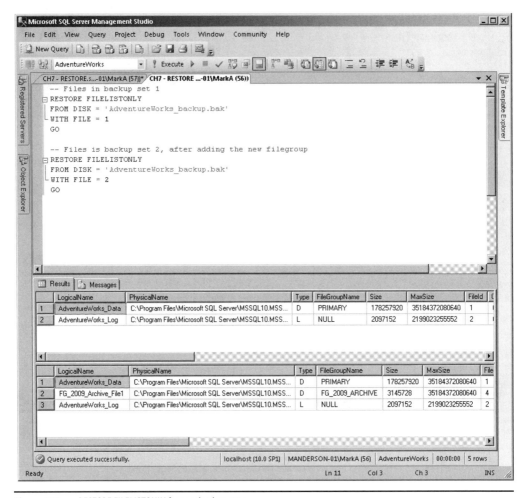

Figure 7-8 *RESTORE FILELISTONLY for two backup sets*

additional database file; this is because, in between the first and second backup, an additional file was added to the database, which was subsequently picked up in the second full backup.

RESTORE VERIFYONLY is used to check that the backup media is readable without having to do an actual restore. RESTORE VERIFYONLY used against a backup that was not backed up using WITH CHECKSUM performs a simple check that the media is readable but does not guarantee that the data is consistent. When the backup has been taken using the WITH CHECKSUM option, RESTORE VERIFYONLY WITH CHECKSUM will check every data page by reading and recalculating the page checksum and will compare it to the recorded page check in the backup to ensure file integrity.

The following is an example of a backup and restore check using checksums:

```
BACKUP DATABASE AdventureWorks
TO DISK = 'AdventureWorks.bak'
WITH CHECKSUM
GO


RESTORE VERIFYONLY
FROM DISK = 'AdventureWorks.bak'
WITH CHECKSUM
GO
```

Restoring and Recovering a Database

The RESTORE statement not only restores the database data files, but also is responsible for recovering the database to make it consistent and accessible.

The basic syntax for a RESTORE statement is as follows:

```
RESTORE DATABASE | LOG database_name
FROM backup_location
WITH recovery_options, general options
```

Database Recovery

It may seem strange to talk about recovery before we look at the restore, but every time you issue a RESTORE, you need to specify whether or not the restore you are performing should have recovery applied. Remembering that full and differential backups contain database pages from different points in time and a portion of the transaction log, and that transaction log backups can contain open transactions, the recovery options are used to specify whether the restore operation should bring the database to a consistent state following the restore operation or keep it in a state that can have further backup files applied. The three available recovery options are

- ▶ RECOVERY
- ▶ NORECOVERY
- ▶ STANDBY

The option of RECOVERY is the default option and will be used if you do not specify one of the others. Using RECOVERY will place the database in an online, usable state by performing recovery on the database at the end of the restore.

When restoring a database using a chain of backups, such as starting with a full followed by a differential backup and finally restoring any transaction log files, you must ensure that after each restore you leave the database in a state in which it can have the next backup in the sequence applied. Performing recovery on the database would remove any open transactions and therefore would break the transaction LSN chain when you attempt to restore the next backup in the sequence, preventing you from restoring further backups. Using NORECOVERY leaves the database in a RESTORING state and able to accept further backup files.

The final option of STANDBY brings the database online by running recovery on the database. Instead of discarding the incomplete transactions, it places the data that it has undone in a separate file so that at a later stage it can be reapplied to the database along with the next backup in the sequence. Restoring a database using STANDBY places the database in a read-only mode so that there is no write activity that would break the transaction log sequence. An example scenario in which you could use STANDBY would be on a database used for reporting that holds the data generated from copying and restoring the transaction log backups from your line-of-business application. Users could use the reporting database to run their queries and then, when the DBA wants to update the reporting system, could restore the next set of transaction log backups from the line-of-business application.

ON THE JOB

If you are restoring from a single full backup (or the last backup in your chain), you do not need to specify WITH RECOVERY to bring the database online since that is the default action. However, it is a good idea to specify it as a matter of course just to get into the habit of always specifying some recovery option with the RESTORE statement. There is nothing worse than restoring a large full backup knowing you have other differential and log backups to apply and realizing you didn't specify the WITH NORECOVERY option, because the only thing you can do in that situation is to start again! A top DBA tip is to always specify WITH NORECOVERY on all your restores so that, when you are sure you have finished, you can issue the statement RESTORE database_name WITH RECOVERY to bring the database online.

Restoring from Backups

For complete database recovery, the process starts with the most recent full backup, followed by the latest differential, and then all transaction log backups since the differential, in sequence.

Let's start with a simple example of restoring a full database backup. In this example, you will be restoring a database back to its original location following accidental deletion. The statement will take the most recent backup set from the AdventureWorks.bak file and restore it back into the instance.

```
RESTORE DATABASE AdventureWorks
FROM DISK = 'AdventureWorks.bak'
WITH RECOVERY
```

NOTE

In the "Backup" section, we covered using one backup set per media set, the common method of backup (that is, one backup per file). If the restore is using a media set that contains multiple backup sets, then you must specify which backup set you want to use by specifying the WITH FILE = n option, where n is the position of the backup set (RESTORE HEADERONLY returns backup set position numbers). For example, if the media set has five backup sets and you wish to restore the second backup set, then the statement would look as follows:

```
RESTORE DATABASE AdventureWorks
FROM DISK = 'AdventureWorks.bak'
WITH RECOVERY, FILE = 2
```

For the rest of the chapter, all examples assume one backup set per media set, removing the need to specify the FILE option.

If you are using full and differential backups together, you would start by restoring the full backup first using WITH NORECOVERY, followed by the most recent differential backup using WITH RECOVERY:

```
RESTORE DATABASE AdventureWorks
FROM DISK = 'AdventureWorks_Full.bak'
WITH NORECOVERY
GO
RESTORE DATABASE AdventureWorks
FROM DISK = 'AdventureWorks_Diff.bak'
WITH RECOVERY
```

If your database was using the SIMPLE recovery model, you only have the options for full and differential backup restore (ignoring partial recovery for now). If on the other hand your database was running in the FULL or BULK_LOGGED recovery model, then your restore would probably include restoring transaction log file backups taken since the last differential backup, making the restore process as follows:

```
-- Most Recent Full
RESTORE DATABASE AdventureWorks
FROM DISK = 'AdventureWorks_Full.bak'
WITH NORECOVERY
GO
-- Most Recent Differential
```

```
RESTORE DATABASE AdventureWorks
FROM DISK = 'AdventureWorks_Diff.bak'
WITH NORECOVERY
GO
-- First log since last Differential
RESTORE LOG AdventureWorks
FROM DISK = 'AdventureWorks_logbackup1.trn'
WITH NORECOVERY
GO
< REPEATED FOR EACH LOG FILE IN SEQUENCE >
-- Last Log file in sequence
RESTORE LOG AdventureWorks
FROM DISK = 'AdventureWorks_logbackup5.trn'
WITH RECOVERY
```

Point-in-Time Recovery

Restoring the log file has some additional options to allow point-in-time recovery. STOPAT, STOPATMARK, and STOPBEFOREMARK all allow you to recover to a specific point. These options are similar to restore points in Oracle, which enable you to specify points in time, log sequence numbers (SCNs in Oracle), or named markers.

STOPAT is used to recover to a specific date and time:

```
RESTORE LOG AdventureWorks
FROM DISK = 'AdventureWorks_logbackup.trn'
WITH RECOVERY,
STOPAT = 'Jan 16, 2010 07:38:00 PM'
```

STOPATMARK and STOPBEFOREMARK, as the names suggest, stop recovery at or before a marker within the transaction log. The marker can be an LSN or custom transaction marker.

Custom markers are placed in the transaction log by naming a transaction and specifying the WITH MARK option on a transaction:

```
BEGIN TRANSACTION transaction_name
WITH MARK transaction_description
<DO SOME WORK>
COMMIT TRANSACTION transaction_name
```

For example, if you were performing an update to your Products table, increasing all your prices by 10 percent, you may decide to mark that transaction as a point to which you can recover. Therefore, when issuing the UPDATE statement, you would mark the transaction as follows:

```
BEGIN TRANSACTION ProductPriceIncrease
WITH MARK '10% Product Price increase update'

UPDATE Store.Products SET Price = Price*1.1

COMMIT TRANSACTION ProductPriceIncrease
```

STOPATMARK and STOPBEFOREMARK can now use this transaction log marker for point-in-time recovery:

```
RESTORE LOG AdventureWorks
FROM DISK = 'AdventureWorks_logbackup.trn'
WITH RECOVERY,
STOPBEFOREMARK = 'ProductPriceIncrease'
```

When a log mark is placed in a transaction log, it is recorded in the dbo. logmarkhistory table in the msdb database, and therefore you can browse the available log marks by querying the table.

You may notice that the STOPAT, STOPATMARK, and STOPBEFORE marks can also be specified when performing a RESTORE DATABASE. It is important to note that this will not restore a database to that point. They are used as a mechanism to check that your database restore is earlier than the point to which you wish to recover. If the backup is later than the target point and cannot be used, an error will be returned.

Oracle DBA Q&A

Q: Does SQL Server have its own version of LogMiner to allow you to inspect the transaction log?

A: No, there is no formal tool like LogMiner in SQL Server. There is, however, an undocumented function called fn_dblog, the details of which you can easily find via a quick search of the Internet. A quick example that will pull back all the information in the current log file is 'SELECT * FROM ::fn_dblog(null, null)'. Most of the fields returned are self-explanatory, and there are many websites and blogs that have good examples of using this function. If you are looking for something a little more formal, you can find log inspection tools from third-party vendors on the Internet.

Restoring to the Last Committed Transaction

In the "Backup" section, we covered tail-log backups. The tail-log backup is used when you want to recover the database to the last committed transaction. For example, suppose your database has suffered serious damage to the media holding the data files and requires a complete database restore. Without a tail-log backup, your recovery point is to your last transaction log backup, but, provided that the media containing the transaction log files has survived and SQL Server is still up and running, a tail-log backup can be taken. The tail-log backup will allow you to capture the log file that has not yet been backed up. Once the tail log has been captured, the database can be restored and recovered as normal:

```
-- Backup the tail of the log
BACKUP LOG AdventureWorks
TO DISK = 'AdventureWorks_taillog.trn'
WITH NORECOVEY, NO_TRUNCATE

-- Restore the most recent Full
RESTORE DATABASE AdventureWorks
FROM DISK = 'AdventureWorks_Full.bak'
WITH NORECOVERY
GO
-- Restore the log files
RESTORE LOG AdventureWorks
FROM DISK = 'AdventureWorks_logbackup.trn'
WITH NORECOVERY
GO
< REPEATED FOR EACH LOG FILE IN SEQUENCE >
-- Restore the tail-log and run recovery
RESTORE LOG AdventureWorks
FROM DISK = 'AdventureWorks_ taillog.trn'
WITH RECOVERY
```

Filegroup-, File-, and Page-Level Restore

Up until now we have looked at how to perform a complete restore of a database. SQL Server also supports repairing parts of the database such as the filegroup, file, and page.

Restoring an individual filegroup or file does not have to come from an individual file or filegroup backup. The files can be extracted from a full backup. The process to recover the files includes taking a tail-log backup, restoring the files from a full backup, applying the most recent differential backup if used, and then applying all log files in sequence, including the tail log.

The following example shows how to restore an individual file using its logical filename (the other steps have been added as comments, as they have been shown in previous examples):

```
-- Backup the tail of the log

-- Restore the missing file
RESTORE DATABASE AdventureWorks
FILE = 'FG_2009_Archive_File1'
FROM DISK = 'AdventureWorks_Full.bak'
WITH NORECOVERY
GO
-- Restore all log backups since full in sequence
-- Restore the tail-log and run recovery
```

To restore a filegroup, simply use FILEGROUP in place of the FILE option. It is also possible to specify several files and filegroups at the same time by adding additional FILE and FILEGROUP parameters to the statement.

```
RESTORE DATABASE AdventureWorks
FILE = 'FG_2009_Archive_File1'
FILE = 'FG_2009_Archive_File2'
FILEGROUP = 'FG_2008_Archive'
FROM DISK = 'AdventureWorks_Full.bak'
WITH NORECOVERY
GO
```

If you are running in the SIMPLE recovery model, then you can only restore read-only files and filegroups because you have no transaction log backups available to roll forward a read-write file or filegroup.

The lowest level of granularity for SQL Server storage is the page, and SQL Server supports page-level restores. In the scenario where a data page has become corrupted, it is possible to replace just that page instead of restoring the complete file or filegroup. A page can be restored from a full, file, or filegroup backup, followed by restoring all log file backups (taken since the file used to perform the restore was created) including a tail log.

NOTE

Although in the previous statement it made reference to restoring the log file backups, it is not actually restoring all of the content of the log files. The restore process performs a scan of the log looking for changes that affect the page you have restored.

The following is an example of restoring a page, in this case in File 3, page 763:

```
RESTORE DATABASE AdventureWorks
PAGE = '3:763'
FROM DISK = 'AdventureWorks_Full.bak'

<Apply all transaction log backups and the tail log>
```

Page restores cannot be used for all types of page. System pages such as file headers, global allocation maps, and boot pages cannot be individually restored and can only be repaired using a full file or filegroup restoration.

NOTE

When a query is issued that hits a page that is detected by SQL Server to be faulty (error codes 823 and 824), it is recorded in the dbo.suspect_pages table in the msdb database.

ON THE JOB

Page-level restore is an excellent feature, but that doesn't mean you always have to resort to it. For example, if the page that has become corrupted belongs to a nonclustered index, then it may be better to rebuild the index than resort to performing a restore. There is less risk in an index rebuild than there is in a restore operation and SQL Server supports online index rebuilds.

In addition, just because a page appears in the suspect_pages table, that doesn't mean it must be restored; it is worth checking if the DBCC CHECKDB command can fix the issue first.

Piecemeal Restore

Piecemeal restore is best described through an example. If you have a 20TB data warehouse and experience a disaster that requires a complete restore, then your total outage time is equal to how quickly you can restore and recover the entire 20TB. Restoring 20TB is going to take some time even if you own a top-of-the-range expensive SAN solution. One possible answer to this problem is piecemeal restore.

Piecemeal restore allows you to recover the database in stages, bringing parts of the database online and available for use before you have finished the complete restore. Piecemeal restore options differ depending on whether you are using the SIMPLE or FULL recovery model.

When running in the SIMPLE recovery model, piecemeal recovery stipulates that you must recover your PRIMARY filegroup and all read-write filegroups before restoring any read-only filegroups. Once the PRIMARY and all read-write filegroups are online, users can start to access the database and start using the data while you restore the read-only filegroups in the background. If the user tries to access data in a filegroup that is not yet online, an error message will be returned to the client.

Let's take a look at an example of piecemeal restore of a data warehouse database using SIMPLE recovery. The database uses filegroups to hold data archives that relate to the year the data was entered. When one year ends, the filegroup becomes read-only and only the current year is read-write:

```
-- Restore the primary filegroup and the 2010 read-write filegroup
RESTORE DATABASE CorporateDW READ_WRITE_FILEGROUPS
FROM DISK = 'CorporateDW_RWFG.bak'
WITH PARTIAL, RECOVERY
GO


/* The database is now online and 2010 data can be accessed by users
2009 and 2008 data is still unavailable and is marked as offline. */

-- Restore and recover the 2009_Data Filegroup
RESTORE DATABASE CorporateDW
FILEGROUP='2009_Data'
FROM 'CorporateDW_RO_2009.bak'
WITH RECOVERY
GO
/* Users can now query the data in the 2010 and 2009 filegroups. */

-- Restore and Recover the 2008_Data Filegroup
RESTORE DATABASE CorporateDW
FILEGROUP='2008_Data'
FROM 'CorporateDW_RO_2008.bak'
WITH RECOVERY
GO
```

Performing a piecemeal restore when using the FULL recovery model differs in that it uses log file restores to roll forward the filegroup as they are recovered. Although this is a slightly longer process, it does allow you to get a database up and running after restoring only the PRIMARY filegroup instead of having to restore all read-write filegroups as in the SIMPLE model.

For example (some steps have been commented, as they appear in other examples):

```
-- Backup the tail of the log

-- Restore the PRIMARY Filegroup, using PARTIAL and NORECOVERY
```

```
RESTORE DATABASE AdventureWorks
FILEGROUP='PRIMARY'
FROM DISK = 'AdventureWorks_Partial.bak'
WITH PARTIAL, NORECOVERY
GO
-- Restore all log file backups since the full backup was taken
-- Apply the tail-log backup WITH RECOVERY

/* The PRIMARY Filegroup is now online and the database is accessible,
all other filegroups remain offline. */

-- Restore the secondary Filegroup(s)
RESTORE DATABASE AdventureWorks
FILEGROUP='SALES'
FROM DISK = 'AdventureWorks_SalesFG.bak'
WITH NORECOVERY
GO

-- Restore all log file backups since the full backup was taken
-- Apply the tail-log backup WITH RECOVERY

/* The secondary filegroup is now online, repeat the secondary
Filegroup(s) restore process until all Filegroups are online. */
```

To take real advantage of piecemeal restore, you should review your physical database design and think about the use of filegroups and how you distribute your objects. For FULL recovery databases, your goal should be to enable quick recovery of your PRIMARY filegroup, followed by the other filegroups in order of importance. In the SIMPLE recovery model, your aim is to restore the PRIMARY and all read-write filegroups as quickly as possible. Thus, a review of whether your filegroups can be made read-only is advisable.

ON THE JOB

Although they can't be used as a primary method of recovery, SQL Server database snapshots (mentioned in Chapter 2) can be used to "wind back" a database to a previous point in time. As a DBA, database snapshots are useful tools to use prior to making any updates to the database as they can be used as a quick way to put the database back to the point in time prior to your making changes. For example, suppose you take a database snapshot of AdventureWorks at 9:00 A.M., prior to performing your database update, and then, following your update, you realize that it didn't go according to plan and you need to revert the database back to how it looked at 09:00 A.M. You can use the database snapshot to wind back the database to that point in time. The syntax is as follows:

```
RESTORE DATABASE database_name FROM DATABASE_SNAPSHOT =
snapshot_database
```

Therefore, to restore AdventureWorks using the AdventureWorks_9AM database snapshot:

```
RESTORE DATABASE AdventureWorks FROM DATABASE_SNAPSHOT =
AdventureWorks_9AM
```

There are caveats and things you should be aware of around reverting to a snapshot, such as it will rebuild the transaction log and break the backup chain. Full details on using snapshots can be found in SQL Server Books Online. Also, it should be noted that in this example you should still perform a proper backup prior to the update; the snapshot simply provided a quick way to revert the database without resorting to a restore from backup.

RESTORE—WITH Options

As with the BACKUP statement, there are several general WITH options for a RESTORE statement. This section covers the most commonly used ones.

Restoring to Alternate Locations

When you are restoring a database, the default action is to restore the database files back to their original location as recorded in the backup set. In the scenario of restoring to an alternate server that may not have the same disk configuration or restoring to the same server but having to use a different disk location, you need to specify where to move the files to by using the WITH MOVE option:

```
WITH MOVE 'logical_filename' TO 'new_location'
```

In the AdventureWorks database, the logical filename 'AdventureWorks_Data' is used for the primary mdf file and 'AdventureWorks_Log' is used for the ldf log file. To restore a backup of AdventureWorks moving these files to a new location, the syntax is as follows:

```
RESTORE DATABASE AdventureWorks
FROM DISK = 'AdventureWorks_Full.bak'
WITH RECOVERY,
MOVE 'AdventureWorks_Data' TO 'E:\SQLData\AdventureWorks_Data.mdf',
MOVE 'AdventureWorks_Log' TO 'F:\SQLLogs\Adventureworks_Log.mdf'
```

Replacing Existing Databases

When using the FULL or BULK_LOGGED recovery model and restoring a database when it already exists within the instance, the following message may appear:

```
Msg 3159, Level 16, State 1, Line 1
The tail of the log for the database "AdventureWorks" has not been
backed up. Use BACKUP LOG WITH NORECOVERY to backup the log if it
contains work you do not want to lose. Use the WITH REPLACE or
```

```
WITH STOPAT clause of the RESTORE statement to just overwrite the
contents of the log.
Msg 3013, Level 16, State 1, Line 1
RESTORE DATABASE is terminating abnormally.
```

The message is telling you that you have not performed a tail-log backup and that your restore operation would result in losing any transactions currently contained within the transaction log that have not been backed up. SQL Server then aborts the database restore. If you are restoring to a previous point in time covered by the backup and have no interest in preserving the transactions within the log, then using the REPLACE option will override the message:

```
RESTORE DATABASE AdventureWorks
FROM DISK = 'AdventureWorks_Full.bak'
WITH RECOVERY, REPLACE
```

Checking Restore Integrity

In the "Backup" section, we covered the use of CHECKSUM for verifying the integrity of the data pages as part of the backup process. When performing a restore of a backup that used the CHECKSUM option, the default action is to re-verify the checksums on restore and, upon encountering any errors, to stop the restore process (STOP_ON_ERROR is the default option). If you want the restore to continue through any errors, specifying CONTINUE_AFTER_ERROR will continue with the restore and report which pages contain errors at the end of the process.

The following restore will verify the backup checksums and will continue through any errors it finds:

```
RESTORE DATABASE AdventureWorks
FROM DISK = 'AdventureWorks_Full.bak'
WITH RECOVERY, CHECKSUM, CONTINUE_AFTER_ERROR
```

It is possible to disable checksum verification by specifying NO_CHECKSUM. Also, if your backup did not use checksums and you specify that the restore should use the CHECKSUM feature, then the restore operation will fail and an error message will be displayed.

Restricted User

When restoring a database, you may not want users to be able to access the database as soon as you have brought it online, as you may need to perform other operations on the database. The RESTRICTED_USER option ensures that following a restore, only members of the sysadmin, db_owner, or dbcreator roles have access to the database:

```
RESTORE DATABASE AdventureWorks
FROM DISK = 'AdventureWorks_Full.bak'
WITH RECOVERY, RESTRICTED_USER
```

Restore Permissions

The fixed server role of sysadmin has all the required permissions to perform a database restore. For administrative users who are not sysadmins, consider making them members of the dbcreator fixed server role. This role is equivalent to granting the ALTER ANY DATABASE server permission and will allow a login to CREATE, DROP, and RESTORE any database on the instance. Logins having only the CREATE ANY DATABASE permission can create new databases and RESTORE and DROP only their own databases.

All of the metadata reading operations, such as RESTORE LABELONLY and RESTORE FILELISTONLY, require the CREATE DATABASE permission.

Restore History Tables

As with the backup history tables, all data relating to restore operations is stored within msdb.

Table 7-4 lists the restore tables with brief descriptions.

Using these tables, it is possible to write scripts to return details of any restore operations that have taken place on your database.

Following is a quick example of how to check what type of restore operations have taken place on the AdventureWorks database and when they were performed and by whom:

```
SELECT rh.restore_date, rh.restore_type, rh.user_name
FROM msdb.dbo.restorehistory rh
WHERE rh.destination_database_name = 'AdventureWorks'
ORDER BY rh.restore_history_id DESC
```

Table	Description
dbo.restorehistory	A row for each restore operation
dbo.restorefilegroup	A row per restored filegroup
dbo.restorefile	A row per restored file

Table 7-4   *Restore-Related History Tables*

This example query could be joined to other tables to provide full details of the restore such as the name of the file and whether or not it was restored to its original location.

Finally, when using tape devices, an additional DMV called sys.dm_io_backup_tapes is available in the master database and will show the status of each tape device.

Restoring System Databases

In the "Backup" section, we covered which of the system databases you should back up and which backup method to use. The restore process for most of the system databases does not differ from that of restoring a standard user database. To restore the model and msdb databases, you would use a standard database restore operation as we have shown in previous examples. A point to note when attempting to restore msdb is to make sure that the SQL Server Agent service is stopped; otherwise, it will hold open a connection to the database, preventing it from being restored.

Restoring the master database is the exception. The master database is fundamental to the operation of SQL Server and, as such, has a specific restore method. If SQL Server is still operational, to restore the master database the server must be started in single-user mode. Once SQL Server is up and running in single-user mode, a normal full restore and recovery of the database can take place.

If SQL Server has suffered a severe failure of the master database, and as such will not start, it is possible to perform a master database rebuild operation using the SQL Server setup media. The rebuild operation replaces the damaged master database and also the model and msdb databases. Once they are all rebuilt and SQL Server is able to start again, you can then attach the user databases or restore the databases using your last backup set.

Restoring Using SSMS

As you would expect, it is also possible to perform a restore without having to write any T-SQL code, by using SSMS. The Restore Database dialog box is accessed either by right-clicking the Databases node and selecting Restore Database (if the database you are restoring does not already exist) or by right-clicking the database of interest and selecting Tasks | Restore. Both methods take you to the same dialog box, although when you start from a database, the dialog box is pre-populated with information specific to that database, including the backup history as recorded in the msdb backup history tables.

Figure 7-9 shows the dialog box launched after selecting AdventureWorks as the database of interest. Instead of using the backup history stored in msdb, the dialog box shows that the 'AdventureWorks_Full.bak' file has been explicitly selected, and the dialog

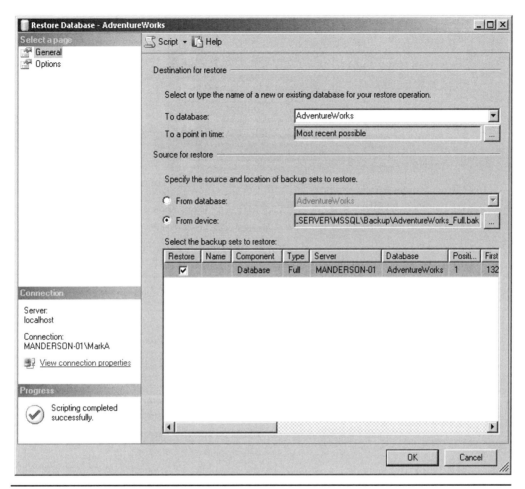

Figure 7-9   *Restore Database dialog box—General page*

box shows the results of a RESTORE HEADERONLY operation on the file. This dialog box allows you to restore over the original database or to specify a new database name. A point in time to recover to (if restoring transaction logs) can also be selected here.

The Options page, shown in Figure 7-10, should look familiar as it allows you to choose the recovery option (RECOVERY, NORECOVERY, or STANDBY) along with options such as moving the files to an alternate location (MOVE) by specifying a new path in the Restore As text box and overwriting existing databases (REPLACE) by checking the 'Overwrite existing database' check box.

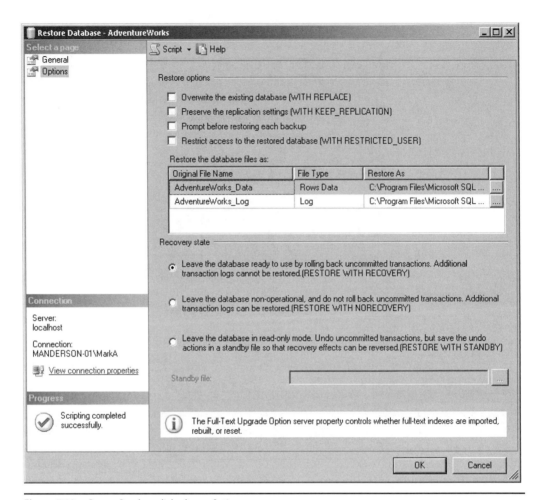

Figure 7-10 *Restore Database dialog box—Options page*

SSMS is great for performing simple restores and saves you time by not requiring you to write any code, but it does not allow you to perform the advanced restore scenarios such as partial restores and the STOPATMARK and STOPBEFOREMARK options.

ON THE JOB

For both backup and restore operations, SSMS is useful for performing quick, simple backup and restore operations, although when it comes to a topic like backup and recovery, which is fundamental to the DBA role, it is important to understand the details behind the operations the GUI is performing for you.

Example Restore Scenarios

In the "Backup" section, we covered two example backup scenarios; let's revisit them following a series of disasters!

Scenario 1: The Company Data Warehouse

It's Wednesday at 4:25 P.M. and a serious disk problem on the array holding your data warehouse database has resulted in the complete loss of the database data files. The rest of your server is up and running, and SQL Server is operational as its system databases were stored on a different disk array.

Your backup regime consisted of weekly full backups followed by daily differential backups that were taken following your load process. The RPO following a media failure is to recover the database to the point of the most recent data load. Therefore, to restore the database you need the full backup from the previous Sunday and the differential backup that was taken following the Tuesday evening data load. To complicate matters, the server hardware engineer is delayed and unable to get to the site to repair the faulty array, and you are under pressure to restore the database so that users can finish running their reports.

The array on which the database data files used to reside was 500GB in total, although the database only consumed 180GB of the available space. Luckily, your server had recently been provisioned with a 200GB disk array in preparation to hold a new data mart that was due to be deployed in the coming months. Therefore, you are able to use this new array to hold your database data file until the hardware engineer can repair your primary location.

You can perform the restore starting with the most recent full backup, which in this case is Sunday, January 17, 2010. Since you are going to be applying a differential backup to this following the full backup, you need to specify NORECOVERY. Additionally, you are moving the primary data file to a new drive array, so you use the MOVE option:

```
RESTORE DATABASE CorporateDW
FROM DISK = 'CorporateDW_17012010_Full.bak'
WITH NORECOVERY,
MOVE 'CorpDW_Data' TO 'J:\SQLData\CorpDW_Data.mdf'
GO

RESTORE DATABASE CorporateDW
FROM DISK = 'CorporateDW_19012010_Diff.bak'
WITH RECOVERY
GO
```

The database is now fully restored and up and running on the new disk array.

Scenario 2: The Line-of-Business Application

A recent unexpected cold spell of weather resulted in some water pipes in your building freezing and bursting. Unfortunately one of those pipes was situated above the data center where your database server is hosted. When the pipes began to thaw, water dripped from the ceiling tiles onto your server, causing a short circuit resulting in the electrical system cutting power to the server.

Following some emergency repairs to the pipes, you are able to get to the server to assess the damage. After a visual inspection you decide it is safe to switch on the server to assess the damage. The server switches on and boots into the operating system, but after you log into the system, it seems that SQL Server has failed to start. A check of the server error logs reveals that several disk arrays have been damaged, including the array which holds the system tempdb data and log files and the data files for your CRM application. The arrays holding your CRM transaction log files and other system databases have survived. The hardware engineer replaces the faulty drive arrays and you now need to recover the system.

The first problem is that SQL Server will not start unless it can create the tempdb database. Since tempdb is re-created every time SQL Server is started, you need to re-create the directory structure that tempdb resided in on the repaired drive arrays. A quick look at the Windows Server application error log reveals that SQL Server is trying to create the tempdb data files in 'E:\SQLData\' and the log in 'F:\SQLLogs\'. After creating these directories, you try to start SQL Server, SQL Server starts up, and you can assess the damage to the CRM database.

The CRM database fails to start, which, according to the SQL Server error log, is because it is unable to find the data files due to the array being replaced. The array on which the transaction log files resided is still intact. Therefore, before performing a restore, you should be able to back up the tail of the log. The outage to the system occurred at 12:43 P.M. and to get the database back online, you need last night's full backup, the differential backup from 12:00 P.M., and all log files up until 12:30 P.M. followed by the tail log:

```
--Backup the tail of the log
BACKUP LOG CRM
TO DISK = 'CRM_TailLog.trn'
WITH NO_TRUNCATE

--Restore full backup
RESTORE DATABASE CRM
FROM DISK = 'CRM_25012010_Full.bak'
WITH NORECOVERY
```

```
--Restore the differential from 12:00
RESTORE DATABASE CRM
FROM DISK = 'CRM_26012010_Diff_1200.bak'
WITH NORECOVERY

--Restore the Log files
RESTORE LOG CRM
FROM DISK = 'CRM_26012010_1215.trn'
WITH NORECOVERY

RESTORE LOG CRM
FROM DISK = 'CRM_26012010_1230.trn'
WITH NORECOVERY

--Restore the tail-log backup
RESTORE LOG CRM
FROM DISK = 'CRM_TailLog.trn'
WITH RECOVERY
```

The CRM database is now fully recovered to the point of the last committed transaction prior to the outage.

Further Reading

This chapter has covered the basics of backup and restore within SQL Server and has enough detail to get you started. In our examples, we have been looking at straightforward, "traditional" databases—the ones that contain tables, views, indexes, stored procedures, and all the other types of standard objects you would expect. It is important to note that using features such as replication, Service Broker, and full text indexes can have an impact on how you perform any backup and recovery. Also, as you may have come to realize while reading this chapter, your database design and layout can also have a profound effect on your backup and recovery strategy, and therefore understanding the SQL Server files and filegroup architecture will help you design a good backup and recovery strategy.

SQL Server Books Online contains details on how to use these features, and there are also many good books available on the subject.

Chapter 8

Performance Tuning and Optimization

In This Chapter

- ▶ **Windows Performance Monitor**
- ▶ **SQL Server Activity Monitor**
- ▶ **Dynamic Management Views**
- ▶ **SQL Server Profiler and SQL Trace**
- ▶ **Database Engine Tuning Advisor**
- ▶ **The Management Data Warehouse**

Performance monitoring, tuning, and optimization are regular activities for the Oracle DBA, and the SQL Server DBA is no different, except that in many cases, with smaller SQL Server solutions, the level of automation included with SQL Server means the solution "just runs." There will always come a point where some fault detection and diagnosis is required, especially when running the larger, mission-critical, Tier-1 solutions for which performance and uptime are critical. This chapter provides an introduction to the tools available in SQL Server for monitoring and tuning performance. The aim of this chapter is to provide you with the knowledge to develop a professional approach to SQL Server performance tuning using the built-in tools that are provided in the Windows Platform and within SQL Server at no extra cost.

In this chapter you will learn

▶   How to check the health of your SQL Server with Windows Performance Monitor

▶   Where to find out what each user connection is currently doing

▶   What DMVs are and which ones are most useful for troubleshooting performance

▶   How to use SQL Server Profiler and SQL Trace

▶   About tuning workloads with Database Engine Tuning Advisor

▶   About consolidating performance data collection using the management data warehouse

Windows Performance Monitor

Performance Monitor (Perfmon) is a Windows tool for capturing and displaying real-time performance data for the operating system and various applications, including SQL Server. Understanding how to use Performance Monitor will help you to narrow the scope of a performance issue to a specific server in a solution, a particular component, or an exact resource within a server. When used with an educated eye, Perfmon can yield quick, accurate results that can form partial or even complete evidence of the underlying cause of a performance issue.

Overview

Performance Monitor was first introduced in Windows NT 4.0 and was renamed System Monitor in Windows Server 2003, although the functionality that enabled you to capture data to a file for offline analysis kept the moniker of Performance Monitor.

In Windows Server 2008 (and clients from Vista onward), what we originally called Performance Monitor has become part of a tool called Windows Reliability and Performance Monitor, which has a much wider scope.

Reliability and Performance Monitor has three main components: Monitoring Tools, Data Collector Sets, and Reports. The Monitoring Tools consist of Performance Monitor, which is used for viewing real-time data, and Resource Monitor, which reports on system stability. Data Collector Sets are used for capturing data over an extended period for offline viewing. The final element which is Reports allow reports to be generated based on data collected by the Data Collector sets providing an easier method to consume and interpret the data collected. Moving forward as you collect more data it is possible to keep just the reports giving you access to performance data without having to retain the full data sets from the original Data Collectors. This chapter focuses on using Performance Monitor and Data Collector Sets in Windows Server 2008, although the principles of what to collect and what to look for are largely relevant regardless of the version of Windows that you're using.

Getting Started

You can launch Reliability and Performance Monitor by choosing Start | All Programs | Administrative Tools | Reliability and Performance Monitor or by simply searching for "perfmon" on the Start button and running the executable that is found.

Resource Overview

When you launch the tool, you'll be presented with the Resource Overview windows, similar to Figure 8-1, which shows a real-time view of the usage of the four key hardware elements: CPU, Disk, Network, and Memory. Each of these can be expanded to break down resource usage and performance by process, and even by file in the case of the Disk view.

Figure 8-2 shows an expanded Disk view on a live server running SQL Server showing I/O details by file and ordered by write throughput. It shows that the SQL Server process is responsible for most write activity during this snapshot, and the database files involved are data files for tempdb and transaction log files. The Response Time column shows the latency, in milliseconds, for I/O requests to each file and is an important metric for disk performance; it is discussed in the section "What to Look For" later in the chapter.

Real-Time Activity Monitoring with Performance Monitor

When you expand the Monitoring Tools and click on Performance Monitor, you're accessing the viewer for real-time server activity that provides you with instant data on the server's workload, performance, and resource consumption.

When you first load the tool, you'll see a line graph showing % Processor Time from the local machine. To add additional counters, right-click anywhere in the chart

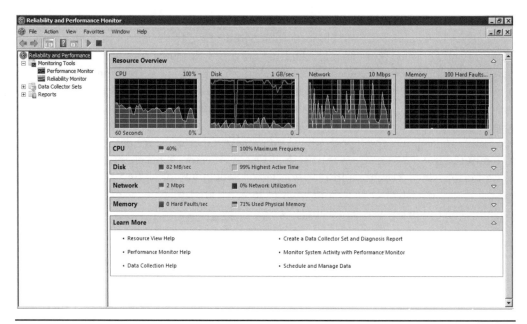

Figure 8-1 *The Resource Overview window in Reliability and Performance Monitor*

area and choose Add Counters. Figure 8-3 shows the Add Counters dialog box, which shows counters from the Local computer being added in this case. In the box below that, the list of counters under the Memory object has been expanded and the Available MBytes counter has been selected and added.

There are lots of counters available to add, even on a basic installation of Windows, and new counters are installed when you set up new applications or roles on a system. For example, every SQL Server instance installed will add its own set of counters to the available list.

Disk		2 MB/sec		3% Highest Active Time				
Image	PID	File		Read (B/min)	Write (B/min) ▾	IO Priority	Response Time (ms)
sqlservr.exe	1388	R:\Data\tempdev4.ndf		14,120,862	26,618,452	Normal	2
sqlservr.exe	1388	R:\Data\tempdev3.ndf		13,083,313	23,966,166	Normal	1
sqlservr.exe	1388	R:\Data\tempdb.mdf		12,549,381	23,112,959	Normal	1
sqlservr.exe	1388	R:\Data\tempdev2.mdf		10,648,686	22,209,705	Normal	1
sqlservr.exe	1388	S:\MSSQL10.B2\MSSQL\TranLog\templog.ldf		0	6,465,249	Normal	2
sqlservr.exe	1388	S:\MSSQL10.B2\MSSQL\TranLog\B2.ldf		61,440	1,332,473	Normal	1
sqlservr.exe	1388	S:\MSSQL10.B2\MSSQL\TranLog\distribution.LDF		0	1,036,360	Normal	1

Figure 8-2 *Expanded Disk view*

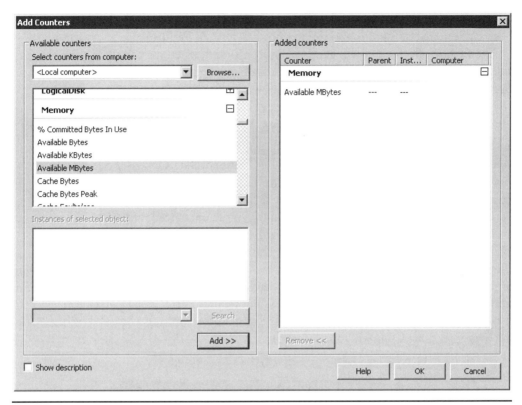

Figure 8-3   *The Add Counters dialog box in Performance Monitor*

After you've added a few counters (recommendations are given in the "What to Look For" section coming up), you can use the highlight feature by selecting a counter and pressing CTRL-H to make the line graph for that counter stand out. This is very useful when you're watching many counters simultaneously and want to focus on just one.

Another nice feature (only available in Windows Server 2008 and later) is the ability to scale selected counters to make the graph easier to read. When comparing counters on the same chart, they very often have vastly different scales, which makes viewing difficult. You can access this feature by selecting one or more counters, right-clicking, and selecting Scale Selected Counters.

Data Collector Sets

Data Collector Sets are groups of data-gathering tools that may include kernel tracing, performance logs, and configuration data. Windows Server 2008 has three preconfigured Data Collector Sets, including a System Performance collector, which consists of a Kernel trace and Performance Monitor log. To use a preconfigured Data Collector Set, expand Data Collector Sets, System, and then right-click System Performance and select Start.

The Data Collector Set will run for 60 seconds and, when it's complete, you'll be able to view a preconfigured report of the data by navigating to Reports | System | System Performance. A sample report is shown in Figure 8-4.

User Defined Data Collector Sets

In addition to using the System Data Collector Sets you've just seen, you can create your own customized versions known as User Defined Data Collector Sets. If you view data only in real time, identifying patterns and trends in performance that may be influencing a problem condition is very difficult. A much better way is to capture performance data over a fixed period and analyze the data afterward.

To create a User Defined Data Collector Set, expand Data Collector Sets, right-click User Defined, select New, and select Data Collector Set. A wizard will take you through the creation process. The first choice will be to create from an existing template or manually. There are three templates available, Basic, System Diagnostics, and System Performance, that you can use to start from, but from a SQL Server perspective, it's easier just to select 'Create manually' and add all the counters yourself (see the upcoming section "Counters to Capture").

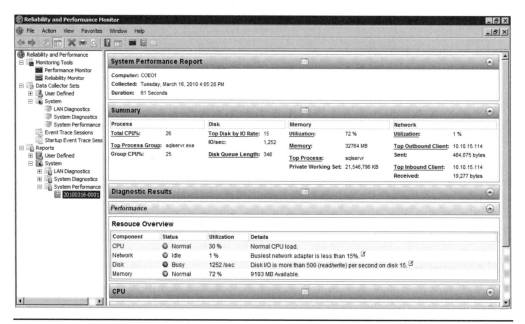

Figure 8-4 *System Performance report*

The Impact of Data Capture on the Server

It is impossible to monitor something without affecting it in some way, so the goal is to minimize the overhead of data capture wherever possible. Fortunately, Performance Monitor is a very lightweight tool in terms of overhead because the counters themselves are constantly being updated by the relevant application whether you're monitoring them or not. The overhead from capturing therefore primarily comes from writing the data to disk during data collection.

The perceived impact of running Performance Monitor on a live server will be more acute on a server that already has resource constraints, and there are a number of factors to consider when trying to minimize the overhead.

The sample interval controls the frequency at which the data is captured. The default is 15 seconds, which is quite reasonable for data captures running for a few hours, but you might want to shorten it to 5 seconds if you're running a short capture (at the expense of additional overhead) or make it longer (maybe 60 seconds) to capture data over tens of hours or even days.

Capturing a large number of counters can also affect the size of the data collection on very busy servers, so you may be able to reduce overhead by being more selective with your chosen counters.

You should also consider the disk to which you're writing the log file and ensure that, at the very least, you're not using a drive that has any file on it that SQL Server uses. Otherwise, your disk performance measurements will be affected by the data collection.

Counters to Capture

For a general-purpose baseline of a server running SQL Server, all counters from the following counter groups will provide everything you need to profile the performance of a server:

IP	SQL Server:Access Methods
LogicalDisk	SQL Server:Backup Device
Memory	SQL Server:Buffer Manager
NBT Connection	SQL Server:Buffer Node
Network Interface	SQL Server:Buffer Partition
Objects	SQL Server:Databases
PhysicalDisk	SQL Server:General Statistics
Process	SQL Server:Latches
Processor	SQL Server:Locks

SQL Server:Memory Manager	SQL Server:Replication Merge
SQL Server:Plan Cache	SQL Server:Replication Snapshot
SQL Server:Replication Agents	SQL Server:Resource Pool Stats
SQL Server:Replication Disto	SQL Server:SQL Statistics
SQL Server:Replication Logreader	SQL Server:Workload Group Stats

The groups prefixed with 'SQL Server' refer to a "default" instance of SQL Server. When using "named" instances, the counter groups will be prefixed with MSSQL$<*instance name*>. You should capture all counters from all instances for a complete server baseline. See Chapter 2 for a description of default versus named instances.

You can remove groups if you know they are not relevant to a server (like replication groups, for example) or choose specific counters within the groups to further filter the collection, but the preceding list provides a solid, all-purpose data collection that is ideal for establishing a baseline and for analyzing results (see the section "Going Beyond the Built-in Functionality" later in the chapter for coverage of a tool to help with this).

Figure 8-5 shows a screenshot of the Create New Data Collector Set wizard with the previously mentioned counter groups added and the default sample size of 15 seconds set. We would expect this data collection to be no more than a few hundred megabytes in size after a few hours.

Oracle DBA Q&A

Q: Slightly off topic, but I have run Oracle on Windows before and have never seen any performance counters for Oracle listed in the available counters. Does Oracle just not supply them?

A: Oracle does ship Performance Monitor counters for its database when installed on Windows, but the counters are not installed by default like SQL Server counters are. They have to be registered and configured on the machine before they will appear in the Performance Counters list. Search for "Performance Monitor" in the Oracle documentation or visit http://download.oracle.com/docs/cd/B28359_01/win.111/b32010/monitor.htm, which takes you to the "Monitoring a Database on Windows" documentation.

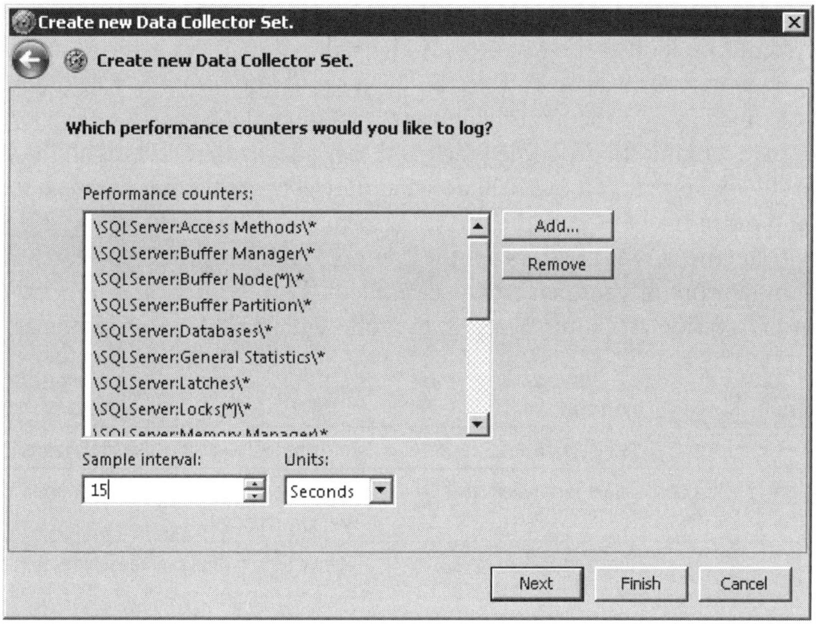

Figure 8-5   *Adding counters to a User Defined Data Collector Set*

What to Look For

When reviewing the performance of a server running SQL Server, it's a good idea to first look at the utilization of the hardware resources on the server, the core of which are memory, storage, and CPU.

   If you can imagine those three resources in a stack starting with memory, you want to start at the top of the stack, ruling out issues as you work your way down, because resource problems further up the stack can cause issues further down the stack.

   For example, under low memory conditions you will be likely to see an increase in storage activity as the system page file starts to be used as a temporary store for committed memory. This can also drive up CPU utilization, as Windows needs to manage the process of paging.

   What you might notice first is that the system is running with high CPU utilization or that the storage system is running slower than normal. Don't be tempted to add more CPUs or faster disks on this evidence alone because, in this example, you'll be missing the underlying problem, which is a lack of physical memory.

It is for this reason that when you troubleshoot performance problems or review an existing system, you look at the resources in the order of memory, storage, and then CPU. As you work your way down the stack, you should be trying to rule out resource problems as much as find the underlying cause.

What you're looking for are some quick and easy checks that will highlight any obvious problems so that you can drill down and investigate further or rule out a resource and move further down the stack. Performance Monitor is ideal for this and, starting with memory, what follows are the counters and thresholds you can use to rule a resource into or out of your performance problem. The counters and target thresholds covered in this section are summarized in the following table for easy reference.

Counter Group	Counter	Target
Memory	Available MBytes	Sustained value greater than 100MB at minimum
SQLServer:Memory Manager	Target Server Memory (KB)	Should be very close to or the same as the Total Server Memory counter
	Total Server Memory (KB)	Should be very close to or the same as the Target Server Memory counter
Buffer Manager	Page Life Expectancy	Greater than 300 seconds for transactional systems
LogicalDisk	Avg. Disk sec/Transfer	Less than 0.020, ideally less than 0.010
Processor	% Processor Time	Less than 90%
	% Privileged Time	Less than 30% of % Processor Time
	% User Time	Greater than 70% of % Processor Time
Process	% Processor Time:sqlservr	High percentage of % Processor Time on a server dedicated to running SQL Server

Memory/Available MBytes

This counter indicates the amount of free physical memory available for Windows. You should aim to keep this at a few hundred megabytes on a busy system, to be sure that there's always enough memory for any unexpected requirements.

If you really want to squeeze every bit of performance out of the server, however, then keeping this counter consistently above 100MB will suffice as long as the server is stable and consistent.

If this counter is consistently low, then you should lower the SQL Server setting for Max Server Memory or review other potential memory consumers on the server.

SQLServer:Memory Manager/Target Server Memory (KB)

This counter represents the amount of memory that SQL Server wants to have. It directly relates to the Max Server Memory setting, if one has been configured, or the equivalent dynamic value if you've left SQL Server to manage memory.

This counter doesn't tell you much on its own, but when you compare it to the next counter you'll understand why it's useful.

SQLServer:Memory Manager/Total Server Memory (KB)

This counter represents the amount of memory that SQL Server actually has. It is closely related to the previous counter and you should compare the two to see whether there is a significant difference between what SQL Server wants and what SQL Server has.

As long as SQL Server has been running for a while or has been busy enough to grow the memory usage, then you should expect these values to be very close if not identical.

If SQL Server doesn't have all the memory that it wants, then make a note that there could be external memory pressure or the Max Server Memory setting might just be too high.

Buffer Manager: Page Life Expectancy

The Page Life Expectancy (PLE) counter was introduced in one of the later Service Packs for SQL Server 2000 and is a great indicator of memory pressure within SQL Server. It will show you the amount of time, in seconds, that SQL Server expects to be able to keep unreferenced pages in cache. If SQL Server doesn't have enough memory to process its workload, then pages will be dropped from cache much quicker than when SQL Server has lots of memory.

On an OLTP system, Microsoft recommends that PLE is at least 300 seconds, which means that SQL Server expects to be able to keep unreferenced pages cached for 5 minutes.

In a data warehousing (DW) environment, it's a bit harder to be so prescriptive because you expect many large queries, which will frequently be causing cache flushes, and that's normal. However, PLE can still be useful as an indicator of how well SQL Server is coping with its current memory allocation, and even in a DW environment you should expect to be averaging a PLE of at least 100 seconds.

Another counter used often to indicate memory pressure before Page Life Expectancy was introduced was Buffer Cache Hit Ratio, which shows the percentage of page requests that were found in cache rather than having to be read from disk. This sounds like a great counter, but the reality is that most servers will always report a very high cache hit ratio, which doesn't fluctuate enough under memory pressure to be of much use. Also, as in Oracle, a high Cache Hit Ratio can indicate poorly tuned queries that are performing an unnecessarily large number of logical I/Os against cached database pages, which can drive the Cache Hit Ratio very close to 100 percent even if workloads are suffering from significant I/O waits.

LogicalDisk:Avg. Disk sec/Transfer

Moving on to look at storage performance, this counter is a measure of the amount of time, in seconds, that it takes Windows to make a transfer to or from disk, which provides a useful high-level indicator of storage performance.

For disks that contain SQL Server database files, you want your disk transfers to be consistently under 20 ms (0.020 second) and ideally under 10 ms.

If you're not getting these performance levels, then you can break down this measurement further to see the split between read and writes by checking these two counters:

- ▶ LogicalDisk:Avg. Disk sec/Read
- ▶ LogicalDisk:Avg. Disk sec/Write

If there's a significant difference between read and write performance, you can then check the controller cache and the RAID level to see if there's anything you can do to rebalance the cache or recommend a faster RAID type.

Processor:% Processor Time

Your main concern when looking at CPU usage is the split between user and kernel mode CPU utilization and the amount of CPU time being consumed by the SQL Server service.

To start with, this counter is just a measure of how busy your CPUs are. Whether or not this value is bad will depend on a lot of factors. Generally, a consistent value >90 percent is considered to be bad, as the server is working very hard and there is very little room for additional workload.

However, if you had just deployed new hardware and saw a consistent value of 70 percent, you might also consider that bad because it might not provide enough headroom for growth.

All you're concerned about at this stage is to find out how busy the CPUs are. Then, you're going to check what they are working on.

Processor:% Privileged Time

This counter will tell you how much of the % Processor Time is spent handling kernel mode operations, which is useful to know because it's a measure of the amount of time Windows is spending managing its resources rather than running applications.

Microsoft guidelines indicate a threshold of 30 percent for this counter, so anything over that could be a problem. A classic example of a problem causing this counter to be high was introduced at the start of this chapter: a low memory condition.

When Windows is low on memory, data will start to be paged out to disk, and the CPU will be working in kernel/privileged mode to handle this. The Processor: % Privileged Time counter will show an increase in value, so whenever you see this you should also check for memory pressure (which is why we review memory first).

Processor:% User Time

This counter, along with Processor:% Privileged Time, makes up the total % Processor Time. Whereas Privileged Time represents time working on kernel mode operations, User Time represents time spent working on applications (like SQL Server), which is what you want the CPU to be spending most of its time on.

Microsoft guidelines indicate that 70 percent or greater is a good value for this counter.

Process:% Processor Time:sqlservr

When you measure CPU utilization, observe high % Processor Time, and see most of that time is spent running user mode applications, it's a good idea to check to see if SQL Server is using the bulk of processor time. You don't want to dive straight into the guts of SQL Server before confirming that's where the problems lies, and this counter is how you can check the CPU utilization for the SQL Server process itself.

There is no threshold for this counter, really. What you're looking for when troubleshooting high CPU utilization is that SQL Server is using more than any other process. If it isn't, then you should be troubleshooting the process that is using the most CPU time.

Going Beyond the Built-in Functionality

Windows Reliability and Performance Monitor is a great tool for capturing performance data, but analyzing it is much harder, particularly when you have an obscure performance problem. To help you analyze Performance Monitor logs more easily, you can download a free open source tool written by engineers at Microsoft, called Performance and Analysis of Logs, from http://codeplex.com/pal. It not only analyzes the data for you but also provides a full report with charts highlighting performance problems and full descriptions of the counters and thresholds involved.

SQL Server Activity Monitor

Activity Monitor provides a quick and easy way to discover who is doing what on a SQL Server instance and how busy the instance is. Activity Monitor was completely rewritten and redesigned for SQL Server 2008 and provides far more features and information than was possible in its previous incarnation. You access the tool by right-clicking the instance name in SQL Server Management Studio and selecting Activity Monitor, which opens the Overview panel, as shown in Figure 8-6.

You're immediately presented with four charts:

▶ **% Processor Time**   Plots the amount of CPU being used by the SQL Server instance that you're connected to, which is particularly useful under high CPU usage conditions to confirm that it is actually SQL Server that's responsible.

▶ **Waiting Tasks**   Plots the number of tasks that are currently waiting for something. This is good to give you a heads-up that something is going wrong.

▶ **Database I/O**   Plots the I/O throughput for all your data and transaction log files, which indicates how much load is on your underlying storage.

▶ **Batch Requests/sec**   Plots the number of batch requests that SQL Server is processing every second, which shows how busy SQL Server is.

Beneath the charts you'll notice four expandable sections, explained in turn next.

Processes

The Processes panel is the place that you most commonly visit once you start using Activity Monitor. It presents a view of all current connections with lots of details, a few of which can be seen in Figure 8-7.

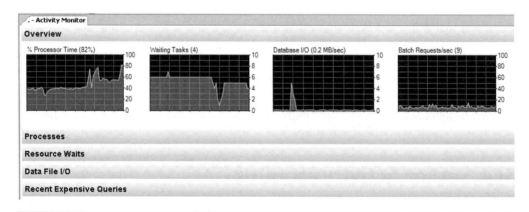

Figure 8-6   *SQL Server Activity Monitor Overview panel*

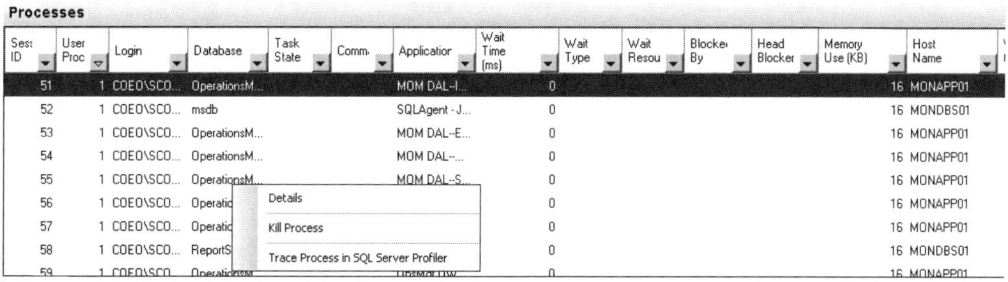

Figure 8-7   *SQL Server Activity Monitor, Processes panel*

The following are the three most useful uses for this view:

▶ You can filter on any column by clicking the drop-down arrow for that column and selecting an option. For instance, you can quickly restrict your view to one particular database, login, or computer name. You can also use it to view all connections that are currently experiencing one particular wait type, are being blocked by another process, or are at the head of a blocking chain. Powerful stuff!

▶ Once you've identified the sessions that interest you, you can quickly kill a troublesome connection by right-clicking the connection in Activity Monitor and selecting Kill Process. But before you do that, you might want to see what the process is working on. To do that, you right-click and select Details to see the last T-SQL batch that was run on that connection, helping you to target the area of the application that caused a problem.

▶ If viewing the last T-SQL batch doesn't give you enough detail, then you can right-click a session and select Trace Process in SQL Server Profiler to launch Profiler using the standard template but with an automatic filter on the session that you're interested in.

Resource Waits

The Resource Waits panel provides aggregated information for current waits by wait type and also shows the cumulative wait time for each wait type. You can read more about SQL Server waits and wait types in the upcoming section "Dynamic Management Views."

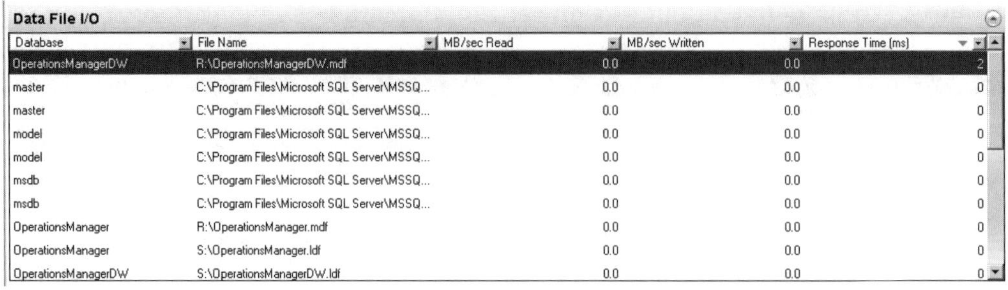

Figure 8-8 *SQL Server Activity Monitor, Data File I/O panel*

Data File I/O

The Data File I/O panel of Activity Monitor provides an excellent view of I/O load and performance that can be ordered by database and even filename. You can see an example snapshot of this in Figure 8-8.

This view makes it very easy to determine which files in which databases currently have the heaviest I/O requirements and, most importantly, the I/O response times for those files, which indicates the latency between SQL Server making an I/O request and actually receiving it.

The response times should be less than 5 ms for a transaction log file and less than 10 ms for a data file on a system that is performing well; anything consistently over 20 ms should be considered unacceptable if you're having perceived performance problems.

Recent Expensive Queries

Finally, the Recent Expensive Queries panel shows you the most expensive queries run in the past 30 seconds. You can view a sample of this in Figure 8-9, which also shows the right-click menu that provides the ability to see the full query text and even to pull the execution plan used out of cache and view it in a graphical format.

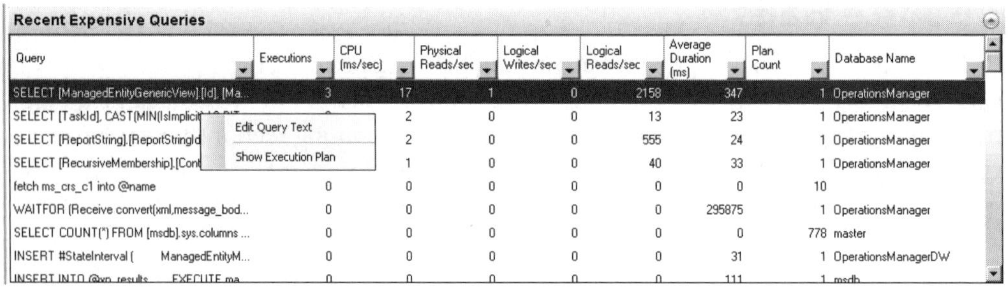

Figure 8-9 *SQL Server Activity Monitor, Recent Expensive Queries panel*

Dynamic Management Views

Dynamic management views (DMVs) were introduced in SQL Server 2005 and provide much greater visibility into the workings of SQL Server than was possible with prior versions of the product. They are basically just views on top of the system tables and internal memory structures, but abstracting away from the physical implementation allows Microsoft to provide a massive amount of useful information through them. They are the SQL Server equivalent of V$ views in Oracle.

The standard naming convention starts with sys.dm_, which indicates that it's a DMV (there are also dynamic management functions, but DMV is still the collective term in popular use), followed by the area about which the DMV provides information. For example, sys.dm_os_ for SQLOS, sys.dm_db_ for database, and sys.dm_exec_ for query execution.

The last part of the name describes the actual content accessible within the view; sys.dm_db_missing_index_details and sys.dm_os_waiting_tasks are both examples that you'll come across in this section.

What Is SQL Server Waiting For?

One of the most useful strategies available for performance tuning in SQL Server is the analysis of SQL Server "waits," and to understand why, you first need to understand some fundamental concepts about how SQL Server manages the scheduling and execution of work.

To recap on the architecture that was discussed in Chapter 2, Microsoft SQL Server only runs on Microsoft Windows, and Windows is designed as an all-purpose operating system, which means that it's not optimized for any particular scenario because it has to provide good performance for a very broad range of applications.

The approach that Windows takes to scheduling and execution of work is to provide each request with a fixed time slice within which to execute on a CPU. This time slice is called a *quantum*, and each request will be scheduled to have one or more quantums in which to run and then they will be stopped to allow something else to run. This allocation of time slices is necessary to provide the illusion of multitasking because a single CPU can only ever do one thing at a time. The way Windows manages the scheduling of work is referred to as *preemptive scheduling*.

Back in the very early days of SQL Server, the Windows scheduler was used by SQL Server to schedule work requests, but the development team soon found that a general-purpose preemptive scheduler wasn't going to provide the level of performance that the product needed so they decided to build SQL Server its very own scheduler.

User Mode Scheduler (UMS) was introduced in SQL Server 6.5 and, in SQL Server 2005, became a part of what we now call the SQLOS. This new scheduling method for

SQL Server is called a *cooperative scheduler* because the execution of work is governed by the fact that workers will voluntarily yield their time on the CPU whenever they have to *wait* for something other than the CPU.

Wait time is dead time, so if you can see what you're waiting for and for how long and then aggregate that across every other worker thread, then you've got a list of the bottlenecks that are impacting SQL Server's performance.

SQLOS uses schedulers to manage the execution of workers, which in turn are assigned to execute a user request. The number of schedulers defaults to the number of logical CPUs in the server because a single CPU can only ever execute one thing at a time, which means that it only needs a single scheduler.

Within a scheduler, the workers assigned to it can be in one of four states: Init, Running, Runnable, and Suspended. Init is used when initializing a worker, but it's the other three states that we're interested in to help understand how waits work.

Only one worker can be in the Running state in a scheduler at a time, and that is the worker that is currently using the CPU. All other workers waiting for time on the CPU are queued in the Runnable state, and any worker waiting for anything other than the CPU is in the Suspended state. Whenever a worker is in the Suspended state, it is considered to be "waiting" and is assigned a "wait type." This is illustrated in Figure 8-10.

In the diagram you can see that session_id 55 is currently executing, four sessions are waiting on resources (which you'll see descriptions of later in this chapter), and two

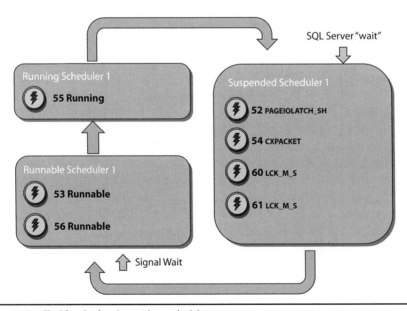

Figure 8-10 *The lifecycle of workers within a scheduler*

sessions are in the Runnable queue. The Runnable queue contains sessions that are waiting to be scheduled some CPU time, so this represents a pure wait on the CPU, which we can translate into CPU pressure. Time in the Runnable queue is measured as "signal wait" time, and is charged to the wait type that the session was in just before it became Runnable.

All waits in SQL Server are categorized into wait types and can be grouped into three areas:

- ▶ **Resource waits**   Occur when the requested resource is unavailable
- ▶ **Queue waits**   Occur when a worker is idle, waiting for work
- ▶ **External waits**   Occur when waiting for an external event

Resource waits, which include I/O, locking, and memory, tend to be the most common and provide the most actionable information.

All this talk of waiting makes it sound like a horrendous thing to find on your system. In fact, it's perfectly normal and expected to see waits. This is how SQL Server scales so efficiently. You're really looking for unexpected waits and large wait times when troubleshooting performance.

The important thing about waits is that they relate directly to users' perceived performance. The total elapsed time of a query is CPU time plus wait time; so if users are complaining about slowness, the wait stats can break down the waits. This is critical because you might look at a system and see high CPU utilization and slow disk response, but 90 percent of the users' waits might be lock waits. Without breaking down the waits by wait type and focusing on the largest waits, you risk optimizing the wrong thing. You might spend a lot of time and money reducing the physical I/O waits by 50 percent, but if physical I/O waits only make up 10 percent of the user waits, then that can only produce a 5 percent improvement in user wait time!

Viewing Wait Information

There are three DMVs available that allow you to view waits directly. You can use sys.dm_exec_requests to view information at the session level, sys.dm_os_waiting_tasks to view information at the task/worker level, and sys.dm_os_wait_stats to see an aggregation of all the wait types and times since the last SQL Server service restart.

sys.dm_exec_requests   This DMV shows all the waiting and blocking information that you would have queried the sysprocesses system table for in SQL Server 2000. However, both sysprocesses and sys.dm_exec_requests are based at the session level, and a better view of performance can be obtained by looking at the task level. System processes can run tasks without a session, so they wouldn't be represented here, and parallel queries are harder to troubleshoot when only a single wait is shown at the session level. Following is a sample script that shows wait information and the T-SQL currently running in each session where available:

```
SELECT    er.session_id,
          er.database_id,
          er.command,
          er.blocking_session_id,
          er.wait_type,
          er.wait_time,
          er.wait_resource,
          st.text
FROM sys.dm_exec_requests er
OUTER APPLY sys.dm_exec_sql_text(er.sql_handle) st
```

sys.dm_os_waiting_tasks   sys.dm_os_waiting_tasks lists all tasks that are currently waiting on something and is the most accurate for viewing current waits. It contains information to identify a task, an associated session, details of the wait, and blocking tasks as well. However, a task only has an entry for as long as it's waiting, so sys.dm_os_waiting_tasks tends to be used for interactive investigations rather than for monitoring purposes. Here is a sample script that shows all the information for waiting tasks with the T-SQL currently running where there is a session_id available:

```
SELECT    wt.*,
          st.text
FROM sys.dm_os_waiting_tasks wt LEFT JOIN sys.dm_exec_requests er
ON wt.waiting_task_address = er.task_address
OUTER APPLY sys.dm_exec_sql_text(er.sql_handle) st
ORDER BY wt.session_id
```

sys.dm_os_wait_stats   This DMV is an aggregation of all wait times from all queries since SQL Server started and is ideal for monitoring and server-wide tuning. You can reset the wait statistics by running DBCC sqlperf ('sys.dm_os_wait_stats',clear) from SQL Server Management Studio. The following sample script provides a way to check for CPU pressure by comparing signal wait times (CPU wait) with resource wait times:

```
Select signalWaitTimeMs=sum(signal_wait_time_ms)
    ,'%signal waits' = cast(100.0 * sum(signal_wait_time_ms) /
                        sum (wait_time_ms) as numeric(20,2))
```

```
,resourceWaitTimeMs=sum(wait_time_ms - signal_wait_time_ms)
,'%resource waits'= cast(100.0 * sum(wait_time_ms -
                          signal_wait_time_ms) / sum (wait_time_ms)
                          as numeric(20,2))
from sys.dm_os_wait_stats
```

If you want to clear the historical data before you run the workload to monitor, don't forget you can run DBCC sqlperf ('sys.dm_os_wait_stats',clear) to clear out data that you're not interested in and give you a fairly clean measurement.

Common or Noteworthy Wait Types

The following wait types are worthy of mention because of their regularity in a system or because their meaning should be understood. For descriptions of more of the wait types, search in SQL Server Books Online for sys.dm_os_wait_stats.

▶ **CXPACKET**   This wait type means that the task is waiting on the synchronization of a parallel execution and is very often the reason for an "all processors running at 100%" scenario. When you see this wait type, it means you have some big queries running that you may want to try to optimize.

▶ **I/O_COMPLETION, ASYNC_I/O_COMPLETION**   These wait types occur when waiting for non–data page I/Os to complete, and you may see them during a long-running I/O-bound operation such as BACKUP. These wait types can also indicate a disk bottleneck.

▶ **LCK_M_***   This wait type indicates a wait to gain a lock on a resource and is one of the reasons why monitoring waits is so effective for performance tuning; it doesn't just highlight resource constraints, but will provide evidence of blocking locks as well.

▶ **LAZYWRITER_SLEEP**   When the lazywriter process is inactive it is considered to be in a sleep state. LAZYWRITER_SLEEP is the amount of time that it has been sitting in this state. It should not be considered in a performance profile.

▶ **PAGEIOLATCH_***   A PAGEIOLATCH is a measure of the time it takes to retrieve a data page from disk into memory and is one of the most likely waits you'll see on a system with a strained I/O subsystem.

▶ **RESOURCE_SEMAPHORE**   All hash, sort, bulk copy, and index creation operations require space in what is called workspace memory, which is dynamically managed between 25 percent and 75 percent of SQL Server's memory. This wait represents time spent pending a memory grant in workspace memory and should be correlated with the Memory Grants Pending Perfmon counter. A consistent non-zero value indicates memory pressure and the wait time tells you how much time you are losing.

▶ **RESOURCE_SEMAPHORE_QUERY_COMPILE** This wait type is set when SQL Server throttles the number of concurrent compiles in the system to limit the amount of memory being used by the optimizer in response to too many compilation requests. If you see this wait type, either reduce the number of compilations by parameterizing queries so that the query plans can be reused in cache or review scenarios that would cause frequent recompiles.

▶ **SLEEP_BPOOL_FLUSH** In SQL Server 2005 and later, checkpoint operations are throttled to prevent them from overloading the disk subsystem, and waiting for this operation is represented by this wait type.

▶ **SOS_SCHEDULER_YIELD** This wait type occurs when a task voluntarily yields processor time and waits to be scheduled again. This cooperative scheduling model was explained earlier in this section. High waits here indicate CPU pressure, in which case further evidence should be obtained by totaling the signal waits (signal_wait_time_ms column in sys.dm_os_waiting_tasks or sys.dm_os_wait_stats).

▶ **SQLTRACE_BUFFER_FLUSH** When the system is waiting for a SQL Trace buffer to be written to disk, a wait state of SQLTRACE_BUFFER_FLUSH is recorded. You will see this on most servers in SQL Server 2005 because a rolling 100MB trace runs permanently by default in the background and is used by the management reports in SQL Server Management Studio. You can normally discount this wait as an ever present feature.

▶ **WAITFOR** A WAITFOR wait state is the resulting wait after issuing the WAITFOR T-SQL command. It is a deliberately instigated wait and shouldn't be considered a performance issue unless its use is a mistake.

▶ **WRITELOG** This also indicates a disk problem, as it's a wait writing to the transaction log file.

Wait Types in SQL Server 2008

SQL Server waits are a great way to troubleshoot performance problems, and Microsoft thinks so too, because it introduced around 250 extra wait types in SQL Server 2008 over what was available in SQL Server 2005.

The most interesting ones were the new PREEMPTIVE wait types. Any code that needs to execute outside SQL Server has to go outside the control of SQL Server's cooperative scheduler (as you've already read) and will use the preemptive scheduling model used by Windows.

Typically these external executions would be very difficult to troubleshoot using wait types because they would either come under a single wait like OLEDB, for example, or wouldn't be tracked at all, like Windows-level functions. The level of detail provided by the wait types even covers areas such as the latency of SQL Server communicating with a Windows domain controller through the PREEMPTIVE_OS_ AUTHENTICATIONOPS wait type. In earlier versions of SQL Server, this type of issue would have been extremely difficult to detect and diagnose.

Another common wait that was difficult to diagnose in SQL Server prior to SQL Server 2008 was the creation or expansion of data files. In particular, database auto-growth, which wouldn't be logged as a wait at all in SQL Server 2005, with SQL Server 2008 we now have the PREEMPTIVE_OS_WRITEFILEGATHER wait type. Being able to track this wait type can help identify the problems associated with the database not being appropriately sized.

Viewing I/O Latency by Database File

In the "Windows Performance Monitor" section, you read about the value of measuring disk latency to assess I/O performance. The counter for this is Avg. Disk sec/Transfer, which provides a Windows view of storage performance, but you can also drill down into SQL Server to look at storage performance more accurately.

The sys.dm_io_virtual_file_stats DMV allows you to view the I/O details for all your database files, and by using the following script, you can view the read and write latency that SQL Server encountered on the files themselves:

```
SELECT  DB_NAME(database_id) AS 'Database Name',
        file_id,
        io_stall_read_ms / num_of_reads AS 'Avg Read Transfer/ms',
        io_stall_write_ms / num_of_writes AS 'Avg Write Transfer/ms'
FROM    sys.dm_io_virtual_file_stats(-1, -1)
WHERE   num_of_reads > 0
        AND num_of_writes > 0
```

Here is sample output from the preceding script run on a SQL Server instance hosting databases for SQL Server Reporting Services and Microsoft Operations Manager:

Database Name	file_id	Avg Read Transfer/ms	Avg Write Transfer/ms
Master	1	7	2
Master	2	2	1
Tempdb	1	0	2
Tempdb	2	0	1

(Continued)

Database Name	file_id	Avg Read Transfer/ms	Avg Write Transfer/ms
Tempdb	3	0	2
Model	1	6	1
Model	2	3	0
Msdb	1	24	1
Msdb	2	5	0
ReportServer$SQL01	1	9	1
ReportServer$SQL01	2	1	0
ReportServer$SQL01TempDB	1	9	0
ReportServer$SQL01TempDB	2	1	0
OperationsManager	1	12	2
OperationsManager	2	6	0
OperationsManagerDW	1	76	137
OperationsManagerDW	2	3	1

Entries with a file_id of 1 show the primary data file for that database, and entries with a file_id of 2 show the transaction log. The only potential cause for concern in these results is the performance of the OperationsManagerDW database primary main data file; with read latency of 76 ms and write latency of 137 ms, it's well outside our target of 20 ms.

In this situation, the first thing to do is to find out who uses this database and ask them if they perceive any performance problems; you don't want to spend time optimizing something when the users don't need it to be faster. Also, the fact that the database is a data warehouse suggests that it will be subject to a large amount of writes during data loads and a large amount of reads when reports are being run. The high latency in this case may be normal because of the heavy I/O pattern and not a cause for concern at all.

Finding Missing Indexes

Whenever you execute a query, the optimizer (whose job is to find a good execution plan for your query) will analyze the best indexes for the query. If the indexes don't exist, then the optimizer will have to use a less efficient execution plan. However, in SQL Server 2005 and later, the information about these "missing" indexes is also stored and is accessible using DMVs and within SQL Server execution plans.

Missing indexes can be viewed by joining together the following DMVs:

- ▶ sys.dm_db_missing_index_details
- ▶ sys.dm_db_missing_index_group_stats
- ▶ sys.dm_db_missing_index_groups
- ▶ sys.dm_db_missing_index_columns

Here is a sample query that produces CREATE INDEX statements from the preceding DMVs and displays the expected performance improvement so that you can target the missing indexes that will have the biggest positive impact to query performance:

```
SELECT
gs.avg_total_user_cost * gs.avg_user_impact *
(gs.user_seeks + gs.user_scans) AS improvement_measure ,
'CREATE INDEX idx_MissingIndex ON '
+ d.statement
+ ' (' + ISNULL (d.equality_columns,'')
+ CASE WHEN d.equality_columns IS NOT NULL
AND d.inequality_columns IS NOT NULL THEN ',' ELSE '' END + ISNULL
(d.inequality_columns, '')
+ ')'
+ ISNULL (' INCLUDE (' + d.included_columns + ')', '')
AS create_index_statement
FROM sys.dm_db_missing_index_groups g
INNER JOIN sys.dm_db_missing_index_group_stats gs ON
gs.group_handle = g.index_group_handle
INNER JOIN sys.dm_db_missing_index_details d ON
g.index_handle = d.index_handle
ORDER BY gs.avg_total_user_cost * gs.avg_user_impact * (gs.user_seeks +
gs.user_scans) DESC
```

In addition to the missing-index DMVs introduced in SQL Server 2005, SQL Server 2008 also displays missing-index information within the graphical execution plan, as shown in Figure 8-11.

Although the missing-index feature in SQL Server is without doubt a very welcome feature, it should also be used with caution. You shouldn't blindly apply all missing indexes but instead should try to justify each index by looking at the query that you think it will fix.

If you go ahead and create all the missing indexes SQL Server reports, you'll likely end up with lots of infrequently used indexes and/or overlapping indexes that create unnecessary overhead for SQL Server to maintain.

A better approach is to find your top ten worst-performing queries and check the missing-index DMVs to see if there are any recommendations on the tables used by those queries. Once you've established that, you can check your filtered recommendations for indexes with overlapping requirements that you may be able to merge together.

Finally, you should check the execution plans to see where the recommended indexes should help before applying them to the database and testing the results.

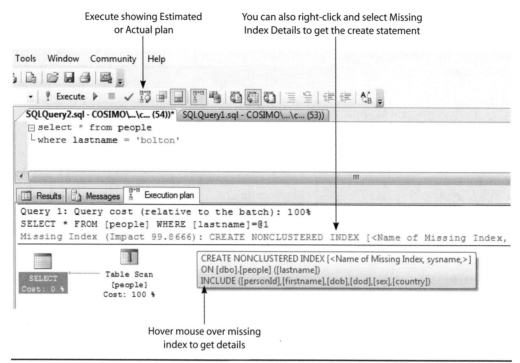

Figure 8-11 *Missing-index details in an execution plan*

Information in the DMVs is reset every time SQL Server is restarted, so you should also make sure that your missing-indexes data includes a representative business cycle to help you get an accurate view.

SQL Server Profiler and SQL Trace

SQL Server Profiler is a GUI tool built around a technology called SQL Trace, which provides access to 180 events that you can collect data on to help you peak inside SQL Server and see what the engine is doing. In this section you'll read about how to reduce the impact of tracing and how to analyze the results, but first you'll learn about the event hierarchy in order to help frame the rest of the section.

Event Hierarchy: Categories, Classes, and Columns

SQL Trace events are grouped logically into *event categories*, some examples of which are Performance, TSQL, and Errors and Warnings. In all, there are 21 different event categories in SQL Server 2008.

The events themselves are bound to applicable columns to create an *event class*. When you set up a SQL Trace, you select the event classes and columns within it that you want to capture.

For example, if you want to see how often sort operations spill into tempdb, you would choose all applicable columns for the Sort Warnings event class in the Errors and Warnings event category.

Figure 8-12 shows the Trace Properties window in SQL Server Profiler with the Sort Warnings event class selected with all available columns; note the check boxes to show all events and all columns.

Knowing what to capture in Profiler is made a bit easier through the use of built-in templates that you can choose from when you define a new trace. The templates contain a preselected list of event classes and columns applicable to what you're trying to achieve. For example, the TSQL_Locks template contains event classes to capture information on lock timeouts, deadlocks, and lock escalations as well as the start and completion events for statements within stored procedures and T-SQL batches so that you can correlate the lock events to what was being executed.

How to Reduce the Impact of Tracing

The impact that your tracing has on the server that you're monitoring will vary depending on exactly what event classes and columns you're capturing. However, the biggest difference you can make to reduce the overhead is not to use Profiler.

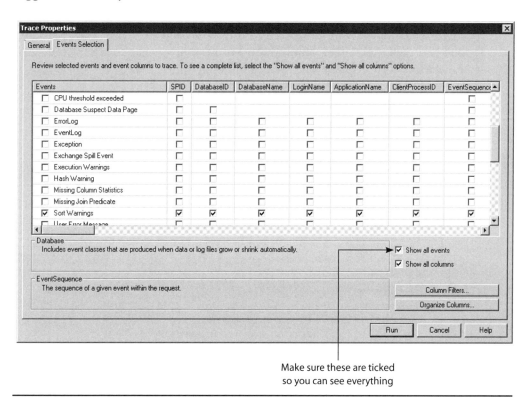

Figure 8-12 *SQL Server Profiler Trace Properties window*

Profiler runs as a process separate from the SQL Server process, and transferring each event to Profiler takes time and resources, which can lead to severe performance degradation of any live applications and sometimes missing events as SQL Server tries to keep up. This is called *client-side tracing*.

The alternative is to run the SQL Trace stored procedures directly, which keeps the tracing within the SQL Server process and reduces the overhead required to capture a trace. This is called *server-side tracing*.

After reading that you might wonder why we have Profiler at all, if it's so bad, but there are still a few scenarios where Profiler comes in very handy:

▶ **Running quick traces with very few events** Setting up and running a trace using the tracing stored procedures isn't a quick operation, so sometimes Profiler can be useful to quickly get some information, as long as you have plenty of free resources on the server. Still, be wary of using it on important production environments.

▶ **Analyzing SQL traces** After you've collected your server-side trace, you can copy it to your desktop and open it in Profiler. See the next section, "Analyzing SQL Traces."

▶ **Creating server-side traces, the easy way** The major drawback to server-side tracing is the complexity in setting it up, but you can actually define your trace in Profiler and then export that definition to a script that you can then run. You can see the correct export option selected in Profiler in Figure 8-13.

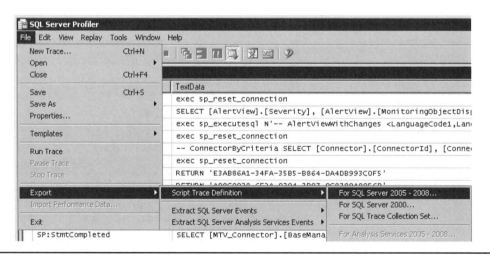

Figure 8-13 *Export SQL Server Profiler Trace definition*

Running a Server-Side Trace

Figure 8-14 shows an annotated image of an export of the Tuning trace template definition from Profiler, which is all you need to run a server-side trace. However, there are a couple of edits you need to make before you start.

First of all, the default max file size is 5MB. This isn't very much at all, so you'll nearly always want to change this to be a reasonable size that you can still copy between machines easily and maybe load into Profiler for viewing. Either 256MB or 512MB is a common value here.

Next, you'll want to set the destination for your trace file. This means specifying the drive letter, folders, and filename (the .trc extension is automatically added); for example, C:\test\mytrace.

Leaving the rest as is and executing the script will run a SQL trace until the output file reaches @maxfilesize and then it will stop. However, defining your data capture simply by the size of the output file isn't that useful, as you'll typically want to wait for your problem condition to occur or to trace for a fixed duration. This is where enabling TRACE_FILE_ROLLOVER comes in handy; instead of stopping when the output file gets to @maxfilesize, SQL Server just starts a new file and keeps going.

Enabling TRACE_FILE_ROLLOVER then creates the problem of exactly how to stop the trace other than by running out of disk space. When you run a server-side trace, it doesn't run in the context of your query window, so stopping it isn't as simple as just stopping your query. You need to run sp_trace_setstatus, which is already in the script and used to start the trace.

When the trace is started by running the script, the trace_id is output to the screen. You'll need to know the trace_id to be able to stop it, so make a note of it. If you lose it, run this code to see the details of all currently running traces to get the trace_id of your trace:

```
SELECT  *
FROM    sys.fn_trace_getinfo(0)
```

When you have the trace_id, you can use sp_trace_setstatus to stop the trace and then delete the definition from the server. Here is the syntax:

```
EXEC sp_trace_setstatus @traceid,@status
```

Use your trace_id for @traceid, and @status can be 0 to stop the trace, 1 to start it, or 2 to delete the trace definition from the server.

```
/****************************************************/
/* Created by: SQL Server 2008 Profiler          */
/* Date: 30/04/2010  14:44:03       */
/****************************************************/


-- Create a Queue
declare @rc int
declare @TraceID int
declare @maxfilesize bigint                        Set the size in MB
set @maxfilesize = 5  ◄──────────────────────────  for each trace file

-- Please replace the text InsertFileNameHere, with an appropriate
-- filename prefixed by a path, e.g., c:\MyFolder\MyTrace. The .trc extension
-- will be appended to the filename automatically. If you are writing from   Change this value to
-- remote server to local drive, please use UNC path and make sure server has   2 to enable
-- write access to your network share                                       TRACE_FILE_ROLLOVER
                                            │
                                            ▼
exec @rc = sp_trace_create @TraceID output, 0, N'InsertFileNameHere', @maxfilesize, NULL
if (@rc != 0) goto error            │
                                     │
-- Client side File and Table cannot be scripted

-- Set the events                     Set your trace file
declare @on bit                       destination here
set @on = 1
exec sp_trace_setevent @TraceID, 10, 1, @on
exec sp_trace_setevent @TraceID, 10, 3, @on
exec sp_trace_setevent @TraceID, 10, 11, @on
exec sp_trace_setevent @TraceID, 10, 35, @on
exec sp_trace_setevent @TraceID, 10, 12, @on
exec sp_trace_setevent @TraceID, 10, 13, @on
exec sp_trace_setevent @TraceID, 45, 1, @on
exec sp_trace_setevent @TraceID, 45, 3, @on
exec sp_trace_setevent @TraceID, 45, 11, @on
exec sp_trace_setevent @TraceID, 45, 35, @on
exec sp_trace_setevent @TraceID, 45, 12, @on
exec sp_trace_setevent @TraceID, 45, 28, @on
exec sp_trace_setevent @TraceID, 45, 13, @on
exec sp_trace_setevent @TraceID, 12, 1, @on
exec sp_trace_setevent @TraceID, 12, 3, @on
exec sp_trace_setevent @TraceID, 12, 11, @on
exec sp_trace_setevent @TraceID, 12, 35, @on
exec sp_trace_setevent @TraceID, 12, 12, @on
exec sp_trace_setevent @TraceID, 12, 13, @on


-- Set the Filters
declare @intfilter int
declare @bigintfilter bigint
                                            Set this to 0 to stop
-- Set the trace status to start            the trace and then 2 to
exec sp_trace_setstatus @TraceID, 1 ◄────── delete the definition
                                            from the server
-- display trace id for future references
select TraceID=@TraceID
goto finish

error:
select ErrorCode=@rc

finish:
go
```

Figure 8-14 *A server-side trace created from Profiler*

ON THE JOB

Here are a great bunch of tips for running SQL Server traces:

▶ *The less you capture, the less impact there will be on the server, so only capture event classes that are necessary.*

▶ *Avoid very frequent events like Lock:Acquired and Lock:Released. There will be an overwhelming number of them even on servers with light usage.*

▶ *Avoid statement-level events like SQL:StmtStarting and SP:StmtCompleted unless you definitely need them. They are expensive to capture and can be very frequent on busy servers.*

▶ *Completed events like RPC:Completed have nearly all the same information as the corresponding Starting events plus all the runtime details, so you can reduce your trace load by capturing just the completed events.*

▶ *The Show Plan Statistics events provide a great level of information but have a much larger CPU cost than most other events, so use them with care.*

▶ *Use column filters to reduce the I/O cost and trace file size at the expense of CPU overhead.*

▶ *Always trace to a locally attached disk that doesn't contain any files that SQL Server uses.*

▶ *If you must use Profiler for data capture, use it locally from the server, not from a remote computer.*

▶ *Test, test, test. Run your traces in a test environment or during a quiet period before running a quick test during a peak period so you know what to expect when you plan your data collection.*

Analyzing SQL Traces

Deciding what events to collect, how to collect them, and for how long is just the first challenge. Let's assume now that you have expertly gathered the information that contains everything you need. How do you analyze it?

Using SQL Server Profiler for Analysis

Your first port of call for analyzing a trace may well be Profiler, and for good reason. Profiler makes reading a trace easy and has a number of features that can help with your analysis.

First of all, filters. It's unlikely that you'll have a nice, clean, short trace to scroll through when looking to troubleshoot a problem, so you're going to want to filter it several different ways as you try to narrow down the problem. The column filters work exactly the same way as when you set them up for a data collection, only this time you're filtering captured data on your own machine, so you don't need to worry about any CPU overhead.

There's also a nice feature that allows you to load a Performance Monitor log into Profiler and to step through it inline with the trace data. You can see an example of this in Figure 8-15.

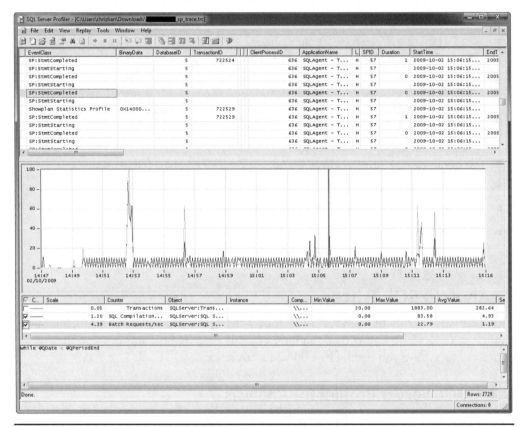

Figure 8-15 *Viewing a Perfmon log with your trace data in SQL Server Profiler*

Things to Note when Viewing Traces in Profiler

▶ There are two important things you should be aware of when viewing traces in SQL Profiler. Use the EventSequence column to check the exact sequence in which SQL Server executed everything in the trace. Hundreds of events can occur within the same millisecond, and only the EventSequence column can be relied upon to show the order in which things happened.

▶ Profiler displays the data in the Duration column in milliseconds even though the data is captured in microseconds. You need to be aware of this if you use other tools than Profiler to analyze the data, as the granularity isn't made clear.

Using Additional Tools

There a several freely available tools that can help you to take your troubleshooting skills further, including:

▶ **Perf Stats Script** This script is a wrapper for a tool called SQLDIAG, which in turn collects Perfmon logs and server-side traces along with other configuration details. The script itself adds to SQLDIAG's features by incorporating a custom data collection that collects information from many more DMVs, including those related to wait stats. Microsoft Customer Support Services uses a version of this script to collect data during customer support requests. It takes a lot of hassle out of creating server-side traces because it's driven entirely by an XML configuration file in which you simply enable the events that you want collected.

▶ **SQLNexus** This tool analyzes the data collected by the perfstats scripts and produces SQL Server Reporting Services reports on wait stats, blocking chains, and aggregated trace data, among other things. It uses Microsoft's ReadTrace tool to analyze traces, which is part of the freely available RML Utilities download.

Figure 8-16 shows an output report from SQLNexus detailing the top ten queries by Total CPU, Total Duration, Total Reads, and Total Writes aggregated across an entire SQL Trace file or files.

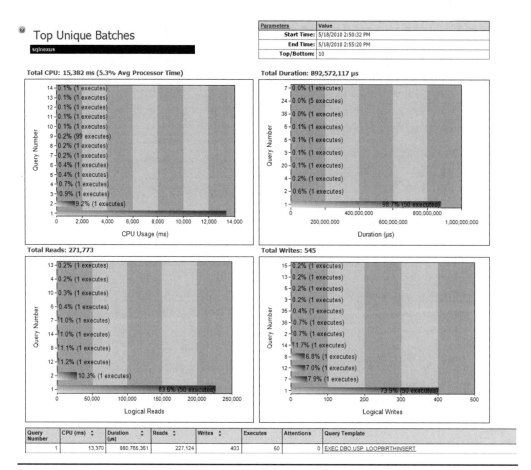

Figure 8-16 *SQLNexus Top Unique Batches report*

Database Engine Tuning Advisor

Database Engine Tuning Advisor (DTA) is a very useful tool for finding performance tuning recommendations based on specific workloads without having to be a SQL Server expert. You can provide the workload to be analyzed as a SQL Server Profiler trace or as a SQL Server script, which allows you to either check for recommendations based on a workload that's representative of a busy period on the server or to narrow it down to a few key pieces of T-SQL that you know are expensive to run.

DTA will generate recommendations on the best mix of indexes, indexed views, and statistics for the workload, whether or not table partitioning would help, and what effects you can expect to achieve if you apply the recommendations. You can see an example report from a DTA analysis in Figure 8-17, which shows a query cost improvement of 99 percent if the highlighted index and multicolumn statistics are created (the auto-create statistics database option only creates single-column statistics).

The tool achieves this by creating a range of different indexes, statistics, views, partition functions, and schemes and uses the optimizer to see what effect they would have on the execution plans required for your workload. From this information, DTA can report on any recommendations that produce performance improvements as well as what level of improvement to expect. To save on the overhead of analyzing lots of real indexes, DTA uses what are called *hypothetical indexes*, which are actually just SQL Server statistics. All the other objects, though, are real.

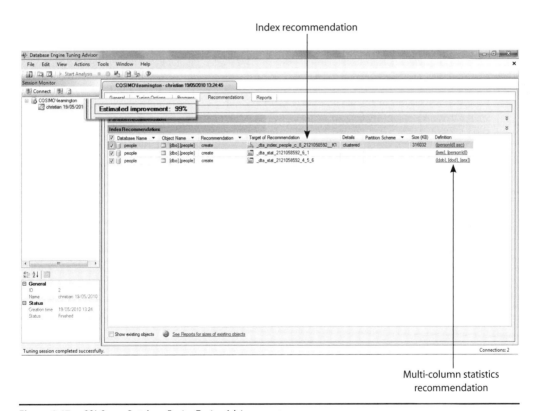

Figure 8-17   *SQL Server Database Engine Tuning Advisor report*

ON THE JOB

As with many things that remove all the "hard work," you should use DTA with caution, so here are a few tips to help you use the tool safely and effectively:

▶ **Never use it in a live production environment**   *The process of creating and dropping all the objects required to test the performance can take time and requires locks that may block users of the system for quite some time. Stopping DTA when it's causing a problem is very difficult and will leave many of the temporary objects in place unless it's stopped cleanly.*

▶ **Do not blindly apply recommendations**   *Always try to understand why the recommendations were made and what they hope to fix. You'll have a far better experience if you use the tool to clarify your understanding rather than using it to replace any thought or logic on your part.*

▶ **Rename any recommendations**   *Applying the recommendations "as is" will create objects with names prefixed with "_DTA" that aren't very user friendly. Applying the recommendations with a standard naming convention helps to show that you've looked at what's being applied rather than blindly applying recommendations and also helps to differentiate your new indexes and other recommendations from what existed before and from any hypothetical indexes or other objects that may be hanging around from a forcefully aborted DTA session.*

▶ **Remove objects left over from an aborted DTA session**   *DTA will always clean up after itself if left to run its course, but occasionally you'll find that people didn't follow tip #1, ran DTA in production, and then had to forcefully kill everything DTA was doing. When this happens, you can be left with a few unnecessary objects. Although the optimizer will ignore them, it's always better to clean them up.*

All the objects that DTA uses during processing will be prefixed by _DTA, so if you follow rule #3, then you'll be able to spot these objects quickly and simply drop them. There is no difference between the statistics, views, partition functions, and partition schemes that DTA uses during processing and the real objects, so knowing which objects should be there is very hard if you don't follow rule #3.

Indexes are slightly different because DTA's use of hypothetical indexes makes these easier to pick out.

Assuming you normally rename any recommendations, you can use this query to find any objects left over from an aborted DTA session:

```
SELECT   [name] AS 'DTA Leftovers'
FROM     sys.objects
WHERE    [name] LIKE ( '_DTA_%' )
```

You can also find just the hypothetical indexes by querying sys.indexes:

```
SELECT   OBJECT_NAME(object_id) AS 'Prent Object',
         name AS 'Hypothetical Index',
         *
FROM     sys.indexes
WHERE    is_hypothetical = 1
```

The Management Data Warehouse

One of the limitations with dynamic management views is that the data accessible through them does not persist through restarts of the SQL Server service. While the data is very useful for systems that have been running for a long time, getting a consistent view of performance data across multiple servers with different levels of uptime requires a solution that goes beyond the capabilities of the native DMVs.

The Management Data Warehouse (MDW) is a centralized repository for performance data from SQL Servers throughout an organization and provides an out-of-the-box solution for anyone responsible for SQL Server performance and capacity planning.

The MDW is populated by data collectors, three of which are provided out of the box, and you can configure your own if required. There is also a customizable reporting solution that is ready to use with minimal effort.

What MDW Doesn't Do

You cannot configure alerts or acceptable performance thresholds for the collectors or reports, so the MDW can't be used as a monitoring solution. It also doesn't provide a real-time view of performance data (which you can get from DMVs anyway) as it's intended to provide a longer-term view of server performance.

The MDW also doesn't allow for an overview of all the servers that data is being collected on, which would be useful for consolidation projects in large SQL Server estates, but it still provides very useful historical performance data on a server-by-server basis with very little setup time.

Finally, the MDW can only collect data from instances of SQL Server 2008 and greater, so it doesn't provide a complete solution for environments containing previous versions of SQL Server, although there are third-party products available that can provide this if required.

MDW Architecture

Logically, the MDW is built around three components:

- ▶ Data collection sets
- ▶ Data warehouse
- ▶ Reports

SQL Server Agent Jobs (covered in Chapter 10) are used to schedule data collection, SQL Server Integration Services (SSIS, covered in Chapter 11) is used to load data into the relational data warehouse, and SQL Server Reporting Services (SSRS) drives the reports.

Data Collection Sets

Data Collection Sets are broken down into two categories: System Data Collections and Custom Data Collections. System Data Collections are preconfigured as part of the MDW setup, and Custom Data Collections are the user-defined sets that you configure yourself.

There are three System Data Collections: Disk Usage, Query Statistics, and Server Activity. Each has one or more collection items that define what is collected.

The *Disk Usage* collection has two collection items, one for data files and one for transaction log files. Both of these collection items use the Generic T-SQL collector type to gather details about the data and log file sizes. By default, they gather the data every 60 seconds, upload it to the data warehouse every 6 hours, and retain it in the data warehouse for 730 days.

The *Query Statistics* collection has a single collection item to gather information on the most expensive queries. It runs every 10 seconds, uploads to the data warehouse every 15 minutes, and retains data from the past 14 days.

The *Server Activity* collection set has two collection items. One gathers data from the following DMVs:

- ▶ sys.dm_io_virtual_file_stats
- ▶ sys.dm_os_latch_stats
- ▶ sys.dm_os_memory_nodes
- ▶ sys.dm_os_process_memory
- ▶ sys.dm_os_schedulers
- ▶ sys.dm_waiting_tasks

The other item gathers data from Performance Monitor counters like Memory, Logical Disk, and Processor for the server as well as counters like Buffer Manager\Page Life Expectancy and SQL Statistics\Batch Requests/sec from SQL Server.

If you want to create your own custom data collections, there are four collection types to choose from:

- ▶ **T-SQL Query** Runs a query and stores the result
- ▶ **SQL Trace** Collects data from a SQL trace (see the earlier section "SQL Server Profiler and SQL Trace")

- ▶ **Performance Counters**   Collects data from Performance Monitor counters
- ▶ **Query Activity**   Captures the query text and execution plan for specific queries

For each Data Collection Set, you'll find two SQL Server Agent Jobs on each of the servers to be monitored, one for data collection and one for data upload to the data warehouse.

Data Warehouse

The data warehouse is the database repository for all the data being captured from your monitored SQL Server instances. It is a normal SQL Server database that needs to be managed in the same way as any other database.

The data warehouse is purged by a SQL Server Agent Job called mdw_purge_data[MDW], which is installed by default and removes expired data from the data warehouse based on the retention policy set in each collection set. It is scheduled to run daily at 2 A.M., which can be changed or even run manually on an ad hoc basis, although this won't reduce the size of an overinflated data warehouse because only expired data is removed, and that is controlled by the configuration of the collection set.

Reports

The MDW reports are SQL Server Reporting Services (SSRS) reports that run against the data collected and stored in the data warehouse. Three reports are provided as standard to provide reporting for the three system data collectors that are set up by default:

- ▶ Server Activity History
- ▶ Disk Usage Summary
- ▶ Query Statistics History

The Server Activity History report, shown in Figure 8-18, shows resource utilization charts for CPU, memory, disk I/O throughput, and network I/O throughput. It also shows the distribution of wait types and duration, to help you identify server bottlenecks, and general activity details like logins/sec, batches/sec, and compilations/sec. The charts also provide the ability to click through for more-granular details on what makes up that measurement. For example, clicking on the Memory Usage chart takes you to another chart that shows the Working Set and Page Reads/sec.

The Disk Usage Summary report, shown in Figure 8-19, shows data and log file growth for all the databases on the reported instance. It includes a trend line to help highlight databases that are growing quickly and the average growth statistics in megabytes per day, which is useful to help with planning your future storage requirements.

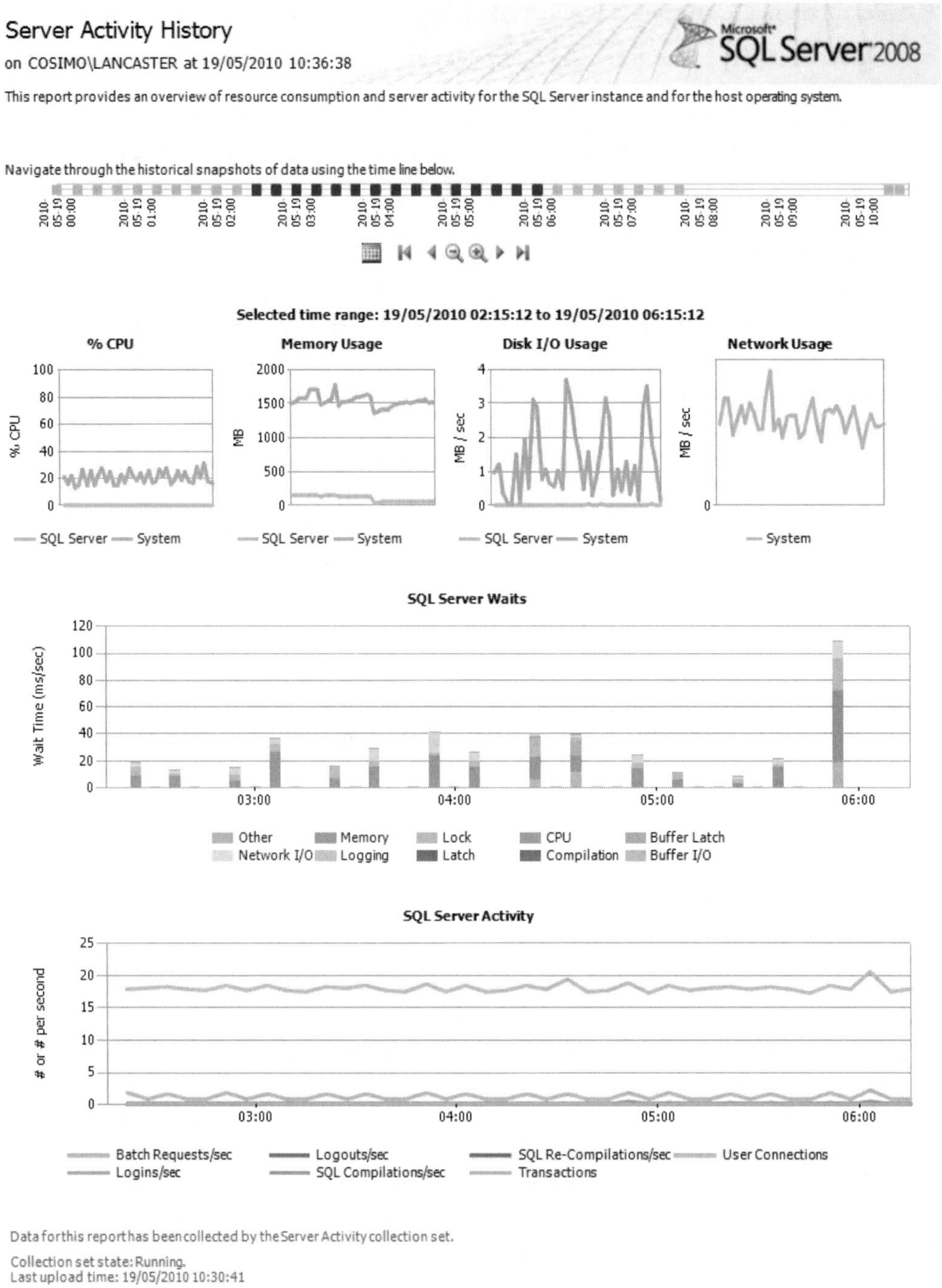

Server Activity History

on COSIMO\LANCASTER at 19/05/2010 10:36:38

This report provides an overview of resource consumption and server activity for the SQL Server instance and for the host operating system.

Navigate through the historical snapshots of data using the time line below.

Selected time range: 19/05/2010 02:15:12 to 19/05/2010 06:15:12

Data for this report has been collected by the Server Activity collection set.

Collection set state: Running.
Last upload time: 19/05/2010 10:30:41

Figure 8-18   *The Server Activity History report*

Disk Usage Collection Set
on COSIMO\LANCASTER at 5/19/2010 7:43:36 AM

This report provides an overview of the disk space used for all databases on the server and growth trends for the data file and the log file for each database for the last 3 collection points between 5/18/2010 11:57:05 PM and 5/19/2010 6:00:33 AM.

Database Name ⇕	Database				Log			
	Start Size (MB) ⇕	Trend	Current Size (MB) ⇕	Average Growth (MB/Day)	Start Size (MB) ⇕	Trend	Current Size (MB) ⇕	Average Growth (MB/Day)
master	4.00		4.00	0	1.25		1.25	0
model	2.25		2.25	0	0.75		0.75	0
msdb	15.50		17.06	1.563	6.75		6.75	0
People	60.50		120.50	60	172.81		593.81	421
PeopleWaitsDemo	500.00		500.00	0	5,121.00		5,121.00	0
tempdb	1,544.00		1,544.00	0	1.00		4.00	3
TempDBDemo	3.00		3.00	0	1.00		1.00	0

Figure 8-19 *The Disk Usage Summary report*

Finally, the Query Statistics History report, shown in Figure 8-20, shows the top ten worst-performing queries and allows you to click through to view more details about the execution statistics for a particular query, including the execution plan.

Oracle DBA Q&A

Q: We decided to use the Spotlight and Foglight products from Quest Software to do our performance monitoring and alerting instead of using the Oracle toolset. Are there similar third-party tools for SQL Server?

A: There are many third-party monitoring and alerting tools available on the market. Taking your example of Spotlight and Foglight, SQL Server versions of these products are available from Quest; therefore, if you want to use the same approach for monitoring SQL Server as you already do for Oracle, then you can do so. This also expands into the management tools; if you use Quest's Toad for management, you can also use the SQL Server version of Toad.

Query Statistics History

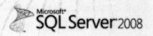

on COSIMO\LANCASTER at 19/05/2010 10:33:23

This report provides an overview of query execution statistics for the SQL Server instance.

Navigate through the historical snapshots of data using the time line below.

Selected time range: 19/05/2010 00:30:08 to 19/05/2010 00:45:08

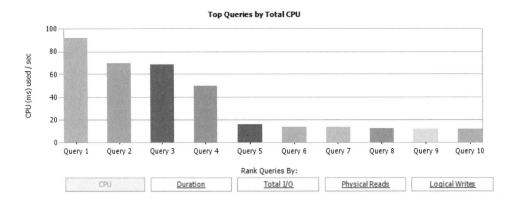

Query #	Query	Executions / min	CPU ms / sec	Total Duration (sec)	Physical Reads / sec	Logical Writes / sec
1	UPDATE people SET lastname = (SELECT lastnam...	200	92	51	0	-1
2	INSERT #boys (personId) SELECT TOP 500 person...	200	69	63	0	0
3	INSERT #girls (personId) SELECT TOP 500 perso...	200	69	63	0	0
4	INSERT people (firstname,lastname, dob, sex)...	7,039	50	114	0	15

Figure 8-20 *The Query Statistics History report*

Chapter 9

High Availability and Disaster Recovery

In This Chapter

- ▶ **Evaluating Business Continuity Solutions**
- ▶ **Cold Standby Solutions**
- ▶ **Warm Standby Solutions**
- ▶ **Hot Standby Solutions**

When we think about high availability and disaster recovery (HA/DR) technologies in Oracle, we tend to think about the two main ones: Real Application Clusters (RAC) and Data Guard. RAC provides clustering capabilities around a single database, and Data Guard provides the ability to create multiple standby databases. This chapter will help you to understand the available HA/ DR technologies that are included out of the box with the Enterprise and Datacenter editions of SQL Server to enable business continuity. In this chapter, we cover

- ▶ How to evaluate business continuity solutions
- ▶ Cold standby solutions
- ▶ Warm standby solutions
- ▶ Hot standby solutions

ON THE JOB

HA/DR capabilities are also included with SQL Server Standard Edition, but just as with Oracle standard edition, there are some limitations to be aware of, such as the number of nodes that can participate in a cluster, the available operating modes (for example, synchronous/asynchronous), and the restriction of certain features to single-threaded operation. Therefore, choose your edition carefully when building a solution that requires some form of HA/DR.

Evaluating Business Continuity Solutions

Microsoft SQL Server has many features out of the box that can be used in part or in whole for high availability and disaster recovery. As you are probably aware, there are many requirements to analyze before you reach the solution that meets your needs. For example:

- ▶ Automatic or manual detection of errors
- ▶ Automatic or manual failover
- ▶ The amount of data loss you can accept (recovery point objective)
- ▶ The time it takes to fail over (recovery time objective)
- ▶ The number of failures you need to be able to survive
- ▶ Granularity: instance, database, table, page, row
- ▶ Cost: hardware, network, additional management
- ▶ Complexity

At a minimum, you need to understand your requirements and the capabilities of each technology to meet specific recovery point objectives (RPOs) and recovery time objectives (RTOs):

- ▶ **RPO requirement**   The amount of acceptable data loss that the solution must provide. For example, if your RPO is 15 minutes, you must be able to restore all the data up to 15 minutes prior to a system failure. The RPO is not concerned with how long it takes to get your data back, only how much of it you can get back.

- ▶ **RTO requirement**   The maximum amount of time that can elapse between a system failure and restoration of the service.

Understanding your RPO and RTO requirements is a critical part of business continuity planning and will help you to choose the most appropriate technology to meet your needs.

Note that although SQL Server provides many solutions for HA/DR out of the box, there are many solutions available that enhance or replace SQL Server features in an HA/DR solution. For example, SAN hardware-level replication technology that integrates with SQL Server can be used for cross-site disaster recovery, and virtualization solutions like Windows Server Hyper-V can move workloads between servers in case of a hardware failure.

Cold Standby Solutions

A *cold standby solution* in SQL Server is one that requires a restore to bring your data back online. It is a perfectly valid solution if your RTO requirements are very flexible and your RPO is reasonable enough to implement with a scheduled backup.

Even if your requirements are greater than those provided by a backup and restore strategy, you should always incorporate a backup solution into your design regardless of which high-availability technology you choose. So, restoring to a cold standby forms the baseline for recoverability in any environment. You can read about SQL Server backups in Chapter 7.

Warm Standby Solutions

A *warm standby solution* is one where most if not all of the data required to bring the service back online to meet your RPO is already restored or available on a server waiting to be used. Warm standby solutions might not have failure detection and do not have automatic failover; they require manual intervention to fail over, to redirect users, or to finalize the recovery process. The technologies available in SQL Server to support warm standby include log shipping, database mirroring (high-performance mode), and SQL Server Replication.

Log Shipping

In Chapter 7 you read about SQL Server's backup and recovery models and learned about full backups and transaction log backups. Log shipping at a fundamental level is simply the continual process of copying and restoring transaction log backups taken of a database to another server until you need to use it. For example, if you want to log ship from Server A to Server B, you would need to

1. Restore a full backup of the database WITH NORECOVERY from Server A to Server B
2. Take transaction log backups of the database on Server A and copy them to Server B
3. Restore each transaction log backup onto Server B WITH NORECOVERY

This is illustrated in Figure 9-1. The restores are made WITH NORECOVERY to enable subsequent transaction log backups to be restored, and when you need to use the

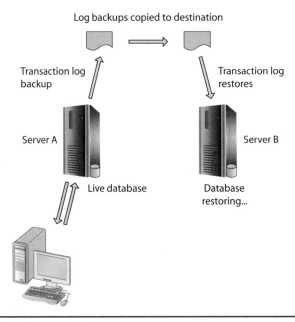

Figure 9-1   *Fundamental log shipping design*

database, you restore the last transaction log backup WITH RECOVERY or simply execute this code to force the recovery:

```
RESTORE DATABASE [database name] WITH RECOVERY
```

This basic model of log shipping has been around almost as long as transaction log backups, and many companies have written their own procedures to automate the process.

The RPO for log shipping is controlled by the frequency of your transaction log backups and the time it takes to copy the backups to the destination server. For example, if you took transaction log backups every 15 minutes and shipped them to another server, you might consider that solution to provide no more than 30 minutes of data loss during a failure. This would allow for a failure just before (or during) a transaction log backup and the previous transaction log backup having not made it to the destination.

The RTO is influenced by the time it takes to finish restoring any transaction log backups on the destination that have yet to be applied, recovering the database, and redirecting your applications to the database on the new server. It is the manual process of recovery and redirection of application traffic that makes this solution a *warm* standby.

Built-in Log Shipping

To make things easier for you, Microsoft has built a set of processes to help automate the log shipping process, all nicely wrapped up and accessed through a wizard that takes you through all the required steps to get up and running. This built-in solution also enables you to set up a third server to act as a monitor for the solution and keep track of all the details in the process, such as when log backups were taken and restored and also backup failures.

ON THE JOB

The fundamental concept of log shipping is very straightforward: it is the continual process of copying and restoring transaction log backups from one source database to either one or multiple destinations. Writing your own scripts to perform this is not too difficult, and in the early versions of SQL Server, that is exactly what DBAs did. Now that the built-in wizard is available, you can build it far quicker than writing your own implementation. Also, using the wizard helps to minimize the risk of the solution because the processes that you're using are supported by Microsoft.

Reporting on the Destination Server

When using log shipping, the database on the destination server is inaccessible because it's running with NORECOVERY. However, it is possible to access the database for read-only purposes between transaction log backups by using the recovery option STANDBY, which was covered in detail in Chapter 7. Using STANDBY places the database in a read-only state by performing recovery on the transaction log restore, but instead of discarding the open and incomplete transactions, they are saved to a file and are later replayed when restoring the next transaction log in sequence to ensure the transaction log chain is maintained. Using the log shipping wizard, this is very easy to implement, as illustrated in Figure 9-2.

The database is read-only when running in standby mode, but SQL Server requires exclusive access to the database to restore a transaction log backup, so you will need to decide whether to kick out all the users from the read-only database before each restore or to let the restores fail and then catch up when the users have finished their queries. The wizard also makes light work of implementing these choices, as shown in Figure 9-2.

Used to make destination database
accessible for read-only queries

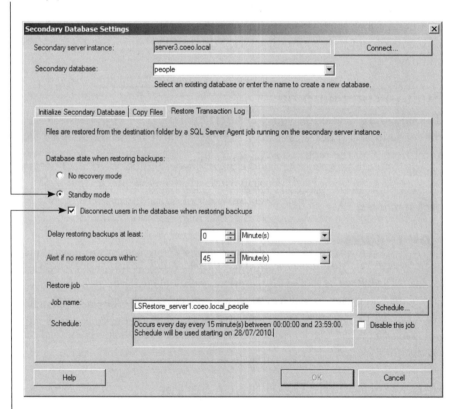

Select to automatically kick out all
users before each log restore

Figure 9-2   *Log shipping wizard*

Other Log Shipping Benefits

As well as all the features and benefits described so far, log shipping can also take advantage of backup compression (see Chapter 7), which was first introduced as an Enterprise-only feature in SQL Server 2008 but then became a Standard Edition feature with SQL Server 2008 R2. Smaller transaction log backups take less time to create, copy across the network, and restore on the destination server, so the benefits in a log shipping scenario are obvious.

Finally, it's very easy for log shipping to support multiple destination servers. Given the fact that the core architecture is so simple, adding another destination is no more complicated than copying the backup files to two different places or having two destination servers read them from the same location. In fact, it's even easier than that because the log shipping wizard will deal with it all for you. All you need to do is to specify all the destination servers that you want to set up.

ON THE JOB

A common pattern for log shipping with multiple destinations is to have multiple destinations that operate with a different time lag; for example, you may log ship to two destinations, with site A only 15 minutes behind the main database as the primary DR site. Site B then may have a delay of six hours or greater for the secondary DR point. This way, if a corruption such as a large amount of data being deleted or incorrectly updated goes unnoticed before the change makes its way to the primary DR site, you have a greater chance of catching it before it is applied to the secondary DR, giving you options to switch to another database while you resolve the problem.

Database Mirroring (High-Performance Mode)

Database mirroring is a feature that was introduced in SQL Server 2005 SP1 and can be thought of as similar to Oracle Data Guard with Redo Apply. Using a similar approach to Data Guard, database mirroring operates by streaming and reapplying transaction log records from the primary (principle) database to the secondary database (mirror).

Just like Data Guard, database mirroring has different modes of operation:

▶ **High-performance mode**   Two SQL Server instances are required, and data synchronization between the principal and mirror databases is executed asynchronously to minimize the overhead.

▶ **High-safety mode without automatic failover**   Two SQL Server instances are required, and replication between the principal and mirror databases is executed synchronously to guarantee no data loss. This mode is usually just a temporary state when the ability to automatically fail over is lost due to the loss of a third server, known as the witness.

▶ **High-safety mode with automatic failover**   Three SQL Server instances are required, and replication between the principal and mirror databases is executed synchronously to guarantee no data loss. The third server, the witness, is required to enable automatic failover. See the section "Hot Standby Solutions" for more details on this mode of operation.

Database mirroring in high-performance mode is comparable to Data Guard operating in its maximum performance mode and is considered to be a warm standby solution because it requires manual intervention to initiate failover and client redirection. It is only available with the Enterprise and Datacenter editions of SQL Server. Figure 9-3 helps to illustrate the basic concept.

With SQL Server 2008 and the introduction of compression into many areas of the product, the log records that are copied across to the mirror are automatically compressed, which uses less network bandwidth and enables faster processing of log records.

Reporting on the Mirror Database

Like log shipping, the destination database can also be used for reporting purposes, but this is achieved slightly differently from log shipping. To be able to read a mirrored database, you need to take a database snapshot (database snapshots were covered in Chapter 2), which is a read-only, point-in-time view of the mirror database, and then read from the snapshot. The advantage to this is that you can take multiple snapshots of the database at different times and continue to use them without affecting the mirroring process or having to disconnect all your users. Figure 9-4 shows a topology in which multiple snapshots have been taken on a mirrored database for reporting purposes.

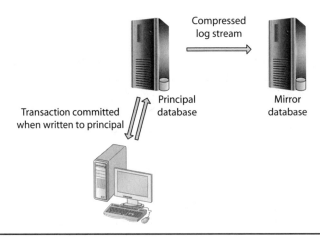

Figure 9-3   *Asynchronous database mirroring basic topology*

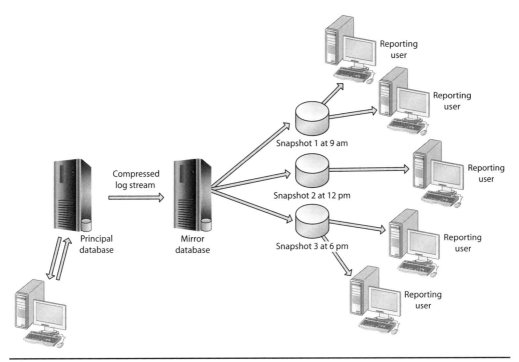

Figure 9-4   *Reporting on a database mirror*

Oracle DBA Q&A

Q: Is it possible to mirror one database to multiple destinations like in Data Guard?

A: It is not possible to have multiple mirror destinations, but you can mix technologies together to achieve a similar approach. For example, you could use database mirroring to mirror the AdventureWorks database from Server A to Server B and then use log shipping to create one or more additional copies on Servers C, D, and E, etc.

Automatic Page Repair

A new feature for SQL Server 2008, automatic page repair will try to fix corrupt pages automatically between a pair of mirrored databases. When a page corruption error is encountered on the principal database (by a user attempting to read the data), details of the corrupt page are written to the suspect_pages table in the msdb database. The principal then requests a copy of the page from the mirror and restores it automatically.

If the page corruption is detected on the mirror, then mirroring will be suspended until the corrupt page is successfully copied again from the principal, after which mirroring will automatically resume.

You can use the sys.dm_db_mirroring_auto_page_repair DMV to track pages that were repaired automatically.

Replication

The last warm standby solution is SQL Server Replication, which is comparable to Oracle Streams or Data Guard with SQL Apply. Replication is particularly useful where there is a requirement to duplicate data and handle write requests from multiple locations. Peer-to-peer replication fits this requirement nicely and allows for multiple copies of the data to be made and writes to be handled from all copies.

The process of committing a transaction on one server and it being replicated to another server is asynchronous; therefore, it is not suitable for zero data loss requirements, and has no automatic failure detection or failover so is considered to be a warm standby solution.

You can read more about replication and peer-to-peer replication topologies in Chapter 11.

ON THE JOB

Although replication can form part of an HA/DR solution, it is mainly used for building data distribution architectures, such as a head office distributing product data to its many stores, or road warriors with laptops containing subsets of customer data synchronizing back to the main database when they are online. Introducing replication can in some cases, depending on the setup, require changes to the actual database schema, such as ensuring tables have primary keys and so forth. Therefore, it requires greater consideration than the other HA/DR solutions.

Hot Standby Solutions

Hot standby solutions have built-in failure detection and automatic failover with no manual interaction required. They are used in business and mission-critical systems where the RTO is very short and the RPO is very small. In Oracle, this is normally when technologies such as RAC or Data Guard operating in maximum protection and maximum availability modes would be used.

Failover Clustering

Failover clustering has been around since Windows NT 4.0 and SQL Server 7, and although the implementation of it has changed significantly over the years, the underlying concept and technology should be considered mature. Failover clustering is a service provided by the Windows Server platform, and SQL Server is able to be installed in such a way that it utilizes the failover capabilities of the platform.

This feature is widely used and aims to provide redundancy at the server level in the same way that multiple power supplies (for example) provide redundancy at the component level.

The basic architecture consists of two or more servers (called nodes) connected to a shared disk array, such as a SAN that contains the data for an application (which in our case are the database files and logs for SQL Server). If the server that is running SQL Server experiences an outage, another "node" in the cluster will take control of the disks, start the SQL Server service, and everything is back up and running again. It is important to note that failover clustering uses a "shared disk" architecture, but that only one node is running the SQL Server instance and has control of the associated disk resources at any one time. Figure 9-5 illustrates this basic design.

Oracle DBA Q&A

Q: Just to clarify, only one node is controlling the instance at any one time. In RAC you can have multiple nodes serving the database at once; can you do that with Windows clustering and SQL Server?

A: You are correct; only one node has control of the instance at any one time. That is why the feature is known as failover clustering: your running instance "fails over" to another node. You can have multiple instances running in the cluster but they all serve their own set of databases, there is no concept of being able to serve a database from multiple machines at the same time such as in RAC.

A failover cluster typically uses a minimum of two networks, one for internal cluster communications (commonly known as the private network), and one for external communications so that users and applications can connect (commonly known as the public network).

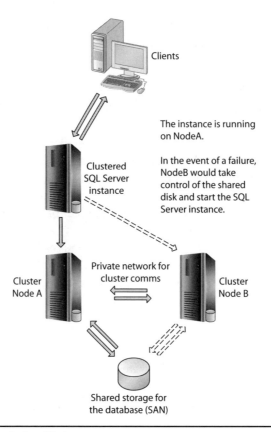

The instance is running on NodeA.

In the event of a failure, NodeB would take control of the shared disk and start the SQL Server instance.

Figure 9-5   *Failover cluster basic architecture*

With the introduction of Windows Server 2008, building supported failover clusters is much easier than it used to be. Prior to Windows Server 2008, all the hardware in your design had to be certified as having been tested for use in a failover cluster, even down to specific firmware revisions; moreover, the complete cluster solution needed to be certified, not just the individual components. This list of approved failover cluster hardware solutions was found on the Microsoft Hardware Compatibility List (HCL), which caused lots of issues for hardware vendors, Microsoft, and Microsoft customers because the list was hard to keep up to date. Inevitably, this meant that the majority of failover cluster installations were running on hardware that was not on the HCL.

The solution to this problem came in the form of self-certification in Windows Server 2008, whereby the installation of a failover cluster requires successful completion of the built-in cluster validation tool. This means that you can build a failover cluster with various different components and firmware levels and self-certify that it all works. Figure 9-6 shows part of a validation report. This also means that you can expand a

Microsoft

Failover Cluster Validation Report

Node:	SQL01.sales.local
Node:	SQL02.sales.local
Started	30/03/2010 10:37:38
Completed	30/03/2010 10:38:22

 Inventory

Name	Result	Description
List BIOS Information	✓	Success
List Environment Variables	✓	Success
List Fibre Channel Host Bus Adapters	✓	Success
List iSCSI Host Bus Adapters	✓	Success
List Memory Information	✓	Success
List Operating System Information	✓	Success
List Plug and Play Devices	✓	Success
List Running Processes	✓	Success
List SAS Host Bus Adapters	✓	Success
List Services Information	✓	Success
List Software Updates	✓	Success
List System Drivers	✓	Success
List System Information	✓	Success
List Unsigned Drivers	✓	Success

 Network

Name	Result	Description
Validate Cluster Network Configuration	✓	Success
Validate IP Configuration	✓	Success
Validate Network Communication	✓	Success
Validate Windows Firewall Configuration	✓	Success

Figure 9-6   *Windows Server 2008 cluster validation tool*

failover cluster over time as your needs increase. For instance, you might start with a two-node cluster, with one passive node and one active node. Later you might add a third server to the cluster, and have two active nodes and a single passive node. This is often referred to as an N+1 cluster, with N (where N = 1 to 15) active nodes protected by one passive node.

Failover Detection and Split Brain

One of the most important jobs of a failover cluster is failure detection. As well as detecting hardware failures that affect the availability of the service like losing access to the public network, the failover cluster needs to be able to decide which node should be running the live service in the event of failure.

For example, imagine you have a failover cluster containing two servers named Node A and Node B. Both nodes are going to be in constant communication with each other to make sure that they are both up and running. This check is known as a *heartbeat*.

If Node A fails to respond to several heartbeat requests from Node B, then Node B will assume that Node A has failed and that it should take control of the resources that were running on Node A.

That's a perfect plan until we come across the scenario where Node A isn't actually down (and is working perfectly serving user requests across the public network) but the inter-node communications are down. This scenario where both nodes are working but can't communicate with each other is known as a *split-brain* scenario because both nodes think that they are the only working node and should be running all the clustered resources. Fortunately, this problem was solved many years ago with the use of a shared disk resource called the *quorum*, and Windows Server 2008 has several quorum configuration options to make cluster deployments even more flexible:

▶ **Node Majority** In order to keep running, each node must be able to contact the majority of the nodes in the cluster. For example, in a five-node cluster where Nodes A, B, and C cannot contact Nodes D and E, and vice versa, Nodes D and E will stop even if they can still service users because they cannot see enough nodes to form a quorum.

▶ **Node and Disk Majority** This quorum configuration also uses Node Majority but adds a quorum disk as an additional safeguard. For example, using just Node Majority in a four-node cluster, the whole cluster will fail if Nodes A and B cannot contact Nodes C and D because they no longer have a majority. Adding a quorum disk ensures that an additional "vote" can be used so that if Nodes A and B can contact each other and one of them can take control of the quorum disk resource, then they have the majority and can continue running.

▶ **Node and File Share Majority**   Each node plus the file share can participate in voting, which achieves the same goal as the previous scenario without requiring a shared disk resource.

▶ **No Majority, Disk Only**   This is the traditional architecture for failover clustering prior to Windows Server 2008 and only uses a shared disk called the quorum to avoid split-brain scenarios. However, it is not considered to be robust enough for many deployment scenarios.

Choosing the best quorum model is usually straightforward, and Windows Server 2008 even gives you advice on which model to choose. You can use Table 9-1 as a guide.

A multisite cluster is one in which the cluster nodes are located in different geographical areas. For example, Nodes A, B, and C are in Seattle and Nodes D and E are in Vancouver. To build a multisite cluster for SQL Server, you need to have enabled synchronously replicated storage between the two sites. This technology is largely provided by your specific storage vendor, so their involvement is necessary to implement this type of failover cluster (which is also sometimes called a geo-cluster or a stretch cluster). A more common solution is to use failover clustering to provide high availability within a single data center, and use mirroring, log shipping, or asynchronous SAN replication to copy the data to a standby data center.

Installation of SQL Server on a Failover Cluster

Chapter 3 covered how to install a stand-alone version of SQL Server. Installing a clustered instance of SQL Server 2008 is fairly similar and is quite straightforward once you have a working Windows failover cluster.

NOTE

To run the installation process, you need to use a domain user account with local administrator access to each of the cluster nodes.

Description of Cluster	Quorum Recommendation
Odd number of nodes	Node Majority
Even number of nodes	Node and Disk Majority
Even number of nodes, multisite cluster	Node and File Share Majority
Even number of nodes, no shared storage[1]	Node and File Share Majority

[1] SQL Server requires shared storage, so this scenario won't occur for SQL Server.

Table 9-1   *Cluster Quorum Recommendations*

There are two options for installation:

▶ **Standard installation**   This option allows you to install a SQL Server failover cluster instance on one node. You can then run setup again and select the Add Node to a SQL Server Failover Cluster function to add additional nodes. These functions are illustrated in Figure 9-7 for a SQL Server 2008 R2 installation.

▶ **Advanced installation**   This option consists of two steps: cluster preparation and cluster completion. The preparation step prepares all the nodes to be operational for the SQL Server failover cluster instance and is run on each node. The completion step, which is run on the node that owns the disk resources, makes the cluster operational. These functions are shown in Figure 9-8 for a SQL Server 2008 R2 installation.

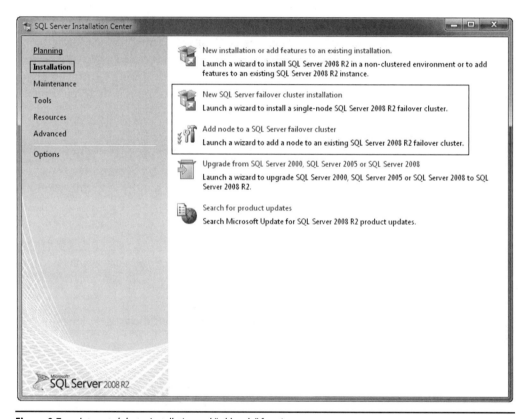

Figure 9-7   *Integrated cluster installation and "add node" function*

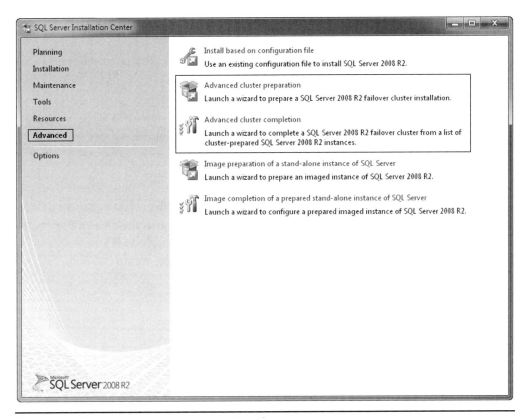

Figure 9-8   *Advanced cluster preparation and completion functions*

The most common installation method is to use the integrated installation option where you start installing on one node of the cluster using the New SQL Server Failover Cluster Installation option. Once you have installed the cluster on one node, you then visit each node in turn, this time using the Add Node to a SQL Server Failover Cluster option, which joins each node to the SQL Server cluster. To remove a node from a cluster, use the equivalent removal option on the Maintenance tab of the SQL Server Installation Center, labeled Remove Node from SQL Server Failover Cluster.

Both cluster installation options can be installed through the command prompt rather than the Windows GUI. See SQL Server Books Online for details.

To install a clustered instance, you need the following:

▶ A Windows Server Cluster Validation Report that shows that all tests were passed. This is a prerequisite check that is run at the start of the SQL Server cluster installation process.

▶ At least one shared storage volume with a drive letter assigned. SQL Server 2008 supports the use of mount points, but you still need a root drive letter to access them.

▶ Domain user accounts for the SQL Server service accounts.

▶ An IP address to assign to the clustered instance (although, DHCP can be used).

▶ A network name and instance name that are both unique in the cluster. For example, in a cluster with two nodes named Node A and Node B and a requirement to install two instances, these instance names would be valid:

   ▶ SQL1\VSQL1 and SQL2\VSQL2

   ▶ Eurocamp\DesOrmes and Keycamp\LesMenhirs

However, these instance names would not be valid:

   ▶ NodeA\VSQL1

   ▶ Eurocamp\DesOrmes and Eurocamp\LesMenhirs

Figure 9-9 shows Windows Server 2008 Failover Cluster Manager connected to a failover cluster running a SQL Server 2008 failover cluster instance.

SQL Server and Windows Server Edition Requirements for Clusters

The Enterprise and Datacenter editions of Windows Server are the only editions that support Windows Failover Clustering. Both editions support up to 16 nodes in a single cluster using Windows Server 2008 R2.

Standard Edition of SQL Server 2008 R2 supports failover clustering up to two nodes, which is by far the most common deployment size. Enterprise Edition and the new Datacenter Edition available in SQL Server 2008 R2 both support failover clusters of up to 16 nodes. Also note that the Enterprise and Datacenter editions also both support a feature known as *fast recovery*, which makes the database available during the undo phase of a crash recovery (cluster failover) or a database mirroring failover.

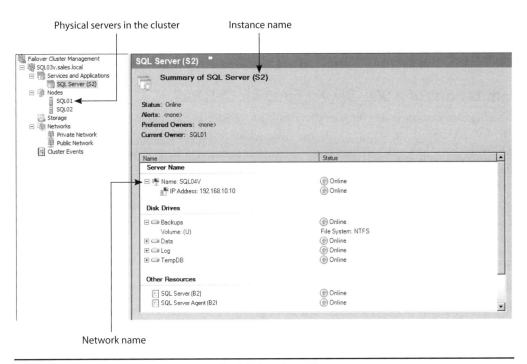

Figure 9-9   *Clustered SQL Server instance viewed with Failover Cluster Manager*

ON THE JOB

Although two-node SQL Server clusters may have traditionally been the most common size of deployment, with the recent trend of organizations moving toward consolidated SQL Server environments, it is now more common to see four nodes or more in a single cluster.

Benefits of Clustering SQL Server

A clustered SQL Server instance will typically take tens of seconds to fail over in a busy production environment, just a bit longer than restarting the SQL Server service, which is essentially what happens, only on another server. As well as providing a hot standby should there be a server failure, manually moving the SQL Server instance between nodes provides you the opportunity to carry out maintenance on the physical server and Windows installation with very little disruption to your users.

In addition, patching SQL Server is far more efficient and less risk-prone on a clustered instance of SQL Server 2008 compared with previous clustered SQL Server versions and even stand-alone installations of SQL Server 2008. This is because you apply Service Packs and hotfixes to all the nodes that aren't running the SQL Server instance first and then manually move the instance to a patched node that will upgrade the databases automatically and complete the installation.

Applying a Service Pack to SQL Server can take between 20 and 40 minutes to complete, all of which is downtime unless you're patching a SQL Server 2008 clustered instance which requires tens of seconds of downtime to complete.

Limitations of a SQL Server Failover Cluster

The biggest weakness of a SQL Server failover cluster is that there is only one copy of your database. It resides on a shared disk, which is controlled by whatever node is currently running your instance. You mitigate this risk by using RAID levels on the storage to protect against physical disk failure, but you can also increase your level of protection by implementing disk-level replication using software from your storage vendor or by combining other SQL Server technologies with clustering (such as database mirroring or log shipping) that do provide another copy of the database.

Database Mirroring (High-Safety Mode with Automatic Failover)

With the addition of a witness server, you can configure database mirroring to execute synchronously with automatic failover. The role of the witness is to act as a third vote to avoid the split-brain scenario described in the "Failover Clustering" section.

In the event that the principal and mirror servers lose contact with each other, they will try to contact the witness server, whose only purpose is to answer the question "who can you see?" If the mirror contacts the witness and the witness can still see the principal, then the mirror knows that it doesn't need to promote itself to be the principal. However, if the witness can't see the principal either, then the mirror has two votes and will promote itself to be the new principal database.

If the previous principal database subsequently comes back online, it will reestablish the mirroring session as the new mirror.

If the witness server becomes unavailable, then the ability to automatically fail over is lost; however, mirroring will still occur synchronously, so there is no data loss.

The overhead of being a witness is so light that it can even be run on SQL Server Express, the free version of SQL Server, which can help reduce licensing costs. The principal and mirror servers must be SQL Server Standard Edition or greater.

What Is the Overhead?

Running database mirroring synchronously ensures that a transaction is not considered to be committed unless it has been applied to both sides of the mirror. This represents overhead for each transaction in the database, which is primarily affected by the round-trip time and bandwidth of the network between the two databases. The overhead is lessened significantly in SQL Server 2008 because the log records are compressed, but having to commit every transaction to two different servers will always add overhead to your transaction throughput.

The question to ask when deciding whether or not to use synchronous mirroring is whether performance or zero data loss with automatic failover is the most important driver for the application. In a high transaction throughput application where speed is critical, synchronous mirroring may not be feasible for the application despite the benefits. However, for many applications, a few extra milliseconds on each transaction may not matter.

ON THE JOB

In high transaction throughput systems, although synchronous mirroring introduces overhead with regard to network round-trip times, which ultimately affect client response times, these delays can be reduced by ensuring fast communication between nodes by using technologies such as 10 Gigabit Ethernet or InfiniBand.

How Do the Clients Know About the New Server After Failover?

Automatic failover of the database is only part of the solution; a technology called transparent client redirection provides the other part of the solution. When a client connects to SQL Server, the client library caches the name of the mirror server. If the client loses connection to the principal and fails to reconnect, transparent client redirection automatically redirects the connection to the mirror server.

You can also specify the principal and mirror servers in the connection string, which is the preferred method because new clients coming online after failover won't have the mirrored server name cached.

You may be thinking, "How fast is it?" The answer is *very fast*; conservatively, under five seconds, and typically under two seconds. For a database to fail over and have all the clients redirected with zero data loss in just a few seconds is very attractive for many customers despite the potential performance overhead.

Database Mirroring Walkthrough

Now that you've read about how mirroring works, this last section is going to take you through step by step how to set up database mirroring in high-safety mode with automatic failover and monitor its status and performance.

To support high-safety mode with automatic failover, you need three instances of SQL Server: a principal, a mirror, and a witness. You also need the database you want to mirror to be running on the server that will become the principal, and you need the database to be in the FULL recovery model to ensure that the log records are kept until they can be copied to the mirror.

The next step is to take a full database backup of the database, followed by a transaction log backup, and restore them both to the mirror server WITH NORECOVERY so that more log records can be applied. Once this is done, you're ready to start the Configure Database Mirroring Security Wizard.

Figure 9-10 shows a quick way to get to the Mirroring page of the Database Properties dialog box. You can also see that on server1 there is a database called people, which will become the principal, and that the database and log file have been restored WITH NORECOVERY onto server3, which will become the mirror. Note also that the server connections have been made using their fully qualified domain names (FQDNs) to make things easier during the later stages of the wizard.

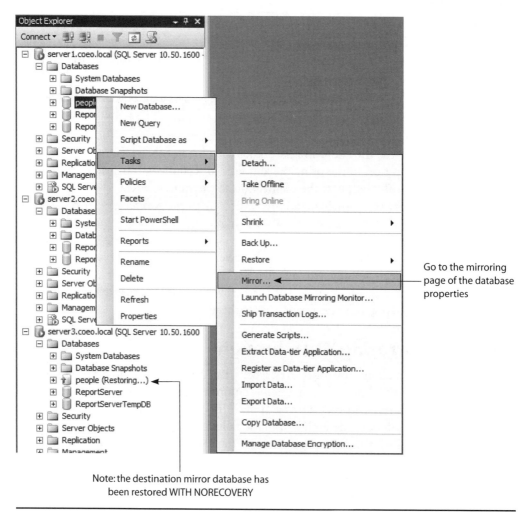

Figure 9-10   *Accessing the Configure Database Mirroring Security Wizard*

On the Mirroring page of the Database Properties dialog box, you'll see a Configure Security button, which you click to start the Configure Database Mirroring Security Wizard. In Figure 9-11 you can see the Configure Security button behind the first decision point in the wizard—whether to configure a witness server. As you've already read, you need a witness for automatic failover, so select Yes and click Next.

On the next wizard screen, shown in Figure 9-12, confirm which servers you want to configure now. As there is no mirroring without a principal and a mirror, the only available option here is to check or uncheck the Witness Server Instance box. Check it and then click Next.

The next screen, shown in Figure 9-13, confirms all the details for the principal server.

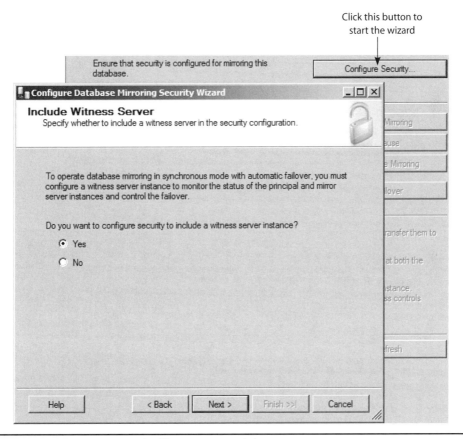

Figure 9-11   *Configuring a witness to be able to use automatic failover*

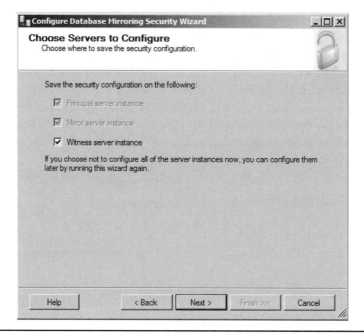

Figure 9-12 *Uncheck the witness if you want to configure it later.*

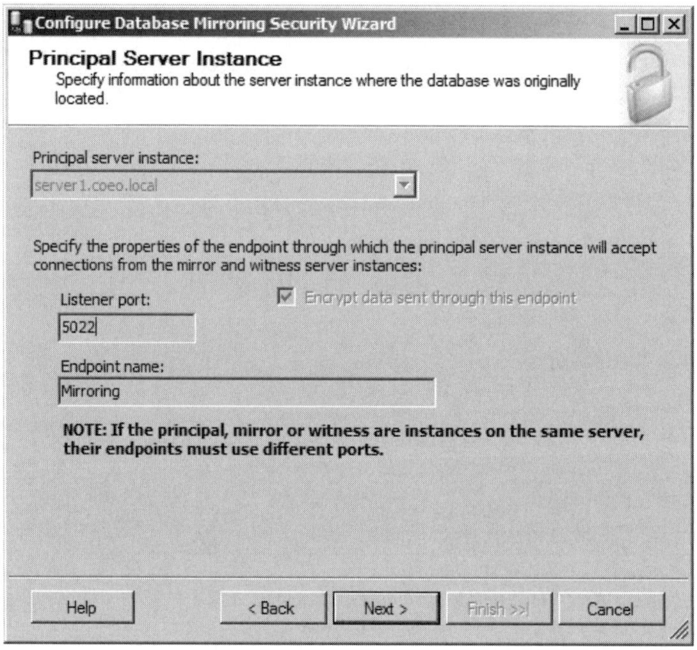

Figure 9-13 *Confirming all the details for the principal server*

There is nothing to configure here because the wizard is being run on the principal server and is already connected. Click Next to move to the Mirror Server Instance configuration screen, shown in Figure 9-14, where all you need to do is connect to the SQL Server instance and then click Next.

In the next screen, shown in Figure 9-15, you need to do exactly the same for the witness server.

Now that the servers have been configured, you're presented with the Service Accounts screen, shown in Figure 9-16, where you need to specify the service accounts for each instance if you're running within a domain environment. This is so that the right permissions can be assigned on all the servers.

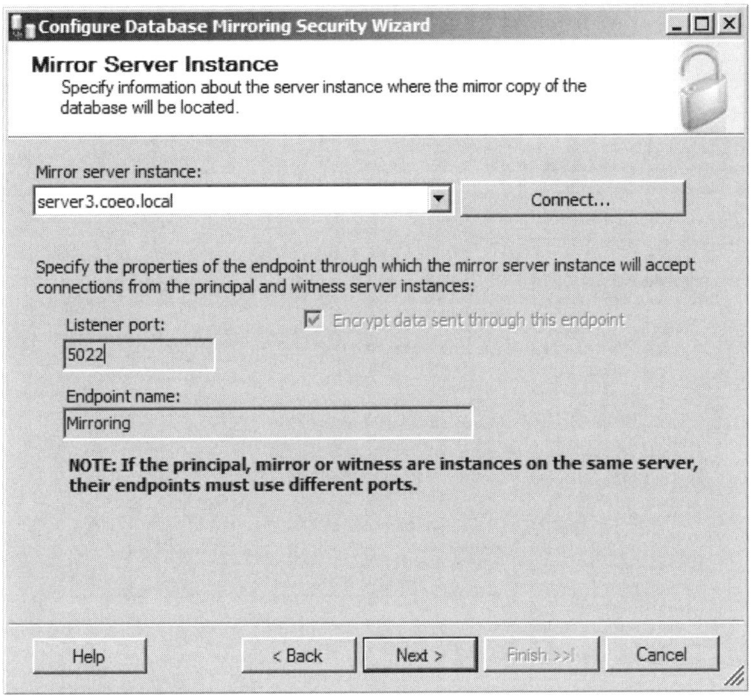

Figure 9-14   *Connecting to the mirror server*

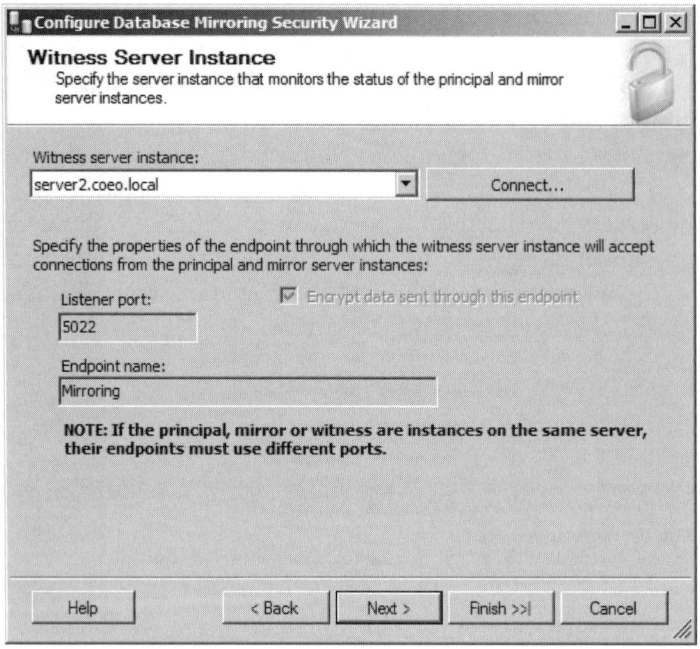

Figure 9-15 *Connecting to the witness server*

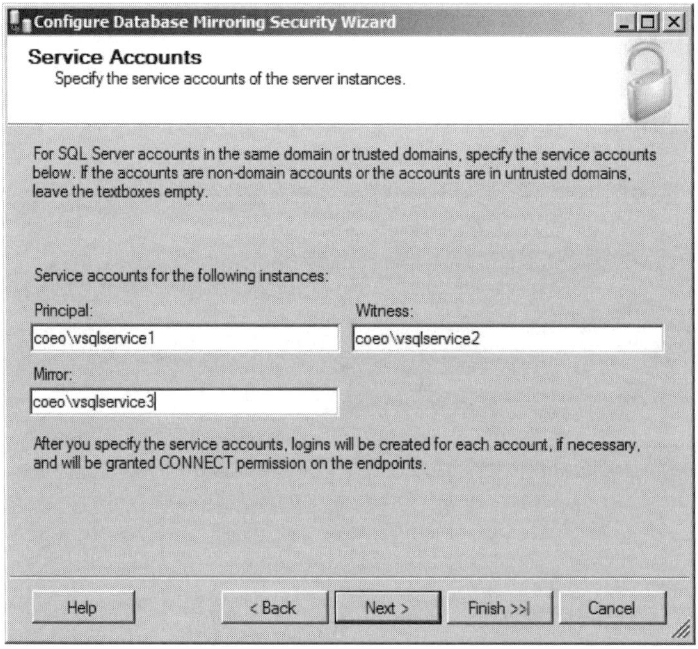

Figure 9-16 *Specifying service accounts for domain environments*

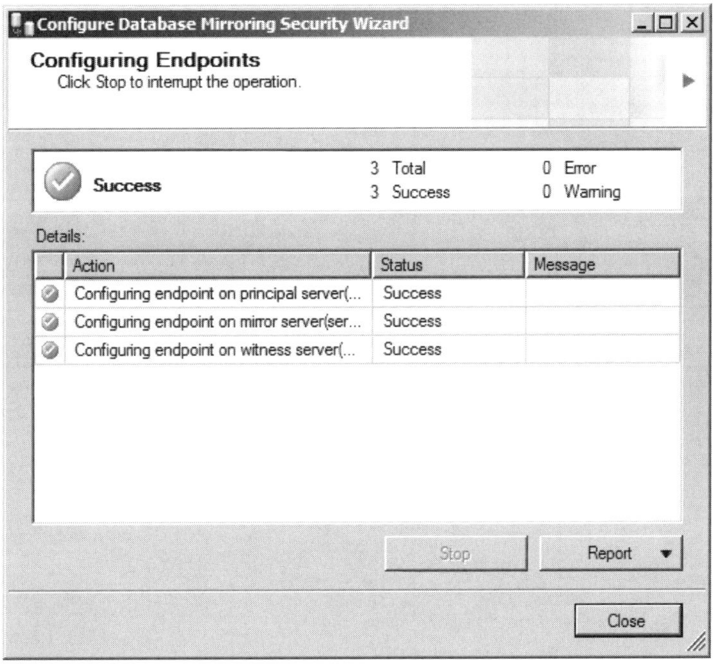

Figure 9-17 *Endpoint creation*

Once you click Next, the endpoints get created, after which you should see three green check marks in the Details column, as shown in Figure 9-17.

The database hasn't started mirroring yet; you've just created everything you need to start. Once you click the Close button, you'll be presented with the Database Properties dialog box shown in Figure 9-18.

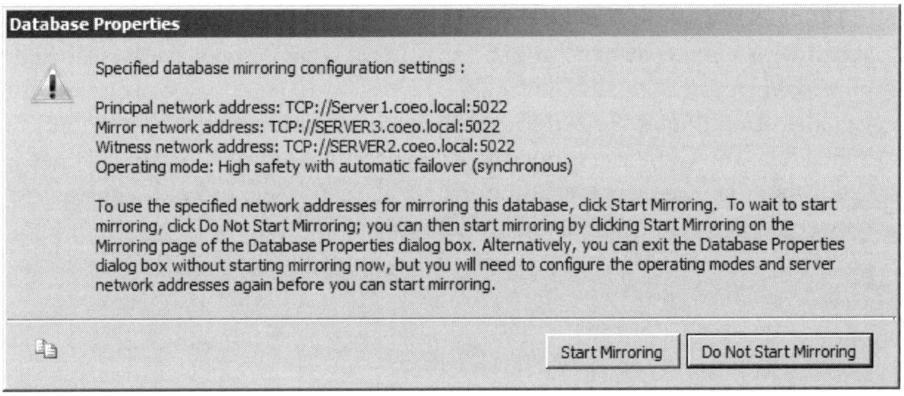

Figure 9-18 *Start mirroring*

Switch to high-performance mode

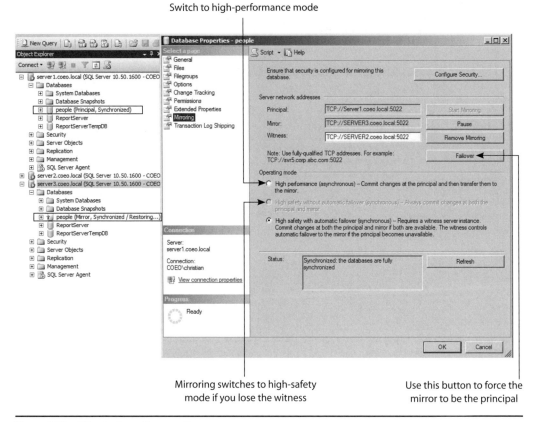

Mirroring switches to high-safety
mode if you lose the witness

Use this button to force the
mirror to be the principal

Figure 9-19   *Mirroring is working correctly.*

Once you click Start Mirroring, you'll finally know if you've done everything correctly. In Figure 9-19 you can see the people database on server1 has been marked as the Principal with a status of Synchronizing, and the database on server3 is labeled as a Synchronized Mirror.

You can also see in Figure 9-19 that a few more options now are available on the Mirroring page of the Database Properties dialog box, including a button to force a failover, meaning that the principal and mirror will swap roles, and radio buttons to switch between synchronous and asynchronous operating modes.

Database Mirroring Monitor

Monitoring the status and performance of a mirrored database is made easy through the use of Database Mirroring Monitor, which is accessible through the Tasks menu, as shown in Figure 9-20.

When run against a working database mirroring setup, your monitor will look something like Figure 9-21. In this example, everything is working fine: new transactions are being generated at a rate of 23KB/sec on the principal, which is matched by the send rate and the restore rate on the mirror. Each committed transaction takes an extra 6 milliseconds to run because of the overhead of writing to the mirror synchronously.

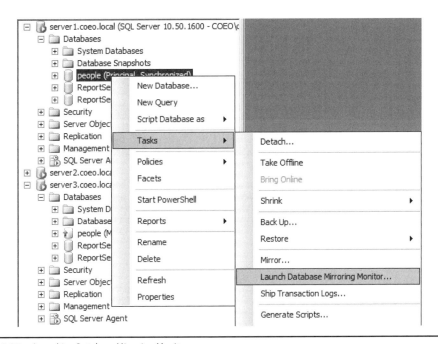

Figure 9-20   *Launching Database Mirroring Monitor*

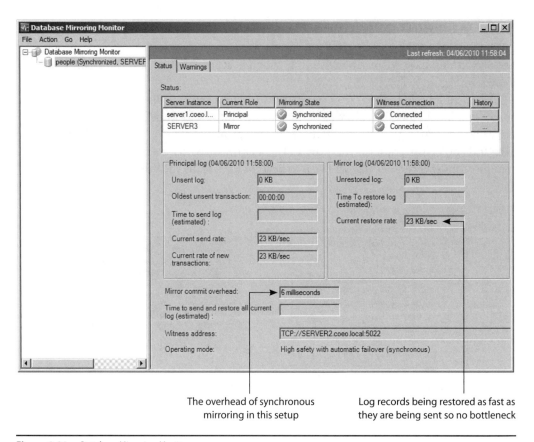

The overhead of synchronous mirroring in this setup

Log records being restored as fast as they are being sent so no bottleneck

Figure 9-21 *Database Mirroring Monitor*

Finally, Figure 9-22 shows the monitor after the principal database has gone offline. You can see that server3 is now the principal and you can still see the witness server. Log records are now being generated on server3 but have nowhere to go until server1 comes back up and establishes itself as the new mirror.

The oldest transaction that hasn't been sent is 1 minute old and approximately 3.5MB of log records have accrued so far.

3.5MB of log records
queuing up

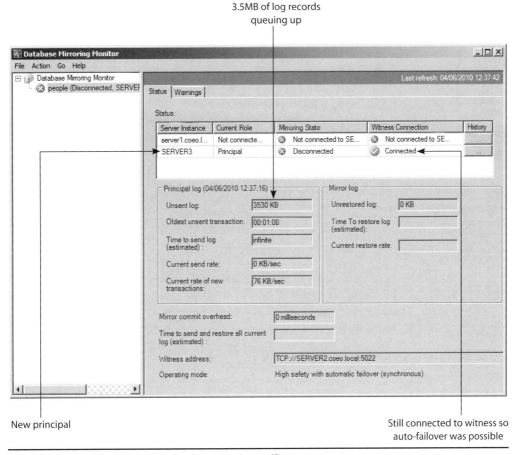

New principal

Still connected to witness so
auto-failover was possible

Figure 9-22   *Database Mirroring Monitor after principal goes offline*

ON THE JOB

This chapter introduced you to the technologies available in SQL Server for high availability and disaster recovery. To further your understanding of database mirroring and clustering, two recommended books are Microsoft SQL Server 2008 High Availability with Clustering & Database Mirroring *by Michael Otey and* Pro SQL Server 2008 Failover Clustering *by Allan Hirt. Also, as previously mentioned, it is always a good idea to check out your preferred hardware supplier's available HA/DR features that integrate with Windows Server and SQL Server. For example, if your preferred hardware supplier is HP and you use the EVA range of SAN solutions, HP provides StorageWorks Cluster Extensions. These extensions integrate with the Windows Failover Clustering feature to enable automatic failover of mirrored storage between sites.*

Chapter 10

Scheduling, Automation, and Alerting

In This Chapter

► **SQL Server Agent**
► **Jobs**
► **Alerts**
► **Maintenance Plans**
► **Policy-Based Management**

Looking after a database server can become very time-consuming without any form of automation, especially since it is likely you are administering multiple servers. Creating automated routines for tasks such as backup, index maintenance, and data import or extract routines takes away the burden of having to manually execute these activities. In addition, you do not want to sit in front of a monitor continually watching for errors. An automated alerting system can tell you when the errors or activities you are interested in happen and, importantly, provide a mechanism to automatically respond to the activity. Finally, keeping your server and database setup configured as per your corporate standards can also be challenging when you have several administrators all looking after the same systems.

On the Oracle platform, you would do job scheduling using either DBMS_SCHEDULER (introduced in 10*g*) or DBMS_JOBS (if using earlier releases of Oracle). If you don't use these internal features, you would probably use a third-party enterprise-scheduling tool or schedule your jobs using the operating system scheduler. For alerting, you would use server-generated alerts and notifications to monitor and notify administrators of issues.

All editions of SQL Server except Express and Compact contain all the required elements to create scheduled operations and provide automated alerting.

In this chapter we will cover

- ▶ SQL Server Agent
  - ▶ Database Mail
  - ▶ Operators
- ▶ Jobs
- ▶ Alerts
- ▶ Maintenance Plans
- ▶ Policy-Based Management

SQL Server Agent

In Oracle, Oracle Scheduler is responsible for providing scheduling capability: system tables store the job definitions, and the job coordinator process is responsible for launching slave job processes to execute the scheduled jobs. Within SQL Server, this capability is provided by SQL Server Agent, which runs as a Windows service and is responsible for all scheduled tasks within SQL Server. SQL Server Agent uses the msdb system database to store information on schedules, jobs, and alerts. Unlike Oracle Scheduler, SQL Server Agent is responsible for more than just job scheduling; it is also used to provide alerting and can monitor the SQL Server relational engine to provide restart capability should the SQL Server process fail. Therefore, unlike the job coordinator process, the SQL Server Agent process is constantly running.

SQL Server Agent is set to manual start by default on a new server installation and therefore has to be started manually; it is possible to set the service to automatically start using SQL Server Configuration Manager (covered in Chapter 3).

SQL Server Agent is used by many out-of-the-box features in SQL Server, such as SQL Server Replication, Maintenance Plans, and the SQL Server Import and Export Wizard. SQL Server Agent is administered through SQL Server Management Studio (SSMS). Figure 10-1 shows SQL Server Agent in SSMS.

Before moving on to the creation of jobs and alerts, there are two supporting elements that provide the ability to send out details of events:

▶ Database Mail

▶ Operators

Database Mail

If you are automating processes and alerts, then using e-mail as a delivery mechanism for sending status information is probably the preferred method. In Oracle, sending e-mail notifications is done via the mail server and account configured in the Notification Methods section of Oracle Enterprise Manager Database Control. It is also possible to programmatically send e-mail in PL/SQL using the UTL_SMTP package to send e-mail to an SMTP server.

SQL Server also has the ability to send e-mail messages via SMTP using the Database Mail feature. Within the wider scope of SQL Server, Database Mail is not just used for

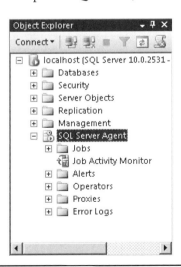

Figure 10-1   *The SQL Server Agent node in SSMS*

sending alerts; it can also be used for any e-mail–related tasks within the database, such as being used as part of an application to send an acknowledgement e-mail to a customer when a new order is placed in the orders table.

Database Mail allows for the creation of multiple mail profiles; these can be either public or private. Public profiles can be used by anyone who is a member of the DatabaseMailUsersRole role, whereas a private profile is restricted to an individual user. In order to be able to send mail using the Database Mail feature, the user account must be a member of the DatabaseMailUsersRole in the msdb database.

Within a mail profile, you specify a mail account. A mail account contains settings such as e-mail account name, reply address, SMTP server, and any connection credentials. It is possible to create multiple mail accounts for a single mail profile. Specifying multiple accounts provides Database Mail with a failover priority capability. For example, if the first mail account is unable to send e-mail because the SMTP server is unavailable, then Database Mail will move to the next mail account in the priority list.

To send e-mail programmatically, you use the sp_send_dbmail system stored procedure located in the msdb database. Making a call to this stored procedure places the e-mail in a queue that is then asynchronously serviced by a process that is external to the SQL Server service. If the external service stops, the mail will continue to queue within SQL Server until the process comes back online.

Oracle DBA Q&A

Q: In Oracle it is quite well known that sending e-mail via UTL_SMTP can impact application performance if you are waiting for a call to the UTL_SMTP package to complete. Therefore, the recommended approach is to submit the action of sending an e-mail to a job that will then send the e-mail asynchronously. If sp_send_dbmail places the e-mail in queue, does that mean it doesn't have the same performance impact?

A: Correct. When sending e-mail via sp_send_dbmail, the call to the stored procedure places the e-mail in an internal queue that is asynchronously serviced, so there is no need to wait for the stored procedure to connect to an SMTP server and all the other actions that can slow down the operation. Another great difference is that if you make a call to sp_send_dbmail within a transaction and that transaction is rolled back, the e-mail never gets sent because it is queued in an internal table that is subject to the same transaction. In UTL_SMTP, if you perform the send action and then later roll back the transaction, you cannot undo the sending of the message.

Similar to the Notification Methods settings in Database Control, when automated features such as jobs and alerts need to send e-mail in SQL Server, the Database Mail profile specified in the settings within SQL Server Agent is used. Figure 10-2 shows the Alert System page of the SQL Server Agent Properties dialog box (accessed by right-clicking SQL Server Agent in SSMS and selecting Properties). E-mail capability has been enabled, and the mail profile SQL Agent Profile has been selected.

Operators

The notification of administrators of events such as jobs completing successfully, jobs failing, or alerts being raised is provided through the use of operators. Operators are quite simply aliases for individuals or groups who you want to be notified when an event has taken place.

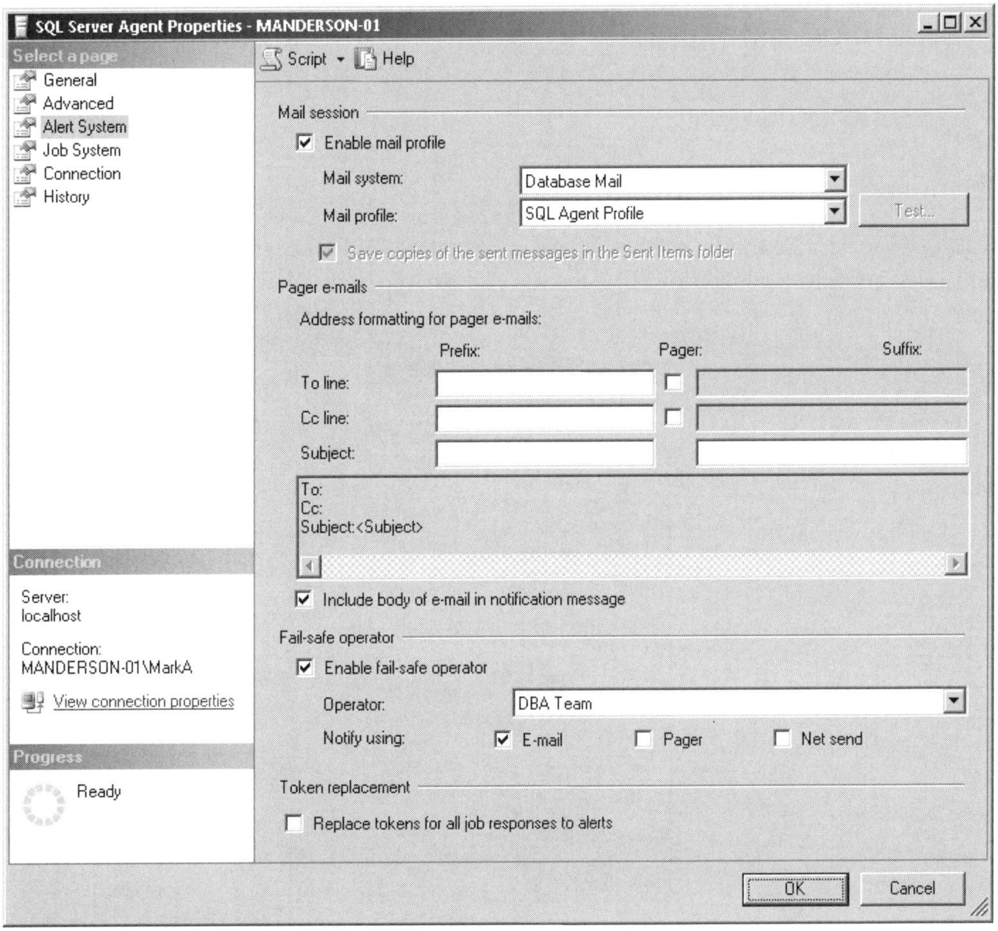

Figure 10-2 *SQL Server Agent Properties dialog box, Alert System page*

Later in the chapter, when we explore setting up jobs and alerts, you will see where operators are used. For now, let's take a look at where they are located and how to create them. Figure 10-3 shows the list of operators on the local server, with a mix of individuals and group aliases such as First Line Support and DBA Team.

There are three system stored procedures for operator maintenance:

- **sp_add_operator**   Creates new operators
- **sp_update_operator**   Updates existing operators
- **sp_delete_operator**   Deletes existing operators

To create an operator graphically, right-click the Operators node in SSMS (shown in Figure 10-3), select New Operator, and complete the relevant fields. Clicking OK creates a call to the sp_add_operator stored procedure.

When you create a new operator, you will notice that there are three notification types that are currently available:

- Email
- Pager
- net send

It is important to note that the Pager and net send options are both due to be removed in a future version of SQL Server and therefore should not be used for any new implementations.

Figure 10-3   *Listing of available operators*

ON THE JOB

The Pager and net send options are a bit of a relic from the past. In days gone by, when pagers were the main method of text-based communication, adding this functionality into SQL Server made sense; these days, with mobile telephones that can receive e-mail and e-mail servers that can convert e-mail to SMS, these options are no longer required. For those of you familiar with the Windows platform, you know that net send is a way to send a message to another Windows workstation. Performing a net send command pops up a dialog box on the desktop of the target computer. The increase of security in network environments has resulted in most firewalls blocking the ports used by net send.

Figure 10-4 shows the creation of a new operator and the disabling of an existing one using T-SQL. The new operator 'Wendy Anderson' has been added using the sp_add_operator stored procedure. The existing operator 'James Fox' has been disabled using the sp_update_operator stored procedure. Disabling an operator prevents them from receiving notifications but does not remove them from the system.

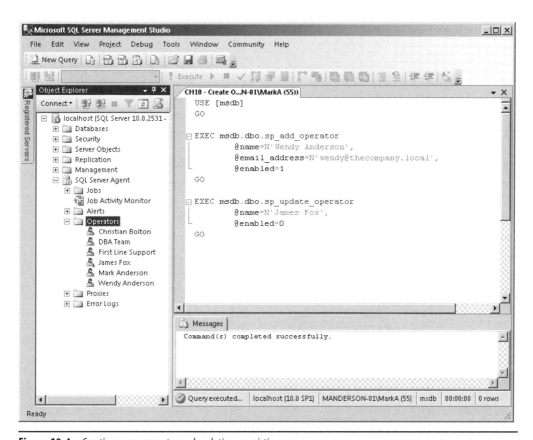

Figure 10-4 *Creating a new operator and updating an existing one*

Jobs

A job in SQL Server is defined as a set of steps, with each step defining a task. There are many task types, including running an operating system script, a T-SQL code block, or an SSIS package. A job can run on demand, on a schedule, or in response to an alert (alerts are covered later in this chapter).

Oracle DBA Q&A

Q: To be clear, in Oracle a job normally just performs one task such as running a block of PL/SQL or calling out to the OS. If you want multiple jobs to run in succession with dependencies between them, you create a job chain. Are you saying that in SQL Server, to create the equivalent of a job chain, you would create a single job with multiple steps?

A: Yes, that's correct. You would create a single job with multiple steps. Also, in the same way as in a job chain in Oracle, you can set some logic to the execution path. For example, "if step 1 succeeds, move straight to step 3; otherwise go to step 2."

SQL Server jobs are used extensively by many features within SQL Server for scheduling, including: the Import and Export Wizard; Maintenance Plans; Policy-Based Management; SQL Server Integration Services; Transaction Log Shipping; SQL Server data replication features; and the Change Data Capture functionality. SQL Server creates jobs to schedule the various activities, which can then be modified by a DBA to add additional logging information and set up notification and alerts on the job.

The jobs engine within SQL Server is quite rich and has many advanced features that we will not cover in this book, such as the Master-Target architecture, in which a single server (Master) can be responsible for holding the job definitions and other servers (Targets) will receive job definitions to run from the Master and return execution results. All these features are covered in the SQL Server Books Online documentation. To get started, let's walk through the creation of a simple job that will back up the AdventureWorks database. In this job, we execute the T-SQL backup command to create a full database backup and we schedule the job to run at 1:00 A.M. every night.

We start the job creation by right-clicking the jobs node located under SQL Server Agent in SSMS and selecting New Job. Figure 10-5 shows the New Job dialog box. We start by giving the job a name and a description. The name is mandatory but the description is not. For now we will leave the job category as Uncategorized; we will cover categories later in this chapter.

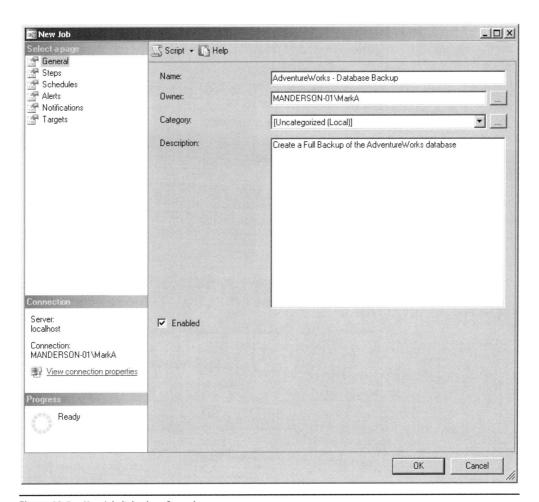

Figure 10-5   *New Job dialog box, General page*

ON THE JOB

It is always a good idea to make the name of a job descriptive and to provide additional detail in the Description field. I have lost count of the number of times that I have sat in front of a SQL Server looking through the jobs only to find names such as "Batch Upload" with no other detail either in the name or description. This can leave you thinking, "Batch upload of what, from where, to where?" Whenever I create a job, I always complete the

Description field to save having to open the steps of the job to work out what the system is doing. Also, I like to use the Description field to keep brief history notes on changes made; for example:

Name: Customer Address Details Update for AdventureWorks
Description: Nightly upload of latest customer address details from CRM system to the AdventureWorks Database
Mark Anderson - 15th October 2009
Updated source server name to point to new CRM system (CRM-SVR01)
John Plummer - 27th July 2009
Added 'AlternativeEmail' field to the import definition.

Now that we have provided a name and description, we select the Steps page on the left side of the New Job dialog box, which presents us with the list of steps. To create a new step, click New at the bottom of the window. Figure 10-6 shows the New Job Step dialog box.

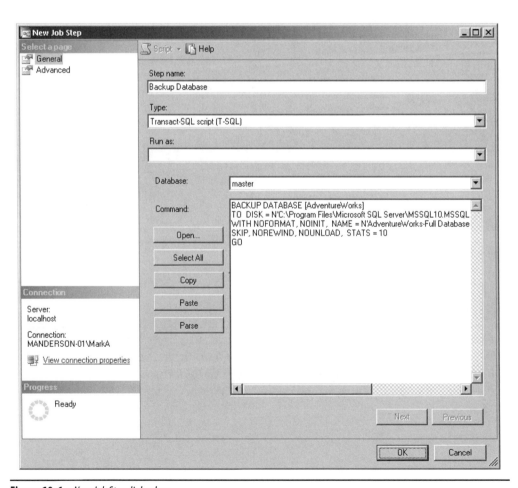

Figure 10-6 *New Job Step dialog box*

In the New Job Step dialog box, on the General page, we define what task we want to perform. We start by giving the step a name, in this case Backup Database. Next, we select the step type, T-SQL. In the Command section, we type the command that we want this step to run. In this scenario, it is the backup command to perform a full database backup of AdventureWorks. Clicking OK creates the job step and returns us to the jobs page (see Figure 10-7). From this window, we could also add additional steps, change the order in which the steps run, or change what happens when a step successfully completes or fails.

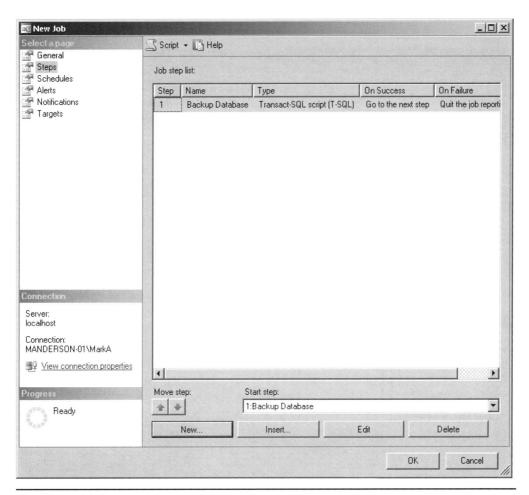

Figure 10-7 *Job Steps page*

Now that we have created the step to back up the database, all we have left to do is create a schedule that the job will run to. Selecting the Schedules page on the left side of the New Job dialog box takes us to the scheduling options (see Figure 10-8). At this point, we are able to create a new schedule or to pick from a shared schedule. Shared schedules are covered later in this section. For now, we will create a custom schedule for this Job.

Clicking the New button takes us to the Job Schedule Properties dialog box, shown in Figure 10-9, where we set the schedule type and the frequency. In this case we want a recurring schedule that operates daily at 1:00 A.M.

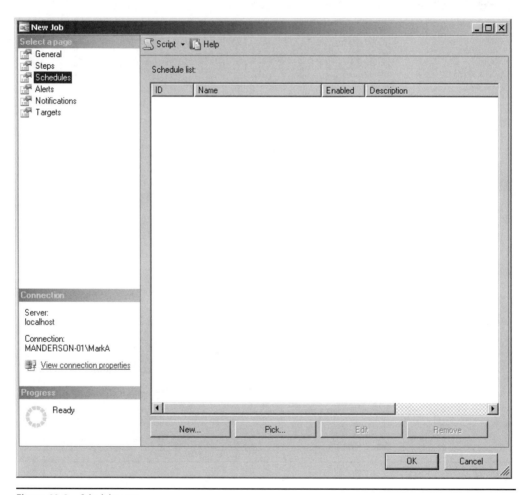

Figure 10-8 *Schedules page*

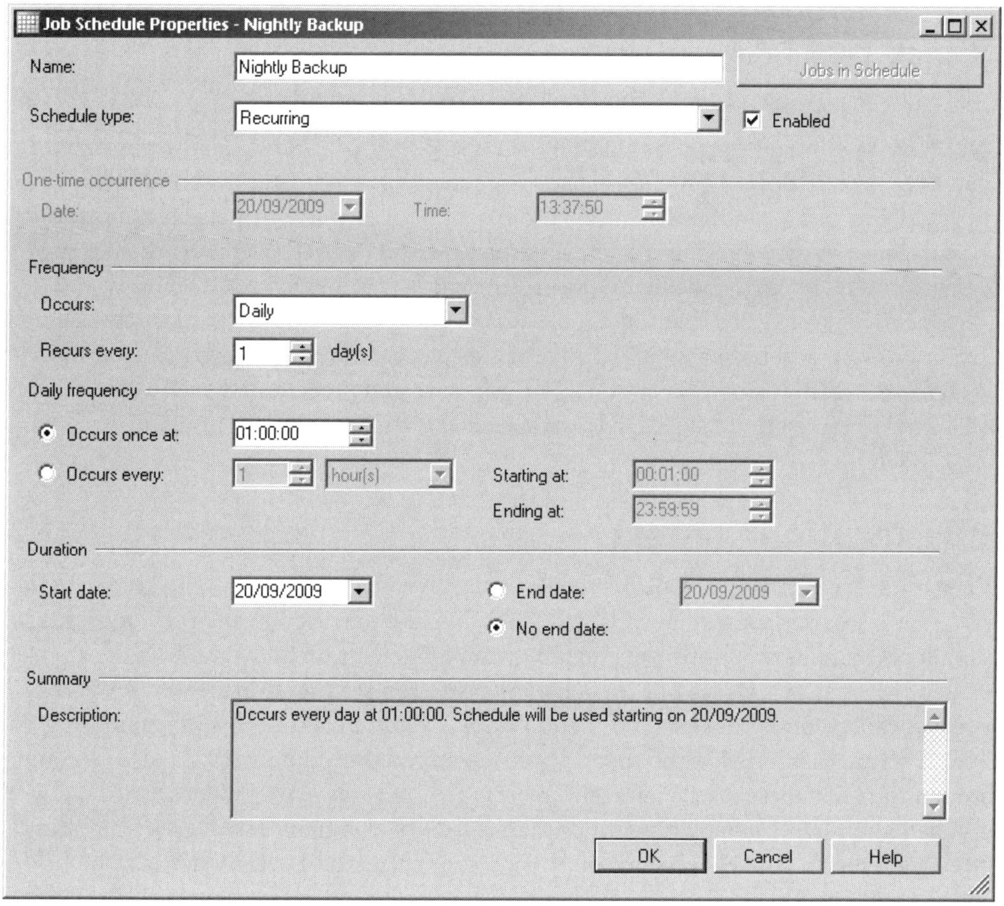

Figure 10-9 *Job Schedule Properties dialog box*

Click OK to create the schedule and return to the Schedules page. If required, it is possible to create more than one schedule for a job. For example, you may want the job to run at 1:00 A.M. every weekday and run in the middle of the day on weekends. To achieve this, you can create a Monday through Friday schedule and a Saturday and Sunday schedule.

Click OK again in the New Job dialog box to create the job.

Oracle DBA Q&A

Q: Does SQL Server have the concept of event-based jobs?

A: It is possible to start jobs based on events or, in the case of SQL Server, based on SQL Server alerts. When an alert is triggered, it is possible to respond to the alert by executing a job. Alerts in SQL Server can be defined as a performance condition, a Windows Management Instrumentation (WMI) event, or [defined as] a response to an error code being raised. Since it is possible to create your own error codes and to raise them in code, you can create an alert that watches for the error or event and then responds by launching a job. Alternatively, you can start a job from T-SQL using the sp_start_job system stored procedure, which you can call from a stored procedure, DML trigger, DDL trigger, or event notification.

Job Execution Context

When a job is executed by SQL Server Agent, each step within the job needs to run under a security context. T-SQL job steps, like the one used in the previous job example, execute in the context of the job owner by default. If you want to make a job step run as a user who is not the job owner, you can set the 'Run as user' property on the advanced properties page of the job step. If you are creating the job step using T-SQL script, then provide the sp_add_jobstep stored procedure with the user account through the @database_user_name parameter.

When a job step is of any type other than a T-SQL command, such as an operating system call, then a Run As account on the job step needs to be set. By default, the only account available for Run As is the SQL Server Agent service account. If you are following best practice guidelines for service accounts, the SQL Server Agent service account should be running with a least privilege account and, as such, should not have permissions to perform many actions. For example, if you are executing a call to the operating system to create a directory, then the account making the call needs the relevant permissions to create directories on the target file system; when running least privilege, it is unlikely that your SQL Server Agent account will have these permissions.

ON THE JOB

It is very tempting to set the SQL Server Agent service account to be a member of a highly privileged group such as the Windows Administrators group, to make life easy, and on SQL Server systems prior to SQL Server 2005, this is exactly what many lazy DBAs used to do. This was not a good security practice and left open potential attack vectors for escalation of privileges. In SQL Server 2005, the concepts of proxy accounts and stored credentials were introduced to ease the administrative burden. That's not to say that the lazy DBAs magically started to use them!

To provide SQL Server Agent with the ability to change security context for job steps to an account other than the SQL Server Agent account, proxy accounts are used. Proxy accounts provide SQL Server Agent with the ability to change security context using stored credentials (refer to SQL Server Books Online for information on stored credentials).

Figure 10-10 shows the Proxies node of SQL Server Agent expanded in SSMS. Below the Proxies node are the available proxy types such as Operating System and SSIS Package Execution.

Let's take the example of a job that will import data to SQL Server using data files located on a remote staging server. The job will contain multiple steps. The first step in the job needs to be to connect to the remote staging server where the data files ready for import are stored, and then to copy the files to the local machine. The second step performs the data import. We are just going to concentrate on the first step, which will be of the type Operating System and will perform a copy command. The step will need

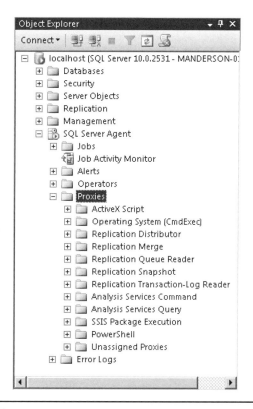

Figure 10-10 *Available proxies*

to run under the security context of an account that can connect to the remote server and read the files and then create a copy of the file locally. The step could simply run as the SQL Server Agent account, but in our setup we have followed best practice and the account does not have the relevant permissions to perform the operation. Therefore, we need to set up a proxy account.

Figure 10-11 shows the New Proxy Account dialog box (launched by right-clicking Proxies and selecting New Proxy). In the example, the proxy account is called StagingServerFileCopy and maps to a set of stored credentials called StagingServerAccount. The stored credentials are for a Windows account that has the relevant file system

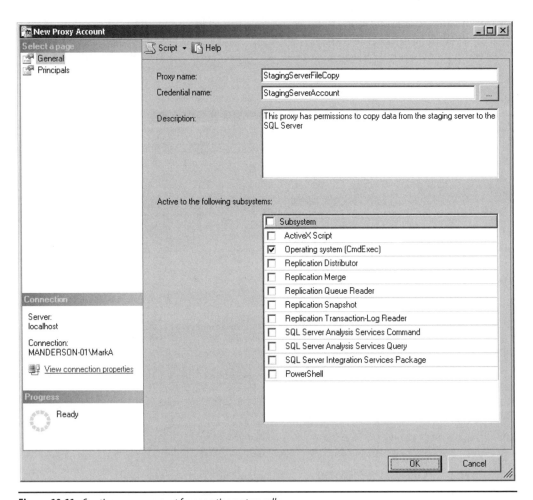

Figure 10-11 *Creating a proxy account for operating system calls*

permission to read data from the external server and copy files to the local server. The account has been marked as available for use with the operating system subsystem.

Now within the job step, the StagingServerFileCopy proxy can be used as the account under which the job step should run. Figure 10-12 shows the job step with the Run As account set to the new proxy account.

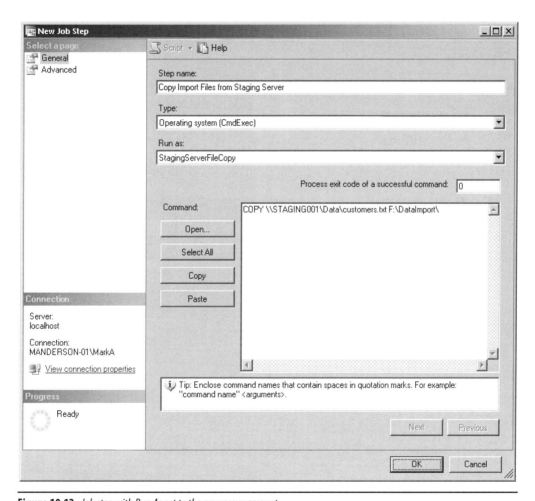

Figure 10-12 *Job step with Run As set to the new proxy account*

Job Categories

SQL Server creates job categories automatically when you set up features such as replication to group all the replication jobs together for ease of management. It is possible to create your own categories and then assign jobs to the categories. For example, you could create a category of Batch Extracts and place all extract jobs into the category. To manage job categories, right-click the jobs node in SSMS and select Manage Categories. Figure 10-13 shows the Manage Job Categories interface. It is also possible to manage the categories via script using the following system stored procedures:

- ► sp_add_category
- ► sp_update_category
- ► sp_delete_category

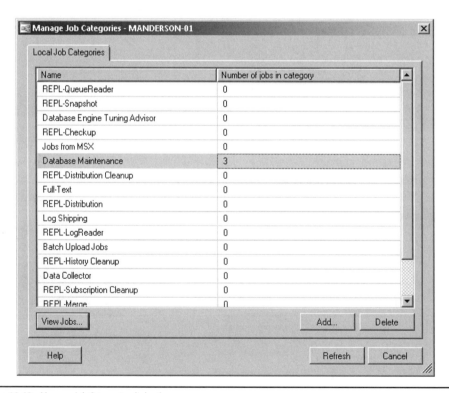

Figure 10-13 *Manage Job Categories dialog box*

Shared Schedules

As you have noticed so far, each job can have its own custom schedule assigned. Although custom schedules offer the ultimate flexibility, there are scenarios where you would want several jobs to run to the same schedule. If that schedule needs to change—for example, you might need to move your backup window—you would only want to modify one schedule, not the schedule for each individual job. Shared schedules give you this ability. A shared schedule is a schedule that can be defined once and then reused by several jobs. Figure 10-14 shows the Manage Schedules dialog box. From here, you can create new and edit/view existing schedules as well as view how many jobs depend on a particular schedule. To access these schedules, right-click the Jobs node in SSMS and select Manage Schedules.

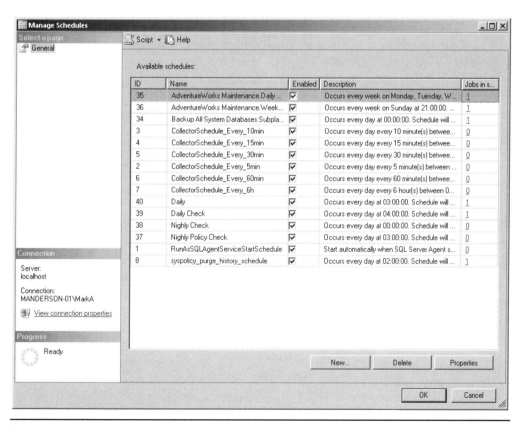

Figure 10-14 *Managing Shared Schedules*

Schedules can also be managed and created by using the following system stored procedures:

▶ sp_add_schedule

▶ sp_update_schedule

▶ sp_delete_schedule

Oracle DBA Q&A

Q: In Oracle there is the concept of a "maintenance window" schedule where a job can be set to run at any point during a predetermined window of time. Oracle decides when the job should start based on available system resources. Does SQL Server have the same concept?

A: No, SQL Server doesn't have the concept of "maintenance window" schedules. A job must be set to run at a preconfigured time. Although not identical, it is worth mentioning there is a concept in SQL Server of being able to run a job when the CPU is considered to be idle. The CPU is considered to be idle based on thresholds that you set. Figure 10-15 shows the Advanced page of the SQL Server Agent Properties dialog box, at the bottom of which the CPU idle condition has been set for when the average CPU utilization drops below 10 percent and remains there for at least 600 seconds (10 minutes).

Job Monitoring and Execution History

To view the current status of jobs and the execution history, two tools are available: Job Activity Monitor and the Job History logs in Log File Viewer.

Job Activity Monitor can be found under the SQL Server Agent node in SSMS, as shown in Figure 10-16. Job Activity Monitor shows the current status of each job, such as whether it is idle or running, when it was last run, whether the run was successful, and when it is due to run again, in addition to some other details.

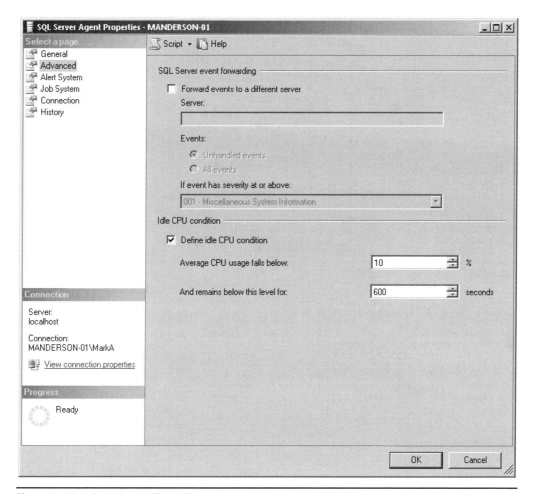

Figure 10-15 *Defining the CPU idle condition*

Job Activity Monitor is launched by double-clicking the Job Activity Monitor node in SSMS. Figure 10-17 shows Job Activity Monitor.

To view complete history details for jobs, you can right-click the jobs node in SSMS and select View History to get all jobs listed, or right-click an individual job and select View History to get just its history. Figure 10-18 shows the viewer with all jobs listed.

Figure 10-16 *Job Activity Monitor in SSMS*

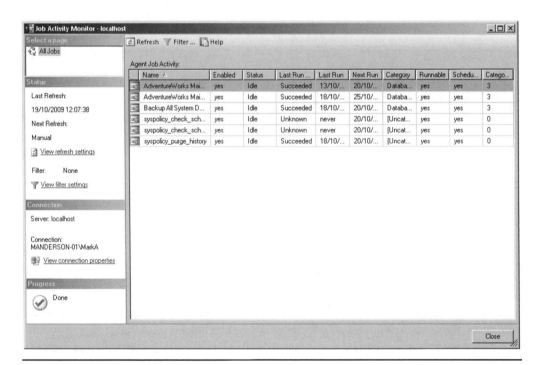

Figure 10-17 *Job Activity Monitor*

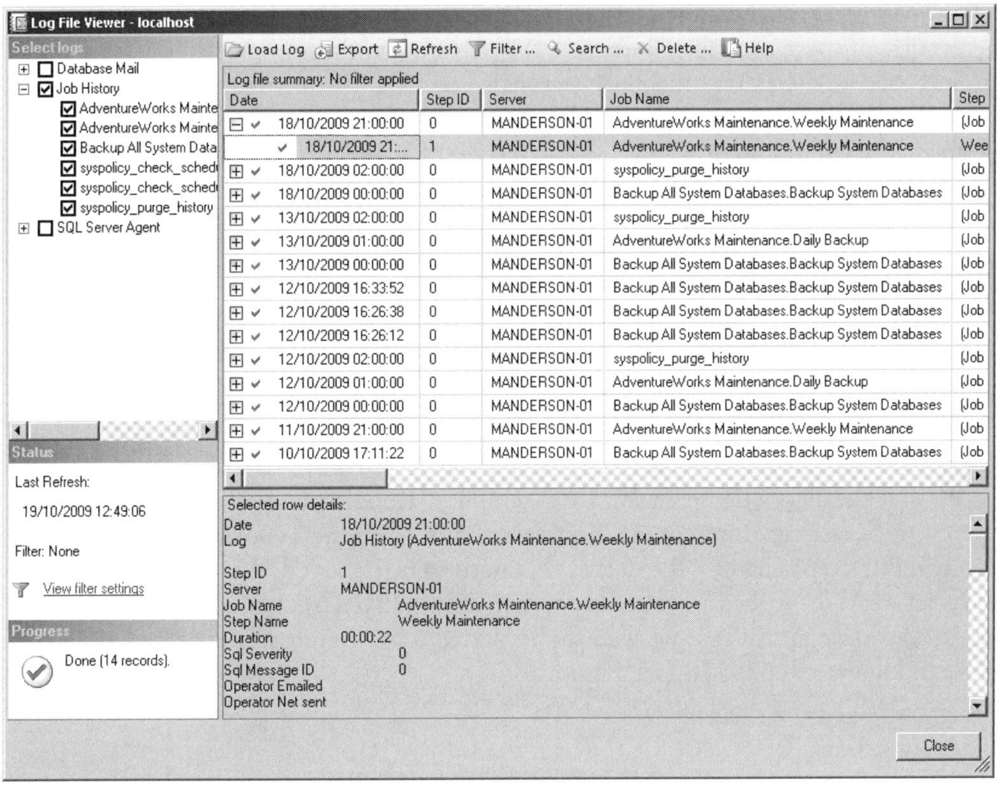

Figure 10-18 *Job History*

Alerts

At an enterprise level, there are many tools that provide network monitoring and alerting for servers and services. Tools such as Microsoft System Center Operations Manager (SCOM), IBM Tivoli, and HP OpenView can be used at an enterprise level to provide the overall view of enterprise operations. Some of the tools, such as Microsoft SCOM, have management packs that can be installed on the SQL Server machine to take alert data that's specific to the SQL Server instance. Although these enterprise tools exist, it is still very common for DBA teams to set up their own level of alerting and to define their own metrics, thresholds, and notification channels at the database server level.

To monitor Oracle, DBAs tend to use server-generated alerts to monitor database operations and notification rules to wrap the alerts with some form of notification for administrators and to perform any corrective action. Even if you have never set up any of your own alerts, there are some default alerts already operating, such as the percentage of space used for tablespaces (85 percent warning, 97 percent critical). In SQL Server, the alerts capability is provided by SQL Server Agent. An alert can be defined as a SQL Server event such as an error code being raised, a SQL Server performance condition, or a WMI event. An alert has the ability to notify operators of the event taking place and can also run a SQL Server Agent job in response to perform any corrective action.

Figure 10-19 shows where the alerts are located in the Object Explorer view within SSMS.

Let's walk through the steps to create an alert using SSMS. The alert we are going to create will notify the DBA Team when available free space in the tempdb system database (SQL Server's temporary tablespace) drops below 10MB.

We start by right-clicking the Alerts node in SSMS and selecting New Alert. This presents us with the New Alert dialog box, as shown in Figure 10-20.

We give the alert a name, in this case "tempdb - Running low on space," and select the "SQL Server performance condition alert" type from the Type drop-down list. Selecting this type changes the details that need to be provided. We select the object SQLServer:Transactions and the Free Space in tempdb (KB) counter. Then we set our alert thresholds; in this case we want to be alerted if the counter "falls below" 10240, the value in kilobytes for 10MB (see Figure 10-21).

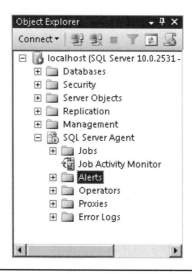

Figure 10-19   *Alerts are located under SQL Server Agent.*

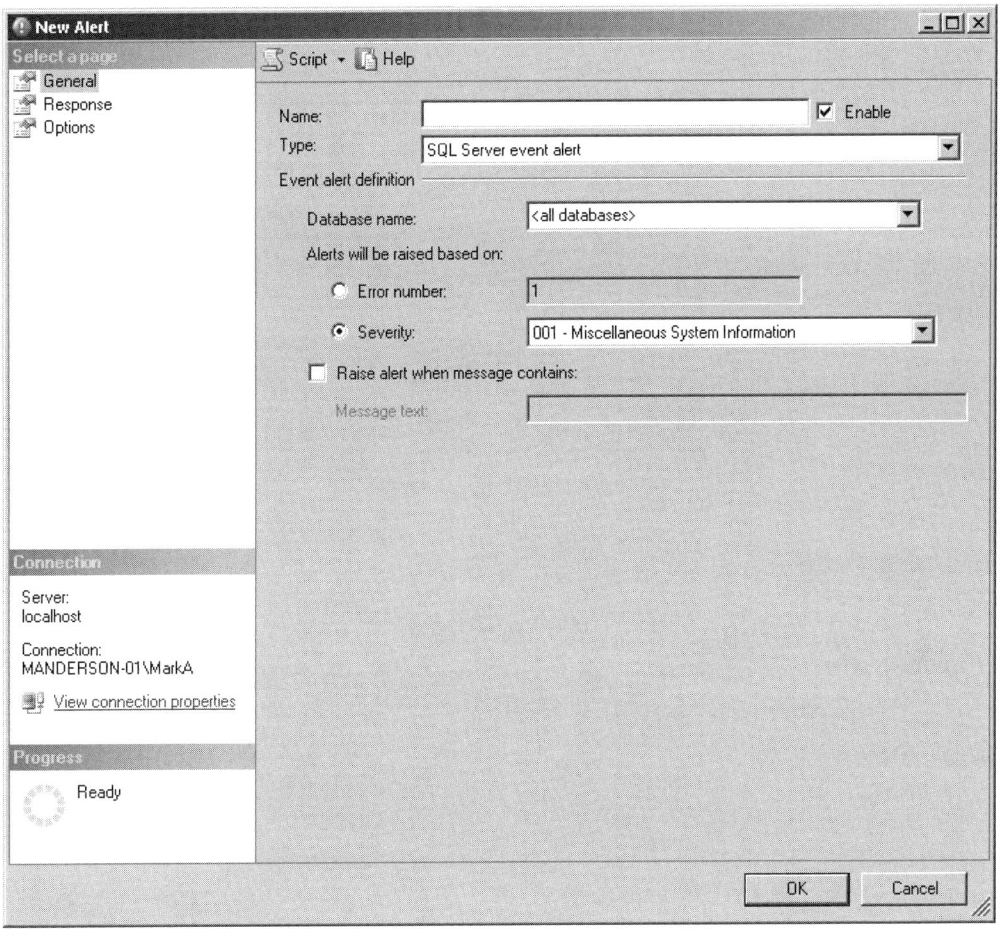

Figure 10-20 *New Alert dialog box*

Full details of all performance objects and counters can be found in SQL Server Books Online. Figure 10-22 shows the details for SQLServer:Transactions in Books Online.

Clicking on the Response page on the left side of the New Alert dialog box presents us with a series of options to determine what to do when the alert has been raised, as shown in Figure 10-23. We have two available options: enable the alert to take corrective action by executing a job, and notify one or more operators. In this example, we have chosen to

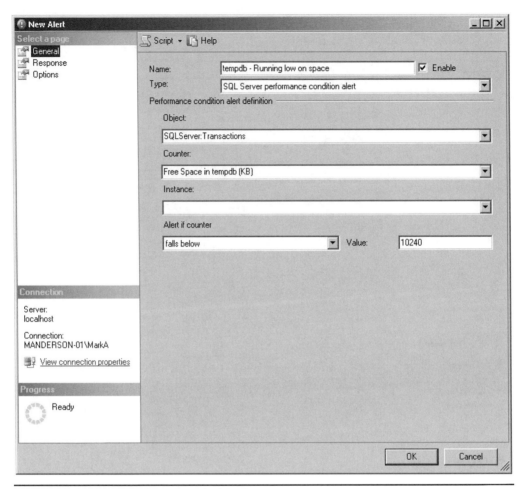

Figure 10-21 *New Alert dialog box with completed details*

notify the DBA Team operator via e-mail that this alert has been raised. On this occasion we have decided not to automate the response with any corrective action.

Finally, we select the Options page (see Figure 10-24) and choose to include in the response e-mail the error text from the alert and some text of our own. The last option on this page is to select the duration of the delay between responses. Depending on the type of event you are monitoring, the event may occur multiple times in a short period. Setting the delay between responses ensures that even if the event occurs multiple times, it will only produce a response to the alert once until the delay period has lapsed. We set our delay to 60 minutes.

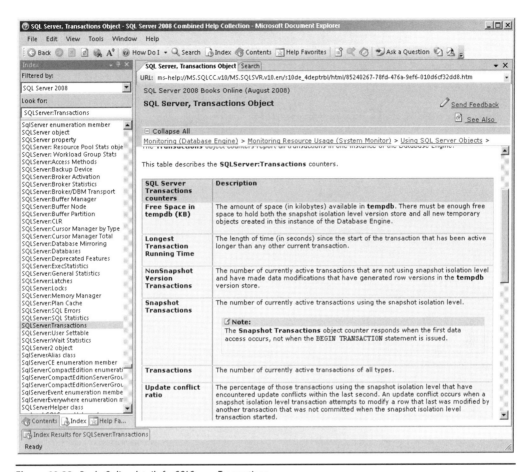

Figure 10-22 *Books Online details for SQLServer:Transactions*

Now that we have completed all the required information for the alert, we click OK. SQL Server then creates the alert and starts to monitor for the alert condition.

In the previous example, clicking OK on the New Alert dialog box creates and executes calls to system stored procedures found in msdb. Three system stored procedures are used for creating, updating, and deleting alerts:

▶ sp_add_alert

▶ sp_update_alert

▶ sp_delete_alert

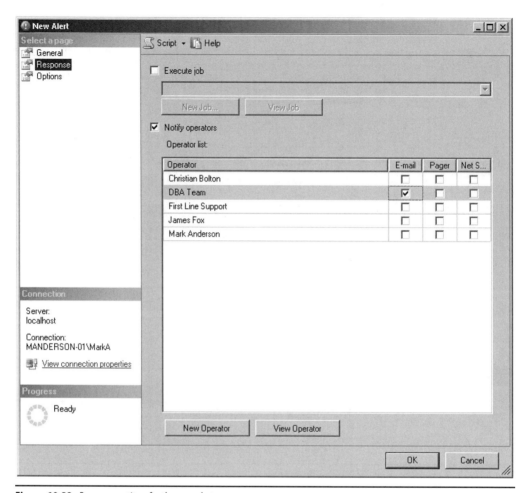

Figure 10-23 *Response options for the new alert*

The notifications are managed separately from an alert and are managed using

▶ sp_add_notification

▶ sp_update_notification

▶ sp_delete_notification

Figure 10-25 shows examples of how to work with alerts using T-SQL script and the system stored procedures. Notice that the initial call to sp_add_alert creates the alert

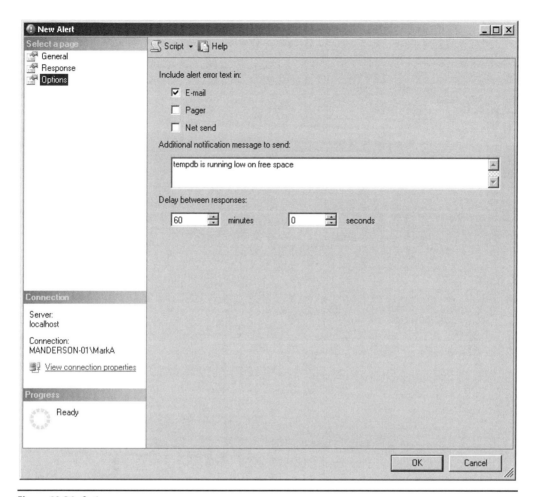

Figure 10-24 *Options page*

definition but does not add the notification. The notification is created with a call to sp_add_notification.

The script also shows how to update the alert using sp_update_alert. In this example, setting the enabled flag to 0 disables the alert, preventing it from responding, but without removing the alert definition from the system. Finally, the script shows a call to sp_delete_alert, which removes the alert from the system. sp_delete_alert also removes

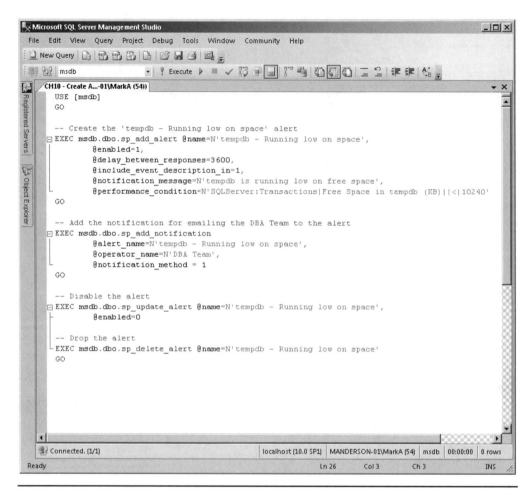

Figure 10-25 *Create, update, and delete alerts using system stored procedures*

any notifications associated with the alert for you so you do not have to make your own calls to sp_delete_notification.

To view how many times an alert has been raised and when it was last raised and responded to, right-click the alert within SSMS and select Properties. On the alert properties screen, select the History page. Figure 10-26 shows the history of the 'tempdb - Running low on space' alert.

Up to this point we have looked at creating alerts based on predefined conditions. It is also possible to create and raise your own errors and to then create alerts that can respond to those events. For example, you may decide to create your own error message

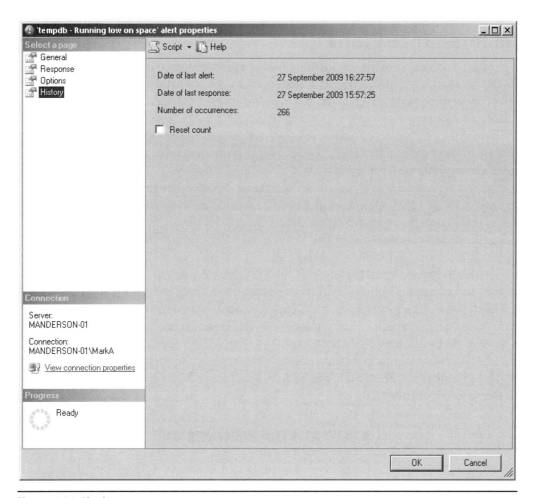

Figure 10-26 *Alert history*

within your application. When the application raises the error, an alert can respond to the error by running a predefined script configured as a SQL Server Agent job.

NOTE

When a feature such as SQL Server Replication (covered in Chapter 11), which is used to replicate subsets of data, is used, it will create its own set of custom alerts in a disabled state. As a DBA, you would then enable the alerts of interest and associate operators with them to receive notifications.

Maintenance Plans

Checking database integrity, performing backups, and reorganizing or rebuilding indexes are just some of the types of maintenance activity that a DBA needs to perform. All of these operations generally tend to be scripted by the DBA and set to run as scheduled tasks.

To remove the burden of having to create scripts and to simplify and automate the process of database maintenance, SQL Server provides a graphical way to describe maintenance routines, through the use of Maintenance Plans. A Maintenance Plan is a graphical representation of a series of maintenance tasks that can be organized to run in a workflow style. Maintenance plans can be created either manually or through the use of the Maintenance Plan Wizard, which automates the creation by asking a series of questions and then producing the Maintenance Plan, which you can subsequently manually edit and apply additional tasks to.

The Maintenance Plans feature uses the SQL Server Integration Services package format and execution engine (SSIS is covered in more detail in Chapter 11). Creating a Maintenance Plan produces an SSIS package that is stored in the msdb database. Scheduling a Maintenance Plan produces a SQL Server Agent job that in turn creates a job step that executes the SSIS package. To create Maintenance Plans, you must be a member of the sysadmin fixed server role.

The Maintenance Plans node can be found under the Management node in SSMS, as shown in Figure 10-27.

Figure 10-27 *Maintenance Plans located under the Management node*

As previously mentioned, there are two ways to create a Maintenance Plan: manually, or by using the Maintenance Plan Wizard.

Let's walk through creating a plan manually. The first step is to right-click the Maintenance Plans node and select New Maintenance Plan. You will be prompted for a name for the new plan; in this case we will call the plan AdventureWorks Maintenance. Click OK. We are then presented with the Maintenance Plan designer surface, as shown in Figure 10-28.

Before moving on to the creation of the plan, it's worth noting that a plan incorporates the concept of subplans. Each subplan is a collection of tasks that can have its own schedule or be executed on demand separately from other subplans. By default, a plan has one subplan.

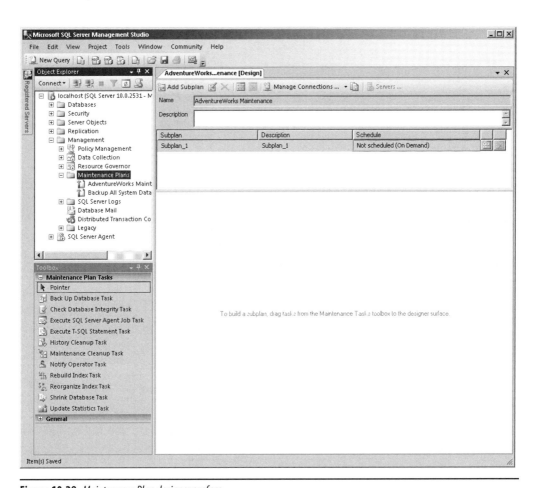

Figure 10-28 *Maintenance Plan designer surface*

In our example, we are going to use two subplans for our AdventureWorks Maintenance plan. The first subplan will run Monday through to Saturday and performs a full database backup. Our second subplan will run on Sunday night and perform additional database maintenance, including running database integrity checks, reorganizing indexes, and updating statistics.

We start by renaming the existing default Subplan_1 by double-clicking the subplan in the designer. Figure 10-29 shows Subplan_1 being renamed to Daily Backup. Clicking the calendar icon in the dialog box enables us to select the schedule to which the subplan will run; in this case, we set it to Monday through Saturday to run at 1:00 A.M., as shown in Figure 10-30.

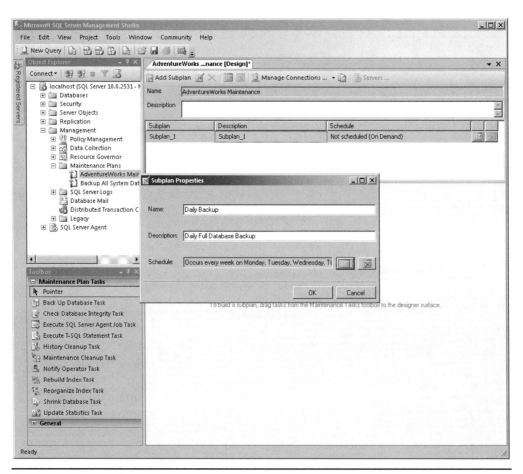

Figure 10-29 *Renaming the subplan*

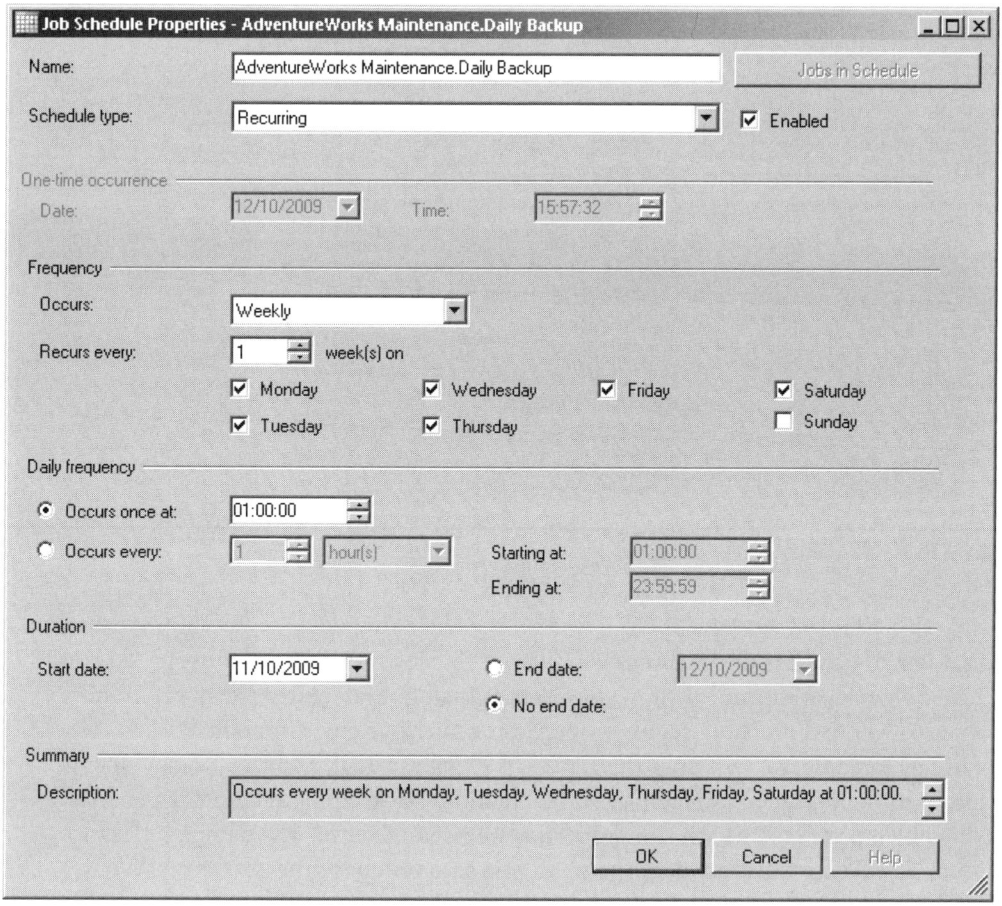

Figure 10-30 *Clicking the Calendar icon enables you to set the subplan schedule.*

Now that we have set the name of the subplan and given it a schedule, we can add the tasks that we want it to perform. The plan is composed by clicking and dragging Maintenance Plan tasks from the Toolbox onto the designer surface; once on the surface, the properties of the task are then set.

Figure 10-31 shows a close-up of the Toolbox that contains the tasks that the Maintenance Plan can perform. The tasks are self-explanatory, such as Back Up Database Task and Rebuild Index Task.

After each task is placed on the designer surface, it needs to have its properties set. Some properties have defaults but others require you to input additional information. For example, if you place a Back Up Database Task on the designer surface, you need

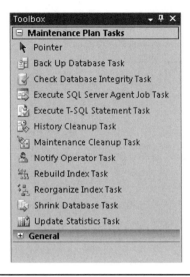

Figure 10-31 *Maintenance Plan Tasks Toolbox*

to set which database or databases you want it to back up; all other settings, such as backup type, location, and compression settings, all have defaults, although in most scenarios you will probably set all properties to suit your environment.

In our example, we will drag the Back Up Database Task and the Notify Operator Task onto the designer surface. We right-click the Back Up Database Task and select Edit, which presents us with the properties we need to set for the database backup. Figure 10-32 shows the property page. In this case we chose the AdventureWorks Database, set the backup location, and set the backup compression setting.

Next, we set the properties for the Notify Operator Task. This task will be used to notify an operator if the backup task fails. We set the operator to notify and set the message as shown in Figure 10-33.

Now that we have the tasks on the designer surface, we need to join them together to define the order of execution and the flow of the tasks. The joins between tasks are known as *precedence constraints*, and there are three types:

▶ **Success constraint**   Ensures that its path is followed upon the successful completion of the previous task

▶ **Failure constraint**   Is followed when the previous task failed to execute successfully

▶ **Completion constraint**   Is followed no matter what the outcome of the previous task

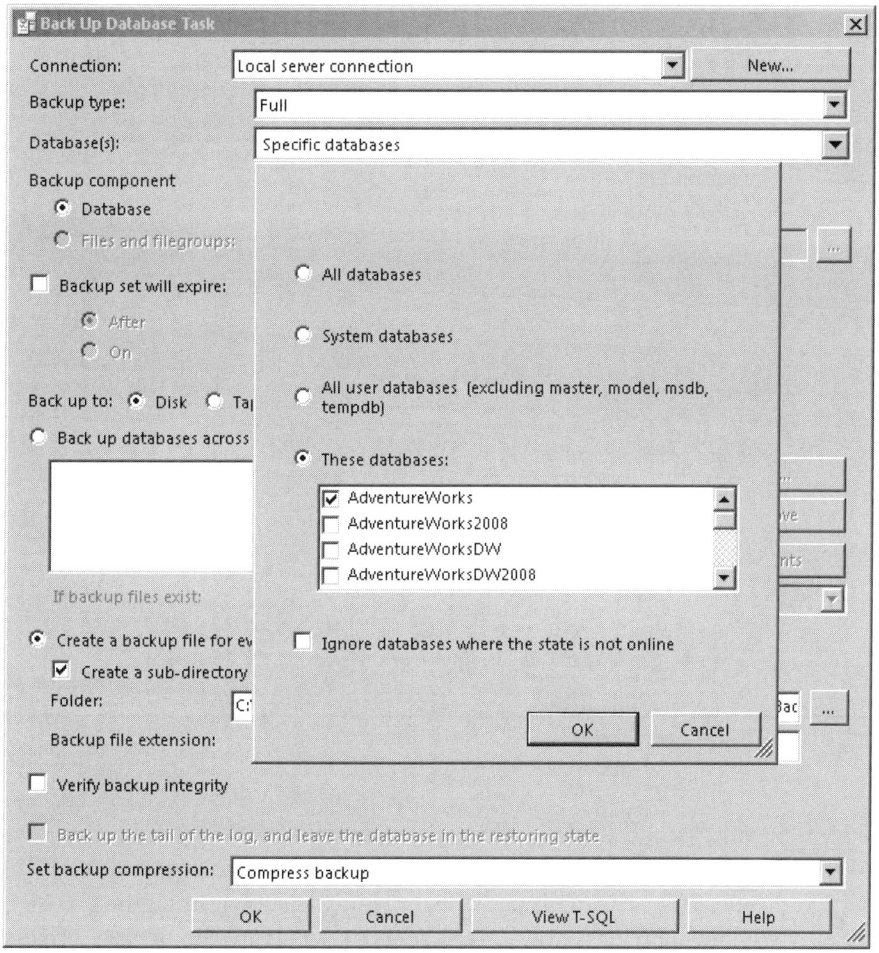

Figure 10-32 *Back Up Database Task properties*

It is also possible to create logical AND and OR constraints for a task. For example, using an AND constraint, a task will only execute if two parallel tasks prior to the next task both complete.

For our plan, we want the Notify Operator Task to execute only when the Back Up Database Task fails. When a task is selected on the designer surface, an arrow icon appears at the bottom of the task, which allows it to be linked to another task. Therefore, we drag the arrow icon from the bottom of the Back Up Database Task and join it to

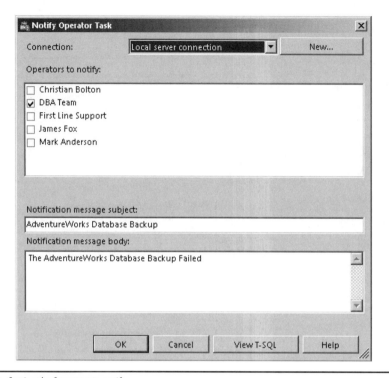

Figure 10-33 *Setting the Operators to notify*

the Notify Operator Task. By default, this will create a Success constraint; that is, the Notify Operator Task will execute when the backup succeeds. To change it to a Failure constraint, right-click the constraint and select Failure, as shown in Figure 10-34.

Our Daily Backup subplan is now complete. We next create the Sunday night subplan, which will perform a series of checks and maintenance. We start by clicking the Add Subplan button in the designer. We then give the subplan the name Weekly Maintenance and set the schedule to run on Sunday nights at 21:00. Next we add the following tasks to the new designer surface: Check Database Integrity Task, Reorganize Index Task, Update Statistics Task, Back Up Database Task, and finally Maintenance Cleanup Task. Next, we join the tasks together to flow in the order in which they were

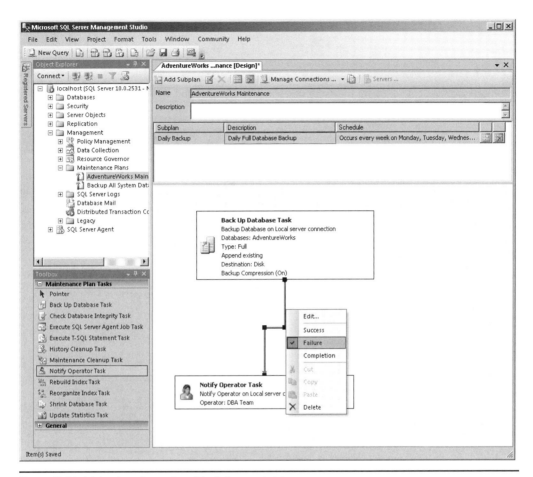

Figure 10-34 *Joining the tasks together with a Failure constraint*

added followed by setting the properties of each task. In the case of the Reorganize Index Task and the Update Statistics Task, we simply let the tasks work with all indexes and statistics. The Maintenance Cleanup Task is set to remove backup sets older than two weeks.

The resulting subplan is shown in Figure 10-35.

At runtime, the T-SQL required for each task is dynamically generated before execution. This ensures that the "catch all" tasks for example on the Update Statistics

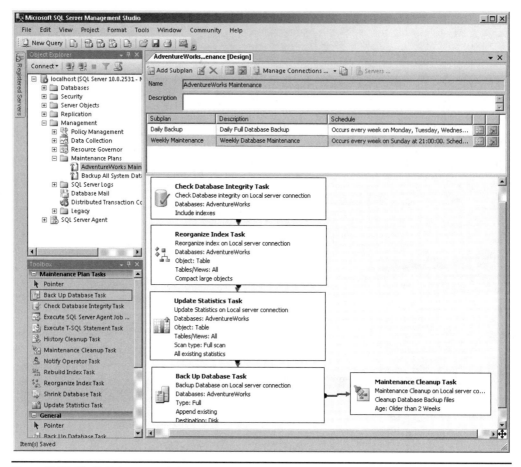

Figure 10-35 *Weekly Maintenance subplan*

Task which update all statistics picks up if more statistics have been added since the creation of the plan. To see what T-SQL would be generated if the plan were run now, simply double-click the task (or right-click and select Edit) and then click View T-SQL. Figure 10-36 shows the T-SQL that would be generated for the Update Statistics Task.

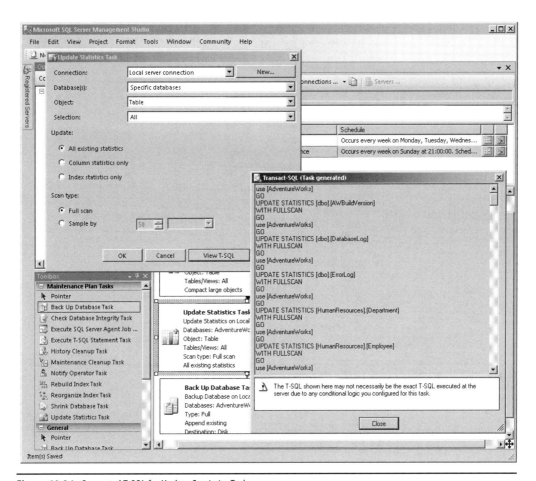

Figure 10-36 *Generated T-SQL for Update Statistics Task*

Our Maintenance Plan for the AdventureWorks database is now complete. Saving the plan creates the associated SQL Agent jobs to run the Maintenance Plan. Figure 10-37 shows SQL Server Agent with the two subplans for the AdventureWorks Maintenance plan.

It should be noted that a Maintenance Plan does not have to be scheduled, although creating a plan always creates a SQL Server Agent job (a nonscheduled plan is a job but

Figure 10-37 *Associated jobs created for the Maintenance Plan schedule*

with no schedule). After a plan is created, it can then be run on demand either by right-clicking the plan in the Maintenance Plans section of SSMS and selecting Execute or by starting the job in SQL Server Agent. If a plan has multiple subplans, then to manually start the subplan, you must use the SQL Server Agent job.

To view the execution history for a Maintenance Plan you can right-click the Maintenance Plan and select View History. Figure 10-38 shows the history for the AdventureWorks Maintenance plan.

The history shown in the Maintenance Plans log of Log File Viewer comes from the log files generated by the Maintenance Plan. By default, a text file will be generated each time the Maintenance Plan is executed and the file will be located in the default

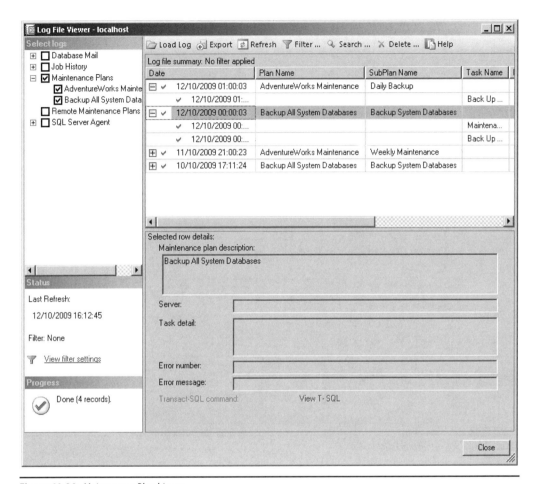

Figure 10-38 *Maintenance Plan history*

log directory location for SQL Server alongside the SQL Server error logs (see Chapter 3 for default installation locations). It is possible to change the logging level and location for each plan by selecting the Reporting and Logging icon within the Maintenance Plan designer. Figure 10-39 shows the Reporting and Logging dialog box with the options to switch off report generation, create a new file per execution,

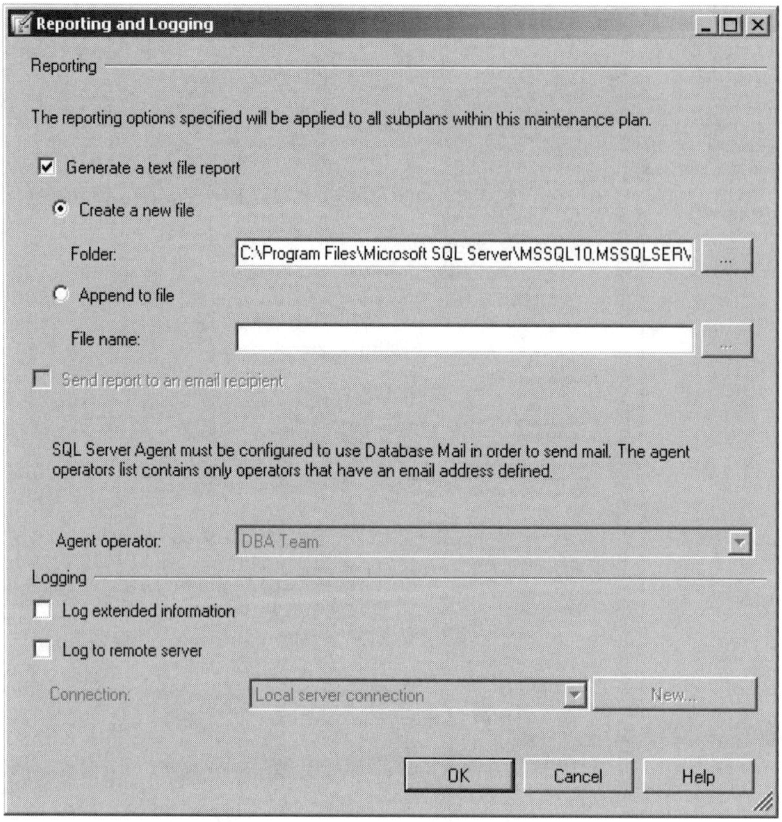

Figure 10-39 *Reporting and Logging details*

or append each execution detail to a single file. The option to change the location of the report file is also available. Other options include logging additional detailed information, sending log details to a remote server, and e-mailing an operator with the report details. Depending on the options chosen for reporting and the logging level for each package, daily, weekly, and monthly executions can result in a large number of report files being generated. To clean up the old and unwanted reports, the Maintenance Plan task Maintenance Cleanup Task can be used to remove old report files. Figure 10-40 shows an example of the setting for the Maintenance Cleanup Task removing report files older than four weeks.

(The following describes the Maintenance Cleanup Task dialog shown in the figure:)

Maintenance Cleanup Task

Connection: Local server connection   New...

Delete files of the following type:

○ Backup files

● Maintenance Plan text reports

File location:

○ Delete specific file

File name: [   ] ...

● Search folder and delete files based on an extension

Folder: SQL Server\MSSQL10.MSSQLSERVER\MSSQL\Log ...

File extension: txt

☐ Include first-level subfolders

File age:

☑ Delete files based on the age of the file at task run time

Delete files older than the following:

4 ÷ Week(s)

OK   Cancel   View T-SQL   Help

Figure 10-40 *Maintenance Cleanup Task removing Maintenance Plan reports*

ON THE JOB

As every good DBA knows, backing up the system databases is essential. Although, there are still many instances of where the DBA has done a good job of creating backup routines, either by using simple T-SQL scripts or by using Maintenance Plans, for their user databases but has neglected to back up their system databases. With Maintenance Plans, you can create a plan that will back up all system databases in less than two minutes!

Figure 10-41 shows a Maintenance Plan that will back up all system databases (master, model, and msdb) every night at midnight. On successful execution of the Back Up Database Task, the plan cleans up any backup sets older than two weeks; on failure of the Back Up Database Task, the Notify Operator Task will e-mail the DBA team so that they can come and fix the problem.

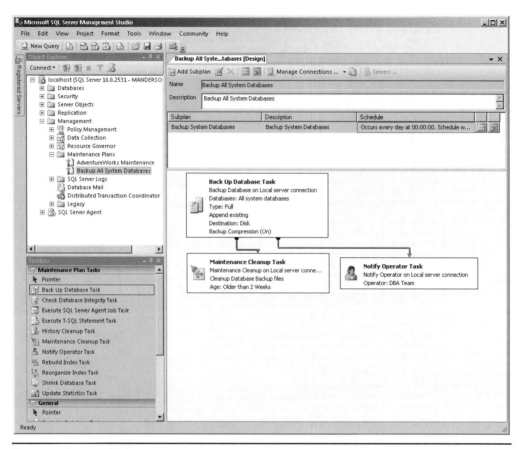

Figure 10-41 *System database backup*

Policy-Based Management

As a DBA you will have either your own standards or a corporate set of standards specifying how your database environment should be configured and managed. For example, there will be rules concerning the placement of log and data files, enabling and disabling database options, and creating objects in certain schemas. Just as Maintenance Plans help with the move away from having to create maintenance routines using scripts, Policy-Based Management allows for the creation of policies that describe your SQL Server environment and the way in which you want it to be, and stay, configured without having to resort to creating scripts to do initial server setup and then retrospective checking of the configuration to make sure nobody has changed your settings.

Policies are stored in the msdb database, and in order to administer policies, you must be a member of the PolicyAdministratorRole role. Policy Management can be found in SSMS under the Management node, as shown in Figure 10-42.

There are five elements to be aware of for Policy-Based Management:

▸ **Facets** Define a group of logically related properties for a particular management area of SQL Server. For example, the Database facet exposes properties related to the database such as the settings for AutoClose, AutoShrink, and AutoUpdateStatistics.

▸ **Conditions** Used to describe the desired state of a single facet. For example, you could create a condition known as 'Standard Database Options' that would describe the desired state of various properties of the Database Options facet such as AutoClose = False, AutoShrink=False, AutoUpdateStatisticsEnabled = True.

▸ **Policies** Take the Condition and specify the target to which the condition should apply. In addition, it also dictates how the policy should be evaluated such as on demand or to a schedule. Polices can also contain information to surface to a user when a policy is violated such as any help text or URLs.

▸ **Targets** Specify the entities to which the policies apply. For example, you may want a policy to only apply to objects in a certain schema within a particular database.

Figure 10-42 *Policy-Based Management in SSMS*

▶ **Categories** Allow for the grouping together of policies. For example, you may create a category called Highly Confidential that contains your policies for database encryption, auditing, and user access. For a database on your server that is classed as containing highly confidential information, you can simply add the database to the Highly Confidential category and all the relevant policies will be applied.

To demonstrate how all these elements work together, let's walk through an example of creating a policy that ensures our corporate database backup standards are being followed. In this scenario, our standards dictate that as a minimum for every database in our environment, the database backup files must reside on a different logical volume from the data files and that the last backup of the database must be less than one day old.

To create this policy we need to start by creating a condition to evaluate the properties of a facet that exposes the data and backup file locations and the last recorded backup properties for a database. In SSMS, we right-click the Conditions node under Policy Management and select New Condition. In the Create New Condition dialog box, as shown in Figure 10-43, we add the name Database Backup Standards and

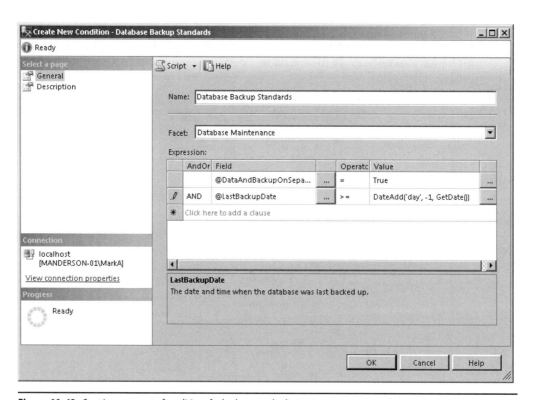

Figure 10-43 *Creating a new set of conditions for backup standards*

select the Database Maintenance facet. The Database Maintenance facet exposes two properties that we are interested in: @DataAndBackupOnSeparateLogicalVolumes, which returns a value of 'true' if the data and backup files are on separate logical volumes and 'false' if they are not, and the @LastBackupDate, which exposes the date of the last database backup.

To check the properties we are interested in, we start by selecting the @DataAndBackupOnSeparateLogicalVolumes property in the Field drop-down menu and setting the evaluation operator to = with a value of True. Next we select the @LastBackupDate field, choose the >= operator, and this time set the value to an expression—in this case, DateAdd('day', -1, GetDate()) to return the date of the previous day based on the current date. Therefore, if the date is greater than or equal to yesterday at this time, then the condition will return 'true'. Our condition is now complete, so we create it by clicking OK.

Now that we have the condition created, the next step is to create a policy based on the condition. In SSMS we right-click the Policies node and select New Policy. Figure 10-44 shows the Create New Policy dialog box, in which we give the policy the name Database Backup Standards Policy. Next we select the check condition we just created from the Check Condition drop-down menu. The Assigned Targets section allows us to create a condition that will determine which objects should be subject to this check condition; in this case, the default of Every Database is selected. We next select the evaluation mode (we will cover evaluation modes shortly). This type of operation has only two types of evaluation mode available, On Demand and On Schedule. We want our policy to be evaluated automatically every day, so we select the On Schedule evaluation mode and then create a new schedule by clicking the New button. The schedule creation screen is the standard one used for creating schedules for jobs. It is also possible to select an existing shared schedule by clicking the Pick button.

Next we move to the Description page of the Create New Policy dialog box, as shown in Figure 10-45. The Description page allows us to put text detail in the policy that will be visible at runtime. Although the detail page is not mandatory, it will assist anyone who encounters the policy by helping them to understand why the policy exists and how and why they may be violating it. We want to provide assistance to anyone who encounters the policy, so we start by providing a description of what the policy is for, and then we complete the additional help text with details of why they have been flagged as being in violation of the policy. Finally, we add a link to an intranet site that contains details about the policy. The last step is to set the policy category. Since this is our first policy, we click the New button. When prompted, we enter the name Corporate Database Standards. This category can now be used to group together any other policies we create relating to standards.

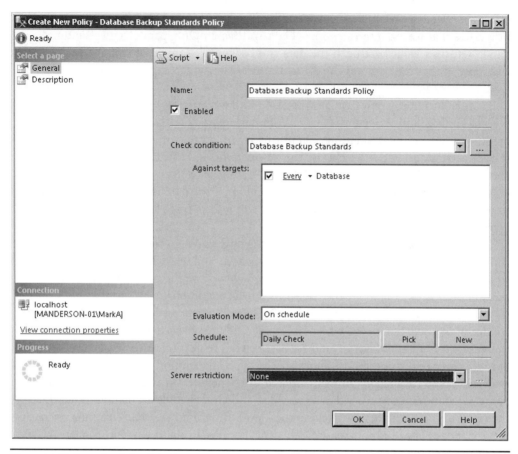

Figure 10-44 *Create New Policy dialog box*

Finally, we click OK and the policy is created along with a SQL Server Agent Job that evaluates the policy according to the schedule we defined. Figure 10-46 shows the new policy and condition created within SSMS.

Policy Evaluation

In the previous example, the policy was created using the On Schedule evaluation mode. The evaluation modes available are dependent on the type of facet being used. Policies have four different evaluation modes:

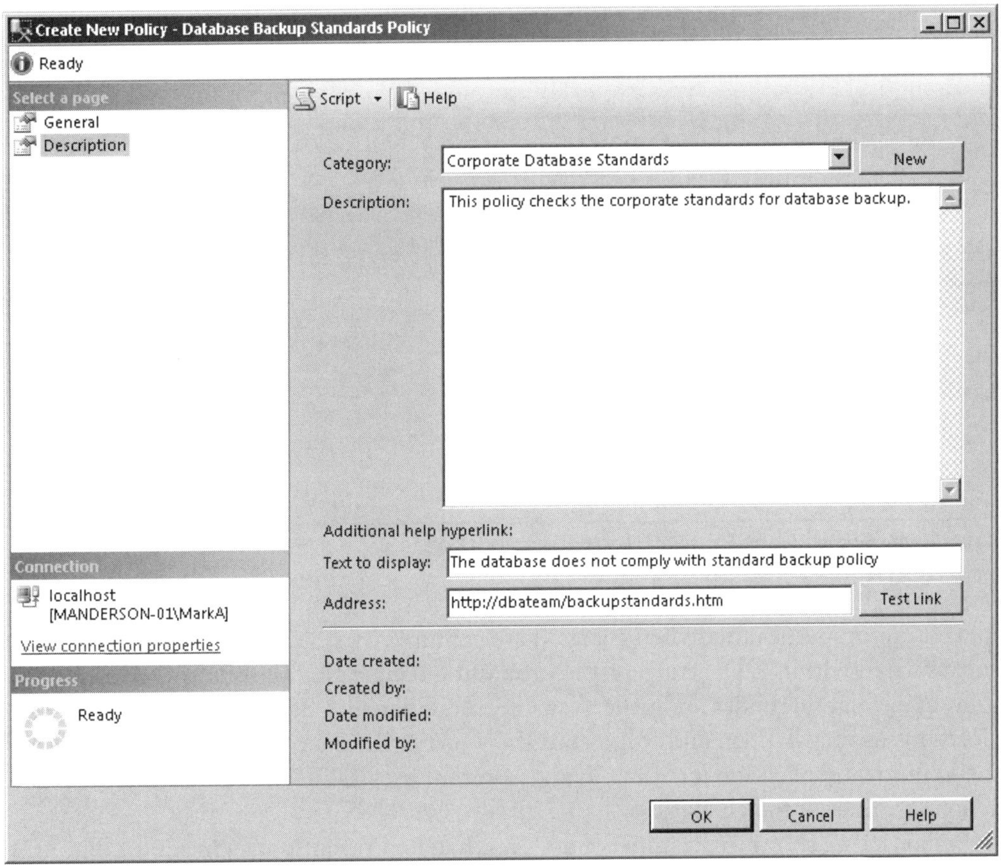

Figure 10-45 *Create New Policy dialog box, Description page*

- ▶ On Schedule
- ▶ On Demand
- ▶ On Change: Log Only
- ▶ On Change: Prevent

All facets support policies using the On Schedule and On Demand evaluation modes. On Schedule uses SQL Server Agent to create a job that will evaluate the policy on a scheduled basis. On Demand policies are effectively manual policies and are only evaluated when a user explicitly selects a policy for evaluation. If the facet being used

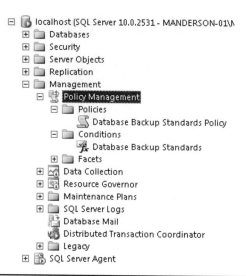

Figure 10-46 *Database Backup Standards Policy and Condition in SSMS*

is exposing properties that when changed are captured by system event tracking or are encapsulated within DDL triggers, then the On Change: Log Only and On Change: Prevent evaluation modes are made available. On Change: Log only watches for policy violations as they happen and will record the violation in the SQL Server error log and the Windows application log. On Change: Prevent uses DDL triggers to intercept the action to roll back the changes.

Figure 10-47 shows an example of an On Change: Prevent policy in action. The policy prevents a user from creating stored procedures with the prefix sp_ in the name. In the example, the attempt to create a new procedure not conforming to the rules is intercepted by the policy engine, the user is given feedback on why their operation failed—with a description of the policy and a link to an intranet site for further detail— and the user is then notified that their attempt to create the object has failed and the transaction has been rolled back.

ON THE JOB

As you may have noticed, all SQL Server system stored procedures start with sp_; therefore, it is strongly recommended that you do not start the names of your own objects with sp_, for two reasons. First, the potential exists for naming one of your own procedures with the same name as a system procedure, which may produce undesirable results. Second, it may be confusing to anyone who is new to administering the system who may think your user created stored procedure is a system stored procedure.

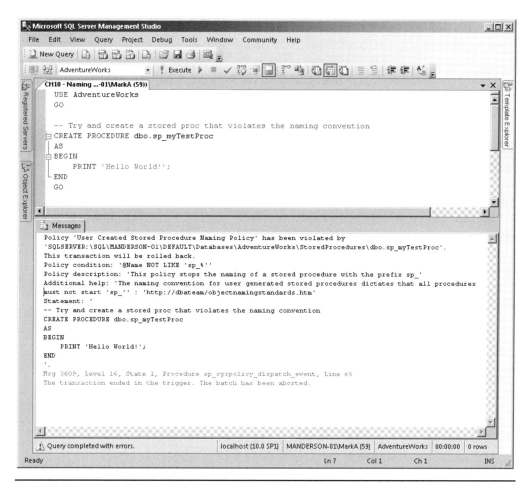

Figure 10-47 *On Change: Prevent policy preventing a policy for being violated*

Oracle DBA Q&A

Q: So I guess I could use Policy-Based Management to help implement a SQL Server version of the OFA (Optimal Flexible Architecture) guidelines, which could be proactively enforced?

A: Yes, you can use Policy-Based Management to describe how your server should be configured and set up, and then the Policy-Based Management engine will be able to alert you to any setup that does not comply with your SQL Server version of the OFA guidelines.

Even if a policy is set to be scheduled, it can also be evaluated on an ad hoc basis. It can be run by right-clicking the policy in SSMS and selecting Evaluate, which will then run the policy, covering its entire scope as defined in the Targets section of the policy; or you can evaluate a policy against an individual database by right-clicking the database and selecting Policies | Evaluate, as shown in Figure 10-48.

Selecting Evaluate presents the user with a dialog box that has all the possible policies that can be run against the database. As an example, Figure 10-49 shows the dialog box that's presented when evaluating policies against the AdventureWorks database. Each policy has a check box next to it, enabling you to select the policies you are interested in running. Once you have selected policies, clicking the Evaluate button will then check the policy against the database.

Once completed, the dialog box will present the results of the evaluation; a red circle with a white × indicates the policy failed, and a green circle with a white check indicates success. Figure 10-50 shows that the policy evaluation failed. In the Target Details section, the Details column contains a hyperlink that, when clicked, will show the detailed results of the evaluation and will highlight which elements failed and which passed. Figure 10-51 shows the detailed view of the policy evaluation.

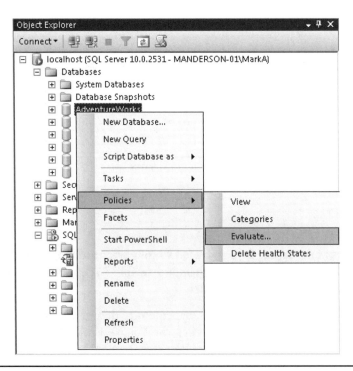

Figure 10-48 *Selecting an ad-hoc Policy evaluation for the AdventureWorks database*

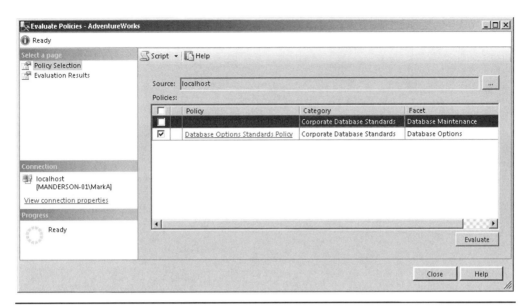

Figure 10-49 *AdventureWorks available policies*

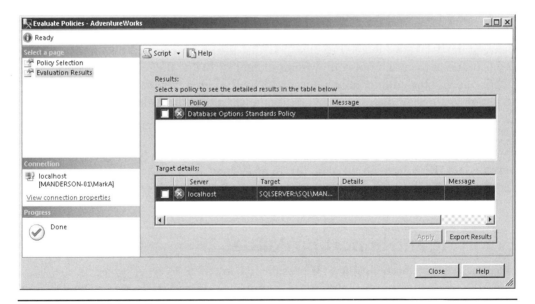

Figure 10-50 *Failed Policy evaluation*

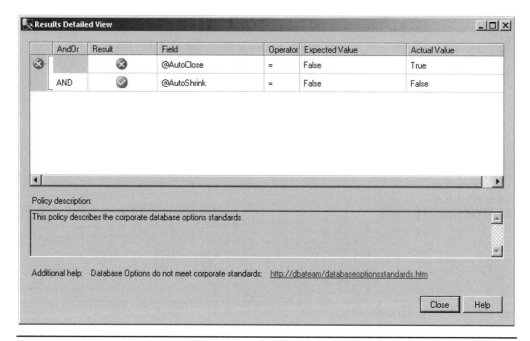

Figure 10-51 *Policy results, detailed view*

In Figure 10-51, the detailed results show that the policy checked two properties and that one of them did not comply with the policy. Below the results, the policy description and the additional help text and hyperlink that were set in the policy definition are displayed to provide guidance on why the policy failed. Clicking the Close button and returning to the Evaluate Policies window, the option to apply the policy to the noncompliant target is available. Selecting the check box next to the noncompliant target and clicking Apply as per Figure 10-52 will produce a dialog box warning that the policy will then modify all properties that do not comply with the policy to the desired configuration, in this example by setting the AutoClose property to False.

Exporting and Importing Policies

Once policies have been created, it is possible to copy them to other servers in the enterprise by using the export and import options within SSMS. To export a policy, you simply right-click the policy in SSMS and select Export. Exporting the policy will take all the details about the condition and the facet used to create the policy and will create

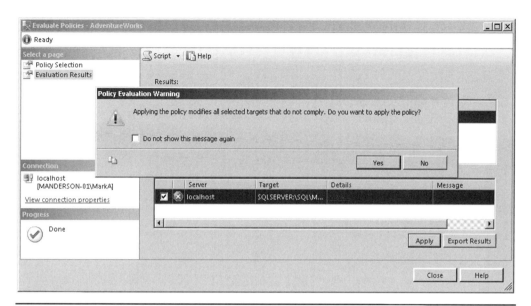

Figure 10-52 *Applying changes to the noncompliant target*

an XML file describing the policy. To Import a policy, right-click the Policies node in SSMS, select Import, and point SSMS to the XML policy definition.

ON THE JOB

Microsoft ships a tool free of charge called the SQL Server Best Practices Analyzer which is available from the Microsoft download site (www.microsoft.com/downloads). You can load this tool on your desktop and connect it to your SQL Server, it then determines if the configuration of your SQL Server is set according to the recommended best practices. The tool produces a report and indicates potential problems in the installed instance of SQL Server. The tool also provides solutions to the problems that it finds.

The best practices are also shipped as a set of policies that you can import into the SQL Server Policy engine. This approach now allows you to pick and choose which of the best practices you want to implement or monitor automatically. You can also make your own tweaks and modifications, which is a great way to get started with Policy-Based Management.

The policies are installed onto the local server and can be found at %Program Files%\Microsoft SQL Server\100\Tools\Policies\DatabaseEngine\1033.

Chapter 11

Data Movement

In This Chapter

- ► **Importing and Exporting Data**
- ► **Moving or Copying an Entire Database**
- ► **Querying Across Servers and Data Sources**
- ► **Data Replication**

"Data movement" can mean many different things, ranging from the simple import or export of a single table through to the setup and administration of complex data-replication architectures to support the publishing of datasets. Regardless of the specific type, some form of data movement tends to be part of the DBA's daily activity. Even if your organization has a data team that is responsible for data quality and movement, it is still highly likely you will be moving or copying databases for development and test environments or using data export techniques to create logical data backups. The aim of this chapter is to introduce you to the various methods available within the Microsoft SQL Server platform for moving data.

In this chapter we will cover the basics:

- ▶ Importing and exporting data
- ▶ Moving and copying databases
- ▶ Querying across databases and servers
- ▶ Data replication

Importing and Exporting Data

Let's start with the basics of importing and exporting data to or from a SQL Server database. Several tools and methods are available for performing these tasks:

- ▶ BCP (Bulk Copy Program)
- ▶ BULK INSERT statement (Import Only)
- ▶ SQL Server Integration Services (SSIS)
- ▶ SQL Server Import and Export Wizard
- ▶ SQL Server Management Studio (SSMS)

In addition to habit and familiarity, factors that might drive you toward a particular method of import or export include the complexity requirements of the load or extract, the environment you want to work in (command line or GUI), the performance requirements, and even the repeatability of the operation (is this an ad hoc request or will it be a regular activity?). For example, if you simply need to extract a few hundred rows of data, you might use SSMS to write a quick query and then copy and paste the results into a document. If your requirement is to import several million rows of data every few hours, you would use SSIS, BCP, or BULK INSERT.

Bulk Copy Program

In Oracle, the simplest method available for bulk importing data into an Oracle database is to use SQL*Loader. SQL*Loader is a command-line tool that takes a flat file containing data and a format file describing the data—along with a few additional options, such as the security type and method of import—and then imports the data into the database.

For import operations in SQL Server, BCP is analogous to SQL*Loader in Oracle. BCP has been in SQL Server since before Microsoft and Sybase parted ways; in fact, Sybase still has its own implementation of BCP in its product today. Although tools such as SSIS (covered shortly) are reported to be the new favorite for data movement, BCP is a fairly simple command-line-driven tool. Due to its simplicity and ease of use, it is still widely used by the DBA community today. BCP uses the bulk-copy APIs of SQL Server Native Client (SNAC) to transfer data to SQL Server and uses ODBC to read data from SQL Server.

One area where BCP differs from SQL*Loader is that it also has the ability to export data as well as import. The export can be a straightforward extract of an entire SQL Server table or it can be the result of a query.

Before moving into the details of the syntax for BCP, let's start with a quick example of BCP in operation. The example in Figure 11-1 shows two BCP commands: the first exports all data from the Employee table in the AdventureWorks database on the default SQL Server instance to a file called hr-emp.dat, and the second command

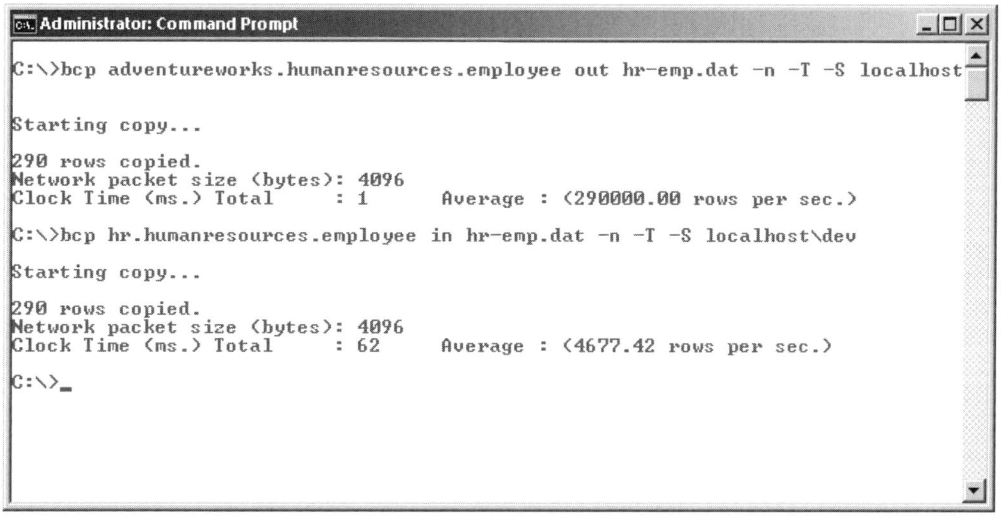

Figure 11-1   *BCP import and export*

imports the file containing the employee data into the Employee table in the HR database on the DEV instance of SQL Server. Both tables are identical in their schema.

Breaking down the commands, the first command starts by calling BCP followed by the object of interest. Using its fully qualified name (database.schema.object), in this case the adventureworks.humanresources.employee table, the 'out' clause indicates an export operation and hr-emp.dat is the name of the file to export to. The -n switch indicates to BCP to use the native BCP file format, -T instructs BCP to connect to SQL Server using a trusted connection (Windows authentication), and finally -S indicates the server to connect to, in this case localhost, which is the default instance.

The second command performing the import calls BCP. As with the first command, this is followed by calling the object of interest, in this example hr.humanresources.employee. 'in' indicates an import operation, with -n indicating the file is in native format. As before, the -T instructs BCP to use a trusted connection. This command also has the -S switch followed by the server name, localhost\dev, which indicates that the server to connect to is the DEV instance on the local machine.

Moving into the detail of the syntax for BCP, a quick and easy way to see the syntax and available switches is to go to a command prompt and type **bcp**, as shown in Figure 11-2.

Table 11-1 breaks down the bcp {dbtable | query} {in | out | queryout | format} datafile command into its various components, including an explanation of each part.

After the datafile parameter, you only need to specify the connection and credential details to start BCP. The connection parameter can use defaults but the credentials are mandatory: you must specify either a trusted connection or the username and password of a SQL Login. Table 11-2 covers the switches you should be aware of.

Component	Description
dbtable	database.schema.object, where both database and schema are optional (if omitted, they will default to the logins default database and the database users default schema, respectively) and object can be either a table or a view.
query	A T-SQL statement used to extract your data. This could be a SELECT statement or a call to a stored procedure. If you use this parameter, you must also specify the parameter queryout. Note: your query text must be in double quotes.
in	Specifies that this is an import process.
out	Specifies that this is an export process.
queryout	Must be specified when using the T-SQL query option for an export process.
format	Creates a format file based on the switch setting of either -N, -c, -w, or -n.
datafile	Specifies the name of the file to import or the name of the file that will be created during an export. This can be the full path name up to 255 characters. The datafile can contain a maximum of 2,147,483,647 rows.

Table 11-1   *BCP Command Components*

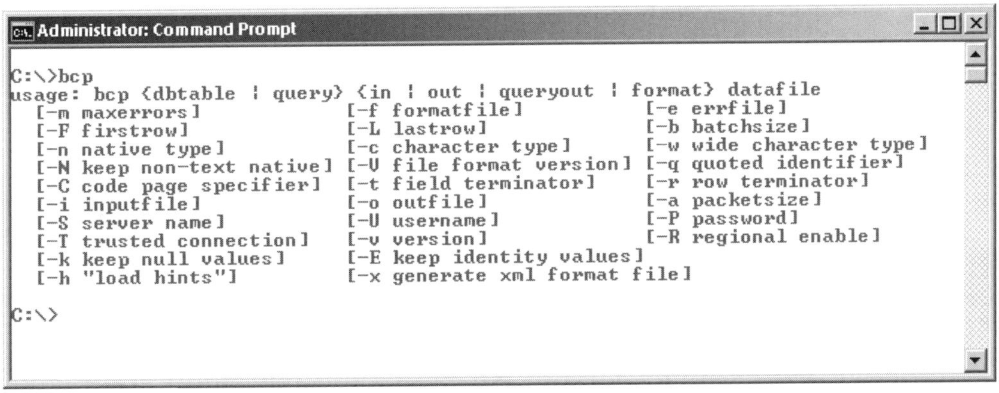

Figure 11-2 *BCP available switches*

There are two ways to run BCP for import and export. The first is interactively, and the second is with a format file.

If you run an import or export operation and do not use either the -c, -w, -n, or -N switch (covered shortly), the process will start interactively, prompting you to specify details such as the storage type, prefix length, and field terminator for the file you are importing from or exporting to. Using a format file eliminates the need to enter all the column and field details, as the prompts are answered in the format file. If you run in the interactive mode and answer all the prompts, at the end of the process you are prompted to save the format file for future use to avoid having to re-enter the details. You can also create a format file without performing an import or export by using the format parameter, covered in Table 11-1.

The remaining switches all provide control over elements such as the format file to use, batch sizes, starting points, and hints. Table 11-3 provides a brief description

Parameter	Description
-S *ServerName*	Sets the server and instance for BCP to connect to. If this is omitted, BCP will connect to the default instance on the machine you are executing BCP from. Otherwise, -S is used in the format *ServerName\Instance*.
-T	Uses a trusted connection to SQL Server, which means that BCP will attempt to connect to SQL Server in the security context of the user that executes BCP. Trusted connections are considered best practice from a security perspective.
-U *UserID*	When not using a trusted connection, -U sets the SQL Server login username to connect to the database with, it is used in conjunction with -P for providing the password.
-P *Password*	Used to specify the password to connect to the database.

Table 11-2 *BCP Connection and Security Parameters*

Parameter	Description
-e *err_file*	The full path to an error file in which BCP can place rows that it cannot import into the database.
-m *max_errors*	The number of errors BCP can sustain before it cancels the operation. Errors include data conversion and constraint violations. The default is 10.
-f *format_file*	When using a format file for an in or out (import or export) operation -f allows you to specify the location of the format file to use. When -f is used with the format for creating a format file the option is used to specify the location that the format file will be created in.
-x	When used with the -f switch and format option, it creates the format file using the XML format.
-F *first_row*	The first row in the file to import from or the first row in the table to start the export from. The default is the first row.
-L *last_row*	The last row to import from the data file or export from a table. The default is the last row.
-b *batch_size*	A batch is committed as a single transaction. Specifying a batch size creates a transaction around each batch of rows. If a batch fails, only the failing batch is rolled back. Omitting this parameter will insert the entire import as a single batch. Do not use this at the same time as the -h ROWS_PER_BATCH option.
-V (70 |80 | 90)	Allows data types from earlier versions of SQL Server to be used for the bulk copy operation (70 = SQL 7, 80 = SQL 2000, 90 = SQL 2005).
-a *packet_size*	Overrides the server setting for the number of bytes per network packet sent to and from the server.
-k	Preserves null values.
-R	Specifies that all currency, date, and time data should adopt the locale of the client machine.
-C *codepage*	Specifies the codepage of the data in the data file. The default is to use the client codepage.
-E	Uses the identity values specified in the import file for the identity column (similar in concept to an Oracle sequence) in place of the server-generated values.
-h *loadhints*	Specifies hints that can be used in the load process, including ORDER, ROWS_PER_BATCH, KILOBYTES_PER_BATCH, TABLOCK, CHECK_CONSTRAINTS, and FIRE_TRIGGERS.
-q	Sets the use of quoted identifiers; use this option when a database, schema, or table name contains a space or single quotation mark.
-r *rowterminator*	Sets the row terminator; by default, a newline character (\n) is used.
-f *fieldterminator*	Sets the field terminator; by default, a tab character (\t) is used.
-c	Specifies character mode for transferring data in ASCII format.
-w	Specifies wide mode for transferring data in Unicode format.
-n	Specifies native data mode for SQL to SQL transfer.
-N	Specifies native data mode for SQL to SQL transfer but with character data converted to Unicode format.

Table 11-3 *BCP Parameters*

of these. An in-depth explanation of all parameters can be found in the SQL Server Books Online documentation.

As indicated at the end of Table 11-3, there are three main operating modes for BCP:

▶ Character mode (-c)

▶ Wide mode (-w)

▶ Native mode (-n and -N)

Character mode and wide mode represent data in ASCII and Unicode, respectively. These modes would typically be used when importing data from or moving data to another platform such as Oracle or if the end user wants to export data into a tool such as Microsoft Excel for processing.

If you are transferring data between Oracle systems, then you would normally use Data Pump, as it has its own native file format, negates the need to perform conversions, and is often the better choice for performance. SQL Server has the equivalent in the native mode file format. As well as providing performance benefits, if you are using native mode and the destination table is the same structure (number of columns, names, data types etc.) as the source table, then you need not specify a format file as part of the import. Using this method increases performance because there is no need for conversion of data types and character formats. If the two structures are different, native mode can still be used with a format file to provide the column mapping. The -n switch should be used

Oracle DBA Q&A

Q: In SQL*Loader, do you have the option of using DirectPath, which bypasses the database cache and appends the data above the high-water mark in the data file? Also, where is that option in BCP?

A: Like SQL*Loader, BCP has a fast mode and a slow mode. The fast mode is the default where CHECK_CONSTRAINTS and FIRE_TRIGGERS are set to off and TABLOCK is on, meaning that the load process will bypass any check constraints on the table and will not fire any triggers, and the TABLOCK hint will take out a table lock to ensure it has exclusive access to the table. Switching off TABLOCK and turning on CHECK_CONSTRAINTS and FIRE_TRIGGERS forces BCP to behave like a normal client, similar to SQL*Loader conventional path load, which is useful for loading data while other workloads are concurrently accessing the table. No matter what data load type you use, you do not have the option to bypass the data cache.

for transferring data between non-Unicode systems, whereas -N is used for double-byte character systems; in the -N mode, BCP keeps non-character data fields as the native database types and converts the character data fields to Unicode character format.

There are certain security requirements at the server and database level for executing BCP. For export operations, the SELECT permission is required on the referenced tables and views; the EXECUTE permission is required on a stored procedure if a stored procedure is being used via the queryout option. For import operations, the minimal permissions are SELECT and INSERT on the destination table or view. The ALTER TABLE permission is required if the default behavior for CHECK_CONSTRAINTS and FIRE_TRIGGERS is used. In addition if the -E switch is used to enable inserting into identity columns then ALTER TABLE is also needed. ALTER TABLE is required in this situation because BCP needs to make schema modifications to prevent things like constraints being checked. Permissions to read or write the import or export files on the relevant file systems are also required.

Oracle DBA Q&A

Q: I like to supplement my RMAN backups with logical backups of certain tables. I normally use Data Pump to create these backup files. Would you suggest using BCP for the same purpose of logical backups?

A: Absolutely, you can use BCP to create logical backups of your data. Just note that if you decide to use BCP as a logical backup mechanism for your data, it is important to create a format file because a BCP extract contains no information about the schema or format from where it was exported. Therefore, if a table is dropped and you want to use BCP to restore the data, you may not be able to do so without the destination schema and format of the export.

Now that we have looked at the switches and syntax in detail, let's take a look at another example of how BCP can be used to export a subset of data from a table using a query. The example in Figure 11-3 shows BCP using a SELECT query with a WHERE clause to extract a subset of data and then outputting the data into an ASCII file format using a comma for the field delimiter and a newline character for the row terminator. Connection to the server is omitted, indicating the default instance on the server it is executing, and -T is used to access the SQL Server using Windows authentication.

```
C:\>bcp "select firstname, lastname, emailaddress from adventureworksdw.dbo.dimc
ustomer where lastname like 'A%'" queryout cust-a.txt -c -t "," -r "\n" -T -S lo
calhost

Starting copy...

842 rows copied.
Network packet size (bytes): 4096
Clock Time (ms.) Total     : 203     Average : (4147.78 rows per sec.)

C:\>
```

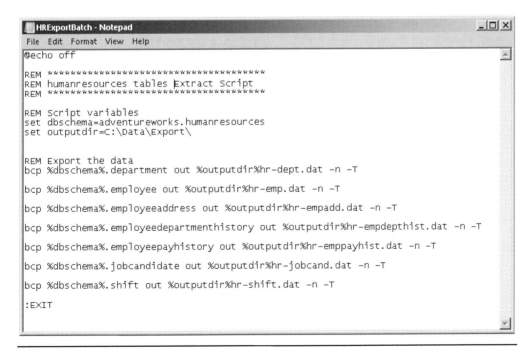

Figure 11-3 *Using a SELECT query to extract data*

Finally, because BCP is a command-line tool, it can be used as part of a Windows batch process or as part of another scripted operation such as a Windows PowerShell script. Figure 11-4 shows an example BCP batch script to extract all the tables in the HumanResources schema within AdventureWorks using the native extract format and a trusted connection.

```
@echo off

REM ****************************************
REM humanresources tables Extract Script
REM ****************************************

REM Script variables
set dbschema=adventureworks.humanresources
set outputdir=C:\Data\Export\


REM Export the data
bcp %dbschema%.department out %outputdir%hr-dept.dat -n -T

bcp %dbschema%.employee out %outputdir%hr-emp.dat -n -T

bcp %dbschema%.employeeaddress out %outputdir%hr-empadd.dat -n -T

bcp %dbschema%.employeedepartmenthistory out %outputdir%hr-empdepthist.dat -n -T

bcp %dbschema%.employeepayhistory out %outputdir%hr-emppayhist.dat -n -T

bcp %dbschema%.jobcandidate out %outputdir%hr-jobcand.dat -n -T

bcp %dbschema%.shift out %outputdir%hr-shift.dat -n -T

:EXIT
```

Figure 11-4 *Windows batch file making calls to BCP*

BULK INSERT Statement (T-SQL)

If you want to import data from a file as part of a T-SQL script or batch process or to wrap the import within a user-defined transaction, then the BULK INSERT statement is a good way to do this.

BULK INSERT is similar to BCP with regard to the switch options of the command, but a major difference exists in the way it interacts with SQL Server: BULK INSERT is a T-SQL statement that executes inside the SQL Server engine. Source data files are opened directly by the SQL Server process and the data is converted into an OLE DB row set, which is then inserted into the table by the query processor. There is no client process interaction as there is with BCP. BCP is no different from a client application connecting to SQL Server.

From a security perspective, there are some additional considerations over those found with BCP. First, in order to execute the BULK INSERT statement, the user's login must have the ADMINISTER BULK OPERATIONS server-level permission. If the login isn't a sysadmin, you can add the login to the bulkadmin fixed server role or grant permission directly. The second consideration involves how the account executing the BULK INSERT statement reads the source and format files. If you are connecting to SQL Server using a SQL Server login and you execute a BULK INSERT statement, it will try to open the source file using the security credentials of the SQL Server service account, whereas if the login account uses Windows authentication, the credentials of the user executing the statement will be used to open the file. This could present a challenge if you are using SQL Server logins and your SQL Server service account is running as "least privilege" (at least you should be following that principle if you are adhering to best practice security guidelines!), as you would have to grant the service account access to the location where the files are located.

If the file you wish to import is located on a remote server, BULK INSERT will allow you to open files from remote machines, but you must specify the file path using its full UNC (Universal Naming Convention) path. From a security perspective, the same rules apply. A Windows authentication account will have its credentials impersonated to the remote machine in order to access the file, and a SQL Server Login will use the SQL Server service account user.

The syntax for BULK INSERT contains arguments that are almost identical to the BCP switches; for example, KEEPNULLS is the same as -k, and BATCHSIZE is the same as -b *batch_size*.

A full list of all the switches and options can be found in the SQL Server Books Online documentation by using the Index and typing in BULK INSERT, as shown in Figure 11-5.

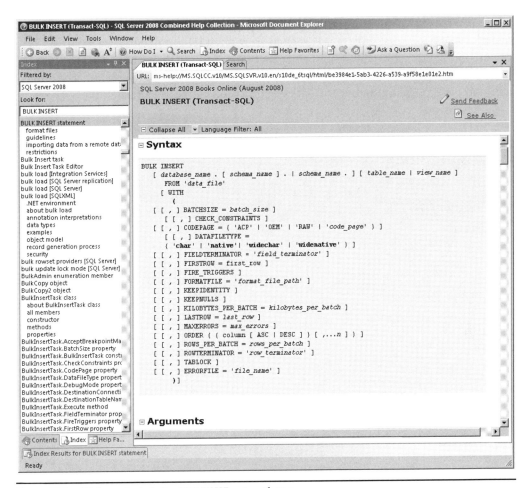

Figure 11-5   *SQL Server Books Online BULK INSERT syntax reference*

Oracle DBA Q&A

Q: So if BCP and BULK INSERT are very similar, which one should I use to import my data?

A: The general best-practice advice is that if you are importing from flat files located on the SQL Server, then BULK INSERT is the better choice, and if you are importing from remote files, use BCP or SSIS, although it is advised to benchmark each method.

Figure 11-6 shows the importing of the Employee data we extracted in the BCP example. The Employee table was extracted from the HR live database in a native format, and Figure 11-6 shows importing that data into the development system using the BULK INSERT statement. Because the destination table is identical to the source table and we exported in native format, we don't need to specify a format file.

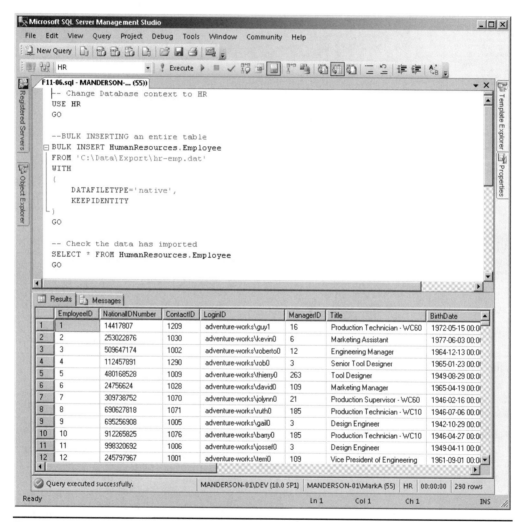

Figure 11-6   *Using BULK INSERT in SSMS*

Oracle DBA Q&A

Q: Oracle external tables allow me to look inside and query a file without actually importing it into the database; this is really useful when I want to browse the contents of the file using SELECT statements, and it allows me to pick out data of interest to import it, such as to restore pieces of data from a logical backup following accidental deletion. How can I do that in SQL Server?

A: In SQL Server, there is a method of opening a file and browsing the contents without having to import it into the database. OPENROWSET allows you to return data from an OLE DB data source in an ad hoc fashion. Using this method, you can specify the file you want to open with a format file that describes the data layout. From there, you can query the data using SELECT statements or use it as part of an import using an INSERT with a sub SELECT statement. Figure 11-7 shows two statements; the first is opening the employees export file and searching for items that match a WHERE clause, and the second is performing an INSERT into the Employee table using a sub SELECT statement that is reading from the export file.

SQL Server Integration Services

SSIS is the Microsoft extract, transform, and load (ETL) offering in the SQL Server product stack. If you are looking for a comparison to the Oracle product set, it is analogous to Warehouse Builder, although SSIS in SQL Server can be used for much more than just moving data.

Developing SSIS packages for data movement may or may not be something that you do as a DBA, depending on how involved you get in data movement operations. Some organizations have data teams that deal with all the data movement and general master data management, and they would probably be the ones creating the SSIS packages. Your job as a DBA would be to host, schedule, and monitor the packages. Because of this and (mainly) because SSIS is such a large product, it deserves an entire book of its own (and there are many SSIS books out there). The purpose of this section is to give you a high-level overview of the concepts and the tools used to build and edit packages.

Even if you do not build packages from scratch, you will encounter the SSIS format when using maintenance plans, the Import and Export Wizard, and the Copy Database Wizard. Having this basic knowledge will allow you to make further modifications to and customize these system-generated packages.

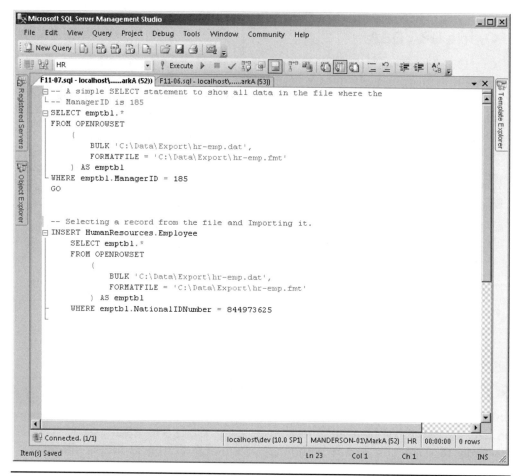

Figure 11-7 *Using OPENROWSET to open and query a file*

There are three parts to SSIS:

▶ **SSIS package** An XML-based file defining the data or maintenance operation

▶ **SSIS engine** Executes the packages

▶ **SSIS Windows service** Allows management of the packages through SSMS

To create, design, and debug an SSIS package, you would use Business Intelligence Development Studio (BIDS), which is installed as part of the SQL Server client tools.

BIDS uses the Microsoft Visual Studio development environment shell to develop SSIS packages and the other Business Intelligence components of SQL Server, namely the reports for SQL Server Reporting Services and the OLAP cubes for SQL Server Analysis Services (SSAS). BIDS lets you create your SSIS packages and then save them to the file system or publish them into a SQL Server repository.

ON THE JOB

SSIS does not have to be used exclusively for moving data in and out of SQL Server. We have worked with customers who have adopted SSIS as their choice of ETL tool and are using it to move data between systems such as Oracle, DB2, and Teradata without a SQL Server source or destination in sight.

Creating SSIS Packages

An SSIS package is the unit of work for SSIS. It contains a workflow of operations that can range from maintenance tasks and server operations through to data movement and manipulation tasks. SSIS packages are created graphically using a drag-and-drop interface in the BIDS tool and ultimately are saved as an XML-based file with a .dtsx extension.

The following are the main components to the design of an SSIS package:

▶ Control Flow

▶ Data Flow

▶ Tasks

▶ Precedence Constraints

▶ Connection Managers

Figure 11-8 shows a blank SSIS package created in BIDS. The Control Flow tab in the center panel is currently selected and therefore the Toolbox panel on the left side shows Control Flow Tasks. The panel below the Control Flow design surface is the Connection Managers panel, and the two panels to the right show the properties of the selected item or task and the details of the SSIS project.

The first two elements of an SSIS package, Control Flow and Data Flow, are used to orchestrate the ETL process and data movement of the SSIS package. Think of the Control Flow as a visual scripting language for ETL processes. In a control flow, you can manipulate files, execute processes and other SSIS packages, and run SQL commands, to name but a few operations. A Data Flow is a data movement pipeline, where data is moved from a source, through zero or more transformations, and sent to one or more destinations.

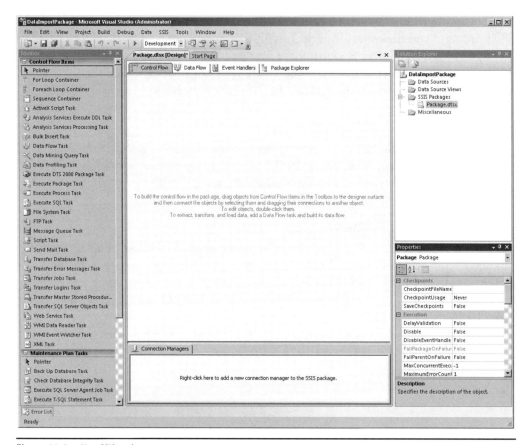

Figure 11-8 *New SSIS package*

In Oracle it is very common to use a combination of shell scripts, SQL*Loader, and SQL*Plus to implement an ETL process. In SSIS the Control Flow is analogous to the shell script, and the Data Flow is roughly analogous to the SQL*Loader or SQL*Plus calls.

A package has only one control flow but can have as many Data Flow components as it requires. It is quite common to see an SSIS package that has just one component on the Control Flow, which is a Data Flow component. Within the Data Flow component, the extract, import, or other relevant data task takes place.

Tasks are the operations that take place on both the Control Flow and Data Flow elements of the package. Which tasks are available for use depends on whether you are working on the Control Flow or Data Flow design surface.

When working on the Control Flow part of the package, the Toolbox contains tasks such as FTP, Send Mail, Execute SQL, and Data Flow components (Data Flow components are containers for the set of Data Flow Tasks). Control Flow also has containers such as For Loop and Foreach Loop, which allow looping operations over a set of tasks placed inside them. For example, suppose you want to create a package that imports the data from all files in a directory into a table. This could be accomplished by placing a Foreach Loop container on the Control Flow and configuring the loop setting to "Foreach file in this directory." Inside the container, a Data Flow component would be placed with the import operation defined within it. Then, as the loop iterates over the files in the directory, the name of the file would be passed as a variable through to the import process. The Toolbox also includes a section of Maintenance Plan Tasks for operations such as backing up databases, rebuilding indexes, and updating statistics.

When working on a Data Flow, the Toolbox of tasks changes to data-oriented operations, such as source and destination objects for reading and writing data, and tasks for data manipulation and cleansing, such as sorting, aggregation, fuzzy lookup, splitting, and merging. A Data Flow streams data from a source, runs it through a transformation pipeline in the SSIS engine, and loads it to a destination. Source and destination can be flat files or any OLE DB, ODBC, or ADO.NET data source. A Data Flow can actually contain multiple sources and multiple destinations, and SSIS will try to run them all in parallel. As powerful as the SSIS transformation pipeline is, some SSIS packages don't use Data Flows at all, instead preferring to use Control Flows to bulk load data from flat files into staging tables, and manipulate it using SQL statements and stored procedures on the destination system.

Precedence Constraints only apply to the Control Flow and are the wiring for the various tasks. There are three types of precedence constraints: On Success, On Failure, and On Completion. Control Flow Tasks can be joined together in a workflow style using these constraints to create a logical path through the package. An example of the On Success and On Failure options could be an FTP task that has two possible branches. The first is an On Success branch, which means the files have been transferred successfully and can then move to the next stage in the process. The second branch is an On Failure constraint that is linked to an e-mail task. On failure of the FTP task, an e-mail is sent to the administrator to warn them of a problem. The final constraint, On Completion, moves to the next stage no matter what the outcome of the previous step was.

Finally, the last components to SSIS package design we are going to cover are Connection Managers. Connection Managers are used within SSIS to define connections to data sources. They contain details such as the data provider to use and the connection credentials. Connection Managers are then referenced by tasks on the Control Flow and Data Flow tabs. Centralizing these connections makes connection management easier and allows for changing of connection criteria at run time. Working with connection managers is a common task for production DBAs, as the SSIS packages need connection details and credentials for production environments that may not be available to the person developing the package. Packages can use external configuration files to contain connection details, or the DBA can override the connection details in a package when it is scheduled to run in SQL Agent or on the command line through dtexec.exe (more on package execution later in this section).

Let's review an example of an existing package. Figure 11-9 shows an SSIS package opened in BIDS. The package is used to create a development version of a database, first by dropping any existing tables in the destination database, then re-creating the tables in the development system, and finally populating the tables with data from another database.

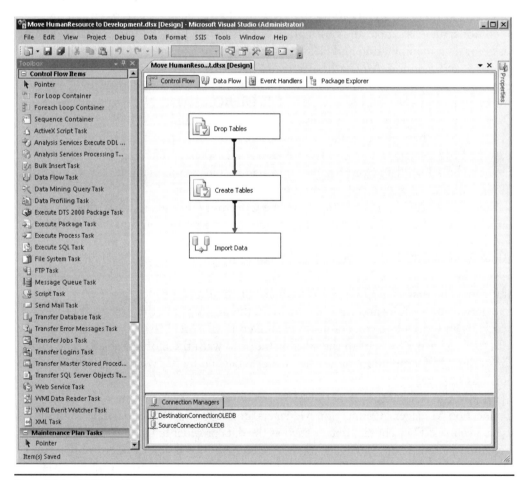

Figure 11-9 *SSIS Control Flow*

Figure 11-9 shows the Control Flow tab. In this control flow, there are three steps. The first two steps execute blocks of T-SQL script. The first Execute SQL Task is called Drop Tables. This step runs the T-SQL DROP TABLE commands. On success of this component, the package moves on to the next stage. The Create Tables step re-creates the tables. On success of the Create Tables statement, the control flow moves to run the Import Data Data Flow component. Double-clicking the Import Data Data Flow task moves the designer to the Data Flow tab.

Figure 11-10 shows the Data Flow tab opened. This data flow has five pairs of source and destination objects to move data into the five destination tables. Because this is a simple export/import operation, moving data from one identical table schema

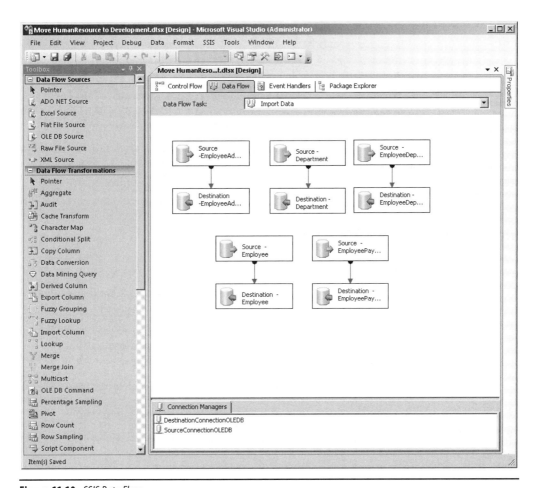

Figure 11-10 *SSIS Data Flow*

to another, the data flow is quite straightforward. The source component reads the data, and the destination component inserts the data into the destination.

Because these five pairs are not chained together in a serial fashion, all export/import operations will run in parallel, but the data flow step itself will not complete until the last export/import operation has finished.

At the bottom of both Figure 11-9 and Figure 11-10 you will see a panel that shows the connection managers for this package. Each of the steps on both the Control Flow and Data Flow tabs that need to interact with a database, such as the Drop Tables step or the Import Data step, references the connections in the connection manager. Therefore, if you needed to change the source server, you would only need to change the connection manager, not all of the individual components.

Each task on the design surface has properties that can be set to configure the task. The Execute SQL Task, for example, has properties for the connection to use and the script block it needs to execute. Figure 11-11 shows the properties dialog box for one of the data destination objects. The dialog box shows the connection manager it is using to import the data and the data access mode and the destination. If you are eagle-eyed, you may spot that the options for this data load look familiar. That is because the "Table or view – fast load" mode selected uses the same bulk-loading APIs that BCP uses.

As you can see, the main difference between an SSIS package and BCP or BULK INSERT is that an SSIS package can be used to implement and orchestrate an entire ETL process, including file management, pulling data from enterprise data sources, loading multiple tables (in parallel), calling stored procedures to do bulk operations on the destination, and performing cleanup operations.

Managing and Executing SSIS Packages

Once an SSIS package has been created, you need to find somewhere to store it and a way of executing it.

The easiest way to store packages, which could be called the "unmanaged approach," is to simply store the packages on the server in any folder of your choice. The second approach, which could be called the "managed approach," is to run the SSIS service, which runs as a Windows service and allows the management of SSIS via SSMS.

Running the SSIS service provides the ability to perform the following tasks with SSMS:

▶ Import and export SSIS packages to and from a managed storage location

▶ Execute SSIS packages

▶ Stop SSIS packages

▶ View currently running packages

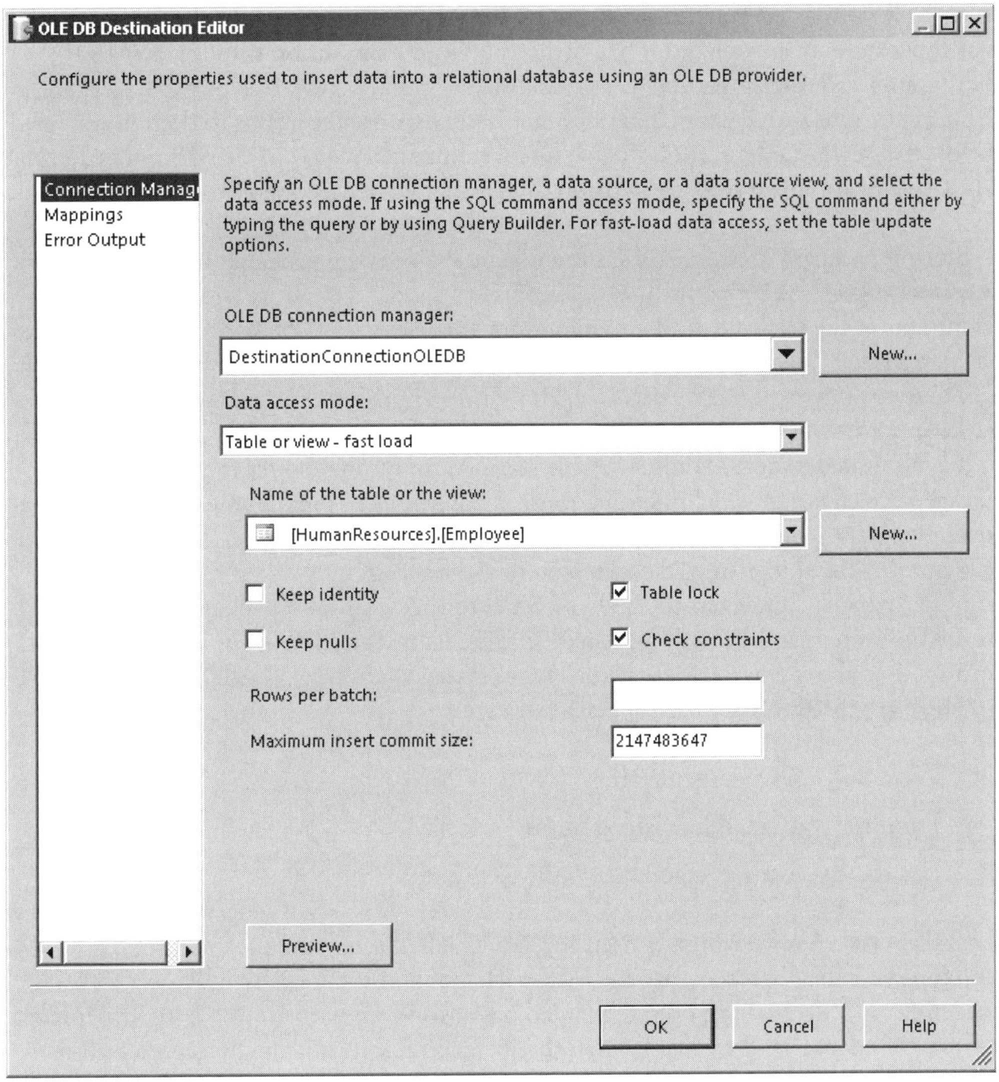

Figure 11-11 *OLE DB Destination Editor properties dialog box*

There are two managed storage options for SSIS packages: store your packages on the file system in a location that the SSIS service is aware of, or store the packages in the msdb system database.

Storing your packages on the file system means your packages are treated as normal files, and therefore backing up your packages must be done outside of SQL Server using your normal file backup methods. By default, the location on the file system in which packages will be placed when using the file system option through SSMS is %ProgramFiles%\Microsoft SQL Server\100\DTS\Packages\. It is possible to change this path to your own custom location, such as F:\ssis\pacakges, but to do this you need to edit the XML configuration file MsDtsSrvr.ini.xml, located in the %ProgramFiles%\ Microsoft SQL Server\100\DTS\Binn directory, and change the <StorePath> value to your preferred location.

Storing packages in the msdb system database places the packages in a table called sysssispackages. Using the msdb approach has the added benefit of providing a security wrapper over the packages and also allows for the packages to be backed up when you back up msdb.

There are other pros and cons to each storage approach. For example, importing packages in the file system approach can be done by simply placing the package definition in the monitored folder location, whereas storing it in msdb requires the use of the import routine. The choice of which method to use is purely one of preference on how you wish to administer the system.

Figure 11-12 shows SSMS connected to the SSIS Windows service. The Object Explorer pane is connected to the local SSIS service with two packages, one stored in the file system and the other located in the msdb store. The right panel shows information about the ADW – Data Transfer package.

There are three ways to run an SSIS package:

▶ Use a SQL Server Agent Job

▶ From the command line (dtexec.exe)

▶ Use the Execute Package Utility (dtexecui.exe)

SQL Server Agent, which is used for server scheduling and automation, has a Job step type specifically for executing SSIS packages and is generally used as a way of executing an SSIS package on a scheduled basis (for example, running a nightly import process). Underneath the covers, when the job executes, it calls the dtexec.exe program. More information on SQL Server Agent can be found in Chapter 10.

To run a package manually, you would use either the command-line option or the Execute Package Utility. The command-line tool dtexec.exe is used to execute an SSIS package at a command prompt, but to use it you must build the execution string, including all the various switches and options. The easiest method is to use the Execute Package Utility, shown in Figure 11-13, which allows you to set the options for executing the package graphically. The utility can also be used to build

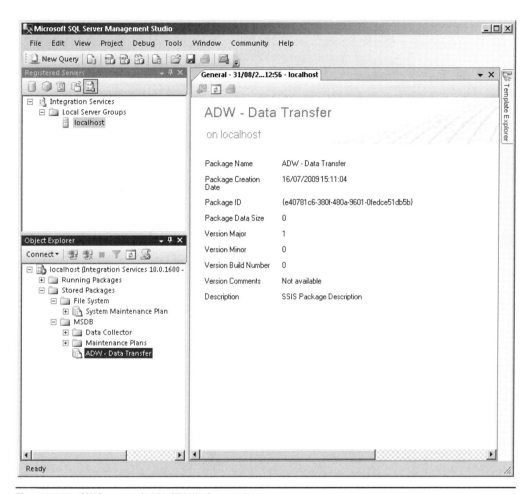

Figure 11-12 *SSMS connected to the SSIS Windows service*

the command-line string that can be used with dtexec.exe. To open the utility, right-click the package in SSMS and select run package. From there, you can set a variety of options and then execute the package.

It is important to note that, as a DBA, you will more than likely be running SSMS and the other tools on your admin workstation connecting to remote SQL Servers in the data center. If you run dtexec.exe or dtexecui.exe from your workstation, the process will execute the SSIS package on your local workstation and all data will flow from the source through your workstation to the destination. For small datasets and

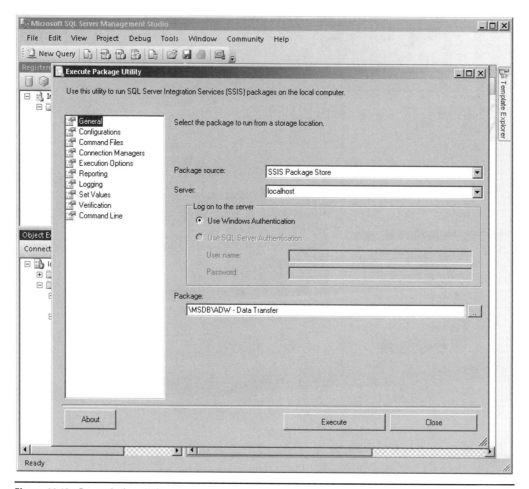

Figure 11-13 *Execute Package Utility*

one-time operations, such as importing a small file or exporting some data to a file on your workstation, this probably isn't an issue, but for large datasets, such as batch uploads or where some real data crunching and manipulation is required with server-class hardware resources, this is going to slow down the operation. To ensure that the package runs at the server, either schedule the execution as a SQL Server Agent Job at the server or log onto the server where SSIS is installed and execute the package.

Advanced SSIS Topics

In this section, we've covered the basics of a package and how to schedule and execute packages, but to fully exploit the power of SSIS, there are many other features that you should be aware of, including:

► Package configurations

► Checkpoints

► Creating custom components

► Event-driven activities

► Error handling

► Logging

All of these features can be used to develop ETL packages that can deal with the most demanding and complex of requirements. Detailed information is available through many reference books and through SQL Server Books Online.

Moving from Data Transformation Services

SSIS is the successor to a feature called Data Transformation Services (DTS), which was introduced in SQL Server 7 and continued into SQL Server 2000. DTS provided a simple way to graphically describe simple data flow and transformation. It also allowed you to add some of your own logic using either T-SQL or ActiveX scripting. Although now deprecated, DTS is worth knowing about as you may inherit SQL Server instances that have been upgraded from older versions such as 7 and 2000 and it is possible that there may be some DTS packages around running in Legacy mode.

In SQL Server 2005/2008, Microsoft provides a Legacy hosting option for DTS. The idea behind the Legacy hosting option is to ensure that DTS will not hold up a migration to the latest platform due to packages having to be rewritten.

Although at the time of writing, Microsoft has not announced the deprecation date of this hosting feature, you would be wise to start migrating or rewriting DTS packages in SSIS. Apart from the obvious reasons for doing so—that it will soon disappear and you will have no way of running the packages if you upgrade—there are many benefits to SSIS, including performance, management, and simplicity.

It should be noted that although the migration tool provides a good way of upgrading packages, you should consider reviewing the design of the upgraded packages. The wizard will move the package from the old format to the new format, but it will not rewrite the package to take advantage of new features.

Import and Export Wizard

When importing and exporting data in Oracle, you would normally use Data Pump Import and Data Pump Export to move the data to or from either operating system files or directly from database to database across a network link.

The SQL Server equivalent is the Import and Export Wizard, which walks you through the steps of an import or export operation. The wizard is a stand-alone tool that you can either find in the SQL Server program group on the Start menu or launch from within SSMS by right-clicking a database, selecting Tasks, and choosing either Import Data or Export Data (SSMS simply launches the stand-alone tool).

The Import and Export Wizard creates an SSIS package, which can be run immediately, saved and scheduled through SQL Server Agent, or run later using dtexec.exe.

Unlike Data Pump, where initiating a Data Pump job launches server-side processes, it is important to note that if you select the "run immediately" option and/or save the package locally and use the client-side execution tools for the package, the process will run as a client-side application as per the same behavior described in the SSIS section. Therefore, the wizard is normally used on the client side to create the package definition and then the package is moved to the server for execution.

Because the wizard uses the standard SSIS package format, it is possible to make your own modifications to the package once the wizard has finished, by opening it in BIDS. This allows you to build other actions around the basic import/export operation, such as manipulating or obfuscating the data on its way to the test system or adding e-mail tasks that notify people that the operation has taken place.

Out of the box, the wizard allows connections to data sources (and destinations) such as flat files, Excel, Access, SQL Server, Oracle, and other OLE DB providers. If you have installed SQL Server on a 64-bit server, then both 32- and 64-bit versions of the Import and Export Data Wizard are available. At the time of writing, data sources such as Access and Excel only have 32-bit drivers available and therefore will not work using the 64-bit version of the wizard.

To use the wizard, certain permissions are required, which can include the following:

▶ Permission to connect to the source and destination location database server or file share

▶ Permission to read data from the source file or database (SELECT permission on source tables or views, read permission on files)

▶ Permission to write data to the destination file or database (INSERT permission on the destination table, write permission on files)

▶ CREATE TABLE/CREATE DATABASE permission if you are using the wizard to create the destination in SQL Server, or the permission to write to the file system if using a file destination

▶ Permissions on the SSIS store to save the package into the SSIS repository

There are several ways to launch the Import and Export Wizard:

▶ From the Start menu, choose All Programs | SQL Server 2008 | Import and Export Data.

▶ In SSMS, right-click a database and choose Tasks | Import Data (or Export Data).

▶ At a command prompt, type **DTSWizard.exe**.

Let's walk through an example of using the Import and Export Wizard to copy a subset of data from the AdventureWorks database located on the default instance. Using the wizard, we will copy all tables that exist in the HumanResources schema over to a new database called HR on the SQL instance called DEV. At the end of the wizard, we will execute the package immediately.

The first step is to launch the wizard. In SSMS, right-click the AdventureWorks database and select Tasks | Export Data, as shown in Figure 11-14.

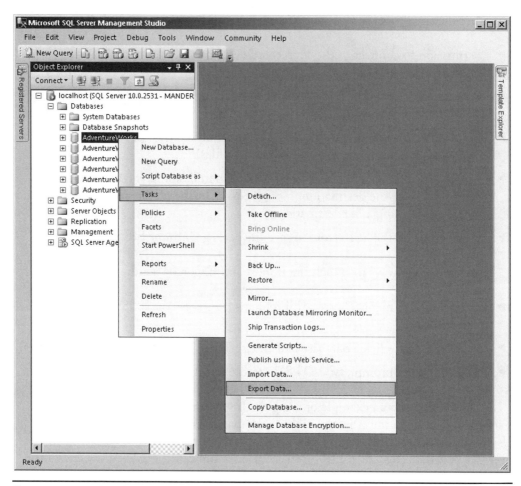

Figure 11-14 *Launching the SQL Server Import and Export Wizard using SSMS*

The Import and Export Wizard launches and presents us with an initial Welcome screen that describes what the wizard does. Click Next to progress to the Choose a Data Source step (see Figure 11-15). Because we launched the wizard from the right-click menu on the database, the server and database details are prepopulated for us, so simply click Next.

The next page, Choose a Destination (see Figure 11-16), asks us to choose our destination server and database. We set the server to localhost\dev and the database to the HR database. If the destination database did not already exist, this screen would allow you to create a new database on the destination server by clicking New; instead, click Next to continue.

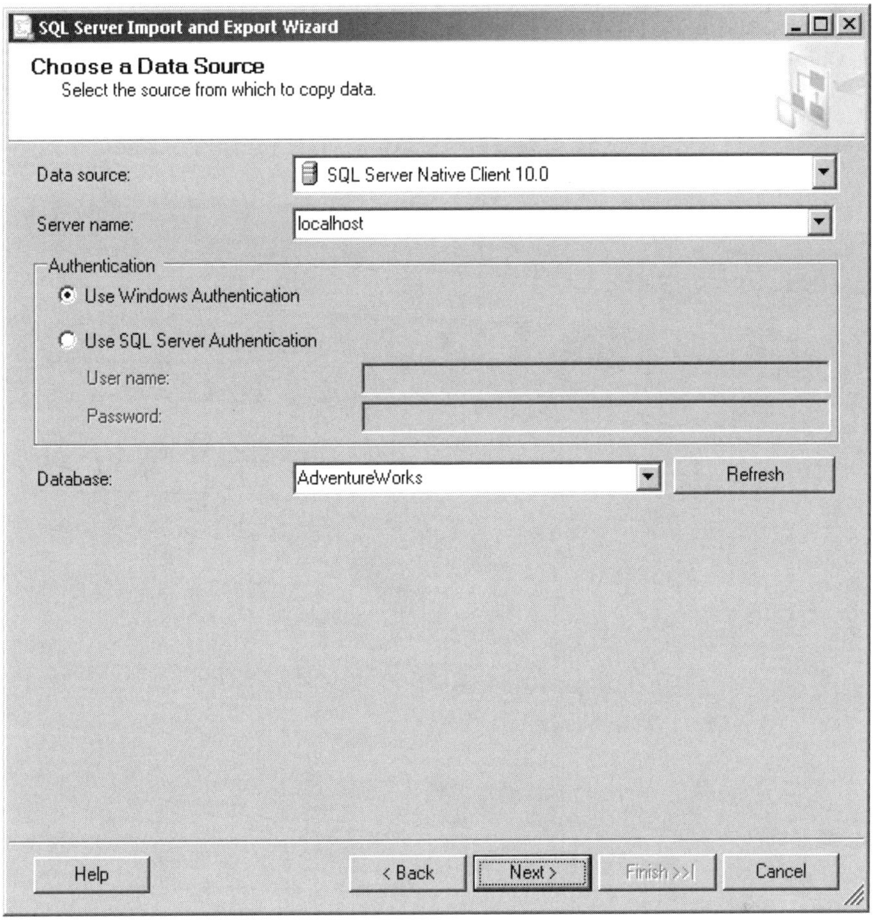

Figure 11-15 *Choosing a data source*

The wizard now asks whether we wish to copy data from existing tables and views or write a query to specify the data we want to export (see Figure 11-17). In our scenario, we want to select the first option, as shown, and then click Next.

NOTE

Selecting to copy data from a view does not create the view definition. In the remote database, it creates a table using the view definition and populates this with the relevant data.

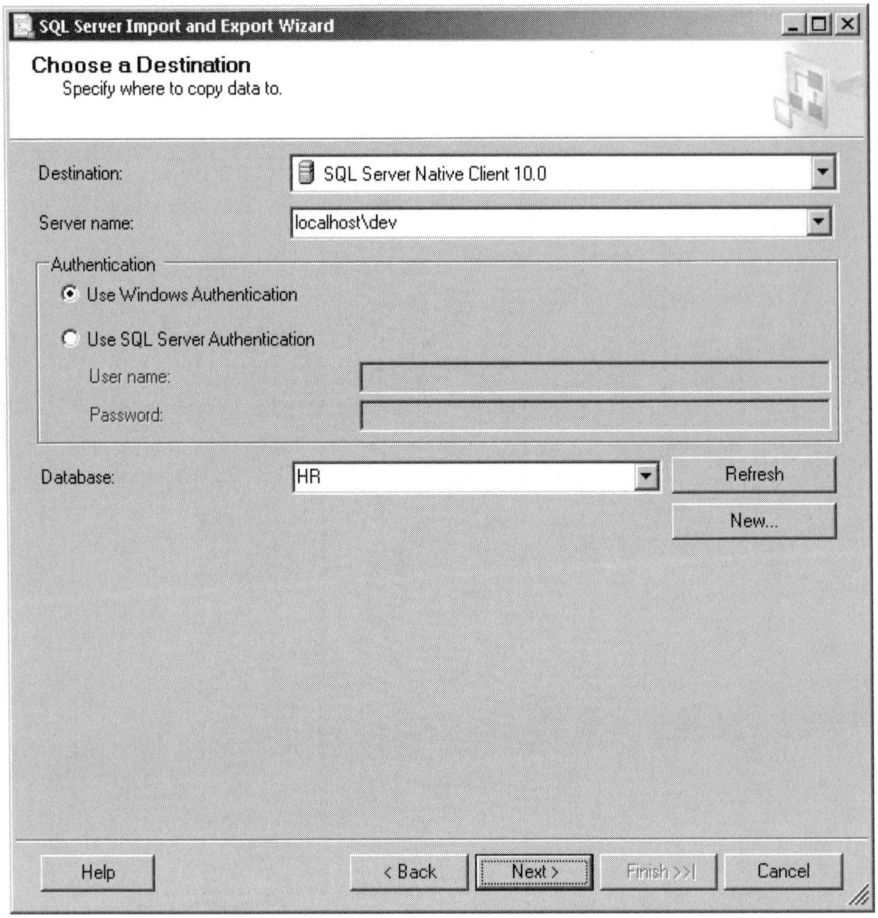

Figure 11-16 *Choosing a data destination*

We are now presented with a list of tables and views that are available to copy. Because we are performing a straight table copy into an empty database, we simply select all the tables in the HumanResources schema (see Figure 11-18) and click Next. If you wanted to map to tables with different names, remove columns, or tell the wizard to drop the destination table if it already exists, then you would click the Edit Mappings button, which provides a dialog box in which to customize these properties and others on the destination table.

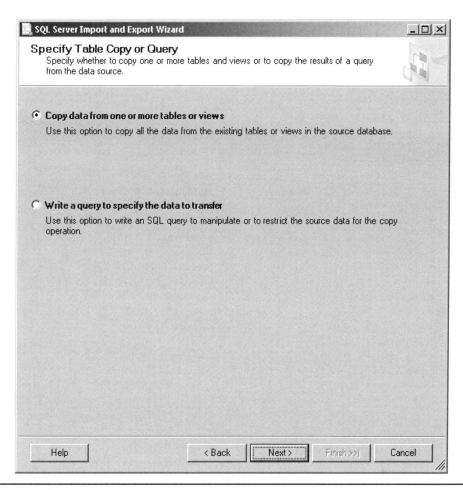

Figure 11-17 *Choosing to copy one or more tables*

NOTE

When creating destination tables, the Import and Export Wizard just creates a simple table with matching columns; it does not script out the source table and re-create it on the destination. To create a full-fidelity copy of an existing table, you need to script the table using another method, such as right-clicking the table in SSMS, selecting Script Table As, and then selecting Create to... for an individual table, or using the Generate SQL Server Scripts Wizard to script multiple tables at once. (The wizard is launched by right-clicking a database, selecting Tasks followed by Generate Scripts.)

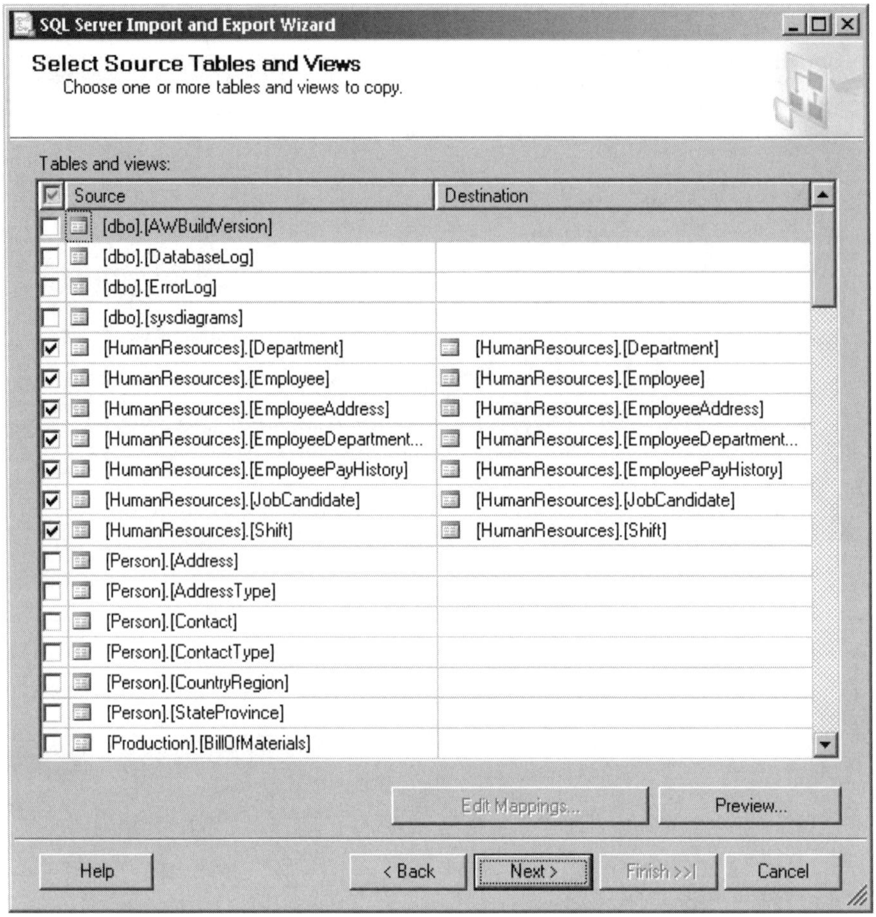

Figure 11-18 *Selecting the tables to copy*

We have now provided the wizard with enough detail on what we want to move and where to. In the next step (see Figure 11-19) we are presented with the option to run the package immediately or save the package into the SSIS package store. We want to run the package now, so choose Run Immediately and click Next.

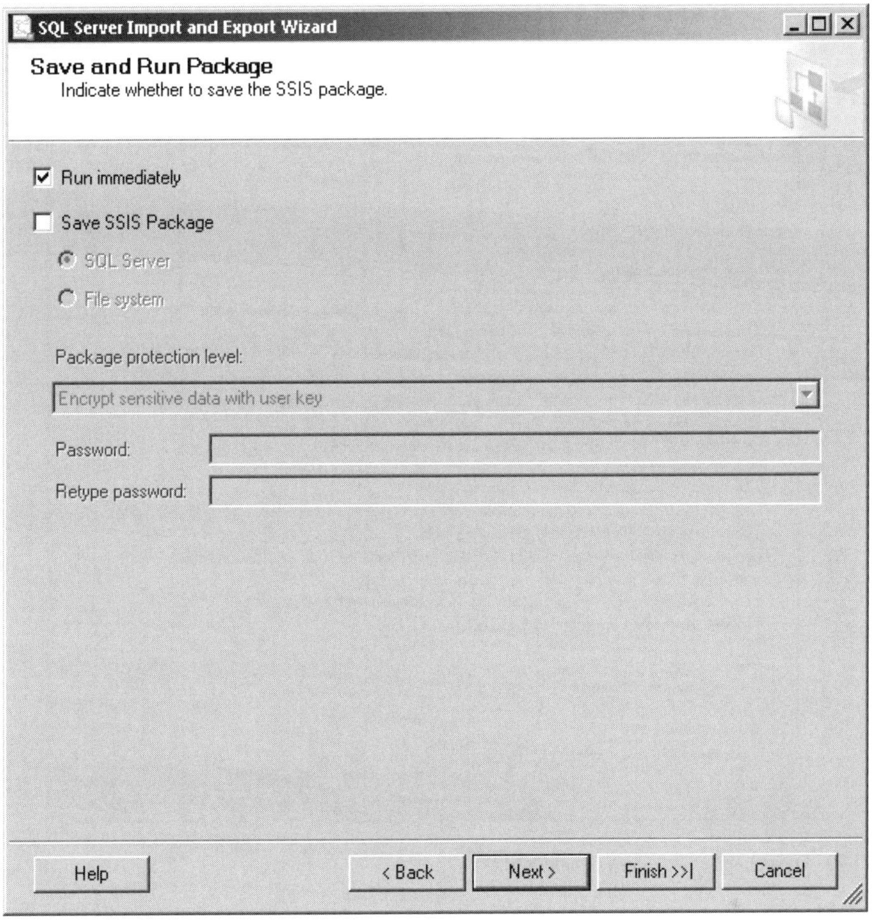

Figure 11-19 *Choosing to run the package immediately*

The wizard now has enough information and is ready to execute, so it displays a final summary screen (see Figure 11-20) for us to check that we have selected the right options. After reviewing the options, click Finish.

The wizard starts to execute the package and displays a progress screen while the package executes. Once the package completes, the status of the actions and details such as row counts are reported back to the user. Figure 11-21 shows the package has completed successfully.

Figure 11-20 *Import and Export Wizard summary screen*

Oracle DBA Q&A

Q: How do I transfer objects other than data from tables, such as stored procedures, functions, and so forth?

A: If you just want to script out one or two objects, then you can simply right-click the object in SSMS and select Script *object_type* As. Right-clicking a stored procedure presents a Script Stored Procedure As option, shown in Figure 11-22, from which you can select the type of script (in this case, a CREATE script) and select where you want the script to go, such as to the Windows Clipboard or to a file. If you want to script out multiple objects, then right-click the database and select Tasks | Generate Scripts, which launches the Generate SQL Server Scripts Wizard allowing you to script the entire database.

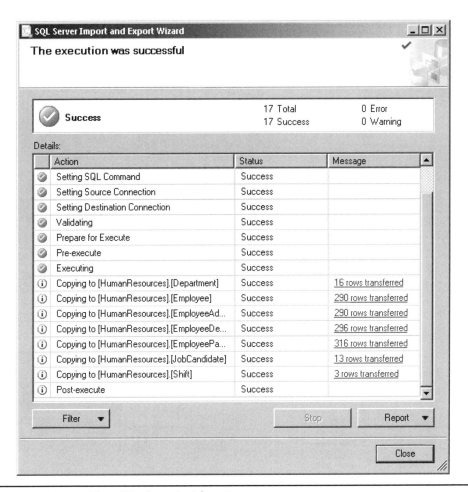

Figure 11-21 *Import and Export Wizard execution information*

SQL Server Management Studio

While we are discussing importing and exporting data, it is worth mentioning a few quick tips for using SSMS to extract a small amount of data as an ad hoc operation. These options are great for when you decide that using tools like BCP and SSIS is too much work for the small amount of data you require.

The previous options discussed for exporting data require some sort of setup or configuration to extract the data. What if we just want to write a query, execute it, and copy the results into a file or even just paste them into an e-mail?

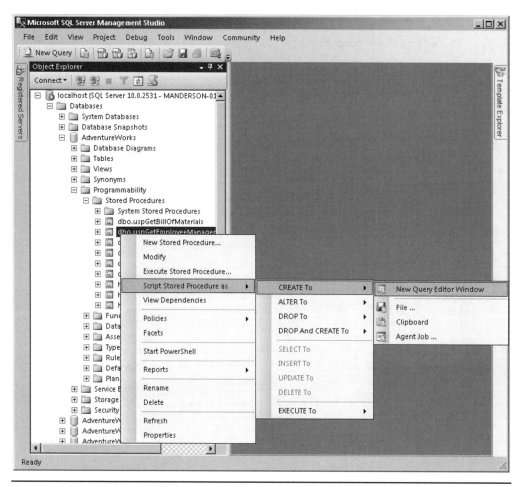

Figure 11-22 *Using SSMS to script a stored procedure*

Similar to using SQL Developer in Oracle, where you would write/execute your query, right-click the results set, select Export Data, and choose the format options, you have a similar approach within SSMS to output a query result set to a text file. Figure 11-23 shows selecting the option in SSMS for sending the results of the query to a file. When the query is executed, a File Save dialog box appears for you to enter the filename and, if required, to set the encoding format (UTF8, ANSI, Unicode, or Chinese Simplified).

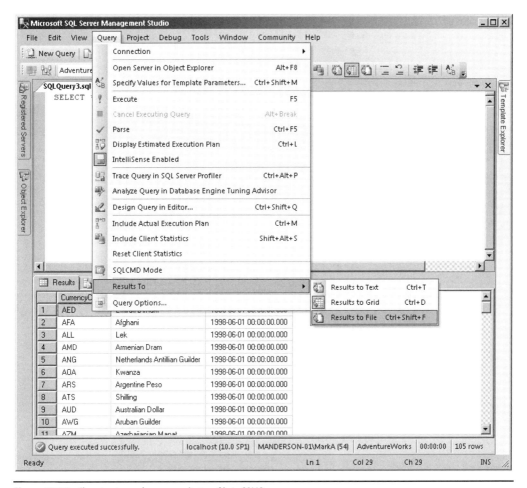

Figure 11-23 *Choosing to send query results to a file in SSMS*

If sending the results to a file is still too much work for you, then SSMS also allows you to copy result sets from the output grid to the Windows Clipboard. Figure 11-24 shows a simple query with the results grid. Right-clicking the Name column presents the option to Copy or Copy with Headers the data, which will then be copied to the Windows Clipboard in the same way as any other copy operation in Windows. Selecting the top-left cell of the results grid selects all columns and data, as shown in Figure 11-24.

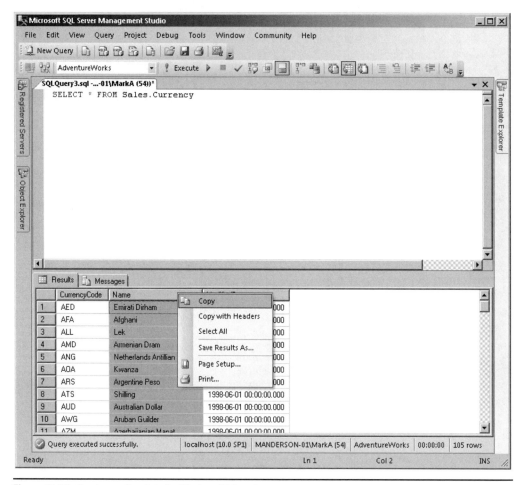

Figure 11-24 *Copying results sets to the Windows Clipboard*

Performance Considerations for Importing and Exporting Data

Having covered the various techniques available within SQL Server for importing and exporting data, we will spend a moment discussing what can affect the performance of an import or export operation.

Performance tuning the export of data from SQL Server is quite straightforward; if you are exporting data, you are in effect performing a SELECT query on the database, so normal performance-tuning rules for reading data from a database apply.

Importing data, on the other hand, has many more considerations; it is important to understand the various dependencies for achieving an optimal import performance.

Obvious server-level performance considerations are whether the CPU has enough spare cycles, whether there is sufficient memory, and whether the disk subsystem performs sufficiently. Assuming your server is sized correctly and has enough capacity to meet the hardware requirements, then other areas that you need to look at include the client side of the import, the destination database, and the table you are importing into.

Many factors can affect a loading process, but the following tend to be the places you should look first before delving deep into the engine. Let's start with the database and table to identify potential bottlenecks and then move to the client side.

At the database level, there are two main things to consider: the database recovery model, and the amount of space currently allocated to the data files. As discussed in Chapter 7, the database recovery model affects how transactions are logged in the database. During a bulk import operation, the FULL recovery model can cause the transaction log file to grow quite large, quite quickly, because it fully logs all transactions. This might not be too much of a problem until you run out of space for the transaction log and find yourself having to roll back the entire load. The other two recovery models, SIMPLE and BULK_LOGGED, are better for bulk-logged operations because they both support minimal logging.

Minimal logging in SQL Server means that SQL Server records in the transaction log that an operation took place and the details of the space it allocated, not the data itself. Before moving between different recovery models, it is essential that you understand the effect it could have on your backup or, to be precise, any recovery process should the database fail while you are in BULK_LOGGED mode. For example, if you normally run in FULL recovery mode, then you should back up the transaction log before moving to BULK_LOGGED mode; then, when your loading process has finished and you move back to FULL recovery mode, you should immediately take another transaction log backup.

Note that in the BULK_LOGGED recovery mode, although the details of your bulk-logged operations are not captured in the transaction log, they are captured in the next transaction log backup, and you cannot do a point-in-time restore to any point covered by a transaction log backup containing bulk-logged operations. This is why you want to switch to BULK_LOGGED mode just before performing bulk-logged operations, and take a transaction log backup both before and after.

The second thing to watch at the database level is how much space is allocated to the data files where the table you will be loading into resides. If you run out of space and the files have hit their MAXSIZE and cannot grow, then the operation will stop. If you run out of space and the files are smaller than the MAXSIZE, the files will grow, but growing files can be expensive because, under the default settings, zeros have to be written in the new file space before it can be used. During a bulk load operation, this type of behavior normally presents itself as the process appearing to pause during a load. Depending on the autogrowth setting, it may take from seconds to several minutes to grow the data file while your data load is paused.

Figure 11-25 shows the SSMS Disk Usage report. This report shows that during a recent data load, 5 data file autogrowth events took place at 20MB each, along with

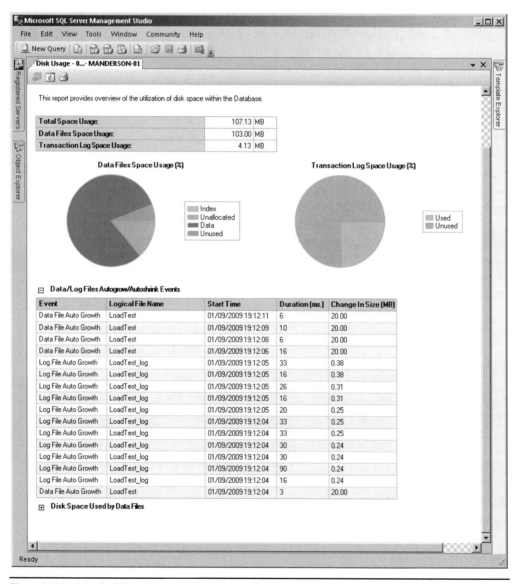

Figure 11-25 *Using the Disk Usage report to view autogrowth events*

11 log file autogrowth events. The length of time each event took to execute is displayed in milliseconds. On this simple demo database, these autogrowth events lasted only a few milliseconds, which is not going to cause a problem, but when you multiply this out to a large-scale database with gigabytes of data being loaded, then setting the autogrowth settings incorrectly can slow down the overall load process. This can be mitigated by ensuring the data files are correctly sized before starting the data load.

At the table level, it's all about the constraints, triggers, and indexes that you have located on the table. In general, the more of these you have on the table, the more work the SQL Server Database Engine has to do.

Constraints in SQL Server perform the same function as they do in Oracle. They are used to enforce business validation rules over the data, such as the format of the data.

By default, BCP and BULK INSERT are both set to ignore constraints during a bulk load operation, to ensure the fastest load possible. However, doing this marks the constraint as is_not_trusted, which means the system is not sure whether or not the data that bypassed the constraint during the load conforms to the constraint definition; therefore, at some point a revalidation of the constraint across the entire table will need to take place.

To enable and validate all the constraints on a table, you can use the following command:

```
ALTER TABLE table_name WITH CHECK CHECK CONSTRAINT ALL
```

Because invalidating a constraint will require a complete revalidation of the table, it is recommended that you enable constraint checking when performing incremental data loads. In most cases, the performance hit of real-time constraint checking versus a complete table revalidation will be considerably less, especially if loading data into a large table. Having said that, there are occasions where disabling constraint validation during a load makes sense, such as when loading into an empty table where it can be applied post load, or when loading into a table where you know the data you are loading violates the constraint but you plan to clean it up following the load process. For the second example, it would be more efficient to clean the data prior to loading in a tool such as SSIS and then run with real-time constraint checking on the database.

Triggers in SQL Server are also analogous to triggers in Oracle. They are blocks of code that fire for a particular type of operation. In the case of loading data, only INSERT and INSTEAD OF triggers are of interest during an import operation.

For both BCP and BULK INSERT operations, the behavior for triggers is the same as for constraints; that is, they are disabled by default but can be enabled with the appropriate switch or argument. When triggers are enabled, they are executed once for each batch. It is also worth noting that when triggers are enabled for a bulk import, the inserted/deleted rows are stored in the tempdb database, and therefore the size and performance characteristics of tempdb should be taken into account.

Standard INSERT statements always perform constraint checks and fire INSERT and INSTEAD OF triggers.

Finally, a point on indexes: indexes are great for improving query performance, but the more of them you have, the more you have to maintain. Therefore, each row that is inserted into the table will need to have any corresponding indexes updated accordingly. You could consider dropping indexes prior to a bulk update, but if you are incrementally loading into a table, then the cost of rebuilding the indexes after the load may outweigh the benefits from removing them in the first place. It is possible to disable indexes in SQL Server, but if you disable an index in order to reenable an index, you must rebuild it.

ON THE JOB

It is generally better to disable and rebuild indexes than to drop and re-create them, because when you drop an index, you have to store the index-creation DDL and use it to re-create the index. This requires careful coordination of your index design and ETL process implementation, and it's easy to lose an index this way.

The last part of the puzzle to cover is the client side of the loading process. Which tuning techniques you have available depends on the method of import, but in general there are several things you should consider. When using BCP and BULK INSERT, there are several optimizer hints and properties that you can set that can affect the performance of an import operation, for example, setting the batch size. Setting the batch size determines how often SQL commits the data to the transaction log which means there is not one large commit process at the end of the load. It is also possible to add locking hints such as TABLOCK, which will lock the table from all other activity to ensure your load process has exclusive access to the table to perform its load. You should also consider, when loading large amounts of data, the possibility of splitting the data up into smaller imports and running them in parallel from multiple clients.

SQL Server Books Online has detailed information on achieving optimal load performance.

Moving or Copying an Entire Database

Sometimes you need to move more than just a subset of data in a database and are required to either move or copy an entire database from one server to another. This could be for relocation onto a server with greater hardware resources, for making a copy for development and test environments, or for creating databases for reporting purposes. In Oracle you would normally achieve this by using features such as Data Pump, transportable tablespaces, or RMAN to restore to an alternate location.

SQL Server has several methods to accomplish this task. As you would expect, there are scriptable and graphical wizard-based options that can be run from the SSMS interface. Some options allow for the source database to remain online while the process takes place, whereas others require the database to be temporarily unavailable while the copy or move is carried out.

There are four main methods available, each of which has its own set of pros and cons:

- ▶ Manual Detach-Copy/Move-Attach
- ▶ Scripting the database
- ▶ Copy Database Wizard (online/offline)
- ▶ Backup and restore

It should be noted that if you are using a SAN (Storage Area Network) solution to host your databases then there are also options available at this level for creating copies of SQL Server databases. Check with your hardware vendor.

Detach-Copy/Move-Attach Method

The Detach-Copy-Attach method (or Detach-Move-Attach method, depending on your objective) is a quick way of copying (or moving) a database to an alternate location. For brevity we will refer to the operation as a copy for the rest of the section, but keep in mind that it is the same process for a move operation, with the exception of moving the files and not copying them.

Similar to the concept of transportable tablespaces, it is possible in SQL Server to detach a database from one instance, copy the data files to another location, and reattach to another instance. Detaching a database simply removes the reference to the database from the master system database and releases any locks SQL Server has on the database files. When a database is detached, it is no longer accessible or visible in SSMS. Using this method involves downtime for your database but can be significantly faster than leaving the database online and performing a data export to another system. Your trade-off for speed is availability.

You have two ways of detaching a database. The first is to right-click the database in SSMS and select Tasks | Detach Database. This opens a Detach Database dialog box, where you are presented with two additional options. The first is to drop all current user connections, and the second is to update the database statistics before disconnecting. The second option of detaching is to use the sp_detach_db system stored procedure. No matter which method of the two you use, you are ultimately doing the same action. The Detach Database option in SSMS creates a call to sp_detach_db. If you have selected Drop Connections, this will also script the setting of the database to single-user mode, rolling back any currently open transactions before attempting a detach. Figure 11-26 shows the T-SQL that is created from using the Detach Database option with both Drop Connections and Update Statistics options selected.

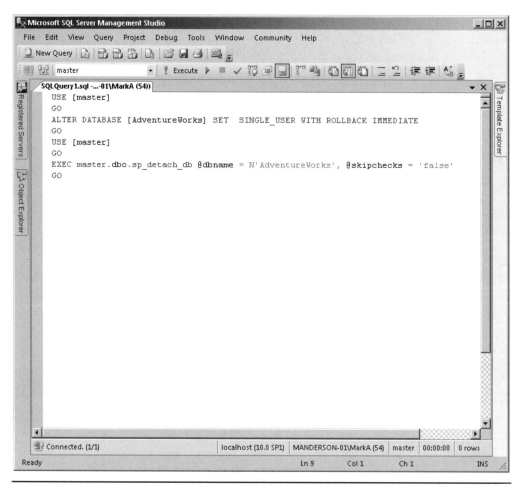

Figure 11-26 *SSMS-generated code for detaching a database*

Once the database is detached, you can copy the data and log files to the alternate location. In the case of the AdventureWorks database example, the procedure is quite straightforward because there is only one data and log file (AdventureWorks_Data.mdf and AdventureWorks_Log.ldf). In the real world, it is more likely that you would have added additional file groups and files for spreading the load and separating objects.

When using the manual detach and attach methods, you need to be aware of which files make up the database, as you will need to copy them all. There is a dynamic management view that you can query (before you detach!) that will list all the files associated with the current database and their locations:

```
SELECT * FROM sys.database_files
```

You will need to make a note of these and ensure that all files are copied across to the new location.

Once you have copied the files to the new location, you are ready to attach the database files to the instance. Again, as in the detach process, you can use SSMS or a system stored procedure, but now you also have the alternative to use a CREATE DATABASE statement with a FOR ATTACH clause. When you use SSMS and ask it to create the attach script for you, it will use the CREATE DATABASE approach.

NOTE

The stored procedure used for attaching databases, sp_attach_db, has been marked for deprecation in future releases of SQL Server. Therefore, you should avoid using this and instead use CREATE DATABASE with FOR ATTACH or the SSMS GUI.

It is possible to make a copy of the database on the same instance to, for example, create a copy for reporting or to test an upgrade. You can detach the AdventureWorks database, copy the data files to a new location (or the same location with a different filename) on the same machine, and then reattach, but since you cannot have two databases with the same name in an instance, the option to Attach As is available, which allows you to rename the database as it is joined to the instance.

For now, we will simply reattach the AdventureWorks database that we detached previously (as shown in Figure 11-26). To attach a database in SSMS, right-click the Databases node and select Attach to open the Attach Databases dialog box, shown in Figure 11-27.

To attach a database, you need to point SSMS to the database primary data file (.mdf). The primary data file contains information on the additional files that make up the database. Clicking Add presents a dialog box to navigate to the primary data file, as shown in Figure 11-28. Select the file and click OK.

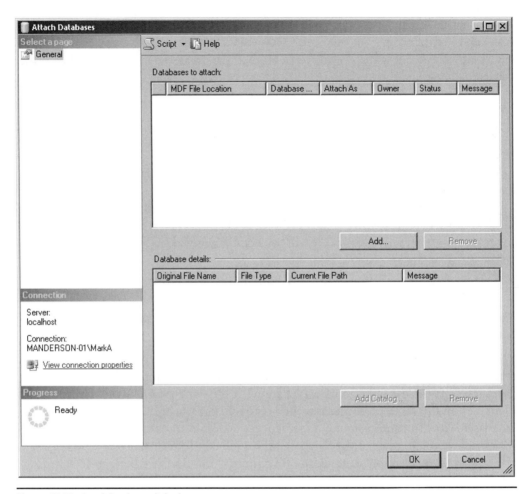

Figure 11-27 *Attach Databases dialog box*

The Database Details pane of the Attach Databases dialog box is now populated with the files it expects to attach (see Figure 11-29). Because we haven't moved any files, the paths that are populated for us are correct, but if they were not, we could simply point SSMS to the new file location. The Attach Databases dialog box allows you to attach many databases at once by simply selecting more primary data files. For now we are happy with just attaching our AdventureWorks database, so click the OK button.

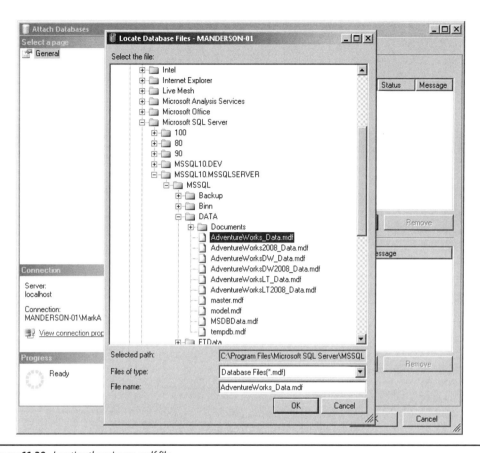

Figure 11-28 *Locating the primary .mdf file*

Oracle DBA Q&A

Q: Like transportable tablespaces, are there any additional considerations, such as file formats, when moving databases to another platform, such as from 32-bit to 64-bit?

A: Because the processor architectures that SQL Server runs on are all little endian format, no conversion needs to take place. The SQL Server on-disk storage format is the same for both 32-bit and 64-bit environments. If your production servers are 64-bit and your development servers are 32-bit, it is possible to just copy the data files over from one server to the other. Another example would be if you are running on a 32-bit production server and need to move the database to a server with greater resources, such as a 64-bit server; it is possible to use this detach and reattach method without having to make any changes to the data files.

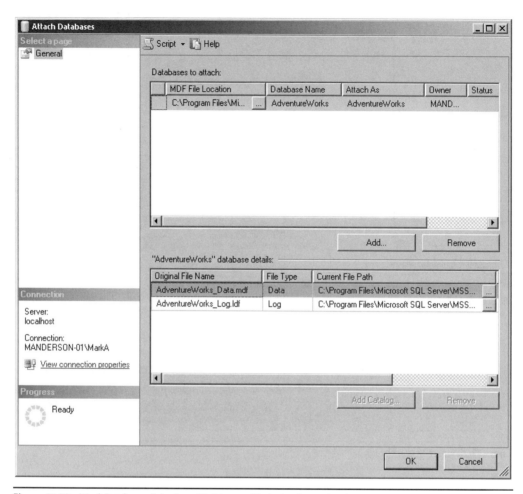

Figure 11-29 *Attach Databases dialog box with AdventureWorks details populated*

It is important to remember that when moving or copying databases between instances, there may be dependent objects outside of the database that need to be re-created on the destination instance, such as logins, maintenance jobs, custom error messages, and so on. Probably the most common objects that need to be transferred are Logins. It is possible to create a piece of T-SQL script to transfer the logins, but doing so is not a trivial task. Microsoft has supplied a set of scripts on its Microsoft Support website (http://support.microsoft.com) under knowledge base article 918992, which can be freely downloaded and used. A quick and easy way would be to use SSIS. SSIS has a Transfer Logins Task that can be quickly set up and executed. If you wanted to be clever, you could create an SSIS package and parameterize the options such that you could pass it the source, destination, and database for the logins you need to transfer, and then you could simply execute the package with the three parameters whenever you needed to transfer logins for a database.

Scripting the Database

If you don't want to take your database offline to copy it or you simply want to take a copy of the database schema and objects with no data, SSMS enables you to script out your entire database using the Generate SQL Server Scripts Wizard. To access the wizard, right-click the database of interest and select Tasks | Generate Scripts, as shown in Figure 11-30.

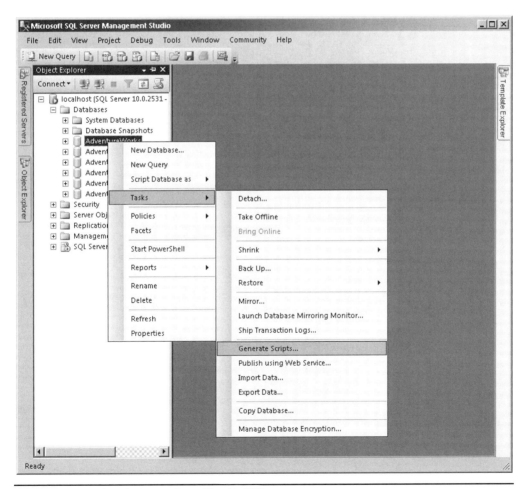

Figure 11-30 *Launching the Generate Scripts Wizard in SSMS*

The steps of the Generate Scripts Wizard, which generally are self-explanatory, give you fine-grain control over how the scripts are created. You can choose to script the entire database or simply a subset of objects. For example, if you want to create a database to use as a reporting system, you might want to script only all the tables and views, and not the logic contained in stored procedures and functions.

The wizard also enables you to include the actual data within the scripts. If selected, the data is placed in the scripts as individual INSERT statements, one per row. Figure 11-31 shows the option to script the data. As you would expect, adding the

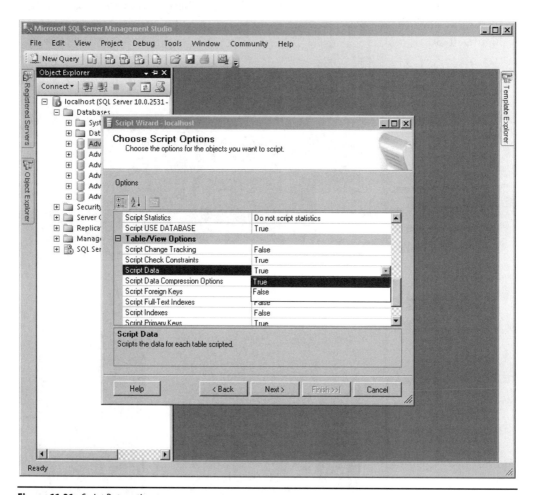

Figure 11-31 *Script Data option*

data as individual INSERT statements to the script potentially will cause the script to become very large, so you should use this option with caution. A better option would be to use the Import and Export Wizard to move data.

Copy Database Wizard

The Copy Database Wizard (CDW) in SSMS provides the ability to copy or move one or more databases either by using the detach and attach method or by scripting the objects, re-creating the database, and performing an export/import of the data. The CDW uses the SSIS package and engine to perform this operation in the same way as the Import and Export Wizard.

The primary difference between the two operating modes is that using the detach and attach method takes your source database offline temporarily. The second mode uses SQL Management Objects. This method allows the database to remain online while the operation takes place by scripting out all the objects and then exporting and importing the data. This method is normally slower than the detach and attach method, but it does allow you to avoid database downtime.

Let's walk through the process of copying the AdventureWorks database from the default instance to the DEV instance while keeping the database online. Starting the process in SSMS connected to the default instance, proceed as follows:

1. Right-click the AdventureWorks database and select Copy Database. The Copy Database Wizard is launched and presents you with a Welcome screen. Click Next.

2. In the next two screens, provide the source and destination servers to connect to and the credentials to access them. Click Next after each screen.

3. Select the transfer method. You want the source database to remain online, so select the SQL Management Object method (see Figure 11-32). Click Next.

4. Select the database that you want to include in this run, AdventureWorks, and select the Copy method (see Figure 11-33). Click Next.

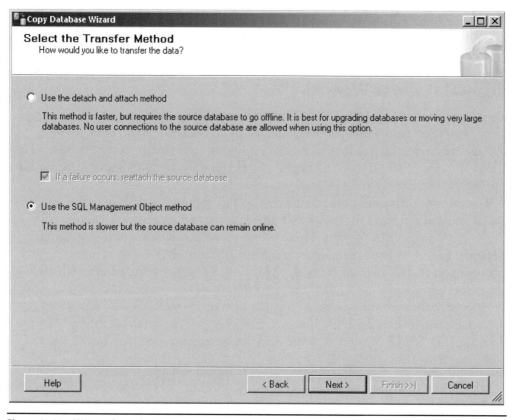

Figure 11-32 *CDW transfer method selection*

5. Specify the destination database name to use and where the files are to be located, as shown in Figure 11-34. Notice that the destination folders have been populated with the default data directory of the destination instance. The CDW also presents the choice of stopping the transfer if a database with the same name exists on the destination server (the default) or dropping the existing database and overwriting any files with the same name. Go with the default and click Next.

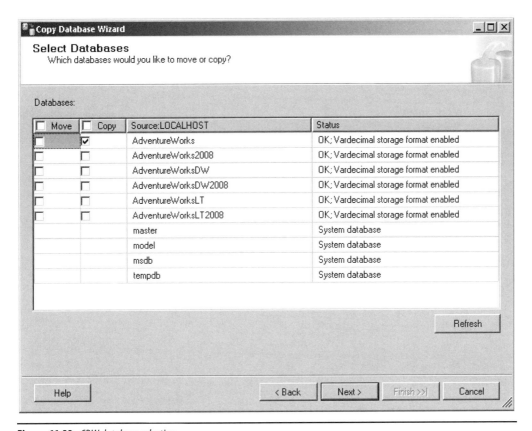

Figure 11-33 *CDW database selection*

6. You are now given the choice to select any server-level objects that you need to copy with the database (see Figure 11-35). This is where the wizard provides an advantage over the manual methods, because using the manual detach and attach methods requires you to be aware of the dependencies and move them independently. The wizard can provide this function. Because you are copying to a development environment and all you want are the server logins to be created, accept the defaults and click Next.

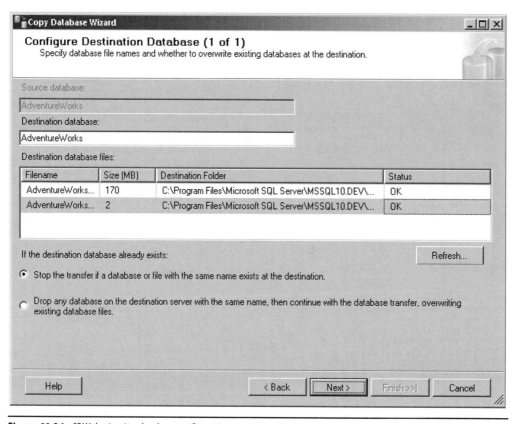

Figure 11-34 *CDW destination database configuration*

7. On the Configure the Package screen (shown in Figure 11-36), give the package a name and click Next.

8. Now that the package has been defined and saved, you are presented with the option of running it immediately or setting a schedule (see Figure 11-37). The schedule could be for a one-time-only operation or to create a recurring job. If you want to refresh your development database on the DEV instance on a weekly basis, you could set a weekly recurring job to run this package. Since you want this to happen now, select Run Immediately. At the bottom of the screen there is also an option to select the Integration Services Proxy account (proxy accounts are covered in Chapter 10). The proxy account is required if you are scheduling the package. The proxy account being used must have the ability to execute SSIS packages. Click Next.

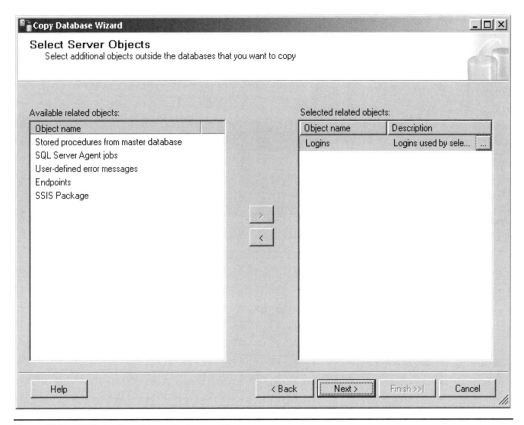

Figure 11-35 *CDW selection of dependent server objects*

9. You have now provided the CDW with enough information to carry out the copy operation. The summary screen (see Figure 11-38) provides an overview of the settings you provided. To start the operation, click Finish.

10. The CDW now executes the package and reports its progress as it runs (see Figure 11-39).

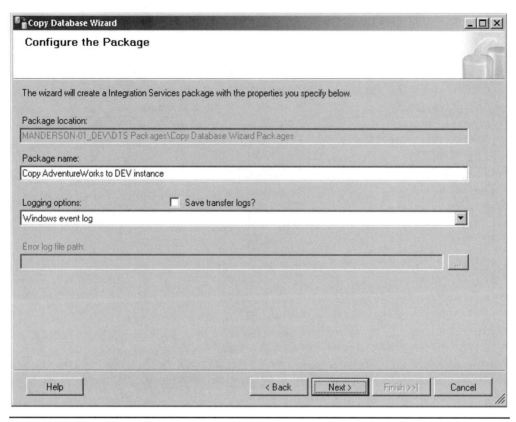

Figure 11-36 *CDW package configuration*

Once the CDW has completed, it is possible to review a detailed report of what has taken place by selecting the Report button, or you can simply close the dialog box.

Backup and Restore

It is possible to use backup and restore as a method for moving or copying databases within your environment. Although, as with the detach and attach methods, moving a database to an alternate server will still require that you also copy other dependent objects such as logins separately.

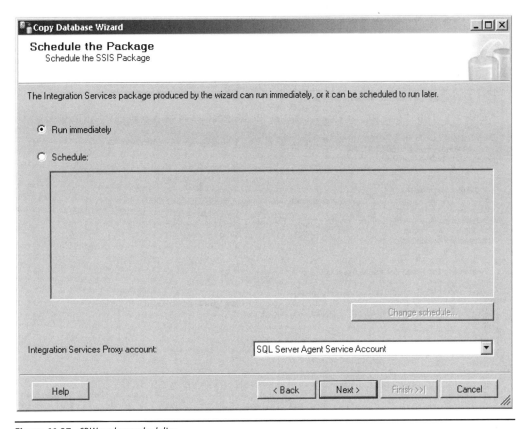

Figure 11-37 *CDW package scheduling*

The techniques for performing a backup and restore operation are covered in Chapter 7.

It is very important to note that if you want to create a copy of your database using your last scheduled backup (that is, the one you use for normal recovery of the database), the procedure is straightforward: copy the backup you want to use and perform the recovery at the alternate location. Although, you may decide that you want an "up to date" copy of your database and therefore since SQL Server allows online backups then what is

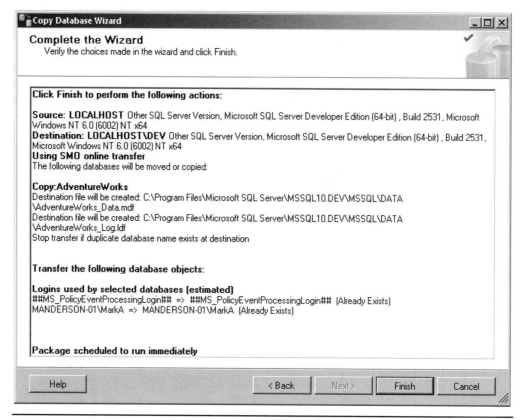

Figure 11-38 *CDW summary*

wrong with running a full backup of the database outside of the normal backup schedule? The answer to this question depends on what types of backup your backup regime uses. The problem arises if your backup regime includes the use of differential backups, then taking a full backup resets the differential base meaning that any differential backups taken from that point forward (on the normal backup schedule) rely on your 'out of schedule' full backup. Since the person taking this backup was doing so for refreshing a test it is highly likely they will move or copy and delete the backup file. Therefore, without the differential base which you are now missing your differential backups are now useless!

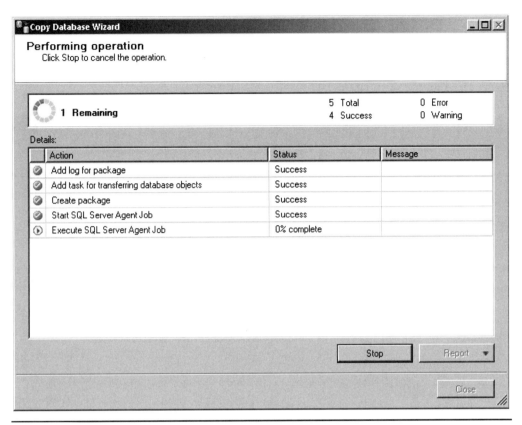

Figure 11-39 *CDW progress feedback*

To avoid breaking the backup chain, there is an option for taking a Copy Only Backup (see Figure 11-40). A Copy Only Backup is a full database backup that does not affect the backup chain and is therefore not required for recovery. Restoring a Copy Only Backup is no different from any other restore operation.

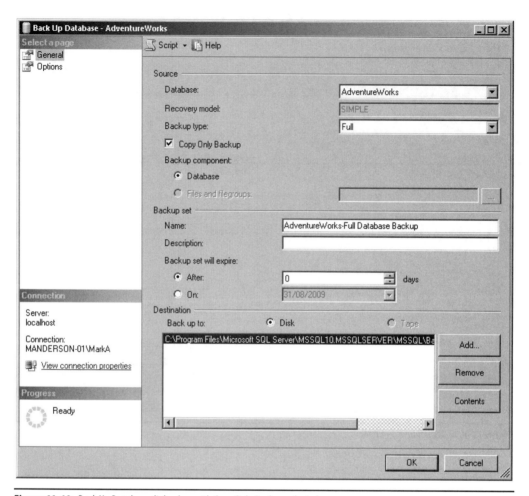

Figure 11-40 *Back Up Database dialog box with Copy Only Backup selected*

Querying Across Servers and Data Sources

These days it is highly likely that the database landscape of the organization you work in has more than one database server, perhaps from more than one database vendor. At some point, it is quite probable that you will need to integrate the data sources together without having to extract and import data from one system to the other. For example, a user working in a sales application may need to query the data in the warehouse application to check if an item they recently sold has been shipped. Instead of having a process where warehouse shipping data is constantly being extracted and loaded into the sales system, it would be more efficient to give the sales system the ability to pass through a query to the remote warehouse system. To set up this type of solution in Oracle, when both of the databases are Oracle databases, you would use Database Links to allow a query to be sent to database A and passed through to database B. To query across to a non-Oracle system, you would use Database Gateways. SQL Server has a concept similar to Database Links and Database Gateways known as linked servers.

Using SQL Server linked servers enables you to issue distributed queries and distributed transactions across heterogeneous data sources using OLE DB. Connections to Oracle and DB2 are available along with a list of Microsoft sources such as SQL Server, Access, Excel, Exchange Server, and Active Directory. Linked servers are part of the SQL Server base product and are not a separate, chargeable module. If you need to connect to systems such as VSAM, Adabas, Enscribe, and other more-exotic platforms, solutions are available from third-party vendors that plug into SQL Server to extend its functionality.

Linked servers use OLE DB providers for connections to other data sources. The OLE DB providers use rowset objects as the mechanism for exposing and manipulating data in a tabular format (a row set is an internal OLE DB object type for representing rows and columns). Therefore, whenever a user executes a distributed query, SQL Server converts the call into a rowset request, which is then sent to the OLE DB provider. The OLE DB provider services the request and returns the data back to SQL Server for additional processing before returning the results set to the user.

Because linked servers use OLE DB, there is an asymmetry to the performance of operations against linked servers. INSERT, UPDATE, and DELETE operations against a linked server are relatively inefficient as these operations are performed on a row-by-row basis in OLE DB. However, reading data from a linked server is substantially more efficient, as a single row set can be used to stream the results from the linked server. You should be cautious in writing distributed queries that join local data with linked server data, as they may require the movement of large amounts of data across the network.

The actions that can be performed using a linked server are dependent upon the support of certain interfaces by the OLE DB provider. For example, in order to take part in distributed transactions, the provider must support the ITransactionJoin OLE DB interface. Without ITransactionJoin support, only read-only operations are allowed.

When performing a distributed transaction across linked servers, you need a distributed transaction coordinator to manage the overall commit or rollback operation. Distributed transaction support is provided by the Microsoft Distributed Transaction Coordinator (MSDTC). MSDTC runs as a Windows Server service (see Figure 11-41). In order to create distributed transactions, the MSDTC service must be running.

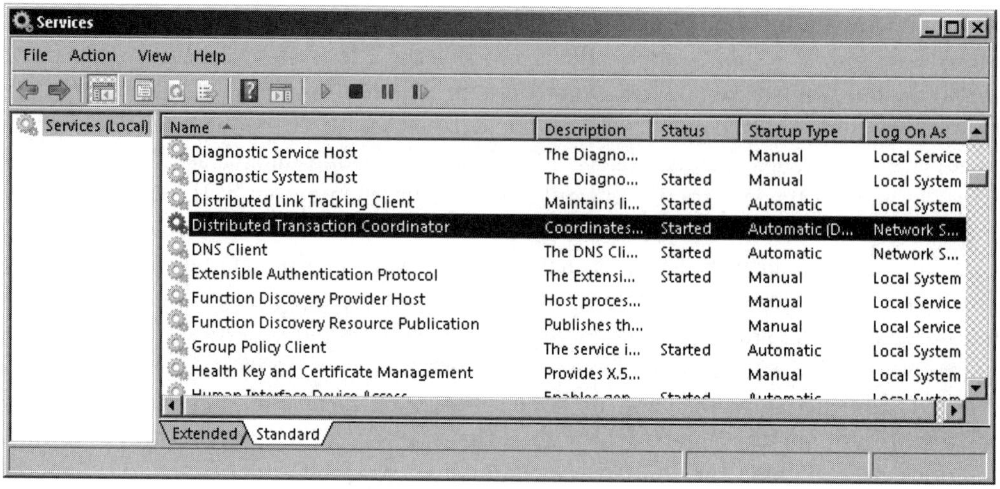

Figure 11-41 *Windows services management*

Linked servers are created and managed either graphically using SSMS or by calling system stored procedures. To create and manage linked servers using T-SQL script, you need to be aware of the following five procedures:

▶ **sp_addlinkedserver**   Adds a linked server

▶ **sp_addlinkedsrvlogin**   Adds login mappings to the linked server

▶ **sp_serveroption**   Sets server options on linked servers

▶ **sp_droplinkedserver**   Drops a linked server

▶ **sp_linkedservers**   Lists existing linked servers

We are not going to cover the syntax for these procedures as they are well documented in SQL Server Books Online; instead, we are going to look at the use of SSMS for creating and managing linked servers. Even if you are a script junkie who likes to do everything using T-SQL, there is an option in SSMS that allows you to fill in the prompts via a GUI. You can then use the Script button at the top of the dialog box to script out the T-SQL that would be executed if you were to click the OK button. This way, you can see what the Microsoft toolset could do on your behalf. Of course, after scripting you can amend and run this manually if you want to.

In SSMS, linked servers are located under the Server Objects node in Object Explorer (see Figure 11-42).

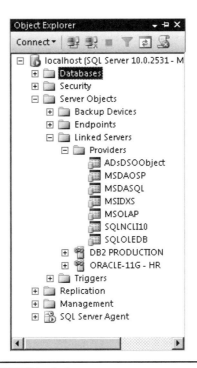

Figure 11-42 *Linked Servers node in SSMS Object Explorer*

Under the Linked Servers node, any previously created linked servers are listed alongside the available OLE DB providers. Opening the Providers node lists all the currently installed data providers and allows you to set any global properties that would affect all linked servers using that provider, such as allowing nested queries or disabling ad hoc access. Right-clicking the Linked Servers node in SSMS presents the option to create a new linked server graphically. Completing the details in the presented New Linked Server dialog box and clicking OK will make the relevant calls to sp_addlinkserver, sp_addlinkedsrvlogin, and sp_serveroptions.

An example of creating the equivalent of a database link between two SQL instances is shown in Figure 11-43. In this example, we will create a linked server on our default instance connecting to the DEV instance installed on the same machine. For the security options, we will specify that we want the credentials of the user making the connection to the linked server to be passed through to the DEV instance. Finally, we will construct a query that spans the two servers.

Figure 11-43 shows the New Linked Server dialog box. Because the server we are connecting to is another SQL Server instance, we start by simply selecting the SQL Server

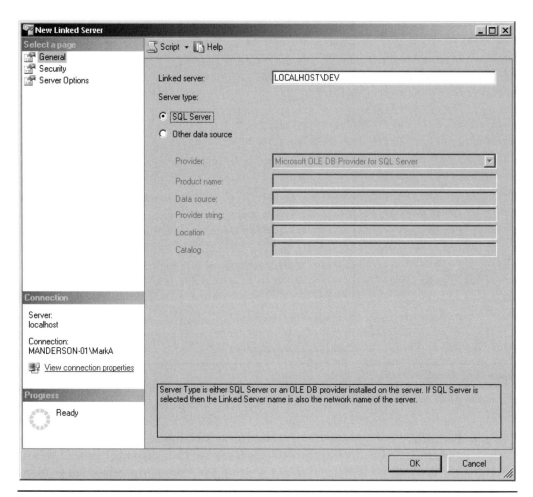

Figure 11-43 *New Linked Server dialog box, General page*

radio button under Server Type. This removes the need to provide any information to the data provider other than the name of the destination server. In selecting the SQL Server option, we are required to set the name of the linked server to the name of the SQL Server instance we wish to connect to. In this case, because the DEV instance is on the same machine as the default instance, we have set the name to LOCALHOST\DEV. By comparison, to connect to Oracle we would have to select the relevant Oracle provider and complete the other property fields to specify the TNS name to use and so forth.

Next, clicking the Security page on the left side of the dialog box presents us with options for how we pass security credentials to the remote server (see Figure 11-44). It is possible to list local logins and to map them to the remote server logins or specify that SQL should impersonate the user at the remote machine. If you choose not to

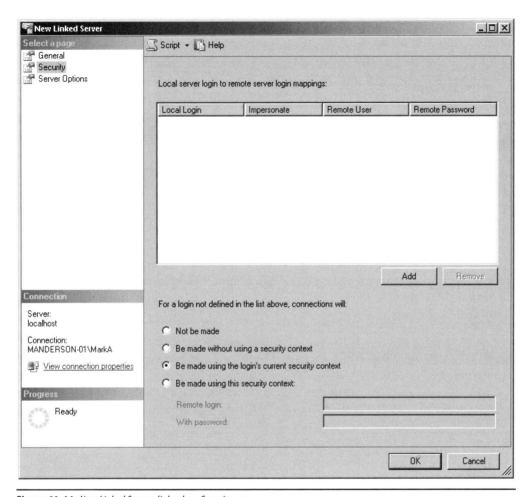

Figure 11-44 *New Linked Server dialog box, Security page*

use this fine-grained method, you have four other options that are global settings for anyone who is using the linked server or is not defined explicitly in the list.

▶ **Not be made**   Denies connection by any login that is not listed in the login table.

▶ **Be made without using a security context**   Connections are made without any credentials passed (that is, connections are anonymous, such as when connecting to an Excel spreadsheet).

▶ **Be made using the login's current security context**   Connections are made with the caller's credentials passed in.

▶ **Be made using this security context**   Enables you to specify an account the linked server should use when connecting to the remote data source.

For our example, since we are connecting to SQL Server with Windows authentication and we want to use the same credentials to connect to the linked server, we will not list any users and will instead select Be Made Using the Login's Current Security Context. This will pass through the credentials of the user accessing the linked server and we will only be allowed access to objects on which we have permissions defined at the remote server.

NOTE

To allow SQL Server to delegate Windows credentials around a network, some additional setup and checks are required at both the server and user account level. The user account must not have the Account Is Sensitive and Cannot Be Delegated option selected in Active Directory, and both of the servers must have SPNs (service principle names) configured; more information on this can be found in SQL Server Books Online. In the real world, this is normally something that would require the assistance of your Windows administration team.

Selecting the Server Options page now lets us fine-tune the details around certain options for our connection (see Figure 11-45). For our example, we are going to accept the default values, but for reference Table 11-4 contains a brief description of the common Server Options.

Option	Description
Collation Compatible	For distributed queries. If this option is set to True, SQL Server assumes that the linked server and local server are using the same character sets and sort orders; therefore, it will send comparisons on character columns to the provider for evaluation. If this option is set to False, SQL Server will evaluate any character comparisons locally.
RPC	When set to True enable RPC from the linked server.
RPC Out	When set to True enable RPC to the linked server.
Use Remote Collation	When set to True, the collation of the remote columns is used for SQL Server data sources and the collation specified in the Collation Name option is used for non–SQL Server data sources. The default collation of the local server is used when set to False.
Collation Name	Sets the name of the collation used by the remote data source. When the Use Remote Collation option is set to True and the data source is not a SQL Server data source, the name must be one of the collations supported by SQL Server. Use this option when accessing an OLE DB data source that is other than SQL Server but whose collation matches one of the SQL Server collations.
Connection Timeout	Timeout period for connecting to the linked server. A value of 0 uses the configured server default.
Query Timeout	Time period before a query times out. A value of 0 uses the configured server default.
Lazy Schema Validation	A value of True skips checking the schema of the remote tables at the start of a query.
Enable Promotion of Distributed Transactions	If set to True, MSDTC will be used to start a distributed transaction when calling a remote stored procedure.

Table 11-4 *Common Server Options for Linked Servers*

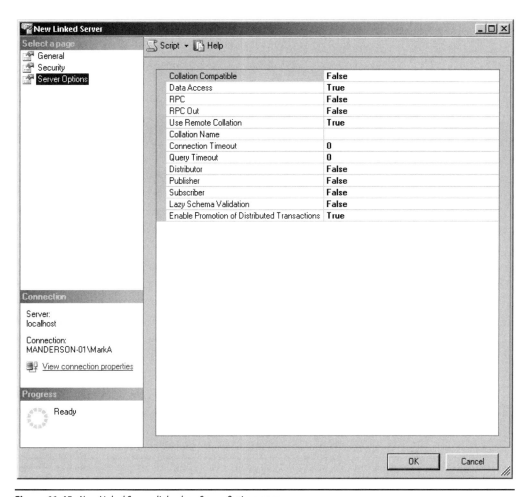

Figure 11-45 *New Linked Server dialog box, Server Options page*

Clicking the OK button creates our linked server. Once created, we can view this in SSMS. Object Explorer shows the Linked Servers node expanded with the new LOCALHOST\DEV linked server listed (see Figure 11-46). Drilling down into that node shows the available catalogs (databases). In the "Import and Export Wizard" section of this chapter, we used the Import and Export Wizard to create an HR database and populated this database with tables from our AdventureWorks database; these tables are now visible through the linked server. To show the linked server in action, the query window to the right of Object Explorer shows a query taking the Employee table in the AdventureWorks database on the default instance and then

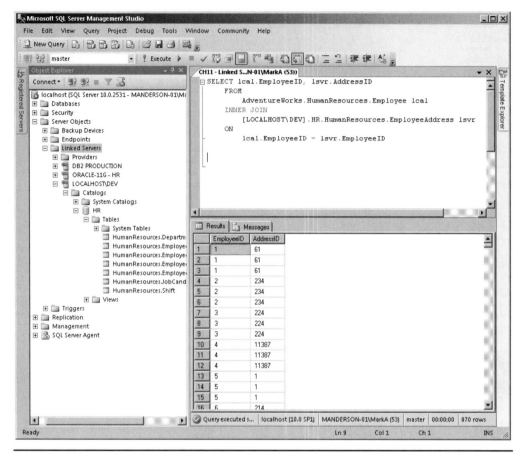

Figure 11-46 *Querying across two SQL instances using a linked server*

joining it to the EmployeeAddress table on the DEV instance. Notice the DEV instance is referenced using the four-part naming convention of *linkedserver.database. schema.object*.

One of the Oracle DBA Q&A questions asked in the "Importing and Exporting Data" section of this chapter is whether SQL Server has equivalent functionality to the concept of Oracle external tables: the answer is to use the OPENROWSET method, which allows OLE DB access to external data sources. OPENROWSET can be used as an ad hoc method of performing queries across data sources without having to set up a linked server. Figure 11-47 shows two queries with identical results; the first uses an OPENROWSET function to create an ad hoc connection to the remote server, and the second uses the linked server we created in the previous example.

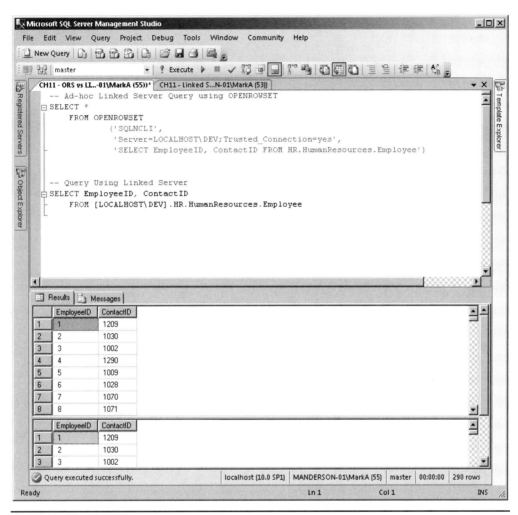

Figure 11-47 *OPENROWSET vs. linked server*

From a readability and maintainability perspective, linked servers are the better choice because if you reference them several times in code and then need to change an option or setting, you would need to change only the linked server definition, not every query that contains an OPENROWSET method.

> **Oracle DBA Q&A**
>
> **Q:** Do I need to create a linked server to query across two databases if they are in the same instance?
>
> **A:** No, you can simply reference the table using the qualified path of *database. schema.object.* You should also note that cross-database queries do not have the performance concerns of linked-server queries, and do not require MSDTC to handle transactions because the databases are all managed by a single instance of SQL Server.

Data Replication

Up until now, all the technologies we have looked at for data movement have been primarily for bulk movement of data or for passing through queries to other data sources. What about the scenarios where we need to provide a constant stream of updates in near real time or create a synchronization model where devices containing data are only occasionally connected to the network? In Oracle you would build these solutions using Oracle Data Guard or Oracle Streams. SQL Server has its own set of technologies to provide these solutions: SQL Server Replication.

Replication in SQL Server allows you to create data replication architectures for building a variety of solutions ranging from near-real-time incremental data replication through to scheduled complete data refreshes. SQL Server Replication also allows for a heterogeneous architecture where Oracle can be used as a data source or destination.

Replication Architecture

Let's first take a look at a high-level architecture diagram for replication in SQL Server. Figure 11-48 shows the hierarchical replication model with the three main components: Publisher, Distributor, and Subscribers. Think of the data flowing from the Publisher to the Distributor and out to the Subscribers. The Publisher, Distributor, and Subscriber can be on the same or separate servers and, depending on the replication type being used (covered shortly), a Subscriber can also push data back up to a Publisher.

Taking a closer look at the components, a Publisher is a server with databases that are made available for replicating to other servers. A Publisher server contains publications, which in turn contain articles. An article is a database object—for example, a table of data or a stored procedure—that you want to make available. Many articles are grouped together to make a publication that is then subscribed to.

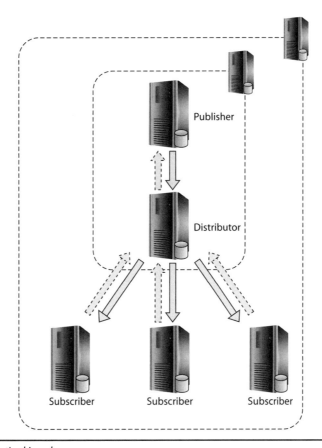

Figure 11-48 *Replication hierarchy*

The role of the Distributor is to distribute replication data to the subscribers. Each Publisher connects to a single Distributor. A single Distributor can act on behalf of several Publishers. When a server is set up as a Distributor, it will contain a system database called Distribution that keeps track of the status of publications and metadata and, in some cases, depending on the replication type, stores the actual data for distribution. A Distributor and Publisher can be on the same machine or they can be separated onto different servers.

Subscribers are the end consumers of the publication. A Subscriber is the recipient of a subscription. A subscription defines the data that the Subscriber will receive and on what schedule. A subscription can be either push or pull. A *push subscription* is where the Distributor pushes updates out to the subscribers without the need for the subscriber to request data. This frequency at which the updates can be distributed can be continuous, on-demand, or on a scheduled basis. A *pull subscription* allows the Subscriber to determine when it would like to receive new updates. In a push subscription, the agents that are responsible for data movement reside at the Distributor; when a pull subscription is being used, the agent is run at the Subscriber. A Subscriber database can contain data from multiple publications and, in some replication models, can send data back to the Publisher.

Replication Types

There are three main replication types in SQL Server, listed next. The type that you choose depends upon several factors, including the amount of data to transfer, whether the subscribers need to update the data, and the schedule on which data needs to be refreshed or updated.

- ▶ Snapshot
- ▶ Transactional
- ▶ Merge

Snapshot replication is the most basic of the replication types. The data that is marked for publication has a snapshot taken of its current state and this is delivered out to the subscribers. When a refresh of the data is required, a completely new snapshot is taken and delivered to the subscriber. Snapshot replication is ideally suited to small volumes of data in which the data does not require regular refreshing. For example, a corporate headquarters may decide to maintain its product catalog centrally and deliver a new copy of the catalog to local branches every night by using snapshot replication. An advantage that snapshot replication has over the other types is that when changes are made in the publication database, changes to the data do not need to be tracked because the data will be completely refreshed, which reduces the resource overhead of replication on the publisher. The disadvantage to this approach is that as data volumes increase, so does the time and network bandwidth required to deliver the new snapshot. Snapshot replication is also used to initialize subscriptions for other replication types.

Transactional replication is typically used for server-to-server configurations, such as when you require data to be available at the subscriber within a short period of time of the data being inserted, updated, or deleted at the publisher, normally within seconds. Transactional replication updates are continually being sent from the publisher to the subscriber in the original order in which they happened. Transactional replication is initially set up either by using a snapshot to initialize the dataset at the Subscriber or, for larger implementations, by restoring a database backup to the subscriber before establishing a replication partnership. By default, transactional replication subscriptions are read-only, although it is possible to configure "Updating Subscribers" that can send back updates to the master dataset for subsequent replication back out to all other subscribers. Transactional replication is often used for creating systems to offload reporting and batch processing from the main database or to push out near-real-time updates to branches or stores. It can also be used to simply create remote copies of the database as part of a disaster recovery strategy.

Merge replication is typically used for server-to-client architectures, where a client may synchronize data while connected to the network, then go and work offline with the data, and finally reconnect to a network at some point in the future. When reconnected to the network, any updates made at the client and server are merged together. An example scenario for merge replication would be where a traveling salesperson connects his laptop to the corporate network when in the office to download the latest product and client data, such as client contact details, from the corporate Sales application. After the salesperson has visited clients, taken new orders, or amended client contact details, these datasets are merged back into the corporate Sales application the next time the salesperson is able to establish a connection.

Merge replication is similar to transactional replication in that a new subscriber is initialized with a snapshot of the dataset. From there, all changes are tracked at both server and client level. When the client is reconnected to the network, the data that has changed is sent up to the publisher, where the datasets are merged. With two disconnected datasets independently updating their own data, it is likely that conflicts may occur. Merge replication allows you to create conflict-resolution rules that specify how to deal with a data conflict.

Figure 11-49 shows the replication objects in SSMS. In this example, a selection of tables (*articles* in replication terminology) from the AdventureWorks database has been published under the publication called AdventureWorks - Sales Data as a transactional publication. A new subscriber database with the name ADW-Sales has been created on the same machine and a subscription has been created. The ADW-Sales database has been expanded to show the tables that are being replicated to it, and the Replication node in Object Explorer has also been expanded to show the AdventureWorks - Sales Data publication and the subscription objects. Because this server has taken on all roles (Publisher, Distributor, and Subscriber), the distribution database is present on this server, as shown in the System Databases node.

Replication in SQL Server has the ability to work in a heterogeneous environment where both the Publisher and the Subscribers can be swapped for non-Microsoft platforms.

At the Publisher, SQL Server supports the use of an Oracle database for both the snapshot and transactional replication types. This provides an architecture in which Oracle can be used as the main data Publisher with a SQL Server Distributor and Subscribers.

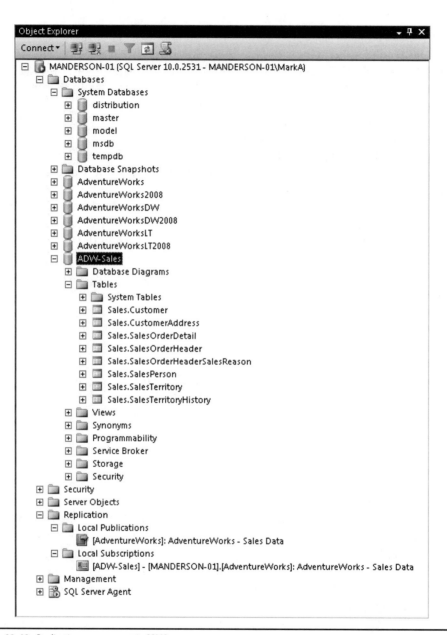

Figure 11-49 *Replication management in SSMS*

To use Oracle as a Publisher, Microsoft provides a script to run on the Oracle database that creates a user account and the relevant permissions on the schemas that you wish to publish (you can review the script before running). Oracle publication uses triggers and tracking tables in this new schema to track changes to the published tables. Once the script has been run, the process can be completely managed from within SSMS. Oracle will be available as a publisher so that you can publish tables as articles for your Subscribers.

At the Subscriber end of the solution, it is possible to have non–SQL Server Subscribers. The two supported non-Microsoft Subscriber types that are used are Oracle and DB2. Both of these platforms can be used to subscribe to snapshot and transactional publication types using a push subscription.

Oracle DBA Q&A

Q: If Oracle can be used as a Publisher, does this mean I can create SQL Server data marts using replication as the method of moving data from my Oracle-based data warehouse?

A: Yes, this is exactly the type of scenario where Oracle-to-SQL replication would be useful. If your data marts each had a different focus, such as Sales or Marketing, you could create publications and articles that only publish the subsets of data that each mart requires for its reporting requirements.

Peer-to-Peer Replication

Peer-to-peer replication is used to create scale-out solutions where all peers in the solution maintain their own copy of the database and propagate changes to each other as they occur.

In a peer-to-peer topology, each machine is in effect its own Publisher and Distributor, and at the same time is a Subscriber to all of its peers. It is possible to have a remote central Distributor, but this is not recommended because it creates a single point of failure. Peer-to-peer replication uses the transactional replication type to propagate transactions between each peer in the solution in near real time.

Take the example of a call center for a worldwide company. The company operates on a global basis providing 24×7 support for its customers. The company has three global call centers, located in New York, London, and Mumbai. As one call center closes, the next call center comes online to continue providing service. If a customer telephones the call center and logs a call with a Mumbai agent, the details of the call must be replicated to both London and New York so that at the end of Mumbai agent's shift, the call details are available to the agent in London to carry on working with the customer. London can pass the call to New York and New York back to Mumbai. In this scenario, if we were to use the standard hierarchical replication architecture with a single publisher and make all three call center Subscribers the challenge would be where does the Publisher reside? In a peer-to-peer model everyone has a copy of the data and if one call center has a failure, two other call centers are available to take over. Figure 11-50 represents the architecture.

Another purpose for which peer-to-peer replication can be used is load balancing. Consider the scenario of the corporate website that takes orders from the Web and provides details on company products. Instead of building one large server to handle all of the requests, it would be possible to put several servers in a peer-to-peer model and load-balance the web requests across each server. Figure 11-51 shows an example of

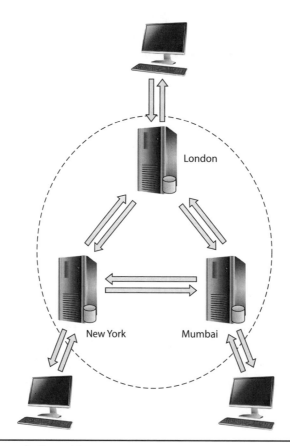

Figure 11-50 *Peer-to-peer replication model*

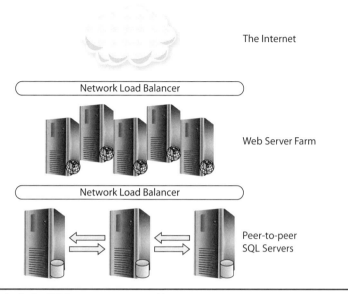

The Internet

Network Load Balancer

Web Server Farm

Network Load Balancer

Peer-to-peer
SQL Servers

Figure 11-51 *Example of using SQL Server peer-to-peer architecture*

a web farm taking requests from the Internet and then pushing the requests via a network load balancer to a farm of SQL Server instances. This approach allows for scale-out of the solution and the ability to take servers down for planned maintenance. It should be noted that peer-to-peer replication has limited conflict resolution, so when using peer-to-peer replication in a scale-out solution, it is recommended that the application guarantee that the same data is not modified on multiple nodes in short succession.

Chapter 12

Upgrading and Migrating to SQL Server

In This Chapter

► **Upgrading from Older Versions**

► **Migrating from Other Databases**

Administrators upgrade SQL Server databases from older versions for exactly the same reasons as those used as drivers for upgrading any other database system. These can include ensuring that a system remains under vendor support and receives security updates, or taking advantage of new features or performance gains. Equally common is for IT departments to look to reduce the number of versions of server products and operating systems that they maintain and to make more efficient use of their hardware resources. This chapter highlights the different approaches that can be taken when upgrading SQL Server databases and then looks at how a project might be planned and executed when the aim is not to move from an older version of SQL Server but from an entirely different database technology.

This chapter is largely concerned with upgrading to SQL Server 2008. At the time of writing, SQL Server 2008 R2 is the most recent version, but this is a minor-version release compared to SQL Server 2008. The implications of this being a minor version release are discussed in this chapter, but this chapter concentrates on how to move to the most recent major version of SQL Server, which is 2008. The tools, processes, and guidance presented in this chapter are equally applicable whether the target of an upgrade from an older version is SQL Server 2008 or SQL Server 2008 R2. In fact, apart from when this chapter discusses the differences between 2008 and 2008 R2, the two versions can be considered interchangeable.

NOTE

For the purposes of this chapter, applying a SQL Server Service Pack is not considered to be an upgrade. Considerations for applying Service Packs are covered in Chapter 3.

Upgrading from Older Versions

Whatever the driver for upgrading a SQL Server database, the process is the same: identify or create an instance of the newer version and then add the database to this instance, upgrading it as you do so. SQL Server provides support for automating some or all of this process. This section discusses the options available to administrators looking to upgrade a database, the tools available to help ensure that the project runs as smoothly as possible, and how to perform any manual tasks that may be carried out.

Upgrade Considerations

Strictly speaking, many upgrade projects don't upgrade a SQL server installation at all; instead they create a new installation (often on new hardware) and move the required databases into the new environments. In this section, we look at the relative merits of upgrading an existing instance and creating a new installation and highlight some key

SQL Server features that administrators will use when choosing an upgrade strategy and carrying out the upgrade.

In-Place Upgrade

SQL Server provides the *in-place upgrade* option to automatically upgrade instances of SQL Server 2000 and SQL Server 2005, including all user and system databases. An in-place upgrade installs an instance of SQL Server 2008, upgrades all data files to the newer format, attaches these files to the new instance, and then stops and uninstalls the older instance from the server (this includes removing the binaries). With an in-place upgrade, all instance and database configuration options are preserved.

There are a number of prerequisites and considerations for performing an in-place upgrade:

▶ Your production environment (the hardware and the operating system) must be supported with SQL Server 2008.

▶ The earliest version of SQL Server for which you can perform an in-place upgrade is SQL Server 2000, Service Pack 4 (version 8.00.2039).

▶ Cross-version instances of SQL Server are not supported. This means that version numbers of the Database Engine, Analysis Services, and Reporting Services components must be the same within a given instance (Integration Services is not a per-instance component; see Chapter 3). If your installation contains components other than the Database Engine, then you must plan to migrate and test artifacts belonging to these additional components at the same time.

▶ It is not possible to downgrade the instance's edition as part of a version upgrade. That is, you cannot move from an edition with greater functionality to one with lesser functionality during the upgrade. An instance upgrade is permitted. Given that SQL Server editions represent collections of functionality (as well as available tools and scalability limits), moving to a higher edition should never result in a previously used feature becoming unavailable, but you should verify that the functionality you are currently using is supported in the edition to which you are upgrading.

▶ Cross-platform upgrade is not supported. You cannot upgrade a 32-bit instance of SQL Server running on 64-bit hardware to native 64-bit.

▶ You cannot add instance components as you upgrade. Any additional features you require could be installed at the previous version and then upgraded as part of the instance upgrade, but it is much more likely that you will carry out the upgrade first and then add the new components to the upgraded instance.

Situations in which an in-place migration might be recommended are

▶ A large amount of instance or database configuration has been carried out in the older system. This includes supporting objects such a Logins. With an in-place migration, these objects and settings will be automatically re-established in the new instance.

▶ The instance contains a large number of user databases and all must be upgraded together.

▶ No new hardware is available and clients cannot be modified to accommodate a change in the instance name or network configuration (see the section "Side-by-Side Installation" for details of how network settings may need to change).

Side-by-Side Installation

In a side-by-side installation upgrade, a new instance of SQL Server 2008 is installed alongside the older SQL Server 2000 or SQL Server 2005 instance, either on the same server or on new hardware, and the data files are manually moved between the two. The databases are automatically upgraded as they are added to the new instance. Because the requirements and process for installing a SQL Server instance on new hardware are covered in Chapter 3, the only other installation scenario we will look at here is installing a newer version of an instance on the same hardware as an older version. A key characteristic of such an upgrade is that the new instance cannot have the same name as the older instance, as there will be a period where they coexist on the same server. Also, if dynamic ports are not in use (see Chapter 3), then the new instance must be configured to listen on a different IP address or different port from the older instance.

Hardware and software prerequisites permitting, instances of SQL Server 2008 can exist on the same hardware as instances from versions 2000 onward and, from an installation point of view, major versions of SQL Server can be treated as separate entities with very few dependencies or shared components with other major versions. The components that are shared between different major versions include:

▶ SQL Server Browser service
▶ SQL Server VSS Writer service

These components are automatically upgraded to the latest version when an instance of a newer version of SQL Server is installed.

ON THE JOB

To prevent any potential "downgrade" of these components, if you're creating a multiversion installation of SQL Server (for example, as part of a hardware-only refresh), you should install SQL Server versions starting with the earliest required and finishing with the latest.

SQL Server 2008 R2 shares the same major version number (10) with SQL Server 2008, so there are additional considerations if these two versions are installed side by side. The list of components that are shared between instances with the same version number is potentially more significant, including:

▶   The management tools

▶   Integration Services

▶   SQL Server Native Client

▶   SQL Server Upgrade Advisor (discussed later in the chapter)

Installing these components for SQL Server 2008 R2 will replace the 2008 versions (but only if you select them as part of the installation), and you should test your existing applications that use these components before putting such a deployment into production.

Components that are installed per-instance are unchanged in that they have no impact on any instance (at any version, major or minor) already installed on the server.

Situations where a side-by-side installation might be recommended are

▶   Only some of the existing databases need to be upgraded.

▶   The overall downtime for the database(s) must be minimized. Where there are a large number of user databases, the automatic in-place migration can take a long time to complete, and the instance is unavailable during this period. For a side-by-side migration, the database is only unavailable as the data files are moved between instances, and an administrator has the option to move different databases at different times.

▶   Complex application testing is required. A side-by-side installation gives the opportunity to use the new SQL Server instance for testing before upgrading the production environment.

▶   Some ability to "roll back" an upgrade is required (see the upcoming section "Compatibility Levels and Database Versions").

Backward Compatibility

SQL Server considers four categories of change when it comes to differences between major versions of the product:

- **Behavior change**   Behavior changes affect how features work or interact with each other when compared to earlier versions of SQL Server. For example, several changes have been made to the optimizer since SQL Server 2005.

- **Breaking change**   These changes might break applications, scripts, or functionalities that are based on earlier versions of SQL Server. For example, the cpu_ticks_in_ms and sqlserver_start_time_cpu_ticks columns have been removed from the sys.dm_os_sys_info dynamic management view. Queries referencing these columns will fail.

- **Deprecated feature**   These features are scheduled to be removed in the next, or a future, release of SQL Server. Deprecated features should not be used in new applications. For example, the WITH PASSWORD option for the BACKUP statement has been marked as deprecated.

- **Discontinued feature**   These features are no longer available in SQL Server 2008. For example, in earlier versions of SQL Server, an administrator could issue the command BACKUP TRANSACTION; this is now replaced by BACKUP LOG.

ON THE JOB

Post upgrade, review all queries containing optimizer hints and all plan guides to ensure that they still provide a performance benefit. If possible, time should also be set aside to check for missing or superfluous indexes.

Compatibility Levels and Database Versions

SQL Server databases have a configurable option called COMPATIBILITY_LEVEL that governs how the instance executes commands and queries against the database. Databases created within an instance always have a compatibility level that represents the version of that instance, but it is possible for databases moved or copied from older instances to maintain a compatibility level that represents some older version of SQL Server.

The compatibility level values that might be found for databases attached to SQL Server 2008 (and SQL Server 2008 R2) are based upon the product major-version number:

- 80 = SQL Server 2000

- 90 = SQL Server 2005

- 100 = SQL Server 2008 & SQL Server 2008 R2 (R2 is considered a minor release and so the version for compatibility remains the same)

Where the compatibility level for a database is lower than that of the instance to which it is attached, this can provide some partial backward compatibility with earlier versions of SQL Server and potentially allow clients to continue to use the database post-upgrade without changes. A full list of changed syntax and behaviors that can be preserved in a database attached to a SQL Server 2008 instance can be found in the SQL Server Books Online article "ALTER DATABASE Compatibility Level (Transact-SQL)," but compatibility level should be used only as an interim migration aid to work around version differences in these behaviors; you should work toward converting applications that use changed features to work in accordance with SQL Server 2008. The reasons for using lower compatibility level only temporarily are

▶ Performance may suffer.

▶ The compatibility level will eventually become discontinued, forcing an upgrade to the current earliest version. If it is possible, it is usually advantageous to carry out all upgrade testing and modifications in one project.

▶ Maintenance overhead. Administrators and developers working within a SQL Server instance need to be aware that certain databases exist at a lower compatibility level and remember the differences between versions.

▶ Changing the compatibility level and upgrading SQL Server versions both require testing, so it saves time to do both together.

For example, an application targeting a SQL Server 2000 database may use the *= and =* operators for outer joins. If the database is added to a SQL Server 2008 instance with the compatibility level left at 80, the application will not need to be changed. However, as soon as the compatibility level is changed to 100 (or even 90 in this case), these particular queries will fail with an error.

The syntax for setting the compatibility level for databases under SQL Server 2008 is

```
SET COMPATIBILITY_LEVEL = { 80 | 90 | 100 }
```

The following other compatibility levels exist, but they cannot be used by databases attached to SQL Server 2008 (or R2) instances:

▶ 60 = SQL Server 6.0

▶ 65 = SQL Server 6.5

▶ 70 = SQL Server 7.0

The new compatibility setting for a database takes effect for queries when the database is next made current (whether as the default database on login or on being specified in a USE statement). Changing the compatibility level causes all stored procedures in a database to be automatically recompiled.

To view the compatibility level for a database, you can query the compatibility_level column of the sys.databases catalog view:

```
USE master
GO
SELECT compatibility_level FROM sys.databases
     WHERE name='AdventureWorks2008'
GO
```

When a database from a SQL Server 2000 or SQL Server 2005 instance is attached or restored to SQL Server 2008, the compatibility level setting from the older version is preserved. Databases upgraded from versions earlier than 2000 have their compatibility level set to 80.

Separate from a database's compatibility level is its internal version number. Whereas the compatibility level is largely an indication of how statements issued against the database are parsed and executed, the internal version represents the format of the database's physical data files and can never be anything other than a number relating to the instance to which the database was last attached. The version of a SQL Server database is stored in the database header (in the primary data file) and can be returned by the following query:

```
USE master
GO
SELECT DATABASEPROPERTYEX (
     'AdventureWorks2008','version')
GO
```

For a database attached to SQL Server 2008, this query returns the value 655, and this value will not be changed by setting the compatibility level. When a database from an earlier version is attached or restored to a newer instance of SQL Server, the database's data files are automatically reformatted and the internal version number is updated. There is backward compatibility when it comes to database versions, but no forward compatibility, so once a database has been moved to a newer instance (and so upgraded), it cannot be moved back.

The internal version numbers for SQL Server databases from version 2000 onward are as follows (note that the physical database version has changed between SQL Server 2008 and SQL Server 2008 R2):

▶   539 = SQL Server 2000

▶   611 = SQL Server 2005

▶   655 = SQL Server 2008

▶   660 = SQL Server 2008 R2

NOTE

To date, the database version supported by a SQL Server instance has never been changed by a Service Pack.

As an example, attaching a database created under SQL Server 2000 to a SQL Server 2008 instance causes the database file format to be modified to the 2008 format. Leaving the compatibility level at 80 means that this database can continue to use features changed or discontinued since version 2000; however, you cannot now take this database and reattach it to the SQL Server 2000 instance—there is no forward compatibility between database versions. The error returned when attempting to attach the database will be similar to

```
The database 'PUBS.MDF' cannot be opened because it is version 655. This
server supports version 611 and earlier
```

The key point to take from this is that even after a side-by-side upgrade, once a database has been put into production and new transactions have been processed, this database cannot be downgraded. The closest thing to a downgrade that can be achieved is to put the old database back into production at the point at which the original upgrade was attempted and copy in the newer data manually.

ON THE JOB

An upgrade from SQL Server 2008 to SQL Server 2008 R2 is a somewhat unique case among SQL Server upgrades in that the compatibility level has not changed, so you should expect no behavior changes or discontinued features. However, since the internal database version number has changed, thorough testing is still required because you will not be able to restore or attach the upgraded database to a SQL Server 2008 instance. This situation likely will become more common going forward, as Microsoft has publicly stated that it is aiming for a two-year release cycle for SQL Server, meaning we are likely to see more minor-version releases.

See the section "The Upgrade Process" for details on changing the compatibility level option after upgrade.

Microsoft Assessment and Planning Toolkit

The Microsoft Assessment and Planning Toolkit can be used to discover many different Microsoft services and products running within an organization and is often used as part of virtualization projects. It can be used to discover SQL Server instances and their versions and can aid the planning and analysis phases of large (many instances and databases) upgrade projects.

Specifically, it can

▶ Discover servers and clients. It provides detailed information as to components installed, including version and edition. It also details the host environment, such as the hardware platform and the operating system version and edition.

▶ Conduct assessments. Conducts assessments of the upgrade effort, taking into account the host hardware and operating system environment.

▶ Automatically generate reports and proposals to support the upgrade case.

SQL Server Upgrade Advisor

Microsoft SQL Server 2008 Upgrade Advisor analyzes instances of SQL Server 2000 and SQL Server 2005 in preparation for upgrading to SQL Server 2008. Upgrade Advisor identifies feature and configuration changes that might affect an upgrade, and it provides links to documentation that describes each identified issue and how to resolve it. It is available as a stand-alone download from the Microsoft website or it can be installed from the SQL Server installation media. Microsoft strongly recommends that you run Upgrade Advisor before upgrading to SQL Server 2008. SQL Server 2008 R2 Upgrade Advisor will also analyze SQL Server 2008 instances, but as there are no breaking changes, behavior changes, or deprecated or discontinued features listed between 2008 and 2008 R2, you should expect only very minor issues to be reported. These are likely to be that shared components will be upgraded, as described in the earlier section "Backward Compatibility."

The location where you should install SQL Server Upgrade Advisor depends on what you will be analyzing. Upgrade Advisor supports remote analysis of all supported components except Reporting Services. If you are not scanning instances of Reporting Services, you can install Upgrade Advisor on any computer that can connect to your instance of SQL Server. If you are scanning instances of Reporting Services, you must install Upgrade Advisor on the report server.

Running the Wizard

Upon running Upgrade Advisor from the Start menu, it gives you two options: to launch the Upgrade Advisor Analysis Wizard, or to launch the Upgrade Advisor Report Viewer to view the results of a previous analysis.

If you launch the Analysis Wizard, you can specify a server (computer) name and select which types of SQL Server components should be analyzed, as shown in Figure 12-1.

Clicking Detect causes Upgrade Advisor to preselect each component found on the server in question, and these components can belong to any of the applicable versions.

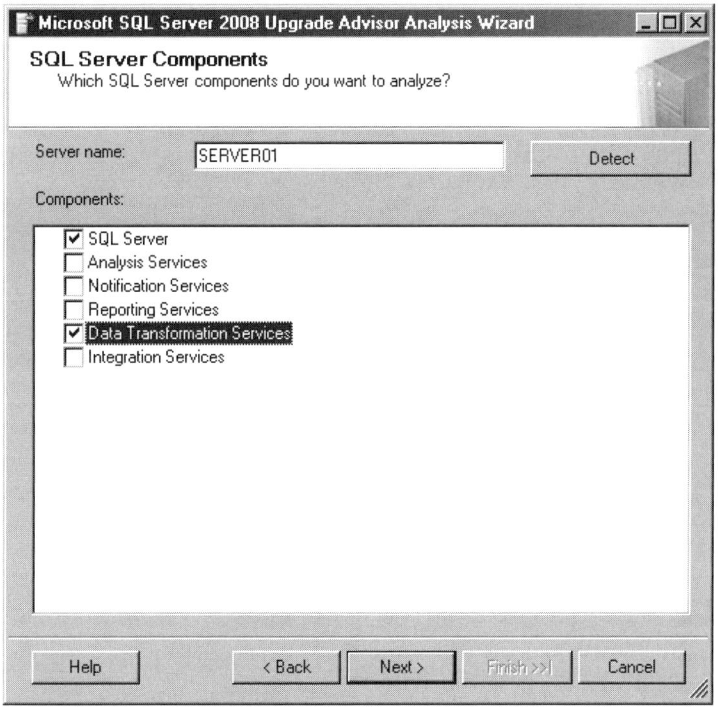

Figure 12-1   *Selecting components for analysis*

There are a couple of prerequisites to analyzing some of the SQL Server 2000 components:

▶ SQL Server 2000 Decision Support Objects (DSO) must be installed on the Upgrade Advisor computer if you are analyzing Analysis Services. You can install DSO from the SQL Server 2000 installation media.

▶ SQL Server 2000 client components must be installed on the Upgrade Advisor computer if you are analyzing Data Transformation Services. You can install the client components from the SQL Server 2000 installation media.

Clicking Next gives you the opportunity to select a particular SQL Server instance to analyze. In this example, we will be analyzing a named SQL Server 2000 instance called LEGACY. In addition, for this example only, SQL Server Database Engine components are being inspected.

As shown in Figure 12-2, we can now select to analyze some or all of the application databases present in this instance. In all cases, the system databases master, model, tempdb, and msdb will also be analyzed. Here we have selected only the pubs database, which is a sample database shipped with SQL Server 2000; in this example, some changes have been made to this database to deliberately introduce errors that will be reported by Upgrade Advisor. Analyzing the pubs database in its original state will cause fewer errors to be reported than those shown in this section.

Another very useful feature of Upgrade Advisor, also shown in Figure 12-2, is the facility to provide both trace files and SQL batch files for analysis. While Upgrade Advisor will inspect procedures, functions, and views found within the target database for SQL syntax and statements that are incompatible with SQL Server 2008, this inspection will miss any incompatible SQL embedded within, or generated by, a client application.

By using SQL Server Profiler (or SQL Trace, as it was known in version 2000) to trace user activity against the database or, if possible, providing a batch file containing

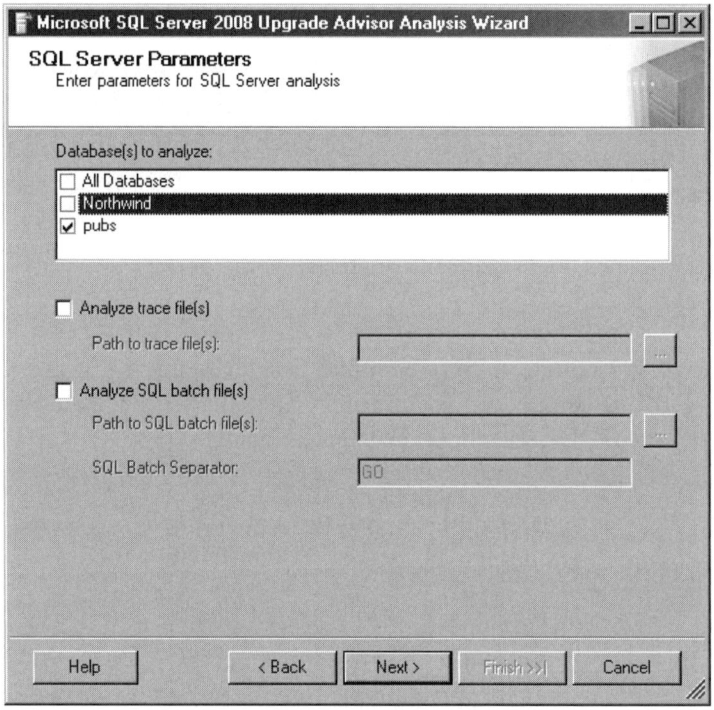

Figure 12-2 *Selecting a database for upgrade analysis*

the SQL statements that an application issues, it is possible to include these queries in the Upgrade Advisor analysis.

Upgrade Advisor can take some time to complete its analysis (for the Database Engine, over 100 rules are evaluated for each database). The results are automatically saved as an XML file under your Documents folder.

Viewing Upgrade Reports

The Upgrade Advisor Report Viewer (shown in Figure 12-3) can be launched either from the Analysis Complete page of the Analysis Wizard or at a later time from the

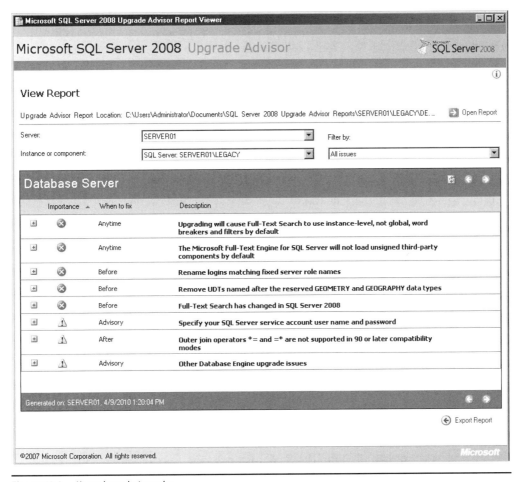

Figure 12-3   *Upgrade analysis results*

main screen of Upgrade Advisor. However the Report Viewer is launched, the results of the last analysis are automatically opened.

As you can see in Figure 12-3, detected issues are categorized as either errors or warnings and, where appropriate, advice is given as to whether the issue should be resolved before or after the upgrade is carried out. Of the issues shown in Figure 12-3, several relate to the Full-Text Search feature, which has undergone significant changes since version 2000. An administrator will need to ensure that any applications that use this feature are thoroughly tested prior to an upgrade. The remaining errors and warnings highlight areas in which the database and instance would need to be changed (and those changes tested) to ensure a successful upgrade.

Finally, a report might contain an "Other Database Engine upgrade issues" item. Expanding this item gives a link to a list of issues that are not detected by Upgrade Advisor but might exist within databases, instances, or applications. This list is in the help file for Upgrade Advisor. You should review the list of undetectable issues and determine whether any changes need to be made due to these undetectable issues.

The Upgrade Process

Carrying out an in-place upgrade using the Upgrade Wizard is a relatively simple process, with a number of screens that capture the required information from you, followed by an automated process of making the required changes on the target server. For the sake of brevity, each wizard screen is not described in detail here. We will continue to use the example scenario of upgrading from SQL Server 2000 to SQL Server 2008 and look at the options available to the administrator carrying out the upgrade. The process would be identical if we were upgrading from SQL Server 2005.

Figure 12-4 shows a SQL Server installation root directory (C:\Program Files\ Microsoft SQL Server) containing a default SQL Server 2008 instance root (MSSQLSERVER) and a named SQL Server 2000 instance root (LEGACY).

To upgrade this SQL Server 2000 instance and all of its system and user databases, the Upgrade Wizard launches a process that is initially identical to that of using the SQL Server Installation Center to install a new instance, namely:

1. The upgrade executables are loaded.

2. Setup support rules are checked, this time to identify any potential problems that would prevent launching the Upgrade Wizard.

3. You are asked to supply a product key for the SQL Server 2008 installation.

   You are then asked to select which of the existing SQL Server instances should be upgraded. As shown in Figure 12-5, all instances and shared components present on a server are listed, although only those at version 2000 or 2005 are available for selection.

Figure 12-4 *A SQL Server 2000 instance root*

The remaining process is

4. Provide an Instance ID for the SQL Server 2008 instance. This option is available because you are upgrading a named instance. The instance name cannot be changed using the Upgrade Wizard, and the instance ID defaults to the instance name; however, you are free to choose another ID. Note that you do not need to supply any version-specific prefix (for example, MSSQL10); this will be added automatically where necessary.

5. Review the disk space requirements. Note that the Upgrade Wizard leaves all data and log files in their current location, even though a new instance root will be created for the SQL Server 2008 binaries.

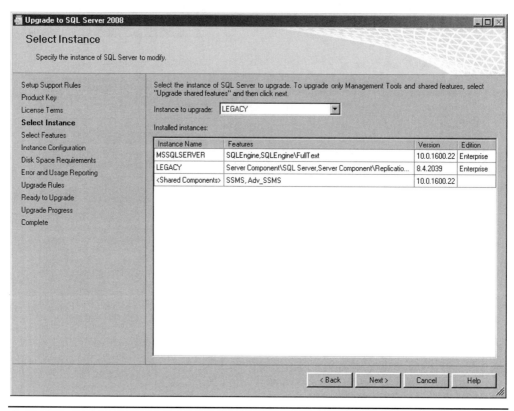

Figure 12-5   *Selecting an instance for upgrade*

6. Review service accounts. The identities associated with SQL Server services will not be changed by the upgrade process. Where services are installed as part of the upgrade that did not exist in SQL Server 2000 or SQL Server 2005, these will be configured to use a default built-in account (usually Local System).

7. Choose how existing full-text catalogs will be upgraded. The options are to import the catalogs without using the enhanced functionality found in SQL Server 2008, or allow SQL Server 2008 to repopulate these catalogs using the new features.

8. Based on all of the choices made in the preceding steps, the upgrade rules are checked to validate whether any issues will cause the upgrade process to fail.

9. The automatic upgrade process starts.

Once complete, any errors are reported to you and are logged to a file. However, assuming that no errors have been raised, you should now see a SQL Server installation root, as shown in Figure 12-6.

Figure 12-6   *SQL Server 2000 instance root post-upgrade*

The SQL Server 2008 instance root MSSQL10.LEGACY has now been created in addition to the existing MSSQL$LEGACY root. By comparing Figure 12-6 with Figure 12-4, you can see that the SQL Server 2000 root (MSSQL$LEGACY) no longer contains a Binn directory; these binaries have been removed as part of uninstalling the SQL Server 2000 instance. However, other directories such as Data have been preserved, and it is very important to remember that, at this point in the example, this Data directory still contains your data and log files, despite the fact that they have been upgraded and added to the new SQL Server 2008 instance. Also, you have to assume that your backups likely are still being written to the MSSQL$LEGACY\Backup directory.

ON THE JOB

Clearly, leaving data files and other artifacts in the instance root of an uninstalled instance is undesirable. You should move database files to the appropriate location in accordance with your physical data design, and you should review maintenance plans for references to directories within this old root. Moving user databases is a straightforward process that has been covered in Chapter 11; however, remember that the instance system databases also will not have been moved during the upgrade. See the Books Online article "Moving System Databases" for details of how to move these databases to the required new location.

Errors during an instance upgrade are not rolled back. Although data files are not removed from the older instance directory, thus preserving the data, it is very possible that the binaries will have been removed and all services will have been uninstalled, meaning that a new installation is the only way of recovering from the error. This is one reason that side-by-side upgrades are more common in enterprise environments.

Manual Database Upgrade

If you are carrying out a side-by-side installation or have established a new SQL Server instance on new hardware (or identified an existing one as a host), then there is no need to run the Upgrade Wizard. After the new instance has been installed, the remaining tasks are to ensure that all required features and configurations are present in the new instance and to move the required user databases(s) (new system databases will have been created when installing the new instance) to the new environment.

There is no automatic way to re-create the configuration of one SQL Server instance on another when manually upgrading. If the older system is SQL Server 2005, then you have features such as the Management Studio built-in reports that can summarize the configurations applied to a system, but if you are upgrading from SQL Server 2000 or earlier, then you will likely need to use sp_configure (as described in Chapter 3) to report the configuration options on the older instance, ensure that these options are valid for your SQL Server 2008 installation, and apply them to this instance.

A very common requirement when moving databases between instances is to re-create Logins from the source instance in the destination, and this remains true for manual upgrades. The document "How to Transfer Logins and Passwords Between Instances of SQL Server" (Article ID: 246133), available from http://support.microsoft.com, details transferring Logins between instances of SQL Server 2005/2008 and between older versions and these instances. Additionally, the Transfer Logins Task in SSIS can be used for this purpose.

Having configured the destination instance, the options for moving user databases are to move the data and log files by detaching, copying, and reattaching them or to back up the database in the old instance and restore it to the new instance. Both of these techniques are described elsewhere—moving a database in Chapter 11, and backing up and restoring databases in Chapter 7—so we will not detail these processes here. As covered earlier in the section "Backward Compatibility," adding a database from an older instance to an instance of SQL Server 2008 does not automatically change the compatibility level flag, so at the point that you are ready to make this change, the recommended procedure is

1. Set the database to single-user access mode.
2. Change the compatibility level of the database.
3. Put the database in multiuser access mode.

Following is an example of the code for this procedure:

```
ALTER DATABASE Adventureworks2008 SET SINGLE_USER
GO
ALTER DATABASE Adventureworks2008 SET COMPATIBILITY_LEVEL=100
GO
ALTER DATABASE Adventureworks2008 SET MULTI_USER
GO
```

As a final point, whether upgrading in-place or manually, the document "SQL Server 2008 Upgrade Technical Reference Guide" (available from the Microsoft website) contains detailed guidance on upgrading from SQL Server 2000 and SQL Server 2005 to SQL Server 2008. This guide includes scenarios such as clustered installations and also covers migrating Analysis Services, Reporting Services, and Integration Services components.

Migrating from Other Databases

So far we've looked at migrating databases from older versions of SQL Server. In this section we'll look at how to migrate a database from another database technology to SQL Server. The most common scenario in which you might undertake such a migration is where a business application has been developed in house and you determine that a change in the database technology can make available new functionality or realize cost savings. Carrying out a database migration can clearly be a very complex undertaking and one that requires detailed planning and specialist resources. However, tools are available that can reduce the required effort in certain circumstances, and we will look at one of them: the SQL Server Migration Assistant (SSMA) in this section. Separate tools and processes exist for migrating Reporting Services, Analysis Services, and Integration Services artifacts.

Migration Tasks

Broadly speaking, a database migration project is likely to contain the following phases:

- ▶ **Planning**   Assessing the business goals and defining the scope of the project; establishing project roles and responsibilities; carrying out risk assessments; and developing a project schedule.

- ▶ **Architecture migration**   Designing and building a SQL Server environment that is equivalent to that of the existing database. Sufficient hardware and software resources need to be made available to support the required database characteristics, and this may include functionality found outside of SQL Server such as third-party backup products or features of the operating system that aid resilience and availability. It is likely that particular attention will need to be paid at this point to configuring storage hardware and developing a physical data design.

- ▶ **Schema migration**   Migrating the database objects, including both storage and programmatic objects.

- ▶ **User migration**   Ensuring that all users and applications can access the new database with the required levels of access and privilege.

- ▶ **Data migration**   Designing the processes and configuring or building the tools that will move the business data from the old database to the new database. This may be carried out in phases or all at once, but either way is likely to require a planned outage of the production environment.

- ▶ **Testing**   Ensuring that each of the preceding phases has met its aims as defined in the planning phase.

It is a common mistake for teams to concentrate on only one or two of these activities at the expense of the others, usually as a result of the background of the team members (application developers will likely focus on migrating the schema, whereas server administrators will likely concentrate on establishing the new environment). Therefore, it is very important to ensure that the project team comprises representatives of as many different disciplines as possible. On large projects this will include Project Management, Application Development, Server Administration, Network Administration, Storage Specialists, and, of course, Database Administration.

Perhaps the other single biggest potential trap is for each of the preceding project activities to be treated separately or even run consecutively. This kind of approach has fallen out of fashion in software development projects for many well-documented reasons that don't need to be restated here, but there are a couple of reasons specific to database migration projects that we will look at. Taking an iterative approach to schema migration, data migration, and testing will reduce project effort in two ways.

First, the iterative approach is likely to identify redundant objects that do not require migration. This is achieved by taking the applications that interact with the database as a starting point for identifying the sets of objects to be migrated, rather than simply working through a list comprising every object in the existing database. The aim is to break down the application(s) into a list of features, each of which represents a discrete user interaction—this might be logging on to the system, performing a search, or running a particular report—and often these features will be closely aligned to individual screens within the application.

By analyzing the application source or by using the appropriate tools to trace the interaction between the application and the existing database (for an Oracle database, the V$SQL table would be a good starting point), it should be possible to identify those objects that are called as a result of the user actions. Testing will identify further objects that were missed during the initial analysis, but by taking this approach, only objects that are in current use by your application(s) will be migrated, not those that belong to deprecated features, older versions of applications, or even applications that are no longer in use.

The second way in which the iterative approach reduces effort is that "errors" in the new database will be identified much sooner and will be much cheaper to fix. In the scenario where objects are migrated by category (for example, all the user-defined data types and functions), followed by all the tables, all the views, and then all the procedures, it is highly likely that nothing can be tested until, at best, procedure migration is under way. At this point, it can be very difficult to marry subtle behavioral differences between the old and new databases to migration decisions that were taken several weeks or months ago, especially where complex combinations of procedures, views, tables, and indexes are all working together to deliver application functionality. By migrating small sets of various types of object (and where necessary their data) and testing using an instance of the application that targets the evolving SQL Server database, it is possible to pick up functional and performance issues far sooner and correct them far more effectively.

SQL Server Migration Assistant

SQL Server Migration Assistant (SSMA) is a tool that can automate schema migration, data migration, and testing tasks when migrating databases to SQL Server from Oracle, Sybase, MySQL, and Microsoft Access. SSMA is freely available to download from the Microsoft website.

While it is unlikely that any automated tool will entirely remove the need for manual effort when migrating databases from one technology to another, there are several features of SSMA that make it a very useful addition to any SQL Server migration project:

- ▶ It can work while disconnected from both the source and destination databases. SSMA builds an internal representation (which it calls a *metabase*) of both the source and destination databases. Once the source metabase has been created, you are free to disconnect from the source database, potentially minimizing the time spent impacting a production system and eliminating the need to create a new database instance to support the migration project. New SQL Server objects are created in the target metabase and only pushed to the destination SQL Server database when required.

- ▶ It can create a detailed assessment of the amount of effort associated with a database migration, highlighting where manual work will be required and the exact nature of those elements that will not be automatically migrated. Although it is unlikely you will build a project schedule around the effort estimates generated, these assessments are very useful in highlighting frequently occurring issues in a migration before the project starts.

- ▶ It can migrate all types of database object, including programmatic objects. Where an object cannot be migrated entirely (usually in the case of a procedure or function), a "stub" object is created, making it as easy as possible for a developer or administrator to visit the object and correct the issue.

This section doesn't give detailed instructions on using SSMA to migrate a database, but it does take a high-level look at migrating Oracle's sample HR schema to SQL Server. Figure 12-7 shows an SSMA project named LegacyMigration; the schema objects have been loaded into the source metabase (although we are still connected to the Oracle database, we could disconnect at this point) and we can now start to set global project preferences such as how we wish to map Oracle data types to SQL Server data types.

Following are particular points to note for Oracle migrations:

- ▶ SSMA can create objects to emulate Oracle system views in SQL Server. The following Oracle system views can be automatically created by SSMA (they will be created in SQL Server when a reference to the view is encountered in the source database):

  - ▶ ALL_CONSTRAINTS
  - ▶ ALL_INDEXES
  - ▶ ALL_JOBS
  - ▶ ALL_OBJECTS
  - ▶ ALL_SEQUENCES
  - ▶ ALL_SOURCE
  - ▶ ALL_SYNONYMS
  - ▶ ALL_TAB_COLUMNS

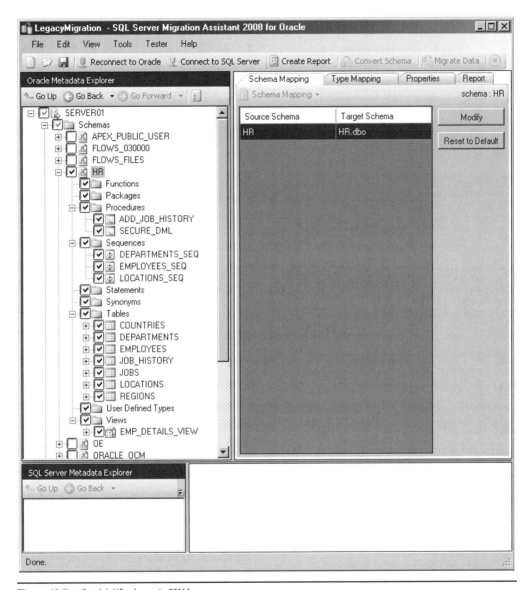

Figure 12-7 *Oracle's HR schema in SSMA*

- ▶ ALL_TABLES
- ▶ ALL_USERS
- ▶ ALL_VIEWS
- ▶ DBA_CONSTRAINTS

- ▶ DBA_INDEXES
- ▶ DBA_JOBS
- ▶ DBA_OBJECTS
- ▶ DBA_SEQUENCES

▶ DBA_SOURCE   ▶ DBA_USERS

▶ DBA_SYNONYMS   ▶ DBA_VIEWS

▶ DBA_TAB_COLUMNS   ▶ GLOBAL_NAME

▶ DBA_TABLES   ▶ V$SESSION

▶ SSMA will create tables and procedures to emulate, as far as possible, Oracle Sequences. Having done this, queries and procedures can continue to use methods such as NEXTVAL.

▶ SSMA seeks to migrate packaged procedures and functions (which don't exist in SQL Server) by using a naming convention (MyPackage.MyProc becomes a SQL Server stored procedure called MyPackage$MyProc) and by, again, creating tables and procedures to emulate the behavior of package-level variables.

Having populated the source metabase, clicking Convert Schema causes SSMA to build SQL Server representations of the selected (or all) objects within its internal target metabase. From here, they can be inspected and, depending upon the type of object, edited or SSMA options can be altered prior to re-running the conversion. Figure 12-8 shows the result of migrating the HR schema and, in particular, the procedure SECURE_DML from Oracle to SQL Server (the SQL Server code is in the lower pane). At this point you can see a reference to a function called to_char_date that has been created in a database called sysdb and in a schema called ssma_oracle.

To take a slightly more detailed look at migrating PL/SQL code, the Oracle and SQL Server versions of SECURE_DML are reproduced next.

Oracle:

```
CREATE OR REPLACE PROCEDURE secure_dml
IS
BEGIN
  IF TO_CHAR (SYSDATE, 'HH24:MI') NOT BETWEEN '08:00' AND '18:00'
       OR TO_CHAR (SYSDATE, 'DY') IN ('SAT', 'SUN') THEN
     RAISE_APPLICATION_ERROR (-20205,
           'You may only make changes during normal office hours');
  END IF;
END secure_dml;
```

SQL Server:

```
CREATE PROCEDURE dbo.SECURE_DML
AS
   /*
```

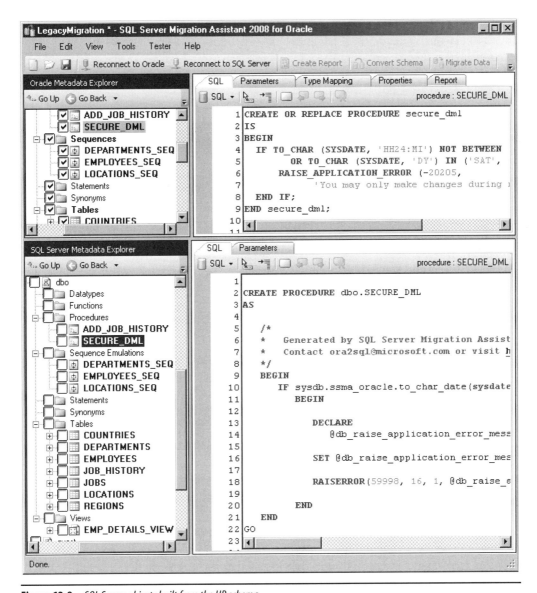

Figure 12-8   *SQL Server objects built from the HR schema*

```
 *    Generated by SQL Server Migration Assistant for Oracle.
 *    Contact ora2sql@microsoft.com or visit
http://www.microsoft.com/sql/migration for more information.
 */
```

```
    BEGIN
        IF sysdb.ssma_oracle.to_char_date(sysdatetime(), 'HH24:MI')
NOT BETWEEN '08:00' AND '18:00' OR sysdb.ssma_oracle.to_char_date(
sysdatetime(), 'DY') IN ( 'SAT', 'SUN' )
            BEGIN
                DECLARE
                    @db_raise_application_error_message nvarchar(4000)
                SET @db_raise_application_error_message = N'ORA' +
CAST(-20205 AS nvarchar) + N': ' + N'You may only make
changes during normal office hours'
                RAISERROR(59998, 16, 1, @db_raise_application_error_message)
            END
    END
GO
```

This is actually an example of a situation where an administrator might decide that the generated SQL Server implementation, while faithful to the original PL/SQL, does not represent the best approach. It is possible to avoid the call to the emulated Oracle function altogether and simply specify the initial IF statement as

```
IF DATEPART(hh, sysdatetime()) NOT BETWEEN 8
AND 18 OR DATEPART(dw, sysdatetime()) NOT BETWEEN 2 AND 6
```

NOTE

Under U.S. English settings, Sunday is considered the first day of the week and Saturday the last. The SET DATEFIRST option can be used to alter this behavior.

This should highlight that even when tools such as SSMA are able to migrate database objects, there is usually still a requirement for the output to be reviewed by an experienced SQL Server developer or administrator.

If there are statements or constructs within a block of PL/SQL code that SSMA cannot automatically migrate, the procedure or function will still be created within the target metabase with the code in question inserted at the appropriate point within a comment block that describes the error. For example:

```
    /*
    *    SSMA error messages:
    *    O2SS0404: ROWID column can not be converted in this
context because the referenced table has no triggers and
ROWID column will not be generated.
    SELECT rowid INTO @p_retval
    FROM JOB_HISTORY
    */
```

Because valid objects are always created (even if they have not been completely migrated and will not yet function as required), you have the option of carrying out the required changes within SSMA, in which case you are editing the metabase, or pushing the procedure to SQL Server as it is and then editing the object. Given the richness of SQL Server Management Studio and the features for team database development present in the Visual Studio Team System, the recommendation would usually be to move partially migrated objects to SQL Server as soon as possible and edit them in place.

Oracle DBA Q&A

Q: Most applications contain at least some SQL statements embedded into the application itself. How can SSMA help with migrating these?

A: This will still be a challenge for anyone migrating such an application. SSMA can't discover SQL statements in your application, but if they can be found either by analyzing the code using other tools or by tracing or inspecting session histories, then these SQL statements can be added to your SSMA project (as Statement objects) and then included in the automated analysis and conversion. Only you will be able to determine whether the effort required to capture these statements and add them to SSMA is outweighed by the savings made in automatically converting them.

When you are happy that you have built a set of SQL Server objects that you are ready to test, SSMA can create them in your destination SQL Server instance. Figure 12-9 shows the Synchronize with the Database dialog box, where you can view and alter which migrated objects will be pushed to your SQL Server database.

In this example, no objects have been created in the SQL Server database yet, so each object is listed as Not Found in the Database column. Things become more interesting when objects already exist in SQL Server. In this case, SSMA evaluates whether the database or the SSMA target metabase contains the newer version of an object and will synchronize accordingly. This means that you can amend objects in SQL Server, potentially test them as well, and then have this newer version pushed back into the metabase. You have manual control over the synchronization of each object, meaning you can omit objects from synchronization, if required, or force an older version to replace a newer one (for example, to abandon a change made to an object in the database). Figure 12-10 shows the migrated HR objects in SQL Server Object Explorer.

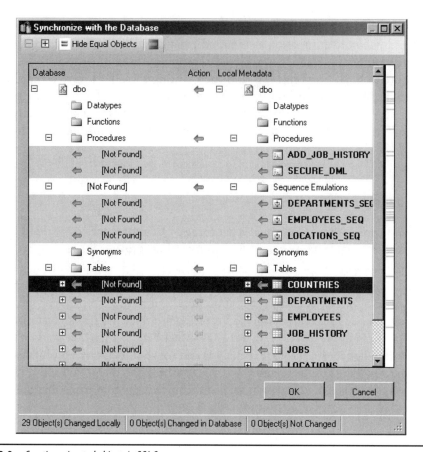

Figure 12-9 *Creating migrated objects in SQL Server*

Data Migration

SSMA can be used to migrate data from the existing database to SQL Server. This built-in functionality can prove very useful as part of the development cycle to allow for testing of migrated objects. One thing does need to be kept in mind: data migration functionality is implemented as a set of procedures and SQL Agent Jobs within the SQL Server database (the functionality does not reside within SSMA itself). This means that even though you have not needed any kind of direct connectivity between your source database and the new SQL Server before now, you will need to establish such a connection at this point. In our Oracle HR example, SQL Server will use the .NET Framework Data Provider for Oracle (which, in turn, uses Oracle Call Interface) to access the data in as efficient a manner as possible. SSMA validates the outcome of any data migration and presents the results to the user.

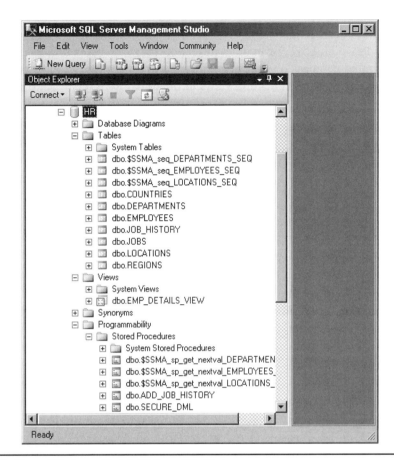

Figure 12-10 *Migrated HR schema objects in SQL Server Object Explorer*

Before the migration starts, SSMA calculates the number of rows in each table that will be migrated, and after the migration completes, SSMA compares this with the target table's row count. If they are equal, the overall migration result is considered to be successful. Otherwise, the user is notified of the discrepancy and can view the source and destination counts.

ON THE JOB

Despite being optimized for efficient data transfer, SSMA's data migration does not provide any facilities for validating the content of the transferred data or carrying out any of the other activities that you might associate with the migration of production business data, such as de-duplication or other kinds of cleansing. For this reason, many projects include the development of routines in a tool such as SQL Server Integration Services to carry out complex extract, transform, and load (ETL) tasks as part of the overall project plan. See Chapter 11 for details of how SSIS can be used to move and copy data.

Automated Testing

The final way in which SSMA can aid a migration project is by enabling automated testing of migrated database objects. SSMA users can build libraries of tests against any or all functions, procedures, tables and views in the evolving SQL Server database (this test configuration information is stored in a separate SQL Server database that can be dropped when testing is complete).

Figure 12-11 shows a test being created that makes two different calls to the procedure ADD_JOB_HISTORY, passing different parameters each time. These procedure calls will be executed against both the source database and SQL Server and the results will be compared. Whatever the type of object being tested, SSMA attempts to analyze the object to determine which other objects may be called and where data may be changed in the database. In this example, SSMA will determine that the table JOB_HISTORY is updated as a result of a call to ADD_JOB_HISTORY and, as well as capturing any exceptions raised as a result of the procedure calls on both the source

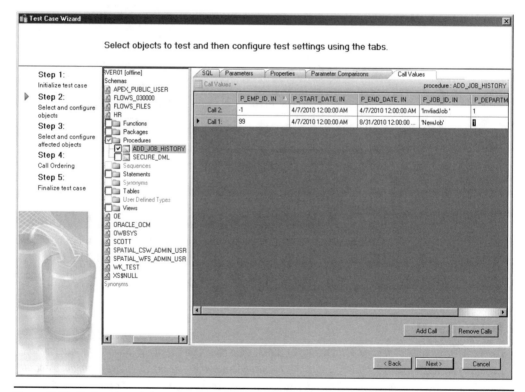

Figure 12-11 *Testing migrated objects using SSMA*

and destination systems, will also inspect this table on both systems to ensure that the data is identical at the end of the test.

Test results for each test run are also stored alongside the test configuration data and can be returned using the SSMA interface at any time. Unfortunately, tests must be run interactively (there is no facility for scheduling test runs), but this kind of object-level testing is still a very useful tool during the development of the SQL Server database. Having said this, another area not covered by SSMA tests is performance—there is no way to gauge whether calls to supposedly equivalent objects in the source and destination systems have the same response times, for example. With this in mind, migration projects will usually still employ significant application-level testing.

The Migration section of the SQL Server website (http://www.microsoft.com/sqlserver/2008/en/us/migration.aspx) contains many detailed guides on migrating from other databases to SQL Server.

Index

...cked with Hundreds of
Powerful, Ready-to-Use Queries

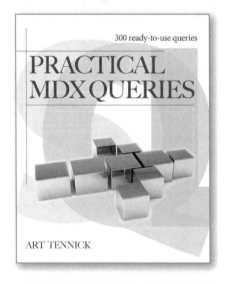

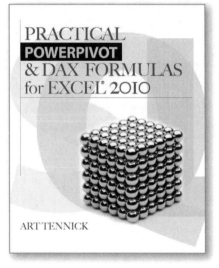

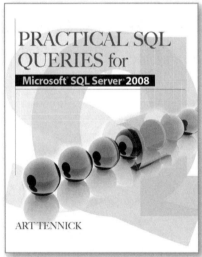

Art Tennick is an expert consultant and trainer in SSAS cubes, data mining, MDX, DMX, XMLA, Excel 2010 PowerPivot, and DAX. His website is www.MrCube.net.